Youth 2.0: Social Media and Adolescence

Michel Walrave • Koen Ponnet
Ellen Vanderhoven • Jacques Haers
Barbara Segaert
Editors

Youth 2.0: Social Media and Adolescence

Connecting, Sharing and Empowering

Springer

Editors
Michel Walrave
University of Antwerp
Antwerp, Belgium

Koen Ponnet
University of Antwerp
Antwerp, Belgium

Ellen Vanderhoven
Department of Educational Studies &
iMinds-MICT
Ghent University
Gent, Belgium

Jacques Haers
KU Leuven
Leuven, Belgium

Barbara Segaert
University Centre Saint-Ignatius Antwerp
Antwerp, Belgium

ISBN 978-3-319-27891-9 ISBN 978-3-319-27893-3 (eBook)
DOI 10.1007/978-3-319-27893-3

Library of Congress Control Number: 2016936661

Printed on acid-free paper

This Springer imprint is published by Springer Nature
The registered company is Springer International Publishing AG Switzerland

Contents

Part III Risks & Empowerment: Supporting & Empowering Youth

List of Figures

(Cyber)bullying Perpetration as an Impulsive, Angry Reaction Following (Cyber)bullying Victimisation?

Changing Unsafe Behaviour on Social Network Sites. Collaborative Learning vs. Individual Reflection

List of Tables

Social Relations: Exploring How Youth Use Social Media to Communicate Signs and Symptoms of Depression and Suicidal Ideation

Compulsive Use of Social Networking Sites Among Secondary School Adolescents in Belgium

(Cyber)bullying Perpetration as an Impulsive, Angry Reaction Following (Cyber)bullying Victimisation?

Changing Unsafe Behaviour on Social Network Sites. Collaborative Learning vs. Individual Reflection

About the Editors and Authors

Editors

Michel Walrave is a professor at the Department of Communication Studies of the University of Antwerp. He is responsible for the research group MIOS which conducts research on, amongst others, young people's uses of digital technologies. His research is centered around online self-disclosure and privacy. He investigates adolescents' and adults' online disclosure of personal information to companies and in interpersonal communication.

Koen Ponnet is an assistant professor and researcher at the University of Antwerp and the Higher Institute for Family Sciences (Odisee). His main research interests are the determinants of risk and problem behaviours of adolescents and adults, both off-line and on-line. In his research, he pays attention to the situation of vulnerable groups, like those who are at risk of poverty.

Ellen Vanderhoven obtained a PhD in Educational Sciences at Ghent University and currently works as a senior researcher at iMinds-MICT, a research group at the Department of Communication Studies at Ghent University. She specialises in research concerning both education about technology (media literacy) and technology for education (educational technology). In both domains, her expertise lies in the design of educational materials, including evaluation studies in authentic classroom settings.

Jacques Haers SJ studied mathematics (Catholic University of Leuven), philosophy (Catholic University of Leuven; Hochschule für Philosophie, München) and theology (Catholic University of Leuven; Oxford University). He is a professor of systematic theology and liberation theologies at the Faculty of Theology and Religious Studies (Catholic University of Leuven), where he also chairs the Centre for Liberation Theologies. He also heads the University Parish at the Catholic University of Leuven.

Barbara Segaert holds a master diploma in Oriental Studies, Islamic Studies and Arab Philology (Catholic University of Leuven, Belgium) and a master in the Social Sciences (Open University, UK). Since 2002, she is the scientific coordinator at the University Centre Saint Ignatius Antwerp where she develops academic programmes on various topics of relevance to contemporary society.

Contributors

Ola Erstad is a professor at the Institute for Educational Research, University of Oslo, Norway. He has been working both within the fields of media and educational research. He has published on the issues of technology and education, especially on "media literacy" and "digital competence". He is leader of a research group at the Faculty of Education, Oslo, called "TransActionslearning, knowing and identity in the information society". Recently, his research interests are directed towards the everyday practices of using different an media, the interrelationship between formal and informal ways of learning and media education in schools.

Janette Hughes is an associate professor and assistant dean of research at the University of Ontario Institute of Technology. Her research focuses on critical digital literacies and investigates the pedagogical affordances and constraints of digital technologies in educational contexts. Dr. Hughes is the recent recipient of the Ministry of Ontario Research and Innovation's Early Researcher Award and of UOIT's Excellence in Research Award as an Early Stage Researcher.

Jennifer L. Laffier is a senior lecturer in the Faculty of Education at the University of Ontario Institute of Technology. She teaches in the field of psychology, child development and mental health. Jennifer is also a counselling psychologist and specialises working with youth and children suffering from mental health issues. Currently, she is developing suicide awareness and mental health training programmes for youth.

Malene Charlotte Larsen is an associate professor at Aalborg University (AAU), Department of Communication, where she is doing research on young people's use of social media. She holds a PhD in Media Communication from Aalborg University. Her research aims at understanding how online social networking is integrated as part of everyday life and how everyday life is represented, mediated and acted out in the digital space. She combines a wide range of data material such as online and multi-sided ethnography, open-ended questionnaires and scene and actions surveys. She is a public speaker and commentator in Denmark on digital youth culture and online social networking.

Koen Leurs is Assistant Professor in Gender and Postcolonial studies at the Graduate Gender Program, Department of Media and Culture Studies at Utrecht University, the Netherlands. He obtained his PhD in 2012. He is a feminist internet researcher who has published widely on digital identities, migration, gender, race, diaspora and youth culture using creative, participatory and digital methods. He is the co-editor of journal special issues on "Digital Crossings in Europe" in *Crossings. Journal of Migration and Culture* (2014) and "Forced migration and digital connectivity in(to) Europe" in *Social Media + Society* (forthcoming 2017), and he published a monograph titled *Digital Passages: Migrant Youth 2.0. Diaspora, Gender and Youth Cultural Intersections* (Amsterdam University Press, 2015).

Rocío Rueda-Ortiz holds a PhD in Education at the **University** of the Balearic Islands in Spain, a master in ICT applied to education and a bachelor diploma in Psychology and Pedagogy, both obtained at the National Pedagogic University, Bogotá, Colombia. Currently, she is a professor in the Inter-institutional Education Doctoral Programme at the same university. Her work in research and teaching can be grouped in three key areas: cyberculture studies, use of ICT in schools and social appropriation of ICT for cultural and political purposes. She has published articles both nationally and internationally in these fields of study.

Sara Pabian is a doctoral researcher at the University of Antwerp, research group MIOS (Media & ICT in Organisations & Society). Her research concerns developmental issues in cyberbullying among adolescents.

Stephen Cory Robinson is a PhD student in the Department of Journalism and Technical Communication at Colorado State University. Cory previously completed a master in Communication and has professional experience in advertising and strategic communication. His research focuses on cultural differences in online disclosure and incentives required for disclosure.

Wouter Martinus Petrus Steijn is a PhD candidate at the Tilburg Institute for Law, Technology and Society at Tilburg University. His research investigates individuals' behaviour on social network sites and their privacy attitudes and conceptions. A special point of interest is age related differences.

Sabine Trepte is a professor for media psychology at the University of Hohenheim. Sabine Trepte's research and teaching interests include media psychology, methodology and media effects' studies. Specifically, her research focuses on online self-disclosure and privacy from a psychological perspective and on knowledge acquisition with media. She holds a master in psychology and a PhD in communication. She won several prices such as the ICA dissertation award and ICA best paper awards and serves on the editorial boards of Media Psychology, Journal of Computer-Mediated Communication and the Journal of Media Psychology.

Ellen Vanderhoven is a senior researcher at iMinds-MICT at the Department of Communication Studies at Ghent University. She successfully defended her PhD at the Department of Educational Studies at Ghent University in 2014, which focused on privacy and security in online social networks. Using a design-based research approach, she developed, implemented and evaluated educational materials to raise awareness about risks on social network sites and to decrease unsafe behaviour. This research fitted in the SPION-project (Security and Privacy in Online Social Networks).

Jolien Vangeel is a PhD student at the Department of Communication Sciences at KU Leuven. She was involved as a scientific researcher in the CLICK project which focused on the compulsive use of computer and Internet in Belgium.

Ellen Wauters is a legal researcher at the Interdisciplinary Centre for Law & ICT (ICRI KU Leuven). She studied political sciences at the KU Leuven and graduated in 2002. She obtained her law degree as a working student at the Vrije Universiteit in Brussel in 2010. She worked as a contracts and licensing administrator at Sony Music and as a legal advisor for Sanoma Media before joining ICRI in February 2012. In the framework of the EMSOC project (user empowerment in a social media culture), she will be investigating the legal challenges of social media and more in particular whether social media can be regulated in a more user-oriented environment, focusing on two policy goals: media pluralism and diversity and the protection of minors.

Co-Authors

Rozane De Cock (PhD in Social Sciences 2007) is a professor at the KU Leuven (Belgium) and member of the Institute for Media Studies (KU Leuven) and the Brussels Centre for Journalism Studies (KU Leuven HU Brussel). Her research focuses on problematic Internet use among adults and youngsters, news consumption and the interdisciplinary field of journalism, justice and law (crime reporting). She teaches courses such as Media Innovation and Research; Qualitative Methods of Communication Research; News and News Effects.

Diana Giraldo is a PhD student in Communication and Information Sciences at the University of Lyon II, France. Her academic background includes an undergraduate degree in Communication and Journalism and a master degree in Philosophy of Language. She has worked in several research projects on the uses of ICT and media at the University of Valle, Cali, Colombia, where she has also been a lecturer.

Annabelle Klein is a director of GRICI (the Interdisciplinary Research group "Communication and Internet") and professor of communication sciences at the "Facultés universitaires Notre-Dame de la Paix" in Namur. She is author of *A galaxie des rumeurs* (EVO, 1996) and *Les pages personnelles comme nouvelles figures* *de l'identité contemporaine* (CIACO, 2002). She has edited *Objectif Blogs! Explorations dynamiques de la blogosphère* (L'Harmattan, 2007) and *Figures contemporaines de la transmission* (PUN, 2009).

Eva Lievens is a senior research fellow of the Research Fund Flanders at the Interdisciplinary Centre for Law & ICT (KU Leuven) and a guest professor at Ghent University.

Gert-Jan Meerkerk is a senior researcher at the IVO Addiction Research Institute Rotterdam, the Netherlands, and Erasmus Medical Centre Rotterdam, the Netherlands. Since 2000, he has been involved in research on Internet addiction, on which he obtained his PhD in 2007 (Meerkerk, G.J., 2007, *Pwned by the Internet, Explorative research into the causes and consequences of compulsive Internet use*, Erasmus University Rotterdam)

Pascal Minotte is a psychologist, psychotherapist and researcher for the Reference Centre in Mental Health (CRéSaM). He works on issues related to problematic Internet use since 2008, mainly as part of research funded by the government. He is also the author of books in French on these issues for professionals in the field, cf. Minotte P., *Qui a peur du grand méchant web?*, coll. Temps d'Arrêt/Lectures, Yapaka, Fabert, 2012; Minotte P., *Cyberdépendance et autres croquemitaines*, coll. Temps d'Arrêt/Lectures, Yapaka, Fabert, 2010; Minotte P., Donnay J-Y, *Les usages problématiques d'Internet et des jeux vidéo*, Les cahiers de l'Institut Wallon pour la Santé Mentale, 2009.

Laura Morrison is currently completing her master at the University of Ontario Institute of Technology. Presently, she is exploring how poetry, drama, writing and technology can be used as tools for students in self-exploration and growth, and in project-based Learning to further engage otherwise disengaged students.

Omar Rosas is currently a postdoctoral fellow in the Institute for Culture and Society (ICS) at the University of Navarra, Spain. From January 2012 to July 2013, he was as a postdoc researcher in the Research Centre for Information, Law and Society (CRIDS) at the University of Namur, Belgium, where he worked on the project *CLICK: Compulsive Computer Use and Knowledge Needs in Belgium: A Multimethod Approach*, funded by the Belgian Science Policy Office (BELSPO). His research interests include ethics and technology, social and psychological consequences of ICT and online journalism.

Tammy Schellens is a professor of Educational Technology at Ghent University in Belgium. Her research focuses on two areas: technology-enhanced instruction (web-based learning, electronic learning environments, the use of technological tools, social network sites, etc.) and innovative instructional strategies (jigsaw, peer assessment, etc.). Central in her research and that of her PhD students is the design, implementation and evaluation of learning environments in authentic classroom settings with a focus on the impact on knowledge construction and motivation, and the question under which conditions these learning environments can be implemented most effectively.

Stephanie Thompson is an elementary school teacher who is currently on secondment as an instructional facilitator at the Durham District School Board in Ontario, Canada. She is also completing her master in Education in Digital Technologies at the University of Ontario Institute of Technology. Stephanie's areas of interest are in digital literacies, critical media literacy and digital storytelling. She has taken part in several research projects involving social justice and the effects of media on adolescents and exploring the use of social networking systems and mobile devices in the intermediate classroom. She is the recipient of the 2013 International Reading Association's Award for Technology in Reading.

Martin Valcke is a full professor of Instructional Sciences at the Ghent University, Belgium, and Head of the Department of Educational Studies. Building on his PhD work in the field of educational information sciences, his main research field focuses on the innovation of Higher Education and the integrated use of Information and Communication Technologies (ICT) in formal and informal educational environments. In addition, he is promoter of studies in the field of performance indicators, teacher education, ICT in primary schools, learning styles and learning approaches.

Peggy Valcke is a research professor at the University of Leuven (KU Leuven) and lectures media and communications law at the University of Brussels (HU Brussel) and the Florence School of Regulation (European University Institute, Florence). She is a visiting professor at the University of Tilburg and at Central European University in Budapest in 2006 and lecturer in the Oxford/Annenberg Summer School.

Heidi Vandebosch is a professor at the Department of Communication Studies at the University of Antwerp. Her main research topic is cyberbullying amongst youngsters. She has published internationally about the prevalence of cyberbullying; the profiles of bullies, victims and bystanders; and the need for prevention, detection and intervention using a multi-stakeholder approach (schools, parents, police, Internet service providers, etc.).

Introduction

The social web has become an integral part of young people's lives. Adolescents have embraced these online and mobile applications, which offer them opportunities not only to consume but also to create and share content. Next to blogs, video- and other content-sharing platforms, social network sites (SNSs) have rapidly evolved as young people's preferred avenue for online communication. How the characteristics of SNSs accommodate needs inherent to adolescent development may explain why adolescents have rapidly and enthusiastically integrated SNSs into their daily lives.

During adolescence, young people develop a unified sense of self and belonging (Steinberg 2011). They gain awareness of who they are and where they belong. While striving for more autonomy from their parents, feedback from peers grows in importance (Buhrmester and Prager 1995). Moreover, young people engage in a broader spectrum of relationships, from casual and close friendships to first romantic encounters (Côté 2009). Throughout these developments, SNSs may play an important role. As most online platforms revolve around one's personal profile, they offer young people a platform to present themselves (Peter and Valkenburg 2011). A profile page thus offers an online stage where a user can, besides communicating with others, also divulge personal data in written and visual form (Siibak 2009). Especially during major life events, users may share experiences and receive support from their (online) contacts. In sharing and responding, young people can further refine their social skills (Boyd 2014). Moreover, SNSs do not only consolidate existing (offline) relationships but also offer opportunities to expand one's social circle. Adolescents can broaden their social network to other people with whom they may share similar interests, concerns or problems.

However, young people's disclosure of personal information when constructing an online profile and sharing significant life experiences has raised concern as to the possible consequences of these disclosures. Indeed, personal information may be misused (Taddicken and Jers 2011). These concerns are related to the characteristics of digital content in general and, particularly, of the personal data disclosed on

SNSs. Digital content is characterised by persistence, scalability, replicability, searchability and shareability (Boyd 2008; Papacharissi and Gibson 2011). *Persistence* refers to the facility of storing digital content that may resurface at inconvenient moments or reach unintended audiences. Conversely, persistence offers users the possibility to keep track of their life course and retain important life events. Moreover, digital content is easy to diffuse. A picture or comment may instantly go viral. Put otherwise, digital data are *shareable* and *scalable*, they can reach a single recipient or be forwarded to a large audience. This is possible through digital data's *replicability*. For instance, holiday snaps, but also intimate conversations, can easily, but sometimes also unintentionally, be shared. Once online, personal information becomes *searchable*. Its diffusion and consultation are difficult to control. In sum, while social media offer important opportunities for young people's identity and relational development through sharing life events, personal information may rapidly spread and reach unintended audiences (Boyd 2008; Papacharissi and Gibson 2011; Peter and Valkenburg 2011).

This raises issues about the implications of digital communication in general, and social media in particular, for young people's development and well-being. As a result, researchers are increasingly turning their attention to the reasons behind the attraction social media have for youth as well as to the benefits and risks they entail. Academic interest is growing in tandem with the policy and media attention regarding the risks young people may encounter, such as threats to privacy due to the diffusion and misuse of personal information.

This tension between opportunities for adolescents' identity and relational development and possible drawbacks for young people's privacy and security was the focal point of a 2-day international conference *Youth 2.0*, organised by the University Centre Saint-Ignatius Antwerp (UCSIA) at the University of Antwerp in March 2013.

The three main themes that constituted the central threads of the conference are developed in the respective parts of this publication.

In the first part of the book, the significance of social media for adolescent identity exploration and development is investigated. Janette Hughes and her colleagues explore adolescent identity construction through online practices in the SNS Ning. They further investigate how online and offline identities are consistent or differ. Malene Charlotte Larsen then explores young people's online identities. She focuses on emotional statements that young people publicly share online and how these disclosures help co-construct their identities. Central to an online profile is its owner's picture. Rocío Rueda and Diana Giraldo analyse profile pictures from Facebook users in more than 20 cities around the globe. How users sometimes stage their image and what meanings they want to express in this way form the subject of a content analysis and in-depth interviews.

In the next chapter, Koen Leurs applies a multi-method approach to investigate the social media use of Moroccan-Dutch youth. He unravels how factual power relations of race, gender and religion are sustained online.

In the chapter concluding this first part, Ola Erstad explores the potential contribution of social media in education. He illustrates this through the case of an online environment created to engage youth at risk in communicative and collaborative activities.

The second part of this book is dedicated to the tension between online self-disclosure and privacy. Why do privacy attitudes sometimes fail to match our online behaviour? This is the central question addressed by Sabine Trepte. In her chapter, the author focuses on three intertwined aspects, namely privacy attitudes, knowledge of privacy mechanisms and behaviour that protects privacy, in order to shed light on the "privacy paradoxes".

It is not just personal attitudes that are important in relation to privacy protection, social norms also play a role in how SNS users regulate their privacy, states Wouter Martinus Petrus Steijn. In this chapter, dedicated to the interplay between norms and users' online behaviour, differences between age groups are elucidated. In the next chapter, Stephen Cory Robinson further investigates how children, adolescents and emerging adults manage their online disclosure. Based on Communication Privacy Management Theory, the author examines privacy protection mechanisms and their implications for media literacy education.

The third and final part of the book is devoted to specific online risks young people are confronted with and how they can be empowered to cope with them. First, social media may be used to emit signs of distress. Jennifer Laffier presents her qualitative analysis on suicide cases reported in the media and to identify these signs with a view to designing a screening tool. In a second chapter, Jolien Vangeel and her co-authors focus on another issue of concern: the compulsive use of SNSs. Their survey among adolescents goes beyond prevalence rates and focuses on significant psychological predictors. Another risk young people may be confronted with is cyberbullying. Sara Pabian and Heidi Vandebosch provide insight into the relationship between prior victimisation that can lead to subsequent perpetration, based on longitudinal data. They found that this link is stronger for former victims who were more angry and impulsive.

The two final chapters highlight possible interventions for empowering young people. Ellen Vanderhoven and her colleagues investigate the effectiveness of online safety interventions. Using a quasi-experimental design, the study proves that an approach encouraging individual reflection has an influence on both young people's attitudes and behaviours, whereas an approach focusing on collaborative learning only raises young people's awareness of online risks. In the final chapter, Ellen Wauters and co-authors assess pertinent issues related to content classification labeling systems, focusing on online content and SNSs. Based on their analysis of these systems and policy documents, they highlight good practices that could further inspire international standards.

The research described throughout the chapters of this book offers an international perspective on its three main themes: the importance of social media for adolescent identity exploration and development, the tension between online self-disclosure and privacy and the empowerment of young people to cope with specific online risks. Concerning the last theme, we witness an increasing number of national and international organisations and events promoting online safety. For example, each year, during the Safer Internet Day, more than 100 countries worldwide promote safer and more responsible use of online technology, especially amongst children and young people (Insafe 2015).

It needs to be acknowledged from the outset that the third part of this book mostly reports research conducted in Belgium. Although it has been found that Belgian children comply with the general standard as regards their use of SNSs, the risks they face and the coping strategies they use (d'Haenens and Vandoninck 2012), we should resist the temptation to generalise. Overall, research on children's online safety is conducted in the global North while insight into children's behaviour in the global South is lacking (Livingstone and Bulger 2013). Researchers reviewing the existing literature indicate a growing need for cross-national comparative studies for a better understanding of children's experiences. Moreover, comparative studies can lead to the international dissemination of good practices (Livingstone and Bulger 2013). Together, the studies in this third part of the book demonstrate emerging research topics and research methodologies with regard to the empowerment and support of youth concerning their online safety. We hope they may inspire other researchers to conduct similar research worldwide.

In sum, this book emphasises three intertwined themes, namely identity, privacy and support or empowerment of youth, and offers a multidisciplinary overview of topical research. The contributing researchers explain relevant theories, answer a variety of pertinent questions, discuss practical solutions and reveal emerging issues that should lead future research and policy agendas.

References

Boyd, D. (2008). *Taken out of context: American teen sociality in networked publics*. Berkeley: University of California.

Boyd, D. (2014). *It's complicated; The social livers of networked teens*. New Haven/London: Yale University Press.

Buhrmester, D., & Prager, K. (1995). Patterns and functions of self-disclosure during childhood and adolescence. In K. J. Rotenberg (Ed.), *Disclosure processes in children and adolescents* (pp. 10–57). Cambridge: Cambridge University Press.

Côté, J. E. (2009). Identity formation and self-development in adolescence. In R. M. Lerner & L. Steinberg (Eds.), *Handbook of adolescent psychology. Vol. 1. Individual bases of adolescent development (3rd ed.)* (pp. 266–304). Hoboken: Wiley.

d'Haenens, L., & Vandoninck, S. (2012). *Kids online: Vaardigheden, kansen en risico's van kinderen en jongeren op het internet*. Gent: Academia Press.

Insafe. (2015). *About safer internet day*. http://www.saferinternetday.org/web/guest/about. Accessed 30 Jan 2015.

Livingstone, S., & Bulger, M. E. (2013). *A global agenda for children's rights in the digital age. Recommendations for developing UNICEF's research strategy*. London: LSE.

Papacharissi, Z., & Gibson, P. L. (2011). Fifteen minutes of privacy: Privacy, sociality, and publicity on social network sites. In S. Trepte & L. Reinecke (Eds.), *Privacy online: Perspectives on privacy and self-disclosure in the social web* (pp. 75–91). Berlin/Heidelberg: Springer-Verlag.

Peter, J., & Valkenburg, P. M. (2011). Adolescents' online privacy: Toward a developmental perspective. In S. Trepte & L. Reinecke (Eds.), *Privacy online* (pp. 221–234). Berlin/Heidelberg: Springer-Verlag.

Siibak, A. (2009). Constructing the self through the photo selection – Visual impression management on social networking websites. *Cyberpsychology: Journal of Psychosocial Research on Cyberspace, 3*(1), article 1.

Steinberg, L. (2011). *Adolescence. 9th international edition.* New York: McGraw-Hill Humanities.

Taddicken, M., & Jers, C. (2011). The uses of privacy online: Trading a loss of privacy for social web gratifications? In S. Trepte & L. Reinecke (Eds.), *Privacy online* (pp. 143–156). Berlin/Heidelberg: Springer-Verlag.

Part I
Identity: Online Identity Construction and Expression

Who Do You Think You Are? Examining the Off/Online Identities of Adolescents Using a Social Networking Site

Janette Hughes, Laura Morrison, and Stephanie Thompson

Abstract The aim of this qualitative research study was to examine the construction, deconstruction and reconstruction of adolescent identities by exploring social practices within the digital landscape of a social networking site called Ning. More specifically, we ask: (a) how are adolescents' identities shaped and performed, as they use a social networking platform to present themselves to the world, and (b) how do offline and online identities correspond and differ in the context of their out-of-school and schooled lives? We share the findings of this study that examines how twenty-three 12 and 13 year old students constructed and presented their identities to their classmates and teacher and how these identities compared to and contrasted with their offline classroom identities, focusing on an in-depth analysis of two students who participated in social practices in ways that both reflect and challenge their online and offline identities.

The out-of-school reality of digital age students now heavily relies on the use of personal mobile devices such as laptops, tablets and smartphones. Through these mobile devices, adolescents interact with a variety of multimodal digital texts and robust communication and social networking tools. Undoubtedly, this influences students' digital literacy and identity development; however, without education, students may only be partially cognisant of this. Remarkably, many education settings have not kept pace with students' out-of-school practices. Schools are hesitant to incorporate these technologies and social networking platforms, ignoring their educational potential. In actively banning students' mobile devices and social networking sites, a marked divide has been created between students' in-school practices and their out-of-school digital realities. As a result, the development of adolescents' digital literacies and their identities are not typically fostered within an education setting where students would benefit most.

J. Hughes (✉) • L. Morrison
Faculty of Education, University of Ontario Institute of Technology, Oshawa, ON, Canada
e-mail: janette.hughes@uoit.ca; laura.morrison@uoit.ca

S. Thompson
Durham District School Board, Whitby, ON, Canada

M. Walrave et al. (eds.), *Youth 2.0: Social Media and Adolescence*,
DOI 10.1007/978-3-319-27893-3_1

Incorporating mobile devices and social networking platforms into a multi-literacies pedagogy encourages students to be active in their learning communities. In this way, students learn not only course content, but also about themselves and their place in their community. Using qualitative case study analysis, this research explores the relationship between a multi-literacies pedagogy and the development of adolescent digital literacies and identities. More specifically we ask, (a) how are adolescents' identities shaped and performed when using a social networking platform to present themselves to the world, and (b) how do offline and online identities correspond and differ in the context of their out-of-school lives and their schooled lives?

As Subrahmanyam and Smahel (2011) point out, "constructing a stable and coherent identity is a key developmental task during adolescence". In this period of their lives, adolescents begin to define and redefine themselves in relation to people around them (Erikson 1968); therefore, understanding developmental change requires us to examine the individual, the social context in which s/he is engaged, and the interaction between the two over a period of time. Kroger (2004) notes that a number of studies have explored identity issues in the context of the diversity of cultural, ethnic and social classes; however, there is now a pressing need to investigate how adolescents make sense of their own identities in the context of their relationships and their surrounding environments. In their study on homepage construction as a way to express social development, Schmitt et al. (2008) found that the online creation of homepages and blogs was related to feelings of mastery, expressions of identity and represented a means to socialise. Subrahmanyam et al. (2006) found that adolescents frequently used online spaces to communicate identity information to others. Given that adolescents are immersed in digital media, there is a growing need for educators to recognise and respond to the needs of adolescents in a digital age.

Adolescents constantly seek ways to express themselves in the process of performing their identities. Therefore, in our digitally connected world, the rapid adoption of mobile technologies has implications for the adolescents who use them. In their work on multi-literacies, Cope and Kalantzis (2000) identify the different domains in students' lives (i.e. Lifeworlds and School-Based Worlds) as discourse worlds and they draw on these various domains to make meaning and create identities. Anstey and Bull (2006) suggest that "these domains or discourse worlds also help form a person's literacy identity, providing a repertoire of resources that a person can draw on when engaging in literate practices". They go on to explain that a student's literacy identity "includes social and cultural resources, technological experience, and all previous life experiences, as well as specific literacy knowledge and experience" (Anstey and Bull 2006). Weber and Mitchell's (2008) notion of identity as "personal and social bricolage" views identity construction as "an evolving active construction that constantly sheds bits and adds bits, changing through dialectical interactions with the digital and non-digital world, involving physical, psychological, social, and cultural agents". The use of an SNS, Ning in this case, allows adolescents to "try on" or play with alternate identities as they continue to develop a sense of self-identity.

Our aim in this research study was to examine the construction, deconstruction and reconstruction of adolescent identities through an exploration of their social practices within the digital landscape of a social networking site similar to Facebook called Ning. We were particularly interested in how students would present themselves on Ning and how the social networking community might bolster the students' "social presence" as defined by Swan and Shih (2005). In this chapter, we share the findings of this research study that examines how twenty-three 12 and 13 year old students constructed and presented their identities to their classmates and teacher and how these identities compared to and contrasted with their offline classroom identities. For the purposes of this chapter, we share an in-depth analysis of two case studies, which explore how two of the students participated in social practices in ways that both reflect and challenge their online and offline identities.

1 Social Presence on Ning

Brady et al. (2010) argue that social networking sites offer great educational potential to enhance the participants' "social presence", defined by Swan and Shih (2005) as the "degree to which participants in computer-mediated communication feel affectively connected one to another", by Picciano (2002) as a "student's sense of being and belonging in a course", and by Rourke et al. (2001) as "the ability of learners to project themselves socially and affectively into a community of inquiry". Our decision to use a social networking site, reaffirms our belief that it is critical for students to articulate who they are and what values, backgrounds, beliefs and experiences they bring to the learning environment. In this context, learning is viewed as a social practice that is culturally, historically and geographically situated, despite the fact that Ning allows us to break down spatial barriers.

In their work exploring how individuals' identities affect discussions, Ke et al. (2011) conclude that identities are critical for extracting meaning from discussions and Kear (2011) points to the importance of beginning from "an inviting place" where "contributions should be friendly, supportive and informal". The students seem to have an intuitive understanding of the social nature of learning, which is evident as they ease into their relationships through casual talk. In their study examining the use of Moodle vs. Facebook, DeSchryver et al. (2009) concluded that there was a positive correlation between social presence and active participation in online discussions, while other scholars (Cobb 2009; Swan and Shih 2005; Brady et al. 2010) confirm that students with a higher social presence online are often more likely to be more engaged in these conversations. Cobb (2009) argues that, "when information is presented in a way that increases social presence, it is better remembered by learners and the learning process is considered more engaging". In a review of the literature surrounding relationships between social presence, motivation and online learning, Bai (2003) states that social presence "can enhance closeness in online learning communities, reduce feelings of isolation and detachment, encourage interactions and facilitate participation in online learning".

There is no denying the popularity of social networking sites like Twitter, Instagram and Facebook. Given the age of the students we could not have used Facebook and opted instead for Ning, which would be deemed more acceptable to parents who are naturally concerned about their children's privacy and safety. Ning was one of a variety of digital tools we used within the larger context of a year-long research project that had students engaging with new media and many online resources. The students had ubiquitous access to wireless Internet and tablets for their learning and they used Ning to respond to media articles, YouTube clips and to extend their literature circle discussions. The research team felt that providing a social networking tool for these purposes would break down the temporal and spatial barriers of the classroom and reach more learning styles. Some students are quieter than others yet still participate fully in their learning. Likewise, some students need more reflection time before they contribute and an asynchronous communication tool allows this.

As boyd (2007) points out, social networking sites enable participants to: (1) create uniquely identifiable profiles that consist of user-supplied content, content provided by other users and/or system-provided data; (2) publicly articulate connections that can be viewed and traversed by others; and (3) consume, produce and/or interact with streams of user-generated content provided by their connections on the site. When we set up the Ning, we asked students to identify by first name and location only and to post a profile picture that did not have to be a personal photo. The discussion forum on Ning is multi-threaded and includes categories, photos and attachments. We enabled the discussion forum feature to allow students to create forum topics, as we wanted to encourage them to take ownership of their learning. Like Facebook, Ning members are able to "friend" other members, send virtual gifts to friends and use the "like" button for photos or comments posted by others. Unlike Facebook, Ning networks are ad free.

While Ning afforded the students a safe online social environment, it also limited the potential to share their work with a wider network of people – something public platforms permit with their webbed connections. Another disadvantage included the limited functions of Ning. Students are used to the integrated games and apps on Facebook, the ability to create "events" and to "like" websites, videos and articles and have this appear on their walls. These additional features keep adolescents returning to check for updates, play games and interact. Furthermore, the limited number of people on Ning makes it less appealing than Facebook. While students may initially exhibit enthusiasm and invest time setting up their profile pages, interest groups and chatting with peers, the lack of additional features or higher volume of people seemingly impacts their long-term interest levels.

2 Methodology

The research followed a qualitative design in keeping with the established practice of in-depth studies of teaching and learning and case studies in general (Stake 2000). A case study methodology was employed, which included detailed field notes, students' writing and contributions to the social networking site (Ning), and also transcribed interviews with students and the teacher. Analysis of the data required several different layers of coding and interpretation. In the first stage the bulk of the data was coded for various themes that emerged. We coded the interview transcripts following traditional coding procedures (Strauss and Corbin 1990) and compared themes across the different students in order to identify recurring and overlapping thematic and structural patterns (Black 2007). The Ning pages created by the students were analysed within a framework of semiotic meta-functions (Kress and van Leeuwen 2001a, b; Jewitt 2008; Burn 2008), which considered design and production as representational, interactive and textual. Our analysis focused on the various modes of expression that the students used (i.e. visual image, gesture, movement) and how these worked in concert to create meaning.

2.1 *Setting Up the Ning Network*

As the designers of the Ning network, the research team chose a colourful, appealing background design but members were also able to customise their profile pages with their own design, choice of widgets and profile applications so that their personal computer view might look very different from the original design. Once students got access to the Ning, it took only 48 h for them to claim it as their own, start making changes to their pages and setting up their friend networks. What follows in the next section is an in-depth analysis of the online activity of two of the twenty-three students in this class, one male and one female, with particular attention paid to their social practices and the way they communicate their online identities. Levi-Strauss once noted that bricolage was about the construction of the bricoleur's identity, moving beyond the simple appropriation of materials (Jenkins 1992). In our analyses, we examine what elements of themselves the students include in their Ning interactions, as well as what they choose to omit. We look at the overall design of their Ning pages – what they have added, deleted or borrowed from others. These analyses are juxtaposed with the teacher's impressions and knowledge of each of the students, as well as with the comments made by the two students, Elyssa and Liam (pseudonyms), in open-ended, follow-up interviews.

We chose to focus on Elyssa and Liam for our case studies as their Ning activity reflected how the other students generally used Ning – personalising their profile pages, completing school assignments and posting personal and work-related comments on each others' walls. However, in other respects they were also exceptional in their use of Ning when it came to their contrasting online and offline identities. For example, Elyssa's classroom personality could be characterised as shy, studious and reserved, while her online personality was outgoing, social and energetic. Likewise, Liam's personality in class was serious, mature and reflective, while his online personality was silly, open and laidback.

3 Case Studies

3.1 Elyssa

Elyssa is a 12 year-old girl of Chinese descent who appears quiet, serious and shy in the classroom. In a pre-project, open-ended survey that asks about students' technology use, Elyssa reports that she does not use any social networking sites other than Ning. She spends on average between 5 and 10 h per week using the Internet, primarily "surfing" for enjoyment and researching for school projects. At home, Elyssa has access to a desktop computer as well as both her own iPad and iPod. She reports that she "normally" enjoys using computer technologies, including mobile devices, in school because it "helps [her] do better in school and get more research done". She also comments that she likes using her iPad in class: "If I have quick access to the Internet, I feel like I have an advantage. Like when I do research on my iPad, it's a lot quicker than going on the computer." When asked whether she felt that technology helped shape a student's sense of identity, Elyssa responded, "No, because I think that kids can develop their sense of identity without using tech items".

Elyssa's Ning page (see Fig. 1) is an interesting juxtaposition of the personal and impersonal; this intersection highlights the anonymity exercised by many online adolescents who choose to omit personal statistical information like real name, age

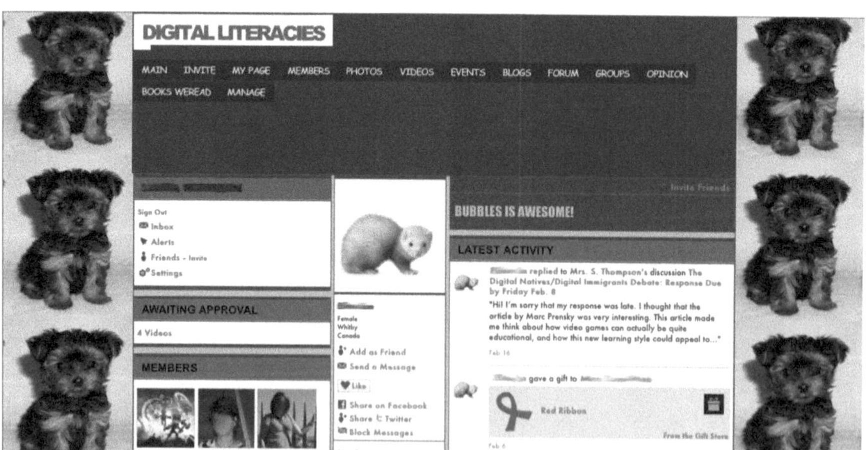

Fig. 1 Elyssa's profile page on Ning

and appearance, but who simultaneously exhibit openness through their intimate status updates, personal comments on friends' walls and publicised discussions posted on discussion boards – all activity in which Elyssa engages. In Elyssa's case the decision to omit personal information comes from a keen awareness of the "dangers" of the Internet. She comments:

> I didn't give personal information because I've learned about the dangers of doing so at school. I also didn't post any personal pictures for the same reason. Also, I am a more private person, and I don't give away personal information like some of my classmates do. I did this consciously, as I was aware of the possible effects.

Interestingly, Elyssa purposely creates a persona that she sees as "opposite" to how she believes her classmates view her.

> On my profile, I made myself seem like the opposite of how my peers see me. On Ning, I seem like a colourful, bubbly girl who is very talkative and confident. This is because I designed my page with bright colours, joined multiple groups, gave gifts, and posted lots of comments.

Elyssa's page is a bricolage of her thought processes: "wow! My response is pretty long!" and then later, "Everyone has long responses. I'm not alone. :D". Her frenetic energy is expressed through her constant status updates and the comments she posts to friends' walls which contain short and erratic sentences and lots of exclamation marks: "f--, when i just saw ur page, i was like woaaahhh. It's awesome!!!!! How did u do it??"

Elyssa has personalised her Ning page and substituted the basic template with a customised layout design. Her profile page has since changed from the original after she learned more advanced layout, design and uploading skills. Her first profile page consisted of a koala bear she uploaded from her computer for her profile picture and a rocky beach for her page's wallpaper. She noted that she would have chosen a puppy or ferret if she had known how up upload a photo from the Internet. Figure 1: Elyssa's Profile Page on Ning illustrates the page she eventually created after learning more skills. Her original profile page included a colour scheme that emphasised colours found in nature like blue, green and yellow. Elyssa did not explicitly comment on these colours and their relation to the natural world and when asked about her design choices she commented: ....

> I left out very dark colours, and I added very few pink. This is because of two reasons. 1. I am not a girly girl, and I despise the colour pink. 2. I don't hate dark colours but I may have added bright colours unconsciously to gain favour from my peers.

Throughout her follow-up interview, Elyssa makes references that demonstrate she is highly conscious of her work being viewed by others. At the end of her interview, she reiterates this idea as she revisits the design of her home page, by saying, "I made it bright and pretty, and I like it. Although I do feel like as if it is because of the fact that my peers would be on it that I made it look that bright."

As someone who is very in tune with nature, her choice of colours furthers her "nature-based" wall theme and supporting wall posts that point to a love of nature and animals: "I have 3 turtles, 2 fish, 3 frogs and a hammy named Bubbles". In a follow-up interview with Elyssa, she mentions repeatedly that she is an animal lover and comments that "animal lover is usually one of five words that someone would use to describe me".

Unlike the chaotic nature of some of her peers' personalised pages, Elyssa's page has maintained order. All the textboxes have highlighted headings and separate boxes for sidebars like "gifts received" "friends", and "blog posts". Elyssa's posts appear in a logical sequence of recent to past posts, and primarily consist of "thinking-out-loud" type posts where Elyssa's internal dialogue is revealed: "is anyone on?"; "what is this?" "…I'm so bored"; "How do you add friends?" and her very supportive and enthusiastic comments to her peers about their work or profile pages: "That's a great response!! I read all of it."; "I really liked your response, Liam. It had many great points!"; "f--, when I just saw ur page, I was like woaaahhh. It's awesome!!!!!!!!!!!!!!!!!!!How did u do it??"; "hi j--. I like ur page."

Based solely on Elyssa's status updates and posts to friends, Elyssa's "voice" is bubbly, enthusiastic and flighty – she uses many exclamation points for emphasis and text-message contractions like "ur" in place of "your" to differentiate her social activity on Ning from her academic activity on Ning's more formal discussion board. In her follow-up interview, Elyssa notes that she is very different online than in class:

> On my ning profile, I am more social than I am at school. On the ning, I go around commenting on many things, when in real life, I am less social. I'm not sure why I did this, but I think that I may be more confident on the ning than in real life (I guess people really do change on the internet.).

Elyssa's teacher agrees that there are noticeable differences in the way Elyssa interacts online versus in person, but that there are also some similarities. As stated, she is a quiet, almost reserved individual in class, so the social comments she makes are not typical of how she speaks in the classroom. However, her positive and encouraging online comments are indicative of her supportive school persona.

Elyssa's exceptional intrapersonal skills enable her to see clearly the contradictions in her online personas and her classroom persona. Indeed, she conducts herself differently depending on whether she is being social on the Ning or whether she is writing a response for her teacher. Her social posts are markedly different in writing style, depth and, where applicable, analysis, compared to the formal discussions Elyssa has posted for her teacher which include a lot of analysis, relevant examples and correct grammar, spelling and sentence structure. From her teacher's perspective, Elyssa's responses to specific school-related assignments express more of her serious in-school personality traits than the comments on her profile page and there appears to be a clear distinction between student-Elyssa and online-Elyssa. To account for the difference in writing styles, Elyssa comments: "These responses are all quite long, as many people describe me as a perfectionist". She also reveals that writing on Ning made her more conscious of what she was saying:

> I left out some of the ideas that I had while writing my responses. I believe that I did this because I thought that it would be unpopular if I did. I did this consciously. I thought of ideas while I was typing, and when I came across a thought that I thought wouldn't be popular with my peers, I skipped it. At school, I normally don't care if my writing doesn't please my peers, but for whatever reason, I do on the internet.

Later, she also says, "at school, I am actually more confident with my teacher than with my peers, so I may have actually responded slightly differently if my peers weren't on the Ning with me".

This controlled, conscious decision about how to write on Ning seems to stand in stark contrast to Elyssa's comments in her interview, in which she states that she feels "happy, relaxed and confident about using the Ning". However, she also adds that she feels "in control" when she is using the Ning for writing:

> In real life, I am not very social, because I am quite shy and I tend to stutter A LOT. However, when I write, I do not stutter and I become creative and colourful in my writing. I feel more in control and confident when I am typing, because I don't get nervous when I'm typing. I prefer to type than to speak because I am nervous standing in front of the class and sometimes, I randomly stutter when I'm talking to close friends! So because of the fact that I don't stutter on the internet, I feel relaxed.

The Ning clearly affords Elyssa an opportunity to convey her thoughts and ideas in a way that provides a high level of both comfort and control. She implies that her shyness is somewhat alleviated when she writes on Ning and that she is freer to express herself. However, she is not entirely free to share all of her ideas and censors the ones that she feels will make her unpopular with her peers. The classroom teacher believes this is likely because Elyssa is a talented writer and does not want to be perceived as "showing off" in front of her peers. This is in keeping with Elyssa's in-class persona, which does not wish to attract much attention.

Elyssa does not participate in the Groups she has been invited to. For the most part the "discussion" in these groups is silly, one-sided banter. This omission of participation perhaps communicates a desire to engage in more meaningful communication. She does, however, engage in the gift-giving trend begun by some of her classmates. She comments:

> On my profile, I gave gifts to everyone. This is not like me in real life, as I am not very friendly with everyone. I chose to give gifts to everyone because I wanted to seem friendly on my ning profile. Also, I gave gifts to everybody because I didn't want to give gifts to some people, but not to others, and I didn't want to give no gifts. Also, I friended a lot of people who weren't actually my friends. When somebody sent me a request to become a friend, I accepted without thinking twice. When I thought about this, I figured that it was because of two reasons. 1. Ning was not like other social websites, as friending someone didn't lead to special things that they could do. 2. I wanted to seem friendly on ning.

Although she has omitted a personal profile picture and chosen to reveal little about herself in her profile, she has allowed all her enthusiastic comments to her peers and their responses to appear on her wall, revealing an effervescent online personality. Her willingness to engage in friending and gift-giving support her claims that she is trying to be more social online than she is in class. It is easy to get a sense of Elyssa's online personality from her Ning wall, even though her personal information is limited. Furthermore, it is the absence of personal information and a personal profile picture that highlights the fact that she does not wish to align her in-person self with the identity she is creating on Ning.

3.2 Liam

Liam is a bright, attentive and articulate 12 year-old boy. In his pre-project, open-ended survey, Liam reports that he does not use any social networking sites other than Ning. He spends on average only 1–5 h per week using the Internet, primarily doing research for school. At home, Liam has access to a desktop computer, as well as an iPod and an e-reader. He reports that he enjoys creating "visual art" on the computer: "I use Microsoft Publisher, Bitstrips, Storybird, Comic Life and Adobe Photoshop Elements (PSE). I enjoy making pictures or stories, and sometimes I also use these to make invitations, cards and comics". Liam comments that he feels more motivated to do school projects and presentations using technology "because without them projects can be dull and boring … and technology opens up huge new opportunities". When asked whether he felt that technology contributed to a student's sense of identity, Liam responded, "Sometimes people will be themselves online, but more often not … Everyone can create an online identity, but it is harder to create one that reflects you in real life, or one that helps you grow."

Liam has personalised his Ning page (see Fig. 2) by including a moving, video-game-looking wallpaper background – a unique feature not included in Ning's pre-made wallpaper selections. In substituting one of the basic background options for this one, Liam communicates that he has the skills and confidence to navigate a program like Ning, which is particularly noteworthy as Liam communicates elsewhere on his wall that he prefers to spend his time outside: "I like to spend as much time outside as I can because I find video games are really boring most of the time." The inclusion of a videogame looking feature is an interesting choice for

Fig. 2 Liam's profile page on Ning

someone who is not particularly interested in them. Liam may therefore have taken this step in the hope of standing out on Ning and appealing to some of the other, more video game-minded students. He receives validating messages on his wall relating to his design like, "ps I like your page☺". Undoubtedly, the attention from having a "cooler" page than others in the class, adds social capital to his online identity.

Liam has also included a slideshow photo gallery that consists of five rotating images pulled from the Internet at the top of his profile page. This is also a unique feature as few of the other students have included this on their profile pages. Each time a photo has been uploaded Liam has received positive feedback from other members in the class through "likes" or comments.

Two photos in the slideshow reference recent popular adolescent movies -- *The Hunger Games* and *Harry Potter*. In his follow-up interview, Liam downplays the importance of the photos, however, commenting: "My pictures show things that I like, but they are not personal, and who doesn't like Harry Potter? The only thing that says anything important about my identity is my profile picture, which is one of my favourite albums, by Radiohead." The Hunger Games photo, which includes an image of the Queen of England and the phrase, "Let the hunger games begin" is satirical, alluding to the idea that the politics surrounding England and the Olympics are comparable to the politics in *The Hunger Games*. It is fitting that Liam included this political allusion as elsewhere on his wall his interest in politics and his knowledge of government is clear. For instance, he posts his thoughts on Ontario's Premier Dalton McGuinty's resignation upon hearing the news: "OMG!!!!! DALTON McGUINTY JUST RESIGNED!!!!!!! OMG!!!!! DALTON McGUINTY JUST RESIGNED!!!!!!! OMG!!!!! DALTON McGUINTY JUST RESIGNED!!!!!!! OMG!!!!! DALTON McGUINTY JUST RESIGNED!!!!!!!" That Liam chose to log onto the Ning and express his surprise indicates Liam wants his classmates to know of his interest in politics. Furthermore, he does not just state the news of McGuinty's resignation, but frames it in the acronym-based and exclamatory language aligned with social networking. He also includes in his "About Me" section, "I am a supporter of the NDP and *not* of the Conservatives or Liberals ($10 you didn't know that!) and I admire Jack Layton." Adding a statement such as this one communicates that Liam sees the Ning as a place where he can divulge information about himself that he may not have had the opportunity to do in class or in person.

Liam omits a personal image of himself, opting instead for the Radiohead album cover of words quilted together that reflect modern North American society: "TV, Fear, Beef, Poor, Aid". He also omits any personal profile information, substituting his real name, and place of residence, Uranus. This transposition suggests that for Liam, the Ning is a place where he is a transposed version of himself. Perhaps the self he would more like to be in person – one that is sillier, more creative and open about his interests. His choice not to reveal much personal information is a conscious one, as he reports: "Even though the Ning is still fairly secure, I still do not trust it to give away secrets or anything, not to sound paranoid".

The emphasis on Liam's wall is primarily silly communication with peers; however, this is interspersed with thoughtful responses to teacher-moderated discussion boards. His wall is a patchwork of comments and images that reflect both the intellectual/academic and the attention-seeking mischief-maker. On peers' walls he comments "DOMO" and "I want a taco. Or a burritto. Don't get killed by the drug scandal. That would mean that I don't get a taco. Or a burrito." And, he leaves comments on his own wall like, "hi". Finally, he posts the most prolific nonsensical comments in the groups he is part of, "Ya you got a morph suit" and "comsfgdfhkbnkjhngfk jcdfoh;pjknk jkdr,vgj,l". Interestingly, in an interview with Liam's teacher, she describes his school persona as anything but silly; bright, dynamic and witty are three adjectives that she uses to describe him. She finds him to be a very interesting student; articulate, sensitive, concerned about social justice, the environment, politics, health and fitness and with a "wisdom about him that comes from being aware of current events and from having frequent conversations with adults on adult issues".

When asked in a follow-up interview about whether the Ning made him feel more aware of what he was writing because the audience was wider than usual, Liam comments:

> It helps me to be more aware, because yes, everybody can see it, but also because on the internet once you put something down it is hard to take it back. On Earth, it is easy to communicate, and take back something. In the computer world, people can misinterpret you and it can really harm you. Often in real life, I try to say things that I would be able to say in front of a crowd or on the computer with a teacher there.

He later adds that it is sometimes easier for him to write things down than to speak them. On the whole, Liam feels that the most important function of the Ning is to connect him to his peers: "If I want to tell somebody something, I can tell them, and it is much easier than calling them on the phone. We can communicate much better, because they can still reply to me even if I miss them by an hour or so." This comment underscores Liam's tendency to use Ning in more social ways than some of his peers.

Liam's page reflects a dual identity in its truest sense with the combination of posts referring to his interest in politics, reading, social issues and nature, all of which are set in stark contrast to the many silly comments that appear on the Ning and the video-game appearance of his personal page. Despite some of the Liam's sillier posts on his wall or to friends, he also presents a studious side when responding to formal discussion posts – this can be seen in a lengthy post detailing the bullying found in the classic Rudolph the Red Nose Reindeer holiday film. Furthermore, he demonstrates the same serious tone when responding to other posts like "Media's Messages" and detailing the three types of media that are the most influential in his life. According to his teacher, Liam's "academic" postings are more in keeping with his in-class persona. He takes all school assignments very seriously and is a critical and analytical thinker as well as a good writer.

4 Building Narratives on the Ning

Psychologist and educator Jerome Bruner (1990, 1996, 2002) has argued that narrative is a natural and necessary part of our lives. We "live most of our lives in a world constructed according to the rules and devices of narrative" (Bruner 1996). We are actors in real-life stories where "we walk on stage into a play whose enactment is already in progress – a play whose somewhat open plot determines what parts we play and toward what denouements we may be heading" (Bruner 1990). We build these narratives up online through the bits of information that we post over time and we can use these posts to get a better sense of how we see ourselves. New technologies are making this even easier. Do these posts, however, which for the students in this study often include photos of pets, vacations and favourite celebrities, really say something important about who they are or are they merely trivial indicators of identity?

Oscar Wilde once said, "There are two principles in life. The first is that one must strike a pose. I cannot remember the second" (Ellman 1987). There is no doubt that the students posture on the Ning but it is clear that they do not set out to deceive their classmates. This was true for all students in the class, but it was most noticeable with Elyssa and Liam. That is why we focused our attention on these two students, who are exemplary for the whole sample.

Elyssa's comments about her selective choices regarding her activity on the Ning indicate that she is fully aware of how she represents herself and for what purpose. Other students may not be as cognizant of the effects their choices might have on their peers. Although both Elyssa and Liam are seemingly candid, their representations of themselves online do not always ring "true", at least when compared to their classroom personas and what the teacher sees in class. It is important to note that identity development is also fluid rather than static, especially at this age when students are "trying on" different identities. To further exemplify this point, we note that both Elyssa and Liam have changed a variety of things about their pages since we first conducted our analyses. As Subrahmanyam et al. (2008) and Subrahmanyam and Smahel (2011) suggest, the online and offline worlds of adolescents are intellectually connected. Ning allowed Elyssa and Liam to explore and construct online versions of themselves, which are undoubtedly connected on some level to their offline personas. It was through the various communication tools on Ning and the less threatening communications that they were able to posture, play and experiment with these otherwise dormant elements of their personalities. All it took was the right environment for them to become animate.

The Ning activities in which they engage can tell us something about these students' identities. The more complex interactions, for example how they interact in an affinity group, post content, select others as friends and offer gifts, give us insight into who they are and how they want to be seen by others. The social discourse of both students indicate that they understand, register and adapt their language use depending on their audience and purpose. Both Liam and Elyssa use a type of stylised writing, in the form of social networking jargon or nonsensical language.

Perhaps this is done as a way of fitting in and, in Elyssa's case, demonstrating that she is "in the know" when it comes to online chat – something she has not been able to share within the parameters of a traditional classroom environment. It is clear that these literacy practices afforded Elyssa the opportunity to engage in identity construction, which is in keeping with Alvermann's (2010) claim that there is a strong relationship between literacy and identity. Literary practices, she relates, "provide an arena for constructing and performing identities, and youth identity production in SNSs [Social Networking Sites] is a pertinent example of this" (Alvermann 2010).

Social networking is a group endeavour and Jones and Hafner (2012) explain that "people's Facebook walls are like stages on which they act out conversations with their friends" and display their personal preferences, interests and activities (Jones and Hafner 2012). Interestingly, depending on the context – a student-created group, teacher-created discussion thread, or their own profile wall – Elyssa and Liam exhibited multiple versions of their online selves. Beach et al. (2011) point out that participation in SNSs enable students to develop a sense of agency through the enactment of online personas; for Elyssa and Liam, one online persona was insufficient when it came to developing this sense of agency. The multiple identities that the students demonstrate are not limited to online vs. in-person personas; a dual identity was noted for both Liam and Elyssa even on the Ning. Depending on the context of the interaction, their personalities varied – for example, responding to a discussion post from the teachers versus chatting with peers or being the only girl in a group discussion filled with boys. The group discourse requires us to examine the choices the students make within the context of the class and what the teacher, the researchers and their peers expect of them. The purpose of Ning must also be considered. Just as LinkedIn is about career building, and other sites are about connecting with friends, the overall purpose of Ning as an educational tool needs to be explicit.

5 Toward a Meaningful Integration of Modern Social Platforms

Our experience using Ning with this group of young adolescents confirms for us the value of this tool in our pedagogical repertoires. As an online learning environment, Ning can foster growth, connection and learning – but building in thoughtful, genuine interaction seems to be a key element in its successful use. We tapped into students' out-of-school literacies to consider how digital technologies like Ning might be used in classroom contexts. It was our intention to create a learning situation that allows students to share their identities and views them as constructors and producers of knowledge.

Building a community is an important priority. Hung and Yuen (2010) argue that sustaining communities of practice can be challenging and that "potential obstacles, such as lack of trust, isolated feelings, and other affective factors" can be barriers to learning. They also suggest that, "hybrid communities mixing online interaction with face-to-face interaction may be ideal" (Hung and Yuen 2010). In follow-up interviews with the teacher and students, there was an overwhelming consensus that combining real-time, face-to-face communication, with the Ning network, which offers flexibility, convenience and opportunities for more informal social sharing, provides a balance that furthers pedagogical goals.

The multimodal affordances of Ning provided the students with an opportunity to convey their social presence in ways that helped them become part of the community. They engaged in collegial social practices such as adding greetings to their posts, referring to peers by first names, writing supportive comments to each other and added personal anecdotes, which offered expressions of emotion and communicated some of their beliefs and values, especially regarding the theme of the project, which happened to be the impact of digital media and technologies in their lives. These online social practices are quite common regardless of the discussion forum or learning space. In addition to fostering a community of learners where each person had the opportunity to engage in collective and collaborative learning and felt comfortable sharing opinions and new understandings, the ability to embed video, images and links and to attach files directly to their comments helped them to enhance and expand their contributions and their social presence on Ning.

In keeping with the understanding that literacy is a social practice and that new social networking platforms offer educational opportunities for students to create or assume social identities beyond the traditional classroom context, we opened up this new space for learning. As important as it is for students to use technologies for thinking, organising ideas and creating multimodal products to represent their understandings, it is equally important to offer them opportunities to connect with each other, build relationships with the people in their learning communities and explore social identities – one of the most crucial tasks of adolescence.

References

Alvermann, D. E. (2010). *Adolescents online literacies: Connecting classrooms, digital media, & popular culture*. New York: Peter Lang.

Anstey, M., & Bull, G. (2006). *Teaching and learning multiliteracies: Changing times, changing literacies*. Newark: International Reading Association.

Bai, H. (2003). Student motivation and social presence in online learning: Implications for future research. In C. Crawford (Ed.), *Proceedings of the society for information technology and teacher education international conference 2003* (pp. 2714–2720). Chesapeake: AACE.

Beach, R., Appleman, D., Hynds, S., & Wilhelm, J. (2011). *Teaching literature to adolescents*. New York: Routledge.

Black, R. W. (2007). Digital design: English language learners and reader reviews in online fiction. In M. Knobel & C. Lankshear (Eds.), *A new literacies sampler* (pp. 115–136). New York: Peter Lang.

Boyd, D. (2007). Identity production in a networked culture: Why youth heart. The role of networked publics in teenage social life. In D. Buckingham (Ed.), *Youth, identity, and digital media* (pp. 119–142). Cambridge: MIT Press.

Brady, K., Holcomb, L., & Smith, B. (2010). The use of alternative social networking sites in higher educational settings: A case study of the E-learning benefits of Ning in education. *Journal of Interactive Online Learning, 9*(2), 151–160.
Bruner, J. (1990). *Acts of meaning: Four lectures on mind and culture*. Cambridge, MA: Harvard University Press.
Bruner, J. (1996). *The culture of education*. Cambridge, MA: Harvard University Press.
Bruner, J. (2002). *Making stories: Law, literature, life*. New York: Farrar Straus & Giroux.
Burn, A. (2008). The case of rebellion: Researching multimodal texts. In J. Coiro, M. Knobel, C. Lankshear, & D. J. Leu (Eds.), *Handbook of research on new literacies* (pp. 151–178). New York: Lawrence Erlbaum Associates.
Cobb, S. C. (2009). Social presence and online learning: A current view from a research perspective. *Journal of Interactive Online Learning, 8*(3), 241–254.
Cope, B., & Kalantzis, M. (Eds.). (2000). *Multiliteracies: Literacy learning and the design of social futures*. London/New York: Routledge/Falmer.
DeSchryver, M., Mishra, P., Koehler, M., & Francis, A. (2009). Moodle vs. Facebook: Does using Facebook for discussions in an online course enhance perceived social presence and student interaction? In I. Gibson, R. Weber, K. McFerrin, R. Carlsen, & D. A. Willis (Eds.), *Proceedings of the society for information technology and teacher education international conference 2009* (pp. 329–336). Chesapeake: AACE.
Ellman, R. (1987). *Oscar Wilde*. London: Faber.
Erikson, E. E. (1968). *Identity: Youth and crisis*. New York: W.W. Norton & Company.
Hung, H.-T., & Yuen, S. C.-Y. (2010). Educational use of social networking technology in higher education. *Teaching in Higher Education, 15*(6), 703–714.
Jenkins, H. (1992). *Textual poachers: Television fans and participatory culture*. London: Routledge.
Jewitt, C. (2008). *The visual in learning and creativity: A review of the literature*. London: Creative Partnerships.
Jones, R., & Hafner, C. (2012). *Understanding digital literacies: A practical introduction*. New York: Routledge.
Ke, F., Chavez, A., Causarano, P.-N. L., & Causarano, A. (2011). Identity presence and knowledge building: Joint emergence in online learning environments? *International Journal of Computer-Supported Collaborative Learning, 8*(3), 349–370.
Kear, K. (2011). *Online and social networking communities: A best practice guide for educators*. New York: Routledge.
Kress, G. R., & van Leeuwen, T. (2001a). *Literacy in the new media age*. London: Routledge.
Kress, G. R., & van Leeuwen, T. (2001b). *Multimodal discourse: The modes and media of contemporary communication*. London: Arnold.
Kroger, J. (2004). *Identity in adolescence: The balance between self and other*. New York: Routledge.
Picciano, A. G. (2002). Beyond student perceptions: Issues of interaction, presence, and performance in an online course. *Journal of Asynchronous Learning Networks, 6*(1), 21–40.
Rourke, L., Anderson, T., Garrison, D. R., & Archer, W. (2001). Assessing social presence in asynchronous text-based computer conferencing. *Journal of Distance Education, 14*(2), 50–71.
Schmitt, K. L., Dayanim, S., & Matthias, S. (2008). Construction as an expression of social development. *Developmental Psychology, 44*(2), 496–506.
Stake, R. E. (2000). Case studies. In N. Denzin & Y. Lincoln (Eds.), *Handbook of qualitative research* (2nd ed., pp. 435–454). Thousand Oaks: Sage Publications.
Strauss, A., & Corbin, J. (1990). *Basics of qualitative research: Grounded theory, procedures and techniques*. Newbury Park: Sage Publications.
Subrahmanyam, K., & Smahel, D. (2011). *Digital youth: The role of media in development*. New York: Springer.

Subrahmanyam, K., Smahel, D., & Greenfield, P. (2006). Connecting developmental constructions to the internet: Identity presentation and sexual exploration in online teen chat rooms. *Developmental Psychology, 42*(3), 395–406.
Subrahmanyam, K., Reich, S., Waechter, N., & Espinoza, G. (2008). Online and offline social networks: Use of social networking sites by emerging adults. *Journal of Applied Developmental Psychology, 26*(6), 420–433.
Swan, K., & Shih, L. F. (2005). On the nature and development of social presence in online course discussions. *Journal of Asynchronous Learning Networks, 9*(3), 115–136.
Weber, S., & Mitchell, C. (2008). Imagining, keyboarding, and posting identities: Young people and new media technologies. In D. Buckingham (Ed.), *Youth, identity, and digital media* (pp. 25–48). Cambridge: The MIT Press.

An 'Open Source' Networked Identity. On Young People's Construction and Co-construction of Identity on Social Network Sites

Malene Charlotte Larsen

Abstract This chapter examines the concept of identity in relation to youth practices on SNSs. The chapter illustrates how writing "I love you" or other emotional statements on each other's profiles on SNSs is not only a common way for Danish teenagers to communicate and practice friendship, but also an important part of their self-presentation online. It examines why these emotional statements are almost always publicly available – or even strategically and intentionally placed on the young people's profiles. In relation to this, it is argued that young people – through their emotional communicative actions – are not only staging their own identity, but are co-constructors of each other's identities, which the author characterises as an "open source", networked identity.

1 Introduction

In addition to being a significant part of children and young people's friendship relations, SNSs are heavily intertwined with self-presentation and the construction of identity. This chapter focuses on the concept of identity and how we can understand it in relation to youth on SNSs. The chapter discusses the concept of identity theoretically and empirically, based on findings from 8 years of ethnographic studies of Danish adolescents' use of SNSs (e.g. Larsen 2010). Specifically, the chapter discusses what role social relations play in the self-presentation of youth and it is argued that to a great extent young people manage and construct each other's identity on SNSs. In relation to this, and based on the concept of networked individualism (Wellman 2002; Wellman et al. 2003), the chapter introduces the term "open source" networked identity (Larsen 2010, 2011; Ryberg and Larsen 2008) as a metaphor for understanding how the collaborative presentation of identity or

M.C. Larsen (✉)
Department of Communication, Aalborg University, Aalborg, Denmark
e-mail: malenel@hum.aau.dk

M. Walrave et al. (eds.), *Youth 2.0: Social Media and Adolescence*,
DOI 10.1007/978-3-319-27893-3_2

identity-through-social-interaction is visible, reinforced and sometimes deliberately used by young people on SNSs.

The chapter focuses especially on a quite specific mode of communication, which the author has found to be typical among Danish teenagers on SNSs. This mode of communication is characterised by a particular Love discourse that exists among best friends, where statements such as "I love you" appear frequently in their interactions and where various technological features are used, refined or even redefined in order to express emotional communication. The way in which young people use this emotional communication reflects what Gee calls discourse with a capital D. Here, we are dealing with "… socially accepted associations among ways of using language, of thinking, valuing, acting, and interacting, in the 'right' places and at the 'right' times with the 'right' objects…" (Gee 1999, p. 17). Based on this understanding the chapter examines how writing "I love you" and using a range of culturally and socially accepted signs, symbols or technological features (often in a very creative or playful manner) has become a common way for Danish youth to communicate and construct not only their own, but also each other's identity online. The chapter investigates why this practice has become so common and what it means to the young people. It discusses the different functions of the emotional communication and analyses the differences between boys and girls and how they critically discuss their own widespread use of the words "I love you". Based on this analysis, the chapter discusses why the emotional statements are almost always publicly available – or even strategically and intentionally placed or highlighted on young people's profiles. As a consequence of this, it is argued that young people – through their emotional communicative actions – are not only staging their own identity, but are co-constructors of each other's identity; an "open source" networked identity.

Theoretically, the chapter is situated within the field of discourse studies where Nexus Analysis (Norris and Jones 2005; Scollon and Scollon 2004; Scollon 2001a, b) is the primary theoretical and methodological approach. Nexus analysis distinguishes itself from other discourse analytic approaches by focusing on central, mediated actions carried out by social actors within a loosely tied "nexus of practice" (rather than focusing solely on discourse). The term nexus of practice refers to the social field where humans, discourses and cultural artefacts intersect and result in social action. In the chapter, young people's use of SNSs is analysed as a nexus of practice where communicating youthful emotions are among the most prominent and central of mediated actions and cycles of discourses.

Empirically, the chapter is based on an extensive amount of empirical data collected over the past 8 years, where the main purpose has been to gain an understanding of the meanings SNSs have for the individual and social lives of Danish adolescents and how they use them as part of everyday life. The primary data referred to in this chapter consist of ethnographic engagement (including participatory observations of young people's use of various SNSs) and a large-scale, qualitative questionnaire aimed at investigating the experiences that 12–18-year-old Danes have using SNSs. In this way, the author has studied the central actions young people carry out across SNSs, as well as the ways in which they discursively construct and articulate their concrete uses and experiences. Before going deeper into the methodological and theoretical grounding, the chapter will start by clarifying how the concept of identity is used.

2 The Concept of Identity

The concept of identity is a diverse concept and its meaning is still being discussed within various theoretical positions. It is closely related to other concepts such as soul, psyche, personality, character, social role, person, self or I, and it is used within various disciplines such as clinical psychology, social psychology, developmental psychology, social philosophy, discourse analysis, cultural analysis or anthropology (Jørgensen 2008; Lemke 2008). Since the concept is being used within several domains, it is impossible to come up with an overarching definition. Thus, there is no single definition of the term identity and its description will always depend on one's theoretical perspective and approach.

Originally, the term identity comes from the Latin *idem*, which means "the same". Nonetheless, the term is being used to describe both similarities and differences. On the one hand, identity is perceived as something unique which each of us possesses that is more or less consistent over time. On the other hand, the term is being used to indicate a certain connection to a wider collective or social group where identification with others is central and where we are expected to behave according to the situation or who we are with (Buckingham 2008). As such, the concept exists in a border area between individual and contemporary culture; between individual psychology and sociology (Jørgensen 2008, p. 13). We are dealing with a dichotomy between identity as something stable, biological and personally psychological and as something societal and socially constructed. As several authors have pointed out (e.g. Jørgensen 2008; Lemke 2008), we can hardly reach an adequate or analytically applicable description of the concept of identity without including perspectives from both sides and trying to bridge the gap between them.

Such a position has been taken up by the discourse analyst Jay Lemke (2008) who rejects the idea that our identity is solely fragmented and socially constructed, but acknowledges the fact that we play different roles in different social situations and act differently according to who we are with. We are, however, always "ourselves", but we highlight certain sides of our personality in different situations. Lemke proposes a distinction of the concept of identity, which involves the terms *identity-in-practice* (or *identity-in-the-moment*) and *identity-across-timescales*. These two terms are heavily intertwined. We are not dealing with two different kinds of identity, but different perspectives on the same concept. A focus on action is more prevalent in the identity-in-practice perspective, focusing on specific social situations and group interactions, whereas a more structured or positional determination is prevalent in the identity-over-time perspective, which involves a focus on social structures and historical aspects of time. Using this distinction Lemke is inspired by e.g. Judith Butler's (1993) notion of *identity performance*, which includes the perception that the more enduring aspects of our identities are inscribed in us when we are acting in specific moments, as well as Bourdieu's (1987, 1990) concept of *habitus*.

2.1 Identity on SNSs

In this chapter the author proposes to use Lemke's distinction when focusing on the concept of identity on SNSs. Thus, we can understand different online situations – e.g. writing a status update, uploading a profile picture or filling out personal information on SNSs – as a performance of identity-in-practice. This form of identity construction appears on the short timescales of situated small-group activity (Lemke 2008, p. 18). Such practices are based on the longer scale perspectives of our identity, which are always inscribed in us when we act in certain ways, in certain moments, with certain people. On SNSs we are continuously constructing our identity in practice by means of the different cultural tools made available to us online. As pointed out elsewhere (Larsen 2007a), young people especially are constantly performing their identity in practice on SNSs. They do so by, for instance, uploading pictures of themselves and asking others to comment on them, creating mini polls on their profiles asking "What do you think of me?" etc. though at the same time they are roleplaying to some extent and trying to appear in a certain way in a certain situation.

Identity – as it is developed across timescales – can, according to Lemke (2008), be generalised in several socially recognisable positions. This is appropriate to larger institutional scales and lifespan developments. As a consequence of the recognisability of identity over time, we can position ourselves – and others – in different groups. This part of our identity is not determined by a single identity performance, but is constituted through many different practices across time and is thereby connected to our habitus. When we log onto SNSs we have many experiences of how we function in different contexts; it is our life story that holds us together as individuals. In relation to this, we can understand SNSs as spaces where we continually relate to and communicate our own life story. This is especially visible on Facebook with the launch of the "timeline". Here, it is possible to gain an overview of all of the information we have shared previously and to add information or important events from before we entered Facebook. This can be seen as an embodiment of our own story about our identity-across-timescales. In relation to this, it is interesting that young people often browse through their profiles and are amused about previous status updates from when they "were kids" or enjoy re-reading previous messages or comments from friends – for instance when they need cheering up (Larsen 2010, 2012a). In this way, we can understand Facebook and other SNSs as spaces where we construct our identity in practice and at the same time give and gain an understanding of our identity across timescales.

The two notions of identity are inextricably linked with each other. Identity-in-practice and identity-across-timescales are thus co-existing concepts on SNSs, but appear in different situations. However, splitting the concept of identity into two can be analytically helpful, as we can get different glimpses into the identity of young people according to what kind of practices we are looking at (Larsen 2007a). This chapter focuses more on practices related to young people's construction of identity in practice on SNSs.

3 Empirical Background

During the past 8 years the author has been following Danish teenagers' practices on SNSs as an ethnographer. The main aim has been to gain an understanding of the meanings SNSs have for the young people's private and social lives and how they use them as part of everyday life. In order to investigate this, the author collected a large amount of different data. The primary data consist of ethnographical involvement and participatory observations within the field. Primarily, the author has conducted virtual ethnographic studies (Hine 2000) with online observations and data collection from the Internet. This required that the author had her own profiles on many of the SNSs, which were the most popular among Danish youth during the period 2005–2013. Here, the research aim has been openly described to the young users and the author has become "friends" with several users who function as informants. Along with observations the author has conducted several chat-based informal and unstructured interviews, carried out focus group interviews and written field notes and taken screen shots.

The ethnographic approach is characterised by a "snowballing" approach (Bijker 1995), according to which discoveries in the field may lead to invitations to move forward (Hine 2000). Such an approach is well in keeping with observations online where users typically move about on different sites and this provides opportunities to move forward together with other users. For instance, the author moved on when her informants quit the once popular Danish SNS Arto and joined Facebook. The result of this approach is that the author has created profiles on at least 25 different SNSs over the past 8 years, though without by any means acting as a participant observer on all the sites. The author only stayed on some sites for a short time and remained comparatively anonymous or passive when observing interactions among users. The short observations have, however, provided an insight into the types of online social networks in question and their application in practice as well as any possible differences from other SNSs used by youth in Denmark. It is, of course, impossible to maintain so many profiles, but as part of this kind of ethnographical investigation it is important to become familiar with the total number of SNSs for children and young people in Denmark, and, subsequently, to carry out more in-depth observations of the most popular sites. Thus, the author has moved among different types of participation – from non-participation to passive participation, moderate participation, active participation and full participation (Spradley 1980).

In addition to the virtual ethnography, the author conducted a comprehensive qualitative online questionnaire survey in which 2400 Danish 12–18-year-olds

(51 % girls and 49 % boys) commented on their experiences of SNSs. The questionnaire consisted of mainly open questions relating to some of the practices, which according to the ethnographic observations have appeared to be central (e.g. practicing friendship, communicating emotions, uploading and commenting pictures and handling risks). In some of the questions, the respondents were asked to state examples from their profiles, e.g. the most recent message or comment on a picture, examples of messages they did not like, messages that had made them happy, etc. Subsequently, they were asked to state who had sent the message/comment and then to reflect on how they felt about it. These questions were included in order to gain insight into the typical messages and comments youth send to each other. Rather than collecting statistical material, the purpose of the questionnaire was to gain insight into the central experiences and practices of children and adolescents between 12 and 18 on different SNSs. The questionnaire data especially shed light on social practices related to the predominant Love discourse since respondents inserted and commented on emotional messages they had received from friends.

In order to create a condensed overview of the data material, the software program Nvivo 8 was applied; it facilitates qualitative data analysis and may qualify the work of coding and categorising large data quantities. Nvivo is based on an approach inspired by Grounded Theory to the coding of qualitative data material. Applying the Grounded Theory approach to data analysis implies, as a rule, that the empirical data are allowed to "speak for themselves", rather than being processed on the basis of certain theoretical frameworks or concepts (Gibbs 2002; Welsh 2002). Several times, the author went through the entire volume of replies to selected questions in the questionnaire and created codes, categories and themes which were gradually refined and related to each other. These have then been analysed in relation to the online observations, screenshots, field notes and interview data. A combination of these different data types have made it possible to examine both the central actions which young users carry out on SNSs, and to analyse the way in which they articulate their concrete use and experiences.

4 Theoretical and Methodological Approach

Theoretically, the research results presented in this chapter are placed within the field of discourse studies with Nexus Analysis (Scollon and Scollon 2004) as the overall theoretical and methodological approach. Nexus Analysis is a wide-ranging and eclectic perspective which, in addition to discourse studies, is theoretically founded using linguistics, anthropology, psychology and sociolinguistics. Rather than an actual theory, it is a theoretical and methodological framework which combines an ethnographic methodological approach with discourse analysis, and whose purpose is to map the central (but not necessarily discursive) practices within a given field of investigation. What characterises Nexus Analysis as a discourse analytical framework is that language does not occupy as central a position as in other discourse analytical approaches; instead the social actions of humans are of primary interest. These actions will always be mediated by technologies or cultural artefacts (mediational means). However, often language, i.e. discourses, mediates social actions but this should not be taken for granted.

Scollon and Scollon themselves characterise Nexus Analysis as "an ethnographic methodological strategy" (Scollon and Scollon 2004, p. 9). The type of ethnography to which they adhere does, however, distinguish itself from traditional ethnography, which is well-known within anthropology and sociology and has more in common with some of the more recent ethnographic trends within internet research, including virtual ethnography (Hine 2000; Larsen 2012b; Leander and McKim 2003). For Scollon and Scollon, ethnography is a theoretical position where mediated actions are centrally located. According to them, no particular group of people can be isolated in order to carry out ethnographic studies, for instance a group of friends, a school class or the users of one particular homepage. Instead, the point of departure is an interest in a certain social issue or certain social practices, and, through involvement in the field, the aim is to carry out an analysis to identify the central, social actors and the central actions they perform. Therefore, the aim of Nexus Analysis is a more general ethnographic theory and methodology which can be employed to analyse the relation between discourse and technology and, at the same time, place this analysis within a broader social, political and cultural context (Scollon and Scollon 2004, p. 7). Thus, Nexus Analysis does not only analyse the concrete social actions but also the repeated everyday actions within a socio-cultural framework.

The place where social actions, actors and discursive practices meet and unfold is termed a "Nexus of Practice" by Scollon and Scollon. A Nexus of Practice is not a physical place, but rather a set of particular activities and the people engaged in these activities (Scollon 2001a, p. 150). The actual concept is comparatively loosely phrased and may therefore cover the interconnection of many different actions. According to Scollon and Scollon a Nexus of Practice is any group that can and does engage in some action (Scollon 2001a, p. 150). We are dealing with a recognisable grouping of a set of mediated actions, which, together with an archive of mediational means, is connected to a major or minor group of people (Scollon 2001a, p. 150). Against this background we may say that all Facebook users in the world are part of the same Nexus of Practice, but we may also say that only the 80–90 people who use the small local launderette on the street corner are a Nexus of Practice. So sizes may vary a great deal and comprise five, five hundred or five million people. Thus, how we consider a Nexus of Practice will depend on our analytical interest.

The author has analysed Danish adolescents' use of SNSs as a Nexus of Practice. This has also meant not analysing one particular friendship group or other close-knit groups of young people and their use of SNSs, but working at a more general level on the central mediated actions which Danish adolescents perform across municipal boundaries and SNSs. The focus on the social actions has turned out to be central. In the following analysis the chapter will present those research results that deal with the ways in which the young Danes communicate emotions on SNSs.

The examples provided resemble central social practices related to the overall Love discourse and were observed by the author across the different kinds of empirical material (counting both the ethnographic observations and the questionnaire data). Thus, the analysis will focus on some of the most common ways for young people in Denmark to communicate emotions and thereby practice friendship online.

5 Analysis

Communicating emotions is one example among many of how adolescents practise friendship on SNSs. It is interesting, however, to examine emotional communication separately because it is a central practice; a practice, which the author has observed on a daily basis during the 8 years of working as a virtual ethnographer. As early as 2005 the author found emotional language to be central on the Danish SNS Arto, and this observation of how adolescents across different SNSs make use of a distinct Love discourse has been confirmed many times since. In this regard it seems that young people make use of many different mediational means to communicate emotions, many of which are not intended for two-way communication between users at all. On SNSs, where users are allowed to identify themselves through user names, the author has seen examples of users who use their user name to send an affectionate message to a friend – by for instance calling themselves "idascarolineforever" (user name belonging to a 12-year-old girl called Ida – Caroline is her best friend), "loveonsigne" (14-year-old girl's user name – Signe is the name of her friend) or "Pernille's-Boy" (15-year-old boy's user name – Pernille is his girlfriend). In this way, user names are used as mediational means to indicate a relation to another user. This is one way of signalling how one person from among all the friends of the user occupies a certain space in the user's heart. It is often seen that such selected friends in similar mediational actions reciprocate emotions.

The Love discourse is especially prevalent in the personal profile texts. The quote below shows how a 16-year-old girl has chosen to present her profile text:

Love you: <33 Christine <3 Nicoline <3 Maria
I wouldn't want to live another second if I knew you weren't here. Cannot live without you.
_I+.<33'
-Have you considered how fond I am of you?
-Have you considered how much I love you?
-Have you considered how much I miss you?
-Have you considered how much you mean to me?
-Have you considered how happy I am to know you?
-Have you considered how proud I am to be yours?
-Have you considered how happy I am that you are mine?
-Have you considered how sweet I think you are?
-Have you considered how beautiful I think you are?
-Have you considered how indescribable you are?
-Have you considered that my love for you is indescribable?
(Extract from 16-year-old girl's profile text on Arto, 2007)

As is often the case in profile texts, the 16-year-old girl does not mention herself; instead, she writes how much she loves her three best female friends, whose pictures she has inserted. It is interesting how an increasing number of users make use of the more personal and profiling functions on SNSs – such as user name or personal profile texts – when writing about their best friends and their fondness for them. This might be related to the sites' use of the metaphor "friend" as a term covering all the contacts a person has. The category "friend" does not actually signify the nature of a relationship, because the term is allocated automatically to a person as soon as they have accepted a friendship application. In the data material the author found several examples of adolescents who carry out a number of mediated actions in order to visualise and select among different contacts, or made use of different mediational means to demonstrate which people are more than "just" friends. With the popularisation of SNSs, we may say that the category of friend is in the process of becoming "the new default mode of social relations" (Boellstorff 2008, 2010). Consequently, young people need to do or say more to signal who among their acquaintances are actually their close relations. And this may be the reason why they often refer to their friends in very affectionate terms in profile texts, user names, etc.

5.1 *"Love on You <3"*

As could be seen in the quote from the 16-year-old girl's profile text above, the heart symbol/smiley (<3) pervades emotional communication among adolescents, and only on very rare occasions does this symbol not occur in communication between best friends. Similarly, the expression "Love on", which appears in the username "loveonsigne" above, is one which the author found many times – for instance when users upload pictures of their friends. Writing "love on" is a less formal way of saying "I love you" – or a way of rephrasing the metaphor "throw your love on". The expression (as it originally appears in Danish) is not grammatically correct, but reflects a special linguistic practice which has spread among young people in particular. Below are publicly accessible status updates from young Danes on Facebook, in which they make use of the expression:

> thanks for the best day yesterday &' today girls :D:D – love on you;*
> good to see you again [name] my lovely girl, [name] tomorrow <3' – looking forward to Rock Under the Bridge with the greatest twins [name and name], love on you!;* (Status updates on Facebook, 2010)

This is a special linguistic jargon which is used almost exclusively by young people, and which is particularly prevalent in their internet communication. We might say that the expression "Love on" – similar to the heart symbol (<3) – has become a "cultural tool" or a mediational means through which adolescents can express their feelings in an easy and informal way. Often, linguistic concepts undergo a transformational process and assume the character of mediational means, which is the result of a lengthy "timescale of internalisation" (Scollon and Scollon 2004, p. 165). The result is that today, few young people would not understand the meaning of the expression "Love on", since it has become internalised into their linguistic practice. If we accept Gee's thoughts about discourse with a capital D, the act of using the heart symbol or the expression "Love on" is more than "just language". It is about behaving, thinking, interacting and speaking in *the right way*, using *the right tools* at *the right time* and *in the right place* (Gee 1999, p. 17). Such symbolic expressions or "cultural tools" are socially accepted forms of expression among young people and form part of the general youthful "Love discourse" or emotional communication on SNSs. It is used as a method of writing themselves into a particular value system; a particular culture and socialisation form which differs from that of adults.

Affectionate language is not only found in user names, profile texts, status updates or together with pictures. What is interesting is that young people on SNSs use all sorts of resources available to them to communicate feelings – even resources and mediational means which were originally intended for other purposes, such as fan groups, blog posts, photo tagging (e.g. "If you are tagged in this picture, I love you!") or even the act of providing information about one's marital status or family relations (e.g. best friends are often "married" or claim to be related on Facebook). Often, young people are creative and playful when it comes to taking advantage of the options available to them.

5.2 The Best Message: "I Love You"

Early on during the observation the author became aware of the affectionate communication form. However, the adolescents interviewed found it difficult to articulate this practice. Therefore, it is relevant to include the questionnaire data, in which respondents specifically commented on the Love discourse as they were asked to give an example of a message they had received in their guestbook which had made them happy. In 47.8 % of replies, such messages were sent by the recipient's best male or female friend, in 23.8 % by a boyfriend or girlfriend and in 23.1 % by another person known to the user. Only in 5.2 % of all replies did the positive messages come from people who were unknown to the user. Not surprisingly, the major proportion of messages selected by the respondents included the words "I love you". Even though a number of respondents stated that such messages were sent from boy- or girlfriends, the chapter concentrates on affectionate messages sent between best friends. It is particularly interesting to include the respondents' explanations of why these particular messages from their friends made them happy, since such replies may indicate the motives behind the widespread emotional communication among young people on SNSs.

Typically, respondents explained that they like the "I love you" messages because "it is nice to know" or "good to be told". Below is a list of characteristic examples followed by the respondents' own comments to them. All the messages were sent by the respondents' "best friends":

- "hello love. I love you. And you are in my thoughts"
  This was from my best friend. Made me happy to know that she thought about me. (13-year-old girl)
- "Mathias ? everybody loves you, and everybody likes you. I wish I were like you – I'd like that".
  Because it makes me warm inside and makes me feel like someone everybody loves:D (15-year-old boy)
- "I love you, and I am just so fond of you.. <'3"
  Because then I know that someone likes me (14-year-old girl)

The fact that respondents feel accepted or appreciated must be seen in the light of the experience of sincerity or authenticity which the respondents have when they receive the affectionate messages. In any case several of them say that they *know* that the sender means what he or she writes. Below are a number of replies to the question "Why did the message make you happy?" In order to save space, the actual message before each reply has been left out, but they were examples very similar to the previous messages, in which the sentence "I love you" appears – either on its own or as part of a longer message.

It means a lot to me when someone says they love me and that I know that they mean it. (15-year-old girl)
It is from a friend... and he means well (16-year-old boy)
It is always nice to know that someone loves you. And because I know that this person means it. (15-year-old girl)
Because I know him, because I know he means it, and because I am just as fond of him <33 (13-year-old girl)

The fact that respondents emphasise that they know that their friends "mean it" may be interpreted in the way that they are aware that there is also a more "empty" Love discourse among friends on the internet, in which the users do not necessarily mean what they write. This points towards an ambiguous attitude to the words "I love you". In the data material there are examples of respondents who state that it makes them mad or irritated if people they do not know very well or "well enough" send them affectionate messages. As the 13-year-old girl pointed out, it made her happy to receive the message for the very reason that she knows the sender and because she is "*just as fond of him*". This indicates that there is a certain requirement as regards the authenticity and genuineness of the communication and the relations who use it.

5.3 "I Love You Brow" – Emotional Communication Among Boys

As it appears, girls are particularly active in communicating emotions. However, during the 8 years the author has acted as a participant observer on various SNSs, she has witnessed an interesting development in the use of emotional communication. Whereas in the beginning (2005) this practice was mostly observed among girls, during the following years it was found that boys also write affectionate messages to each other. Today it is not unlikely that the sentence "I love you" appears in public communication situations among boys on SNSs. Surveys of young people's texting activities for instance, have previously found that girls (here 14–18-year-olds) are more likely to display "socio-emotional orientations" and write longer and more caring messages than boys (Höflich and Rössler 2002). On the basis of these studies (particularly screenshots and questionnaire data) this also seems to be the case on SNSs, without, however, being exclusively confined to girls.

Examining the boys' replies in the questionnaire, emotional messages such as "I love you <3", "LoveYouMyBestFriend <3" or "You are my best friend. <3" are also among the favourite messages of boys. These messages are often from girlfriends and best female or male friends. Like the girls, the boys say that it is nice to know, or that it makes them happy to receive such messages even though some of them use this friendly Love discourse with a certain ironic distance. Below are a few examples from boys, in which the loving message from a friend of the same sex is followed by the respondent's comment on the message:

- "I love you brow <3". (15-year-old boy)
  Because my love for my best friend is mutual. (15-year-old boy)
- "hi homie. Looking forward to seeing you again"
  Well, it's nice to know that your friends think you are good to be with (16-year-old boy)
- "Lalala This is a stupid message saying a lot of smart stuff about [name] and how cool he is and how much I like him and it is vital for our relationship that it is written on Arto or else the whole world might go under" [Name] misses you! Best [name] (don't you dare delete this message)
  Because my best friend is in the USA this year. So I miss him. That's why it's nice to get such messages from him. (17-year-old boy)

In the last example, in which a 17-year-old boy has received a message from a friend who is in the USA, we see an ironic distance, as the sender makes fun of the affectionate communication form. Even though this ironic distance is found in the actual message, the contents are still positive, and the 17-year-old receiver says that "it's nice to get such messages". Thus, this practice matches that of girls, but boys are more conscious that their communication should not resemble the girls'.

The boys' practice of sometimes expressing an ironic distance in connection with emotional communication may be interpreted as a method of breaking with and being different from the romantic and grandiose form which is often found in the language of the girls. This is backed by the fact that boys often use slang expressions from American rap culture in connection with their affectionate messages. For instance, the boys call each other "brow" (short form of brother) or "homie" (short form of homeboy); expressions the author has encountered regularly in boys' communication on SNSs. Such slang expressions are indeed normally used by boys as a method of signalling coolness (Jørgensen and Quist 2008, pp. 93–98), and when they are combined with the words "I love you", they help downplay the romantic tone. With the girls, on the contrary, expressions such as "honey", "baby" or "princess" are used as a method of boosting the affectionate contents, which is another reason for boys to add other – and more masculine – expressions to their affectionate statements. There are also examples of boys quoting from lyrics, and in the questionnaire responses there are several examples of references to popular music. The use of lyrics as part of the emotional communicative practice is yet another way of distancing oneself or removing seriousness from the contents. When in such cases the users "borrow" voices from others or mime emotional expressions, they pass on an affectionate message, while avoiding risking themselves. As Bakhtin would point out, all the words we utter are "half someone else's" (Bakhtin 1981, p. 293), but they also become half our own, since we use them with our own accents and make our own choices of when and in which contexts we borrow them (Jones and Norris 2005). Thus, it is clear that boys as well as girls have a need to communicate feelings and in this way be affirmed by their friends on SNSs, even though this practice is displayed differently among the sexes.

5.4 *Superficial or Precious – What Does "I Love You" Mean?*

The fact that boys who send affectionate messages to their friends of the same sex use irony, slang expressions from rap culture or in other ways downplay their affectionate contents may also be seen as a sign that among the users themselves there is a higher degree of acceptance of the emotional communication practice when performed by girls. The author encountered this attitude particularly in the debate forums of the SNSs. Here the users keenly discuss among themselves the widespread use of emotional communication. Some find that it is ok for boys to use it, while others (boys in particular) find that it is "gross" or even "gay".

The fact that the users themselves bring the Love discourse among friends up as a topic for debate indicates that communication practices have evidently shifted and that the boys are indeed under the influence of the girls' use of emotional communication; a point which makes good sense, considering that Discourses (with a capital D) are always undergoing processes of change, and that boundaries may therefore be challenged (Gee 1999). In spite of this, conflicting views still exist concerning the general Love discourse among friends as to what it actually implies to communicate feelings and to write "I love you" to each other on SNSs. For not all young users have taken the Love discourse to heart. It is evident that young people themselves are aware that an overall discourse of this type exists on the

SNSs, but attitudes vary as to their use. Even though the questionnaire data reveal that it is a very widespread practice, there are examples of young people who consider it far too superficial or exaggerated to write "I love you" to male or female friends on SNSs, and that the words are often misused. Likewise, the author has encountered adolescents who claim that "I love you" has become a "cliché" or "a type of slang".

In this regard, it is interesting that some state that they contemplate their use of "I love you" and sometimes change conduct as regards emotional communication, as can be seen in the following statements made by two 13-year-old girls:

> I am a little careful about saying this; but some.... actually quite a few, I think, feel pressured to do so, because their male or female friends, wtf; write it to them, and then they might be worried about losing that person because they don't write the same in reply, I for one have tried this a couple of times. I know I have misused it. But am trying to change it now. I am also careful about saying it to url friends, because I don't think you can love someone you haven't met. On these Arto profiles I actually also see some girls who have written to each other for no more than 2–3 weeks, and who already loooove each other. (13-year-old girl in the debate section on Arto)
>
> I've experienced periods when I did not take that sentence seriously at all! I regret that very much!... (13-year-old girl in the debate section on Arto)

In these comments we see the demand that if you write "I love you" you have to mean it. Consequently, it may not be the emotional communication practice as such that some users resist, but rather a Love discourse which is empty or devoid of content. As a 16-year-old girl points out, it seems that an explicit demand exists that you *must* have affectionate messages on your SNS profile:

> [...] many when I look have love messages in their guestbooks, think it is particularly abused here on Arto more than on msn&mobile, because of course you must have love messages in your guest book ? hehe ☺ (16-year-old girl in the debate section on Arto)

This may be the reason why several respondents in the questionnaire stress that they "KNOW" that the sender meant what he or she wrote to them on their profile. In this way they dismiss the empty Love discourse – which may characterise the communication of *other* users on the SNSs – and stress that as far as they are concerned these actions are meaningful. Thus, the users must strike a balance within a schism between the superficial and the precious when they receive and send affectionate messages to each other. The fact that some use the word "misuse" about the sentence "I love you" is in itself interesting and indicates that among young people on SNSs there is some self-regulation as regards code of conduct, as pointed out elsewhere (Larsen 2005, 2007b).

5.5 *Youthful Emotions in Public Space*

It is a common feature in all the different examples of emotional communication that they are publicly accessible within the SNSs in question, and that they are examples of an indirect or asynchronous communication form. This is an important point, which indicates how SNSs act as a special "social space" in which such emotional communication is acceptable. As some respondents have explained, they rarely say "I love you" or the like to each other when standing face to face and rarely write such terms of endearment to each other when texting or chatting. In such circumstances it would seem almost too intimate to use these words, but in the public forum of a SNS, the situation is different. This indicates that saying "I love you" has a different meaning on SNSs compared to other situations of communication where communication is more private. This could be explained by what Suler (2004) calls "The Online Disinhibition Effect"; the fact that online, some people tend to loosen up, feel less restrained and express themselves more openly. The lack of contact and face-to-face visibility disinhibits people and the invisible and asynchronous nature of online communication provides them with courage to say things that they would not normally say. Online, it simply feels safer "putting it 'out there'" (Suler 2004, pp. 321–323).

When adolescents use user names, personal profiles, presentation texts, photo comments, status updates, etc. for publishing affectionate messages about (and to) male and female friends, these are public statements, which may often be characterised as one-way communication or mass communication. Thus, it may be argued that the use of emotional communication by adolescents on SNSs is more frequently "frontstage" than "backstage", in Goffman's terminology of theatre metaphors (1959). When things happen frontstage, the interacting parties know that their actions may be watched, whereas backstage is characterised as being the "back room", where it is acceptable not to maintain a front (Goffman 1959, pp. 96–97). So in Goffman's analogy, "front" is understood as the element of "self-presentation" where a person is "performing" and acts in a certain way because they are conscious that an "audience" is present. On an SNS the audience is not only the individual user's contacts on the friend list, but also all other users of the site.

The fact that adolescents on SNSs generally make use of the emotional communication "frontstage" or in public forums where their communication may be seen by others indicates that the Love discourse does not only have the function of maintaining and confirming a friendship. Several of the actions performed by young people when using the Love discourse may be related to the way in which they construct their identities in practice. Thus, it is remarkable that users also employ the messages they have received from their friends as part of their own self-presentation. It may happen, for instance, that profile owners delete messages which are uninteresting or devoid of content from their guest books (such as "what's up" or "just passed by") and consciously leave the positive declarations of love for public show. In relation to this, the author has seen examples of users who, on Twitter or Facebook, have uploaded screenshots of loving messages they have received from friends. This practice can be linked with general developmental aspects of adolescence. It is not new that young people want to be accepted by (and popular among) their peers, but on SNSs they have found a new way of presenting themselves and each other. Their performances of identity-in-practice become a "joint venture" where messages from friends – more or less consciously – are elements in the personal performance of the individual user. The mutual declarations

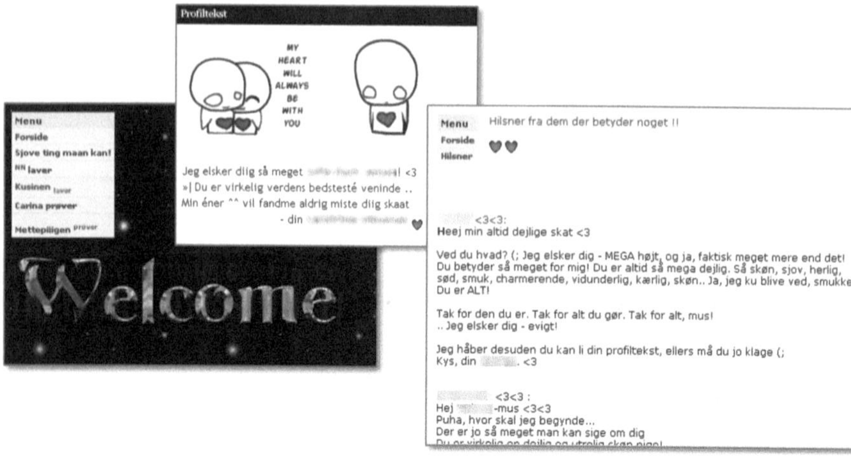

Fig. 1 Profile texts composed by others rather than the users themselves, 2005 and 2008

of praise or love between friends contribute to painting a flattering picture of the profile owner and we are witnessing a co-construction of identity in practice.

5.6 *Friends as Mediational Means*

This is also the case when a user leaves (elements of) his or her profile to friends, presenting them with the possibility of commenting on or describing the person as they wish – a practice which became extremely popular during the period the author made observations. In the figure below are three examples of profile texts whose content was written by people other than the profile owners themselves (Fig. 1).

The first example is the front page of a 14-year-old boy's profile text, which he has divided into five sub-menus ("Fun things to do", "NN makes", "My cousin makes", "Carina tries", "Mettepiiigen (Mette girl) tries"), four of which are reserved for descriptions written by friends. The second screen shot is an example of how the 14-year-old girl has let a female friend write and design the front page of her profile text and the friend uses the front page text as if it were a guest book, writing directly to – and not about – the girl. The last screen shot shows how a profile owner has created her own menu item and inserted a number of "greetings from those who are important to me". In this case, the girl has asked a number of selected friends to write texts which she might insert on the page. The common feature of all the examples is that the users "help" one another create a desirable online identity and it is an unspoken rule that they only write positive descriptions. As the sender writes in the very flattering text in the third example, "I hope you like your profile text – if not, you must complain, of course (;". In this way friends (and their words of praise) act as mediational means in the self-representation of young people online (Larsen

2005, 2007a, b). The young users make conscious and strategic use of their friends' affectionate messages and descriptions to both receive and give an understanding of themselves. Returning to Goffman's theatre metaphor we might find it noteworthy that the distinction between performers and audience is blurred. Instead, the users are co-constructors of each other's identities in the public social space, which is constituted for adolescents by the SNSs (Larsen 2005, 2007a, b).

6 An "Open Source" Networked Identity

The above analysis has shown how young people today are constantly portraying and relating to themselves and each other online. Their emotional practices could be seen as an example of how sociality and identity construction function in today's network society (Castells 2001, 2010). The fact that adolescents on SNSs use their friends as mediational means and are co-constructors of one another's identity-in-practice underlines the ambiguity embedded in the concept "networked individualism" (Castells 2001; Wellman 2002); that on the one hand, social actors go through amplified personalisation and individualisation processes, while on the other hand they become more and more attached to and mutually dependent on one another. The argument here is that young people on SNSs develop a type of "open source" network identity (as also highlighted in Ryberg and Larsen 2008). The term "open source" is often used within software development and open formats, which everyone else can develop further. The point is not that this kind of social form of identity construction is new, nor that it differs from the general development of adolescence. However, it is interesting to see how young people especially take advantage of, and are creative in using, both each other and the features provided by the SNSs to present their identity. Thus, the term "open source" networked identity may serve as a metaphor for understanding the collaborative presentation of identity or identity-through-social-interaction among youth on SNSs.

The idea that young people have an open source networked identity may also contribute to explaining why friendships are (just as) important for adolescents today (as they were previously); why friendships must constantly be maintained through various technological features, and why it is customary to refer to friends in very emotional terms on all possible sites on the internet. The individual users are dependent on their friends as part of their relational networked identity. If we acknowledge this, it is not difficult to understand why "I love you" messages are so highly rated among many adolescents. Even though they question their own prevalent use of the Love discourse and discuss whether it is superficial, "too much" or cliché-like, actions of emotional communication are still part of their practice, which is linked to their networked identity. It seems that adolescents themselves are well aware of what they are staking by keeping the "source code" open and accessible. As a 12-year-old boy wrote in relation to a negative comment on one of his photos, he "was the one who posted the photo and thereby asked for comments on it...". An "open source" networked identity is not one that you can control

100 %, which is why good relations to friends and a flattering profile with positive statements become important elements in the moment-by-moment identity construction of adolescents online.

References

Bakhtin, M. M. (1981). Discourse in the novel. In M. Holquist (Ed.), *The dialogic imagination* (pp. 259–422). Austin: University of Texas Press.

Bijker, W. E. (1995). *Of bicycles, bakelites, and bulbs: Toward a theory of sociotechnical change* (Inside technology). Cambridge, MA: MIT.

Boellstorff, T. (2008). *Coming of age in second life: An anthropologist explores the virtually human*. Princeton: Princeton University Press.

Boellstorff, T. (2010). *Virtual worlds, culture, and change – with Doug Thompson and Tom Boellstorff*. Presented at the 3rd annual virtual worlds best practices in education conference. http://business.treet.tv/shows/bpeducation/episodes/tomboellstorff. Accessed 31 Jan 2015.

Bourdieu, P. (1987). *Distinction: A social critique of the judgment of taste*. Cambridge, MA: Harvard University Press.

Bourdieu, P. (1990). *The logic of practice*. Stanford: Stanford University Press.

Buckingham, D. (2008). Introducing identity. In D. Buckingham (Ed.), *Youth, identity, and digital media* (pp. 1–22). Cambridge, MA: The MIT Press.

Butler, J. (1993). *Bodies that matter*. New York: Routledge.

Castells, M. (2001). *The internet galaxy: Reflections on the internet, business, and society*. New York: Oxford University Press.

Castells, M. (2010). *The rise of the network society* (Vol. second edition, with a new preface). Chichester: Wiley-Blackwell.

Gee, J. P. (1999). *An introduction to discourse analysis: Theory and method*. London: Routledge.

Gibbs, G. R. (2002). *Qualitative data analysis: Explorations with NVivo*. Buckingham: Open University Press.

Goffman, E. (1959). *The presentation of self in everyday life* (Vol. reprint). Harmondsworth: Penguin.

Hine, C. (2000). *Virtual ethnography*. London: Sage Publications.

Höflich, J., & Rössler, P. (2002). More than just a telephone: The mobile phone and use of the short message service (SMS) by German adolescents: Results of a pilot study. In *Estudios de Juventud 57* (pp. 79–100). Madrid: Instituto de la Juventud Redacción Consejería Técnica de Planificación y Evaluación Servicio de Estudios y Documentación.

Jones, R. H., & Norris, S. (2005). Discourse as action/discourse in action. In S. Norris & R. H. Jones (Eds.), *Discourse in action: Introducing mediated discourse analysis* (pp. 3–14). London: Routledge.

Jørgensen, C. R. (2008). *Identitet: Psykologiske og kulturanalytiske perspektiver*. København: Hans Reitzel.

Jørgensen, J. N., & Quist, P. (2008). *Unges sprog*. København: Hans Reitzel.

Larsen, M. C. (2005). *Ungdom, venskab og identitet – en etnografisk undersøgelse af unges brug af hjemmesiden Arto* (Upubliceret specialeafhandling). Institut for Kommunikation, Aalborg: Universitet.

Larsen, M. C. (2007a). Understanding social networking: On young people's construction and co-construction of identity online. In *Proceedings from the conference internet research 8.0: Let's play*. Vancouver: Association of Internet Researchers.

Larsen, M. C. (2007b). Kærlighed og venskab på Arto.dk. *Ungdomsforskning*, *6*(1), 11.

Larsen, M. C. (2010). *Unge og online sociale netværk – En neksusanalytisk undersøgelse af medierede handlinger og offentlige diskurser*. Ph.d.-afhandling, Aalborg Universitet, Institut

for Kommunikation. https://malenel.files.wordpress.com/2010/09/ph-d-afhandling_malene-charlotte-larsen.pdf. Accessed 31 Jan 2015.
Larsen, M. C. (2011). Ungdommelige følelser i offentlige rum. *Barn, 2011*(3–4), 13–38.
Larsen, M. C. (2012a). Børn, unge og sociale netværkssider. Hvad ved vi? In *Sociale netværkssider som tekst og kontekst* (pp. 13–70). Via Systime. http://via.systime.dk/paedagogik-og-socialfag/paedagogik/sociale-netvaerkssider-som-tekst-og-kontekst.html. Accessed 31 Jan 2015.
Larsen, M. C. (2012b). Når dataindsamlingen går online: Udfordringer for den kvalitative internetforsker. In M. H. Jacobsen & S. Q. Jensen (Eds.), *Kvalitative udfordringer*. København: Hans Reitzels Forlag.
Leander, K. M., & McKim, K. K. (2003). Tracing the everyday "sitings" of adolescents on the internet: A strategic adaptation of ethnography across online and offline spaces. *Education, Communication & Information, 3*(2), 211–240.
Lemke, J. L. (2008). Identity, development and desire: Critical questions. In C. R. Caldas-Coulthard & R. Iedema (Eds.), *Identity trouble: Critical discourse and contested identities* (pp. 17–42). Basingstoke: Palgrave Macmillan.
Norris, S., & Jones, R. H. (Eds.). (2005). *Discourse in action: Introducing mediated discourse analysis*. London: Routledge.
Ryberg, T., & Larsen, M. C. (2008). Networked identities: Understanding relations between strong and weak ties in networked environments. *Journal of Computer Assisted Learning, 24*(2), 103–115.
Scollon, R. (2001a). Action and text: Towards an integrated understanding of the place of text in social (inter)action, mediated discourse analysis and the problem of social action. In R. Wodak & M. Meyer (Eds.), *Methods of critical discourse analysis* (pp. 139–183). London: Sage Publications.
Scollon, R. (2001b). *Mediated discourse: The nexus of practice*. London/New York: Routledge.
Scollon, R., & Scollon, S. W. (2004). *Nexus analysis: Discourse and the emerging internet*. London/New York: Routledge.
Spradley, J. P. (1980). *Participant observation*. New York: Holt, Rinehart and Winston.
Suler, J. (2004). The online disinhibition effect. *CyberPsychology & Behavior, 7*(3), 321–326.
Wellman, B. (2002). Little boxes, glocalization, and networked individualism. In M. Tanabe, P. V. Besselaar, & T. Ishida (Eds.), *Revised papers from the second Kyoto workshop on digital cities Ii, computational and sociological approaches, October 18–20, 2001* (pp. 10–25). London: Springer.
Wellman, B., Quan-Haase, A., Boase, J., Chen, W., Hampton, K., Isla de Diaz, I., & Miyata, K. (2003). The social affordances of the internet for networked individualism. *Journal of Computer Mediated Communication, 8*(3).
Welsh, E. (2002). Dealing with data: Using NVivo in the qualitative data analysis process. *Forum: Qualitative Social Research, 3*(2). http://www.qualitative-research.net/index.php/fqs/article/view/865/1880. Accessed 31 Jan 2015.

Profile Image: Ways of Self-(re-)presentation on the Facebook Social Network

Rocío Rueda-Ortiz and Diana Giraldo

Abstract This chapter focuses on the description of the profile image and the entire communicative ecosystem on the Facebook social network. In doing so, it presents the results of the inventory and classification of 7200 profile pictures of Facebook users from 24 different cities around the world. The classification criteria were initially based on a model which includes entity, treatment and framing (ETF) of the image. Although our study does not focus specifically on youth, we also present a number of results in relation to this demographic group, as it experiences digital technologies as an answer to its expressive needs and the kinds of identity exploration which characterise our modern social life. Finally, we introduce some conclusions about the integration of digital technologies into everyday life.

1 Introduction

The present chapter aims to understand the way in which one of the dimensions of identity construction, the presentation of a self-image, arises from the publication of profile pictures on SNSs like Facebook. We state that while during face-to-face interactions people present themselves as if they were playing a role in a play, on Facebook users present their public image as a set of *works of art*, or *opera*.[1] From this perspective, how can we analyse these *works of art*, taking into account not only their representative and expressive function but also their importance as parts of a system of social values? As we cannot make a priori assumptions about the intricate relationships and intentions that people bring into play when deciding to post a certain profile image, we decided to recognise and classify the *formal procedures* behind the

[1] We use here the word *opera* (the plural for *opus*) from its Latin origin: *operari* (operate, labour) which means *a work*.

R. Rueda-Ortiz (✉)
Universidad Pedagógica Nacional, Bogotá, Colombia
e-mail: rruedaortiz@yahoo.com

D. Giraldo
Universidad del Valle, Cali, Colombia

Information and Communication Sciences, Université Lyon 2, Lyon, France
e-mail: giraldodiana@gmail.com

M. Walrave et al. (eds.), *Youth 2.0: Social Media and Adolescence*,
DOI 10.1007/978-3-319-27893-3_3

genesis of that image. In order to study these procedures, we explore how Facebook users exploit – or fail to exploit – digital resources in both capturing and treating their image, and therefore, how technical decisions intersect with social issues.

With respect to technical procedures, we talk about restrictions because all Facebook features, even those that may seem insignificant, will have an influence on how users display their profiles; and we talk about possibilities because, as a complement, users have the resources to manage what it is that they present of themselves and how. In this regard, we would like to emphasise two aspects of Goffman's (1959) approach: first, people do not interact directly but through the use of symbols that contain relevant social data. Second, the presentation of the self emerges from interaction with others; therefore the role to be played is always socially situated. This allows us to say that behind the decision of posting a profile picture on Facebook there are two types of procedures: one that takes into account the affordances and constraints of the website, and another that takes into account its social possibilities and restrictions.

This chapter presents some of the results obtained in a much more extensive study about 'Ways of self-(re-)presentation on Facebook' which focused both on the profile image and the communicative ecosystem of the site. The underlying idea is that there is no technological or social determinism in these new forms of interaction. Instead, new subjectivities emerge from the contingency of everyday use of technologies where our values and culture are being (re-)shaped. Thus, the first phase of this study focused on the selection and classification of 7200 profile images. This procedure was accomplished by following the model previously proposed by Gómez and González (2009, 2011), which explores three categories: entity, treatment and framing (ETF). Our hypothesis was that despite the multiplicity of technical and representational options, people concentrate on very few of these. Therefore, one of our main goals was to find primary tendencies and similarities around different cities in the world.

The second phase of this study was based on an ethnographic approach. This phase consisted of interviews with 12 Facebook users and the observation of their Facebook account activity over 6 months. This ethnography enabled us to understand the dynamic between online/offline self-presentation and the ecology of verbal, graphic and visual pieces found in Facebook pages. We argue that this dynamic is what makes the use of Facebook an *opera*. The present text will only take into account one dimension of the findings of this second ethnographic phase, which corresponds to the interviews with the 12 people selected. In these interviews, we deal in depth with the meaning of photography in general in their lives, as well as the transformations they have observed regarding photography in their respective Facebook accounts.

2 Theoretical Framework

From a sociocultural point of view, the category of identity comprises three dimensions: first, an intrapersonal or subjective dimension, related to the individual's intentions of representation; second, an interpersonal or relational dimension, regarding the interactions with the immediate social circle; and third, the set of roles assumed and played by the individual. The creation of a self-image and the presentation of self to others is therefore a combination of three elements: symbols, interactions and context. The latter is particularly important when it comes to SNSs. We state that digital interfaces play an important role in the forms of self-(re-)presentation today since they are both the technical and the social support of multiple forms of expression and identity co-construction. Facebook or, more precisely, the profile picture, would be just *one* possibility within this wide range. In the following section we present our general framework. Our theoretical starting point is the symbolic interaction approach proposed by Goffman. However, we include some other contributions from sociology, semiotics and cultural studies.

2.1 The Presentation of Self in Everyday Life

Our idea of how people present themselves in the Facebook SNS emerges most clearly from the micro-sociological analysis of Goffman (1959). In his study, the author describes people as performers in a theatre and face-to-face interactions as efforts to manage impressions in front of an audience. In his words: 'While in the presence of others, the individual typically infuses his activity with signs which dramatically highlight and portray confirmatory facts that might otherwise remain unapparent or obscure. For if the individual's activity is to become significant to others, he must mobilise his activity so that it will express during the interaction what he wishes to convey' (Goffman 1959, p. 29).

Throughout Goffman's study, the presentation of self in everyday life is understood as a constant work of creation and negotiation: people carefully select and use settings, appearances and manners in their performance. In sum, they try and display a coherent front. 'Fronts are that part of the individual's performance which regularly functions in a general and fixed fashion to define the situation for those who observe the performance. Front, then, is the expressive equipment of a standard kind intentionally or unwittingly employed by the individual during his performance' (1959, p. 22). More precisely, the front is the sum of the setting (furniture, supplies and props used for the scenery), the appearance (stimuli which reveal the performer's social statuses), and manners (stimuli which function as a warning of the interaction role the performer will expect to play). Thus the presentation of self, rather than a state, is a dynamic process that involves a production (sometimes individual, sometimes collective) in which the author invests effort, time and care.

Similarly, a dramatic realisation is also observable in SNSs. We do not try to extrapolate here each of the concepts proposed by Goffman. We are interested, however, in exploring the dramaturgical metaphor given its general definition of the presentation of self as a management of impressions. In this regard, we highlight two aspects of the presentation of self in everyday life that seem relevant to the analysis of the construction of a self-image in SNSs: first, the active role of the one wishing to present themselves to a targeted audience; secondly, the management of symbolic-expressive equipment according to the specific environment of interaction which involves possibilities as well as constraints, not only in a material but also in a social sense.

2.2 *Photography: An Ordinary Practice*

Frequently, an important relationship is observed between mood, personal narrative and photographs. Some writers – i.e. Barthes (1989), Benjamin (1973) and Sontag (2005) – have formulated that photography is essentially melancholic: a picture recalls the past, refers to what is gone and is associated with loss and death. Even what appears to be a joyous picture could be taken only as evidence that all things pass and fade. But does photography only have a commemorative function? Nowadays, new meanings are being attributed to photography. Taking pictures is not an exclusive practice of artists and professionals; rather, it is an extended activity due to the dissemination of low-cost devices and the advent of new platforms for exhibition. Evidently, Facebook does not institutionalise photography as an ordinary practice, but it does provide other conditions for the creation, publication and distribution of images that did not exist before (Rueda 2012).

Certain perspectives from semiotics and photography theory allow us to explore some aspects of the intricate relationship between the experience of personal photography, the social meanings of daily photographic practices and the uses of emerging technology. For example, Roland Barthes' theory (1989) is ostensibly grounded in the idea of the inseparability of an image from its referent; more precisely, the picture and the object it depicts are of the same nature. For him, the message is therefore a message without a code. This idea leads us to consider how today Facebook users are part of a communicative space where there is not a unique meaning but multiple meanings. We believe that the author is born simultaneously with his *opera*. He is not replaced by another being which precedes or transcends his work. This is because taking pictures no longer designates an operation of recording, of representing, but rather what pragmatics calls a *performative* act.

In contrast, Benjamin was committed to making the past active in the present, because for him, nothing in the past had truly disappeared forever; its traces could be rediscovered and put to use. Thus, it is possible to think of bringing back the past as active within the present and involved in the anticipation of the future. In fact, as Roberts (2011) states, photographs and "photographing" (even with a phone camera) can, in short, stimulate a "rememoration" of people, events and objects and associated emotional and sensory experiences which are placed within contemporary thoughts, feelings and circumstances. The environment that social networks like Facebook offers takes advantage of this new condition of our societies and accelerates it. This acceleration is also related to the need to constantly update one's self-image, apparently motivated by a permanent desire to excel in front of an audience that can be both supportive ("Like") but sometimes critical.

As a complement to this understanding of photography, we consider that Sennett (2009) provides another element: the notion of craftsmanship, which refers to both the desire for quality and the skill to deliver it. Sennett wants to broaden cultural materialism to include the sensations and puzzles aroused by material things themselves; the ways in which abstract thinking and belief develop through practice and practical activity; the forms of social behaviour which emerge from shared physical experience. Sennett views the satisfactions of physical making as a necessary part of being human. We need craft work as a way to keep ourselves rooted in material reality, providing a steadying balance in a world which overrates mental facility. It is in this regard that we see the profile image as a work, as a matter of routine practice and, at the same time, as an individual and collective experience.

2.3 *Identity, Youth and Digital Media*

According to Van Dijck,

> the digital evolution that has shaped personal photography is anything but an exclusive technological transformation. Rather, the shift in use and function of the camera seems to suit a more general cultural condition that may be characterised by terms such as manipulability, individuality, communicability, versatility and ease of distribution. This cultural condition has definitely affected the nature and status of photographs as building blocks for personal identity (2008, p. 70).

In this respect, it is necessary to look at the different studies that focus on the cultural aspects of digital media. Among the large and diverse body of work on youth, identity and the use of digital media, we find the cultural studies account of the appropriation of the Internet in everyday life very useful. Mainly, we highlight Buckingham's (2008) and Livingstone's (2011) contributions. As these authors suggest, today digital media are providing young people with symbolic resources for expressing themselves and constructing their own identities. Although our study does not focus specifically on youth, it is true that this demographic group is the one which most fully exploits digital media as a way to respond to the expressive needs and identity explorations which characterise our modern social life. In this respect, the concept of "reflexivity" is at the core of Giddens' theory. Reflexivity can be defined as a self-defining process that depends upon the monitoring of, and reflection upon, psychological and social information about possible trajectories of life. "The reflexivity of modern social life" writes Giddens, "consists in the fact that social practices are constantly examined and reformed in the light of incoming information about those very practices, thus constitutively altering their character" (1991, p. 28).

Like many of the other authors, Giddens sees identity as fluid and malleable rather than fixed. Richard Jenkins (1996) argues that identity is a fluid, contingent matter – it is something we accomplish practically through our on-going interactions and negotiations with other people. In this respect, it might be more appropriate to talk about identification rather than identity. On Facebook, the identity of a person does not only involve a voluntary act on the part of the users, or even their awareness, because there is a lot of information that "others" (friends) can provide. In this regard, the construction of a self-image on this SNS seems to be more complex than in face-to-face interactions. As Cardon (2008) has pointed out, digital identity is a co-production where platform strategies and tactics of users cross. In fact, the productions made by Facebook users require as much of a *technical manipulation* of the interface as a *social activity* of permanent exchange with other members of the network. In other words, it is necessary to take into account, and at the same level, both the technical and social dimensions, because the presentation of self in SNSs closely articulates the architecture of the site and the calculations that users make to produce a better impression of themselves. There are elements produced, but mostly registered by others, and users must calculate and anticipate this too.

In addition, SNSs not only exploit the relational aspect of the web, inviting us to connect and communicate; as participatory environments they also encourage users to create. But it is important to note that such participation is highly autobiographical. Cardon (2008) suggests that, within the expressionist dynamic of the web, people's identity is increasingly deposited and distributed in the works and products of those actions displayed to others. This type of production fits perfectly in the context of new interactive platforms and digital networks since they can only exist to the extent that users publish their own content. Internet users are invited to be part of a broad and varied range of sites and multimedia applications that require the construction of a user profile.

3 Methodology

3.1 First Phase: Selection and Classification of Profile Images

From November 2011 to May 2012, this study began by selecting and classifying 7200 profile images from Facebook[2] in 24 cities around the world (300 images per city). Selection criteria for cities consisted of: (a) a high degree of urbanisation and infrastructure for access to the Internet, (b) a metropolitan lifestyle, high migratory flow and contrasting cultural populations, (c) a significantly increasing rate of new Facebook users in recent years or high penetration of Facebook, and (d) some socio-political or cultural particularities. We included: Bogota, Buenos Aires, Caracas, Mexico City, Havana, São Paulo, Chicago, Montreal, New York, Toronto, Berlin, London, Madrid, Paris, Rome, Beijing, Bombay, Islamabad, Tel Aviv, Pyongyang, Tokyo, Johannesburg, Nairobi and Sydney. All images were chosen from public profiles by following the random list provided by the Facebook browser after the name of the city was submitted.

The classification process was accomplished by following the ETF model, previously proposed by Gómez and González (2009, 2011), which is based on some

[2] At that time, Facebook had not yet implemented the timeline layout which allows users to upload not only a profile image but also a cover image in their profiles.

Table 1 Types of entity

	Human	Non-human
With Bio-graphics	E1	E3

Without Bio-graphic	E2	E4

E1 Human with bio-graphics, *E2* Human without bio-graphics, *E3* Non-human with bio-graphics, *E4* Non-human without bio-graphics

of the functional and conceptual categories of nonlinear dynamical systems (attractors, self-organisation, phase transitions, state space grids and trajectories). This model is constructed by three categories: entity, treatment and framing. Each category is described by four types, resulting from the combination of two variables, as explained below:

Entity (E) is assessed taking into account what is inside the image. The first variable of this category indicates if the profile picture shows a human figure or an object (non-human). The second variable determines whether the image brings up, or not, some biographical information, a trace about the profile owner. In that sense, we use the term *bio-graphics*. The following table[3] exemplifies the four types of entity resulting from the crossing of the variables mentioned (Table 1).

Treatment (T) relates to the intention of presenting either a natural image or an artificial one. In this category, the first variable oscillates between the presence and the absence of intervention traces. We refer to intervention as digital manipulation or editing. The second variable classifies the image as non-staged, if it is intended to be spontaneous, or staged, if there is an explicit manipulation of the setting. The following table shows examples for each one of the four types of treatment (Table 2):

[3] All images in tables are published with owner's permission.

Table 2 Types of treatment

	Non-intervened	Intervened
Non-staged	T1	T3

Staged	T2	T4
		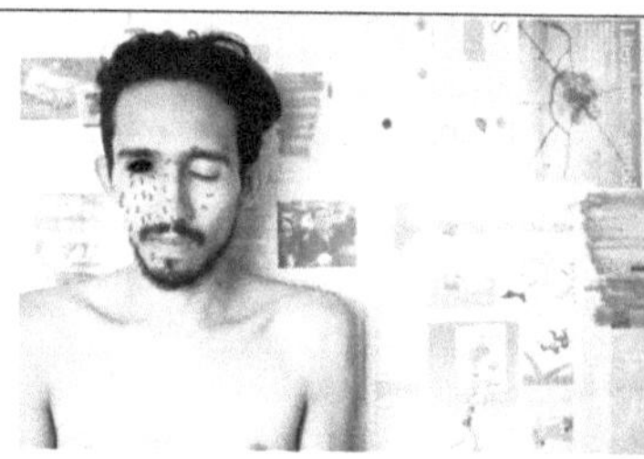

T1 Non-intervened and Non-staged, *T2* Non-intervened and Staged, *T3* Intervened and Non-staged, *T4* Intervened and Staged

Framing (F) refers to the amount of information provided by the image. Here, the first variable indicates how much of the entity is shown: a whole recognisable unit or just a portion of it. The second variable defines the context in terms of wide, if there is enough information to recognise the life context of the profile owner, or limited, if there is very little or none. The following table illustrates the four possible types of framing (Table 3).

Finally, the ETF model makes it possible to create 64 possible configurations (see Table 4) as the result of the combinatorial analysis of the three categories as shown in the following table.

At the end of the classification process, one catalogue was created for each city. Though the catalogues were made by different members of the research team this was not an inter-rater procedure. However, we did try to eliminate subjectivity in several meetings through discussion and verification.

Table 3 Types of framing

	Whole	Portion
Wide context	F1	F3

Limited context	F2	F4

F1 Whole with wide context, *F2* Whole with limited context, *F3* Portion with wide context, *F4* Portion with limited context

Table 4 Configurations

E1T1F1	E1T3F1	E2T1F1	E2T3F1	E3T1F1	E3T3F1	E4T1F1	E4T3F1
E1T1F2	E1T3F2	E2T1F2	E2T3F2	E3T1F2	E3T3F2	E4T1F2	E4T3F2
E1T1F3	E1T3F3	E2T1F3	E2T3F3	E3T1F3	E3T3F3	E4T1F3	E4T3F3
E1T1F4	E1T3F4	E2T1F4	E2T3F4	E3T1F4	E3T3F4	E4T1F4	E4T3F4
E1T2F1	E1T4F1	E2T2F1	E2T4F1	E3T2F1	E3T4F1	E4T2F1	E4T4F1
E1T2F2	E1T4F2	E2T2F2	E2T4F2	E3T2F2	E3T4F2	E4T2F2	E4T4F2
E1T2F3	E1T4F3	E2T2F3	E2T4F3	E3T2F3	E3T4F3	E4T2F3	E4T4F3
E1T2F4	E1T4F4	E2T2F4	E2T4F4	E3T2F4	E3T4F4	E4T2F4	E4T4F4

3.2 *Second Phase: Ethnographic Fieldwork*

The second phase took place between May and October 2012 and consisted of interviews with 12 Facebook users and the observation of their Facebook account activity. Our purpose was to identify what forms of representation remain the same and which others have changed as regards photographic practice in everyday life.

The selection of this group was essentially based on the fact that their Facebook pages were open to the public, that they showed signs of a high level of activity in updating their pages and, above all, that they authorised us to monitor their Facebook pages for 6 months and were willing to participate in interviews. Observation field notes were registered in field diaries and, additionally, fortnightly interviews (either face-to-face or by videoconference) were conducted for which we developed one guide for weekends and another one for weekdays. In these interviews we talked about the entries made and we tried to clarify the meanings of the Facebook activity during this period of time. The study group (12 people) consisted of five women and seven men with the following age distribution: nine people between the ages of 20 and 30 (four women and five men, the youngest age group); two men between the ages of 30 and 50 (the group of adults); and one 70-year-old (an elderly female). Most of the participants in the study group (eight people) belong to a young, middle-class "college-student" generation from the city of Cali, Colombia. Finally, the two adult males have white-collar jobs (in communication and tourism), and the female senior citizen is currently a pensioner. The present text will only take into account results related to the profile image; however, as a result of this ethnographic study, other elements were observed related to the lifeworlds of the subjects, the ways in which they constructed their works or mundane crafts, and also the emergence of forms of a poeticised experience of the self through their works.

4 Major Results and Discussion

4.1 First Phase

The inventory of images was primarily exploratory in nature. Our objective was to test the image classification model (ETF) described above and to identify, despite the cultural and social differences among cities, what appeared to be regularity in the Facebook profile images. We note that it was not our intention to carry out an intercultural analysis of these images. Doing so would have required adopting other techniques to gather qualitative information in each of the selected cities. Accordingly, the general results are presented below, based on the regularities found in the analysis of 7200 profile images.

4.1.1 The Canon of the Facebook Image and the Other Three Types of Images

The most interesting finding is what we called the canon of the Facebook image, i.e. the typical profile image: the configuration E1T1F1 (human with bio-graphics, non-intervened, non-staged, and whole with wide context). As can be seen in Graph 1, of the 24 catalogues of the selected cities, 19 had more than 200 images of this

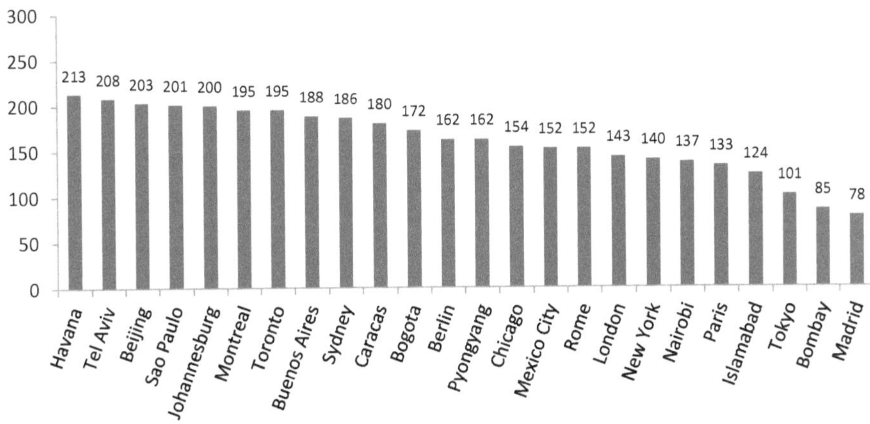

Graph 1 Frequencies E1T1F1

canon type (of the 300 in each catalogue). Moreover, in the five catalogues of the cities with the least amount of typical profile images, at least half of the photos were of this canon type.

When combining the entity and treatment types we found a high concentration of human representations with bio-graphics as well as a more natural treatment of the images; that is, they were neither modified nor theatrically staged. Thus, 83 % of the total images are *natural and spontaneous* photographs, 97.44 % depict whole units (not portions of bodies, faces or objects), which are neither fractioned nor modified nor staged. We found that 90 % of the profile images display human shapes; only 10 % are non-human entities, animals, objects or landscapes. More than half of the images (54 %) show non-intervened and non-staged bodies and faces revealing significant portions of the subject's common surroundings. These findings show a strong tendency towards maintaining the inherited forms of face-to-face presentation forms found in the offline world and an interest in giving auto-biographical accounts. Despite the technical affordances of cameras and the photographic editing and graphic design programs available on the Internet, many of the uploaded profile images were not visually processed, either before or afterwards.

4.1.2 Type E2: Human Without Bio-Graphics

There are very few Type E2 images (see Graph 2). Between 62 and 138 images of this type were found in only five catalogues. In 19 catalogues there were fewer than 50 of these images of the 300 that each catalogue contains. It is interesting to note the absence of the subjects' everyday world in Facebook profiles and, on the other hand, the presence of subjects from media iconography (TV and movie celebrities, journalists, personalities from the sports and music world and the videogame industry) as well as religious cult figures (Buddha, Christ).

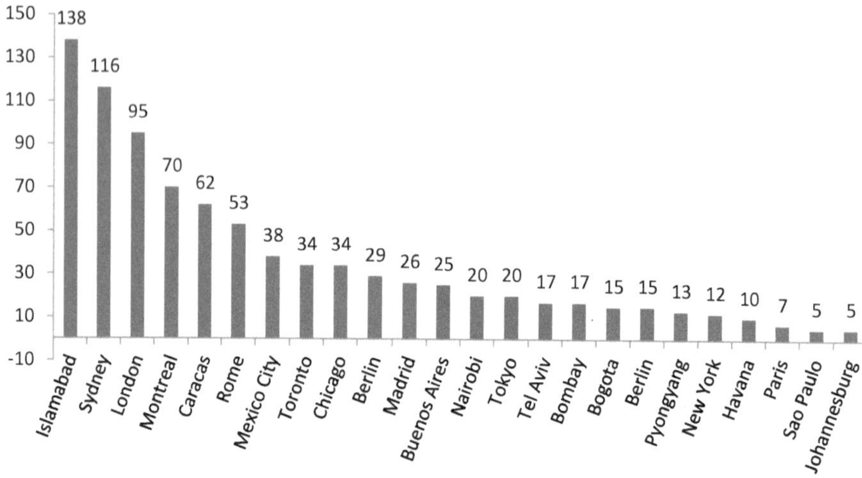

Graph 2 Frequencies E2: Human without bio-graphics

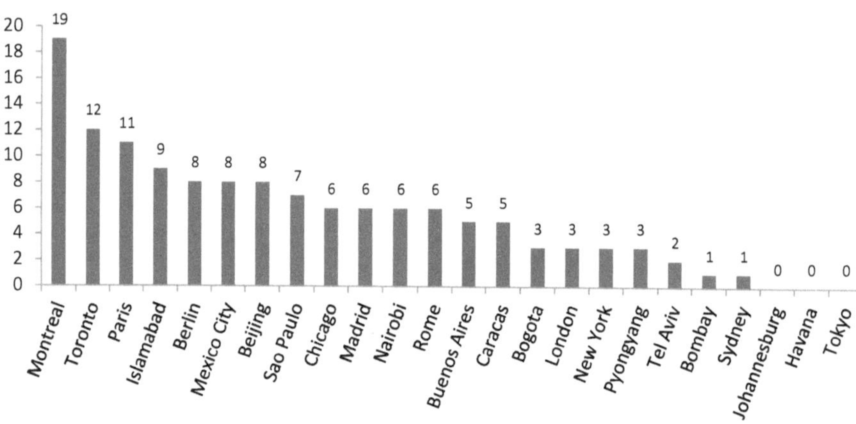

Graph 3 Frequencies E3: Non-human with bio-graphics

4.1.3 Type E3: Non-Human with Bio-Graphics

The non-human with bio-graphics type is the least common (see Graph 3). Of the 300 images available per catalogue, a maximum of between 12 and 19 images of this type were found. In fact, no image of this type was found at all in three of the cities. At least in the samples we analysed, it appears to be uncommon to use non-human subjects with biographical information (pets, objects, landscapes) as profile images.

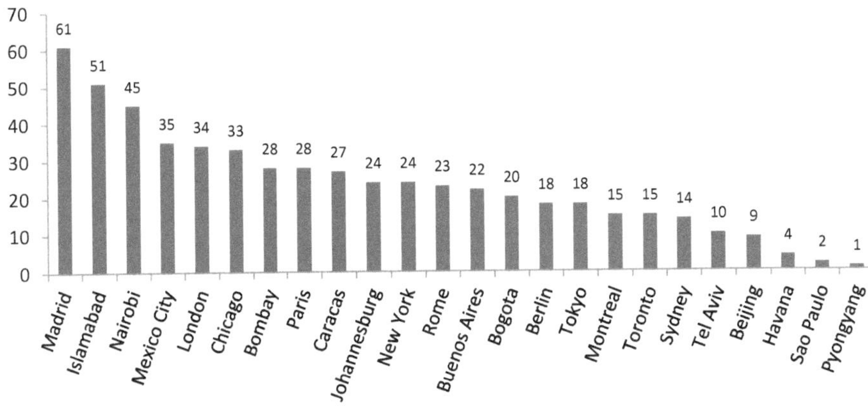

Graph 4 Frequencies E4: Non-human without bio-graphics

4.1.4 Type E4: Non-Human Without Bio-Graphics

Although this type of image is not common (see Graph 4), there are more reported cases than the non-human with bio-graphics type. The case with the largest number of images of this type had 61 images, followed by 51 and 45. The smallest case had one image. Apparently, in this type of image, the subjects are much more likely to resort to images from the cultural industries or from the Internet without traces of their everyday life. Nevertheless, these images also carry a symbolic, communicative power about the lifeworlds of the subjects in relation to interests and lifestyles (sports, music, movie and TV personalities, religion, etc.). Both in Type E3 and in Type E4 the biographical information is quite closely associated with human representations.

Furthermore, in these last two types of images it is important to note that 11 % of the images representing bodies and faces were generated in the digital world and were released by the media and cultural industries with limited context and apparently free of intervention or staging. Whenever an image of the human without bio-graphics type is used, the subject fills the whole of the frame, without showing any signs of the surroundings. That is an extreme use of the front, if we put it in Goffman's terms. Using pictures of widely known personalities from the media and cultural industry seems to be a sort of idealisation of the front, because they express socially accepted values and hierarchies and therefore receive more acceptance and consensus (which for young people is very important). Aside from that, the combination of non-human with bio-graphics is rare; it is often an image taken from the digital world, with no relation to the user´s context, and simply posted on Facebook as a profile image.

According to the data collected, it should be noted that the tendency or canon of Facebook images is configuration E1T1F1: human, with bio-graphics, non-intervened and non-staged. The low levels of graphic exploration, even in cities like New York or London or Buenos Aires, which use high levels of technology, leads us to believe that old forms of self-presentation are still the norm. Therefore, it is not possible to generalise about the innovative character of the presentation of self on Facebook. However, although it is a minor trend, we have observed among younger users a greater interaction with the technological affordances that the social network offers, as well as with other technical devices at their disposal. In fact, when observing the profiles of adults and of younger people, there are differences. While older adults tend to use images without much treatment, framing or staging, younger adults seem to explore to a greater degree the possibilities that the social network has to offer. Thus a greater exploration of technical possibilities seems also to be related to an intense exploration of the processes of youth identification. In adults, issues of identification and the construction of a social universe are not at the forefront; instead, the focus is on communication and maintaining ties with family members and friends.

Profile images on Facebook show, in sum, three tendencies: firstly, people seem to assume *something* (human/non-human) must be present; an entity containing the qualities necessary for users to identify and present themselves, mainly belonging to the human with bio-graphics type (the canon). Thus, despite the fear of hypocrisy and shallowness some people accuse the virtual world of, we found that most users post images of their actual life. In some cases spiritual or religious tendencies greatly influence the choice of image; for example, replacing the self-portrait with an image of a personality from the media or cultural industry or a religious icon. Secondly, as stated above, these *entities* tend to exhibit a certain completeness (faces in medium close-up or entire bodies) creating a great number of images with wide context. Experimentation on profile images with fractioning, detail focusing and extreme close-ups once again complicates recognition of these *entities* (profile images). Nevertheless, even a fraction of a human face or body still preserves some elements that can lead one to identify and acknowledge the subject, a possibility that *seems* to be lost when the representatives are inanimate objects or non-human. Thirdly, although image intervention is rare, it mostly affects the human with bio-graphics type, while non-human objects are seldom modified. Image staging is also infrequent for both human and non-human representatives. Nonetheless, users who only upload and classify spontaneous shots without subsequent treatment, as well as those who like to experiment with their image, are showing us a palette of possible *opera* and forms of *handcraft* of the self-image, and, consequentially, new possible ways of identity exploration. Sennett (2009) proposes that imitation, attention to detail and the appropriation of someone else's secrets to use them in one's own work are worthy abilities that should be valued as part of the process of building our singular profile as craftsmen of our own lives.

Therefore, the profile image as *opus* is sometimes produced through an object of artistic experimentation while in other cases it is produced by finding the appropriate source (the precise time or people, and the scene required). But in many other cases it occurs both in the process of identity exploration during interactions in the everyday world (off and online) and through its capture by image technologies. Thus, everyday life and technologies are mutually instituted through a process of craftsmanship which relies on a continuing involvement. As Sennett (2009) argues, while we are working, submerged processes of thought and feeling are in progress. Almost without being aware we set ourselves the highest standard required when we care about the qualities of our work.

What follows are two of the most important tendencies regarding the grammar of images with respect to treatment and framing, as well as what they allow us to see about permanence and transformations in the forms of presentation of self.

4.1.5 Treatment and Framing: Capturing the Moment, Posing and Posting

Subjects who treat and frame their images through the pre- and post-production of a staged profile image use a different process from that of classic photography (in a studio or *posing* in front of the family camera for special occasions); due to the ability of new technology to multiply the chances of recording all kinds of daily life scenes and events, the capture of the moment is the most extended practice. The existence of several picture-taking devices seems to fuse together the event with its visual record; being somewhere is an occasion to take pictures, which generates disposable images (in the words of Fontcuberta (2010): "Kleenex-images: to use and throw away"). At the same time, we note that experiencing the world turns into an occasion to pose. A wide spectrum of relationship codes, as Barthes (1989) stated, can be observed in photos shared by youths; from simple greeting gestures to more sophisticated expressions that relate affection, sympathy, cordiality, charm or seduction. Thus posting, sending and sharing photos works as a new system for social communication.

Visual Effects and Retro-Aesthetics

On the intervened human with bio-graphics type, which requires post-production work on the digitalised image, it is common to find all kinds of retouching. Young people can then *play* and experiment with their self-image using various technological tools like the editing software Photoshop and others.[4] We also found a strong tendency to use black-and-white pictures in which experimentation with the grey scale produces interesting textures to our colour-tired vision. This tendency (observed in all catalogues) could indicate the comeback of the kind of retro-aesthetics that might have been considered obsolete with the emergence of new technologies of visual recording. Maybe the reappearance of the old and worn out can produce *novelty* in modern communication.

[4] PhotoScape and the online face-retouching tool PinkMirror, among others.

4.2 Second Phase

In the second phase our purpose was to identify what forms of representation remain and which others have changed as regards photographic practice in everyday life. We state that the profile image should be studied in relation, not only to the use of old and new technologies, but, most importantly, in relation to the representation of what a technology can do (Van Dijck 2008). In this respect, we affirmed that although the publication of a personal image in Facebook depends on the affordances of the website, creation depends on the user's symbolic world. That is why, in order to approach this symbolic universe, we are going to base this second phase of our research both on virtual ethnography and on interviews. From the interviews, we were able to identify some of the changes and continuities in photographic practices, and how our artists, in addition to the ability to represent and preserve a memory, also confer on images a narrative, performative, political or relational function. Thus we observe how, while some practices still continue, different values have arisen about what images to show, where, when and to whom.

In interviews, participants revealed having strong connections with photography since childhood and they even had very clear memories about it: family albums, the first camera and its use to document and record trips, special dates and significant biographical events. This is still preserved in the way Facebook is used. Many of our artists consider Facebook as a place of memory and archive their photos there as they once did with family albums. But this is just one of the many uses of Facebook. The representational function coexists with new practices in which the images are considered visual resources to do and say something else.

Storing photos on Facebook makes it possible to exhibit images in a permanent manner. Depending on their interests, users take advantage of this to create a dialogue with friends and other users of the network. Seen as a personal diary, Facebook is a repository of moods and feelings. Seen as a gallery, Facebook is a place to exhibit their visual works. Seen as a blog, Facebook is a place to publish content, generate discussion and engage in activism. This multiplicity of uses reveals a transformation of individual identity, a constant work of creating and recreating oneself in which contemporary individuals, along with the potential of online social networks and digital photography, take responsibility for building the project of themselves (Giddens 1991), among a multitude of options (Fig. 1).

We also found that graphic experimentation is much more popular on user's albums than on profile images. Given that the profile image, as conceived by Facebook, serves to identify users within the network, they may set the need for presentation and acknowledgement against the desire for expressive experimentation using the image. The great trend that we found in the profile image is the use of an image that refers more to representation in its modern sense, that is, as a unit of meaning and *authentic* vision of the world. Experimentation, in this sense, can diffuse and even threaten correct identification of the subject. Albums instead propose an option to reconcile experimentation with identification through a visual narration; many users create thematic albums of different kinds, some with clear

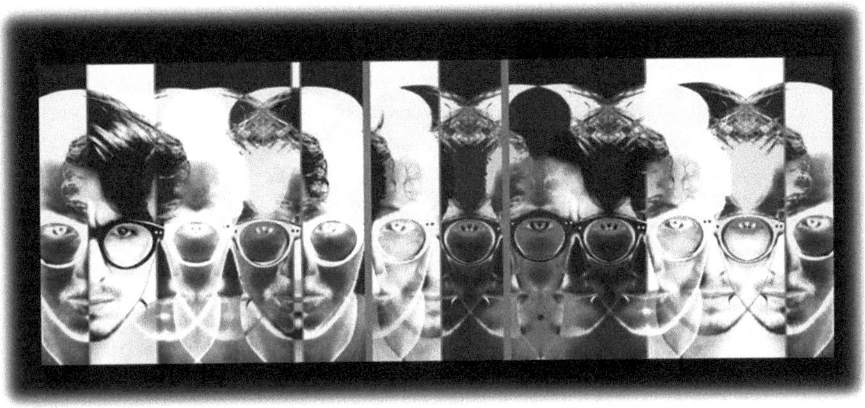

Fig. 1 Image made by one of the participants in the study group (Published with owner's permission)

experimental purposes, while others have a documentary character, registering topics of interest without subsequent treatment. In both cases albums contain cross-references to other subjects (tags, comments, titles) that reinforce bonds within the SNS.

As regards the matter of public display of an individual, a transition seems to be taking place: from the origins of modern photography as a mimetic representation and a realistic and static reproduction of the subject, locally bound, as described by Barthes (1989) and Benjamin (1973), to a proliferation of photographic devices as well as times and spaces to re-present oneself. It constitutes a subjective construction through a semi-public dynamic context which has intense symbolic exchange value. However, the cultural archetypes of face-to-face interaction are reproduced and maintained in technological environments because technological acceleration does not equal cultural acceleration; therefore, users seems to prefer conventional *representation* rules (spontaneous pictures without treatment or staging) that do not threaten their recognition and acceptance on the network. But at the same time, although to a lesser degree, it can also be observed that youths – as is the case in face-to-face interaction – have a need to experiment with their self-image beyond the established rules, staging and modifying images, which are published mainly in digital albums.

In this regard, the image of the self in Facebook acts as a symbol that allows the younger generations especially to share their significant world with a network of family members and friends. Thus, through a new common way of presenting one's self, where thoughts, feelings and attitudes are shared, the interpretation of self and others is learned. We routinely construct our experience of daily life in exactly this manner: stimulating, pushing, suggesting, advising, admonishing, criticising and praising as we create the flow of our actions in the social world. "Well done!", "I like it", we might say to ourselves when surveying the results of our actions; the crucial point here is that such surveying of the territory of the self is always carried out with reference to the reactions of others, as others would view and interpret actions of the self. In Facebook this process becomes much more intensive and reflexive since the actions of our public presentation become permanent works, like written language, to be read over and over again by others. That is why the process of presentation of self is much more complex and difficult to control, as is the case with face-to-face interaction.

5 Conclusions

As stated by Gómez and González (2012) registering or positioning the profile image is the last of a series of procedures involving emotional decisions, calculations and strategies of various kinds, picture taking and file reviewing, as well as proficiency in uploading and downloading picture files and so on. This is a digital *rite of passage*, which celebrates the presence and exposure of the individual on the social network. Thus the Facebook image is the *convergence* of a communicative ecosystem offered by the platform with a set of decisions and procedures, which appear to culminate with the *uploading* of an image to Facebook, but is nevertheless transformed and enriched by the interactions occurring around it, in a process of permanent reflexivity.

The findings about the "canon-type" image could thus be more a demonstration of an intense social exploration than a technical exploration of the communicative environment Facebook offers. However, since the space reserved for the profile image does not offer tools to treat these images, this could be a condition that constitutes a technical restriction of this environment. Those who wish to perform more of a treatment of the image must then resort to other devices and editing spaces outside of the Facebook platform.

We have found that there is a blurring between front-stage and back-stage: what feels like an intimate space for and with friends can exist under the watchful electronic gaze of a large unknown audience, while what is being acted out as a front-stage performance could have no witnesses. In terms of online exchanges in social networks, it can be argued, as other researchers have found (Di Prospero 2011), that the performance is a mixture of attributes from the private and the public. It is a front-stage space entered into from private spaces, and contains personal, sometimes intimate, relationships. Yet it is also open to *outsiders*, demanding skills with codes of communication and exchange in order to convey information and ideas to others. Thus the performativity within an SNS like Facebook emphasises the juxtaposition between the private and the public.

Just as Goffman argued in relation to face-to-face interpersonal contact, we see that users in online spaces perform their roles using codes and signs developed and learned through both online and offline interaction. In doing so, these actors are most of the time aware (to a greater or lesser degree) of other users as well as the *audience* of friends, lurkers, virtual passers-by, and wider social networks. In any case, the possibility of permanently revising one's profile, taking another photo, updating it, retouching it, in an intense conversation with "friends", produces an environment of reflexivity – as Giddens stated – about the presentation of oneself as a work (*opera*). The strong tendency toward one or two types of configuration and the infrequency of cases that do not conform to the traditional or inherited modes of representation, confirm Goffman's idea that the presentation of self is a dialectical process. Certainly Facebook is no longer a mere book of faces, nor an environment of simple superficial consumption, nor is publishing a self-image or an image of a celebrity, a pet, a T-shirt of one's favourite football team, etc., a random act: who can see the image, who can understand it, or what interpretations it allows, are some of the questions that arise.

Although critics have argued that Goffman tends to overstate the importance of rules and to neglect the aspects of improvisation, or indeed sheer habit, that characterise everyday social interaction, we still find his approach very useful for our understanding of young people's uses of digital media. We state that the subjective experience in Facebook is not predetermined but is attached to a set of rules, protocols and conditions of interaction and communication offered by this new technological environment. For example, in Facebook, we found that to assess the profile image, one must read the set of communicative parts that make up the page: a kind of front with settings (pictures, texts, symbols used for the scenery), appearance (information about the Facebook user), and manners (rules and roles of the interaction expected to be played); performance too is very relevant as we have found in Facebook pages. At the same time, Facebook has been adapted and readjusted by social frames where individual and collective experiences take place.

Nevertheless, studying the profile image on Facebook forces us to consider a new aspect initially not included in the Goffmanian approach: the endurance, even if immaterial, digital, of the self-image. Unlike the performance of a real-time role or face-to-face interaction, the profile image in Facebook brings its own *pre- and post-productions* and leaves a *digital trace* which is stored in the SNS. That means that the image is maintained over time. That trace remains throughout time and can be assessed at different times by different people, i.e. by an audience. Therefore the profile image has at least two social functions: on the one hand, the process of exploring and adjusting the ways of the self-image for the actor-author and the observers. On the other hand, it eases establishing and maintaining social liaisons with other people and plays an important role in setting the rules for self-images on the network, and in the recreation and *aesthetic enhancement* of daily experience.

Returning to one of this discussion's starting points, perhaps the most interesting question is that identity and self-(re-)presentation could be approached by means of the (material) support in which they unfolded. Nonetheless, a much deeper understanding of the role of digital ICTs in our lives requires a non-deterministic approach. Often, one of the first ways in which people react to new technology is trying to do what they are already familiar with, before starting to experiment with new uses. While past practices can be redefined and even displaced, they also tend to coexist with the new ones. So it is important not only to look at the changes of photography as an ordinary practice but also its continuities. If we consider Facebook as a real environment creation, instead of associating it with a mere device for the recording and storing of images, we could really understand its constitutive role in the construction of meaning in everyday life. Thus we believe that everyday life and ordinary practices are the contexts in which technologies are inserted and not the other way around. We consider that the integration of digital ICTs in our daily routines is more the result of an evolution, an adjustment, a negotiation between our inherited traditions and the desire to transform our societies rather than a revolution or a radical rupture.

Acknowledgements We would like to express our gratitude to José Joaquín Recasens for partially translating the text from Spanish to English, and for revising and helping to adapt it to the editorial standards required for publication.

References

Barthes, R. (1989). *La cámara lúcida. Notas sobre la fotografía*. Barcelona: Paidós.

Benjamin, W. (1973). *La obra de arte en la época de su reproductibilidad técnica*. Madrid: Taurus.

Buckingham, D. (2008). Introducing identity. In D. Buckingham (Ed.), *Youth, identity, and digital media* (pp. 1–24). Cambridge, MA: The MIT Press.

Cardon, D. (2008). Le design de la visibilité: Un essai de cartographie du web 2.0. *Réseaux, 152*, 93–137.

Di Prospero, C. (2011). Autopresentación en Facebook: Un yo para el público. *Revista Latinoamericana de Estudios sobre Cuerpos, Emociones y Sociedad, 6*(3), 44–53.

Fontcuberta, J. (2010). *La cámara de Pandora. La fotografí@ después de la fotografía*. Barcelona: Ediciones Gustavo Gilli.

Giddens, A. (1991). *The consequences of modernity*. Cambridge: Polity Press.

Goffman, E. (1959). *Presentation of self in everyday life*. New York: Doubleday Anchor.

Gómez, R., & González, J. (2009). Formas de presentación pública de la persona en Facebook. *Nexus, 8*, 54–65.

Gómez, R., & González, J. (2011). *Formas de presentación pública de la persona en Facebook. Informe de Avance. Documento interno de trabajo*. Colombia: Universidad del Valle.

Gómez, R., & González, J. (2012). *Rutas y configuraciones de la imagen de perfil en Facebook. Documento interno de trabajo*. Colombia: Universidad del Valle.

Jenkins, R. (1996). *Social identity*. London: Routledge.

Livingstone, S. (2011). Internet, children and youth. In R. Burnett, M. Consalvo, & C. Ess (Eds.), *The handbook of internet studies* (pp. 348–368). Oxford: Wiley-Blackwell.

Roberts, B. (2011). Photographic portraits: Narrative and memory. *Forum Qualitative Sozialforschung/Forum: Qualitative Social Research, 12*(2). http://nbnresolving.de/urn:nbn:de:0114-fqs110263. Accessed 30 Jan 2015.

Rueda, R. (2012). Formas de presentación de sí en Facebook. Esbozos de una poética y estética dialógica. *Nexus, 12*, 202–215.

Sennett, R. (2009). *El artesano*. Barcelona: Anagrama.

Sontag, S. (2005). *Sobre la fotografía*. Bogotá: Anagrama.

Van Dijck, J. (2008). Digital photography: Communication, identity, memory. *Visual Communication, 7*(1), 57–76.

Digital Divides in the Era of Widespread Internet Access: Migrant Youth Negotiating Hierarchies in Digital Culture

Koen Leurs

Abstract In this chapter I analyse the digital practices of migrant youth as situated, power-laden, pleasurable and sometimes painful everyday experiences. I develop Walter Benjamin's theorisations of the nineteenth century "arcade" or commercial passageway (Benjamin W (1999) The Arcades project. Harvard University Press, Cambridge), together with Nirmal Puwar's understanding of how non-normative bodies become "space invaders" (Puwar N (2004) Space invaders: race, gender and bodies out of place. Berg, Oxford) upon entering certain domains, in order to conceptualise the digital spatial biases of online platforms and their subversions. The argument builds on survey, interview and ethnographic data gathered as part of the interdisciplinary research project *Wired Up. Digital media as innovative socialisation practices for migrant youth* run by Utrecht University. I argue firstly how offline societal power relations related to race and ethnicity, religion and gender relations travel online and create new digital divides that go beyond computer ownership and Internet access. Secondly, I argue how Internet platforms become spaces for the negotiation of power relations, digital belonging and greater cultural understanding in an increasingly multicultural world.

1 Introduction

In order to puncture recurring utopian and dystopian myths of technological determinism, I analyse the digital practices of Moroccan-Dutch youth to argue that contemporary digital media use among ethnic minorities is a situated, power-laden, pleasurable and sometimes painful everyday experience. Contemporary digital culture remains power-ridden, which urges us to reconsider the early notion of the digital divide; more attention is also needed for the empowerment users experience when negotiating digital inequalities and hierarchies. The argument builds on a quantitative survey (n = 1408), qualitative interviews (n = 43) and ethnographic data

K. Leurs (✉)
Department of Media and Culture Studies / Institute for Cultural Enquiry (ICON), Utrecht University, Muntstraat 2a, Utrecht 3512 EV, Netherlands
e-mail: K.H.A.Leurs@uu.nl

M. Walrave et al. (eds.), *Youth 2.0: Social Media and Adolescence*,
DOI 10.1007/978-3-319-27893-3_4

gathered in the context of the Utrecht University interdisciplinary research project *Wired Up. Digital media as innovative socialisation practices for migrant youth.*

As recently shown across the United States (Madden et al. 2013) and Europe (D'Haenens and Ogan 2013), with figures hovering around 90–95 % computer ownership is widespread and broadband Internet access has become the norm across different population segments. Young people of different backgrounds enjoy spending a large part of their leisure time using computers and other digital devices. The same holds true for the Netherlands. *Wired Up* survey data reveal that 98.3 % of Moroccan-Dutch girls and 96.9 % of Moroccan-Dutch boys have a computer in their homes with Internet access. These numbers are comparable to the 97 % of males and 96 % of females among the general Dutch population that own computer hardware and have Internet access (CBS 2014a). However, beyond ownership and access, new situated digital divides need to be taken into account. Considering that social media users are promised new opportunities to contribute to digital culture, it shows that not everyone can participate equally. Excluding obstacles arise from default technological settings that are most often oriented towards (white, male, Western, middle-class) mainstream users and excluding norms emerge from the behaviour of the majority of users downplaying the input of minority users. However, how can we account for the time and energy minority users enjoy spending online? In other words, how can we consider digital inequalities and the empowering subversion of exclusionary practices?

Exploring these questions, the chapter provides a timely intervention in the debate on digital divides, as previous studies "largely fail to address the 'have-nots' as differentiated, possessing agency, or embedded in place, while simultaneously failing to address the crucial importance of intersecting relations of power" (Gilbert 2010, p. 1003). I focus both on how offline societal power relations intersecting race and ethnicity, religion and gender relations travel online and create new digital divides that go beyond computer ownership and Internet access. In addition, I aim to provide new insights into the ways in which Internet platforms are providing spaces for the negotiation of power relations, digital belonging and greater cultural understanding in an increasingly diverse world.

The argument is structured as follows. First, methodological considerations are given and the study is situated in the context of the Netherlands. Subsequently, the theoretical framework is presented by drawing an analogy between mid nineteenth century pedestrian passageways as described by Walter Benjamin and early twenty-first century Internet applications like *YouTube* and *Facebook* to criticise uneven opportunities for peer-production. Subsequently, I transpose the concept of "space invaders" developed by Nirmal Puwar (2004) to digital platforms in order to scrutinise what happens when minority subjects enter spaces that have not been designed for them or that hold positions that they do not meet. The ways in which digital hierarchies are installed through the *sociotechnical and algorithmic cultures of Google* search's autosuggestions are charted and secondly, I elaborate how digital practices of mainstream users can serve to exclude ethnic minority subjects. The final empirical section presents three instances of how ethnic minority users can become "space invaders".

2 Methodological Considerations, in the Context of the Netherlands

The fieldwork was conducted in the context of *Wired Up*, an interdisciplinary research programme (2008–2013) from Utrecht University (the Netherlands) which – in collaboration with Vanderbilt University in the USA – focused on how new digital media practices involving the Internet impact on the lives, identities, learning and socialisation of migrant youth. Bridging approaches from the humanities and social sciences, the primary aim of the project was to develop new conceptual tools and innovative methodological approaches to assess the socio-cultural specificities of digital practices among migrant youth from a comparative perspective (migrants versus native Dutch, youth with a Moroccan background in the Netherlands versus Mexican migrants in the USA, first and second generation migrants and girls versus boys). Combining quantitative and qualitative approaches, the empirical data gathering consisted of three phases.

Firstly, a large-scale online survey was developed, in which a total of 1408 young people were contacted through seven secondary schools in the Netherlands completed on computers during school hours. Out of the total number of 1408 respondents, 344 Moroccan-Dutch youth participated; this group consisted of 181 girls and 163 boys. On average they were 14.5 years (SD = 1.7) old, and, when prompted, 98.5 % described themselves as Muslim. In this chapter descriptive findings are used to present a general impression of digital media use frequencies, attachments to applications and online self-presentation practices. Secondly, I carried out ethnographically inspired in-depth interviews with a group of 43 Moroccan-Dutch individuals, 21 girls and 22 boys, between the ages of 12 and 18 years. With the aim of providing a broad context of identity deployments, a group of Moroccan-Dutch parents, website founders and artists were also interviewed. Through a virtual ethnography with a smaller group of informants texts were gathered from the four digital platforms the informants considered most important: discussion forums, instant messenger, social networking sites and video sharing platforms.

Moroccan-Dutch people are the second-largest minority group in the Netherlands, after those from a Turkish-Dutch background. Consisting of 374,996 people, those of Moroccan-Dutch descent make up some 2.2 % of the total Dutch population of 16.7 million (CBS 2014b). Of this group, 47 % migrated to the Netherlands from the 1960s onwards as guest workers, while the other 53 % were born in the Netherlands, after their parents had migrated. In the context of the Netherlands, young Moroccan-Dutch people receive a lot of attention in media reporting, governmental policy-making and scholarly research. They are systematically stigmatised and made hyper visible by right-wing journalists and politicians such as Geert Wilders and members of the Freedom Party (PVV), who describe them as anti-citizens posing a threat to Dutch society. Prior academic research *has predominantly focused* on *particular behaviour such as juvenile delinquency, radicalisation, mental health problems and early school leaving*. These issues are undeniably important and significant, but they single out only a narrow slice of their experiences (Leurs et al. 2012). Things are going well for the majority of Moroccan-Dutch youth, but their realities remain largely invisible in contemporary debates. For example, more than 40 % of second-generation youth follow higher education and it must be emphasised that this is a remarkable accomplishment; when considering a significant number of their parents were illiterate farmers who generally had received little schooling (De Valk and Crul 2008, p. 84).

My aim is to contribute to an emerging strand of scholarship that does not focus on excesses but that considers the everyday experiences of young migrants. In particular, digital media are taken as an entry point. Similar to young people engaging with the Internet elsewhere in the world, Moroccan-Dutch youth use digital media to circumscribe their individual identities and articulate group belongings. Analysing informants' practices will contribute to breaking down binary polarisations of social categories, by showing how Moroccan-Dutch youth negotiate between seemingly opposing gender, ethnic, diaspora and youth cultural identity positions via digital media. However, due to the dominant focus of previous scholarship on excessive, problematic and negative experiences, as outlined above, gaining access to members of the community has become difficult. In the qualitative fieldwork phases especially, I had to invest substantial energy to gain trust and overcome the suspicions of Moroccan-Dutch youth. I managed to circumvent this obstacle by emphasising my interest in the point of view of the young peoples themselves. It is a fact that these youth are often written and talked about while few people actually talk to these young people themselves. I therefore emphasised my interests in wanting to learn from the informant's personal experience about the role of the Internet in her/his life and her/his views on youth culture, discrimination, ethnicity, religion and gender issues across online and offline spaces. Continuously emphasising the views of the informants as a serious source of knowledge, I noticed how the rapport grew. Increasingly, they showed that they enjoyed being the centre of attention. Taken seriously as co-researchers of their everyday experiences, informants remained in touch for example, sending me links to videos, music and texts after the interviews.

3 Spatial Approaches to the Digital Divide in Online Cultural Participation

In this theoretical section, a brief and not all-encompassing overview is given of scholarship on the digital divide, before a plea is made to address hierarchies in contemporary participation in digital culture from the perspective of space. In particular, an analogy is drawn between Internet platforms and the writings of Walter Benjamin on nineteenth century arcades and Nirmal Puwar's notion of "space invaders" (2004) is transposed from the offline to the online world.

Inequality in/of the Internet has first and foremost been analysed in terms of different digital divides. Scholarship on digital divides initially focused on making visible material divides across geographic scales and across markers of difference. An uneven geographical distribution in terms of ownership of hardware and access to the Internet was noted: the rich, overdeveloped parts of the world were found to be highly connected, while underdeveloped countries in the "Global South" were shown to be disconnected. Ownership and access was also unequally spread across different axes of differentiation: younger and/or white and/or upper class males were found to be more connected versus older and/or non-white and/or lower-class females. The term digital divide is thus ideologically loaded, particular in its proposal that once the gap is closed, a "computer-revolution" will take place, spreading democracy, promoting equality and potentially ending poverty (Murelli and Okot-Uma 2002). Emerging in the early 2000s, the second wave of scholarship on the digital divide shifted focus from access and ownership towards skills and literacies. The gaps between "the information haves" and the "information have-nots" were again purported as operating across geographical and personal markers of difference (Selwyn 2004). Policy makers and government institutions mobilised resources to provide the information have-nots with the skills for a more egalitarian distribution of knowledge. In sum, where previously most digital divide analyses "separate social inequalities from technical processes", today technology is essentialised as distinct from social processes and inequality is perceived as a dynamic that is independent from technology (Halford and Savage 2010, p. 937).

This chapter contributes to a new wave of situated scholarship on digital inequalities to move beyond technologically deterministic utopian and dystopian renderings of social media use. On the one hand, promising alternative ways of being and the collapse of difference, postmodernism and military-industrial neo-liberal progress came together in a Californian ideology that framed cyberspace as a disembodied, equalising, liberating, democratising and empowering world separated from the offline world. On the other side of the spectrum, techno-pessimists have made sweeping dystopian remarks in response to utopian appraisals of the Internet. Most famously, Jaron Lanier warns that digital technologies entail a loss of democracy, devalue individuality and deaden creativity (2010) and Evgeny Morozov argues Internet activism is a delusion that makes us unable to recognise technologies are used for purposes of propaganda, manipulation, censorship and surveillance (2011). These two perspectives do not, however, account for why migrant young people who for example encounter discrimination online still make heavy use of digital platforms.

As social media applications allow more people to have a presence online, scholars need to start acknowledging unevenness in people's contribution to digital culture while also paying attention to the feelings of agency and joy minority subjects experience in their negotiation of digital inequalities (Leurs 2015). Internet applications such as weblogs, social networking sites, video sharing platforms and online discussion forums signal the on-going shift from people being represented by the media to people representing themselves. Internet researchers have reached consensus in seeing the Internet as "an extension of life as it is, in all its dimensions, and all its modalities" (Castells 2001, p. 118). Online, digital spaces augment material, corporal and real offline lives, friendships, romance and socialisation. This is especially true for young people (Boyd 2014). However, little attention is paid to the differentiating power dynamics of the different locations where digital culture is expressed (Graham 2011). The lack of awareness of the spatial configurations of Internet applications is problematic because digital spaces are not neutral and/or innocent.

Building on the analogy of internet platforms as arcades and the notion of invasion of space I carve out a middle-ground position to account for how non-mainstream people in their everyday use are hailed and bound, but not fully determined, by medium-specific characteristics, commercial incentives and user norms. First I posit that Walter Benjamin's work on passages can be transposed to theorise social and symbolic meanings attributed to technological developments. In the mid nineteenth century, arcades or pedestrian passageways ("*passages*" in French) emerged in Brussels, Bologna and Paris among other places. Historically, the term arcade refers to a pedestrian passageway that links two streets. Unlike public space, this glass, iron or brick roofed passage is open at both ends and concentrates a row of commercial establishments (shops, cafés, restaurants) in a small space. In the words of Benjamin, arcades were "the most important architecture of the nineteenth century" (1999, p. 834). It can similarly be argued that internet platforms nowadays play an increasingly fundamental role in the daily lives of millions of people.

Benjamin recognised that these corridors carried an ambivalent meaning since as objects of history they simultaneously contained a "dream- and wish-image of the collective". He observed the dialectic tension between collective desires and exploitative "ruins". Indeed, Benjamin urged to ponder imaginations and to expose whether technology users were truly "emancipated" (Benjamin 1999, p. 115). As a "technical organ of the collective", innovations such as the arcades were imagined as a "new nature": "These images are wish images; in them the collective seeks both to overcome and to transfigure the immaturity of the social product and the inadequacies in the social order". "Caught in a dream", Benjamin added "the new, in order to shape itself visually, always connects its elements with those pertaining to a classless society". The "new nature" furthering utopian imaginings remains "concealed within machines". Instead of these imaginations, Benjamin argued for the figuration of "ambiguity". The role of the arcade is double-faced, as Benjamin illustrated: "during sudden rainshowers, the arcades are a place of refuge for the unprepared, to whom they offer a secure, if restricted, promenade – one from which the merchants also benefit" (Benjamin 1999, p. 31). Neither skepticism nor evangelism captured the dynamics of passages completely, and Benjamin aimed to capture them as a "*constellation saturated of tensions*" (Benjamin 1999, p. 475).

Although focused on the scrutiny of economic power relations in a striated, modernising society, the argument can be expanded to account for the ambiguous power relations which digital technologies sometimes conceal. Passages and insights on spatial power relations in a modern, democratising and urban crowded mass society allow us to draw parallels with contemporary forms of exclusion, distinction and contestation. Similarly, in their scrutiny of Internet culture, critical media and feminist theorists have argued for an ambiguous middle-ground position between the utopian dreams and dystopian nightmare perspectives that were dominant in writings on digital embodiment, identity and activism. Judy Wajcman, for example, unravels the constellation of gendered technologies from the perspective of "*mutual shaping*", "where neither gender nor technology is taken to be pre-existing, nor is the relationship between them immutable" (2007, p. 287). In particular I aim here to conceptually and empirically ground that the negotiating of hierarchies and inequalities online can be empowering.

Focusing on spatial relations in the built environment, Nirmal Puwar argued that British institutions such as parliament, the judiciary, civil service and academia are territories holding privileged positions that are historically "reserved". Recognising that including and excluding mechanisms operate around corporeal specificity, those who enter spaces of authoritative power are measured against the dominant template of "white male bodies of a specific habitus". Those who do not meet these normative expectations are positioned out of place; they become "space invaders" (2004, p. 141–144). Puwar developed the concept of space invaders to understand how ethnic minorities can feel out of place in institutionalised spaces. As they increasingly present themselves in spaces from which they were previously excluded through top-down governmental policies and bottom-up social climbing, she noted women and ethnic minorities may subvert the status quo but have to actively reposition themselves from within the spaces they invade. This re-positioning and decolonisation of dominant spaces relies on agency. Transposing the concept to account for digital spaces, I wonder how hierarchies are constructed and impact upon the digital practices of minority subjects.

Internet platforms increasingly promise users they can become active agents in charge of their own representations. My middle-ground perspective aims to acknowledge twenty-first century Internet platforms – analogous to nineteenth century arcades – as ambiguous constellations full of tensions and hierarchies but with room for subversion. Following Puwar, the question arises what happens when Moroccan-Dutch youth take up "privileged positions" that have not been "reserved" for them in digital space (2004, p. 144). When having to assert themselves against the grain, non-mainstream users become invaders of online territories. Below, I will first give examples of how *digital spaces are constructed as prescriptive, normative spaces*. Subsequently, I will explore how they can be subverted, invaded or transformed by the contributions of subaltern subjects by creating diversity in spaces that were previously defined as neutral and universal.

Across digital space, templates, norms and interface decisions reserve certain dominant consumer, national, gendered, ethnic and racial positions. These socio-technical processes have uneven spatial effects, both online and offline. For example, Fig. 1 displays the dominant positions that the *Google Netherlands* search engine associated with "Marokkanen" (the Dutch word for Moroccans). The auto-complete search query suggestions that *Google* provides appear automatically upon typing Marokkanen in the search box. The auto-complete algorithm offered query suggestions in a drop-down list, predicting behaviour based on queries typed

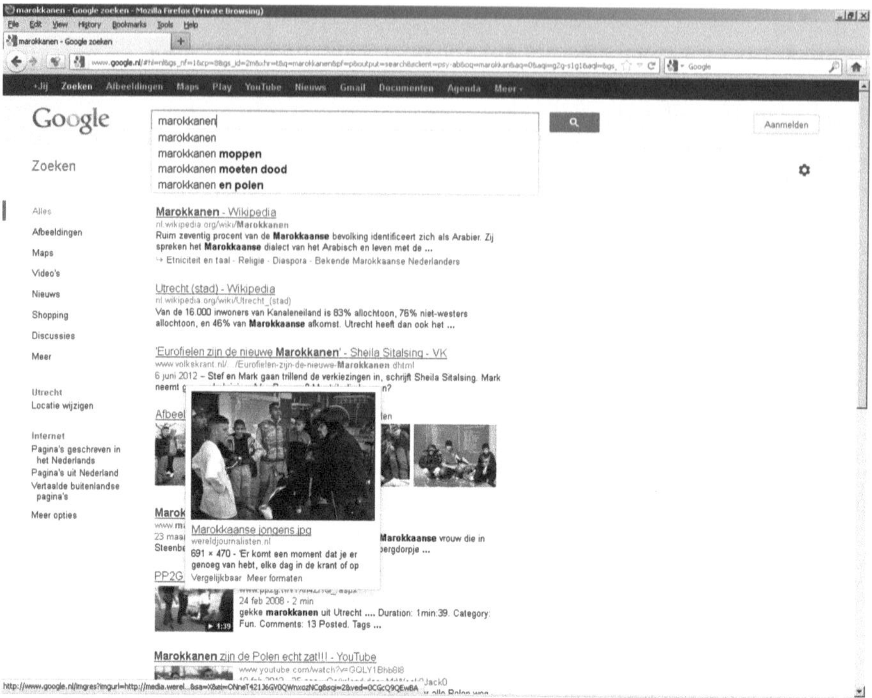

Fig. 1 The construction of exclusionary, normative digital spaces *Google.nl* search "Marokkanen" (June 28, 2012)

previously by *Google* users as well as generating items on the basis of traffic, page visits and recently crawled websites (Google 2012).[1]

Showing how algorithms may convey symbolic violence, the search query suggestions reveal some of the ways young Moroccan-Dutch people are allocated particular, narrow gendered and racialised positions in digital space. Reading from top to bottom they can be translated as follows: "Moroccan jokes", "Moroccans must die" and "Moroccans and Polish people". The suggestions for "Moroccan jokes" provide results of websites that host offensive anti-immigration, anti-Islam and racist jokes. The second suggestion points the Google user towards websites – mostly discussion forums – where white, right-wing extremist Dutch people discriminate against Moroccan-Dutch people. For example, the third result directs the user towards a forum posting on *MeetHolland.com* where the following comments are published in relation to Moroccan-Dutch youth: "Those rotten bastards must die!!!!!!!!! Dirty, cowardly, disgusting, stinking cancer goats" (Wilders 2005). The third suggestion equates Moroccan-Dutch people with a more recent group of guest

[1]The search was carried out in a *Mozilla Firefox* browser, using the 'Private Browsing' settings, without being logged in to a Google account and without having searched for the topic earlier. The results do thus not present my earlier search behaviour or that of my contacts.

workers, Polish people. Simultaneously, without having pressed the search button, Google lists search results, including Google Image Search findings. The four images are all stereotypical representations of aggressive masculine street culture showing Moroccan-Dutch youth as dangerous loiterers and the inclusion of a policeman emphasises Moroccan-Dutch boys as troublemakers.

The auto-complete algorithm (which is partly based on search-term popularity among previous search engine users) exemplifies received ideas that emphasise particular associations and stereotypes of Moroccan-Dutch people – particularly those voiced by populist, anti-Islamic politician Geert Wilders and his “Freedom Party”, PVV – rather than others. Spearheaded by Wilders and a sensationalist press, young people of Moroccan migrant descent are often framed as a problem. Moroccan-Dutch boys are dismissed as “strangers” to Western society, possibly dangerous “Islamic fundamentalists”, “street-terrorists” or “thieves” while headscarf-wearing girls are constructed as either “un-emancipated and backward” or “oppressed by Muslim culture”. The example given in Fig. 1 is not a temporary glitch since a similar search query on 29 May 2012 included the following suggestions: “Moroccans must die”, “Moroccans must exit the country”.

In the context of the United States, danah boyd similarly described that when searching for the name “Mohammed” for example, Google auto-complete provides suggestions related to Islamic extremism and terrorism. She defines this process as a form of “guilt through algorithmic association”, as the search suggestions for Mohammed exemplify how people can be “algorithmically associated with practices, organisations, and concepts that paint them in a problematic light” (Boyd 2011). The auto-complete example reminds us that digital space is not neutral but power-ridden. Similar to how nineteenth century arcades were imagined, a platform on the “Internet hails its audiences”, in a way that is similar to how non-digital environments are intended for particular groups of people (Nakamura and Lovink 2005, p. 65).

The examples discussed above attest to how these ideologies may be perpetuated through commercial algorithms, but participants of digital culture also constitute them themselves. During my fieldwork, many informants shared their frustrations and anger of the ignorance, discrimination and hate-speech they encountered in their engagement with Internet platforms. For instance, 16-year-old Naoul's statements were harsh reminders of the politics of difference on *YouTube*.[2] Naoul said that the comment sections for videos pertaining to Morocco sometimes fill up with verbal abuse and hostility: “when you watch a video on YouTube, they [referring to white, ethnic majority Dutch people] shout cunt-Moroccans and this and that about Moroccans”. Exclusionary majority user norms were also apparent in Dutch video game culture, where Islam was equated with terrorism. A fan of the game *Counter Strike*, 15-year-old Oussema shared that he had bad experiences after he disclosed his ethnic and religious background: “When saying I am Moroccan, I am a Muslim, I get called a terrorist”. Eighteen-year-old Safae told me after her friend who covers

[2] The names of interviewees used in this chapter are pseudonyms, mostly suggested by the informants themselves.

her hair uploaded a picture on the Dutch social networking site *Hyves*, somebody sent her a message typing "a headscarf is out-dated, and it's something of the past". Thus, digital spaces are not mere mute, neutral and external backdrops of identity formation, but distinct expressive cultures filled with ideologies, hierarchies and politics.

4 Space Invader Tactics

Although digital spaces are interspersed with politics and exclusionary practices, during the interviews informants shared the fact that they enjoy spending a lot of their time online and that they have many tactics to keep their use enjoyable. I explore three of those space invader tactics below. Revealing the ambiguous constellation of tensions Internet platforms present to Moroccan-Dutch youth, I will present three examples of their negotiation of power relations here: racial passing, perpetuating common teenager gender stereotypes and appropriating a digital space of their own.

4.1 Racial Passing

The first tactic to be discussed is *racial passing*. During our interview, 15-year-old Ryan explains that he is accepted as a gamer because, as he argued, he does "not look like a Moroccan", in the sense that he was seen as "very different from what normal Moroccan youth in [his] school do". He "mostly only plays games on the computer" and he felt gaming is more white "Dutch culture" as it is mostly white "Dutch kids who play games". He was accepted as he backgrounded his Moroccan affiliations during in-game interaction using voice-chat programs like Skype or Teamspeak: "when I talk I do not appear to be Moroccan". On his Hyves profile page he also subverted the dominant image of Moroccan-Dutch youth: "when someone sees me there, they say I do not look like a Moroccan, but obviously I am one, but I do not let it show". Masking his Moroccan identity, Ryan passed as an ethnic majority Dutch boy. Homi Bhabha, who recognised processes of passing as "mimicry", described the ambivalence of racial passing. Mimicry offers camouflage and can become a site of resistance and transgression. The minority subject achieves "partial presence" by passing for someone one they are not and "becoming a subject of a difference that is almost the same, but not quite" (Bhabha 1994, p. 122–133). Ryan did so by strategically employing dominant cultural repertoires and making less visible the ways he deviates from majority norms while emphasising resemblances. Choosing the pseudonym Ryan during the interview can also be seen as an act of passing, as the informant did not opt for a Moroccan or Dutch but an English first name. Ryan's act of passing offered self-protection but also reflected his desire to be accepted by the majority group. Nakamura noted that "racial impersonation" is a form of passing that "reveals a great deal about how people 'do' race online". However, she rightly argued that passing does keep the foundations of dominant exclusionary, white national identities intact (Nakamura 2002, xvi, 37). Although such digital forms of racial passing offers us insight into the empowerment that may be felt through the temporal dismissal of excluding norms, the foundations of cultural difference and the othering of non-mainstream users remains intact.

4.2 Perpetuating Teenager Gender Stereotypes

Taking and uploading photographs of the self, "selfies" have been recognised as offering innovative tools to "see and shape ourselves" (Walker Rettberg 2014). This section scrutinises to what extent the gendered self-presentation of Moroccan-Dutch youth can be an empowering tactic for migrant youth to forge alliances with mainstream users. In the *Wired Up* survey respondents were asked how they would show themselves in their profile pictures in order to be liked by their friends. With this question we aimed at learning more about *the norms of selfies and displaying pictures among young people*. Answers given to the question allow for reflecting on impression-management, expectations of appropriate self-presentations and ideal beauty-standards among Moroccan-Dutch youth.

The survey findings show that nearly half of the Moroccan-Dutch girls and boys in the survey sample reported they would like to present themselves as "normal" (Fig. 2). In addition to the label "normal", boys and girls chose specific labels to describe their aspired self-presentation. Commonly chosen labels indicate that participating girls specifically desired to look "beautiful", "sweet" or "fashionable/trendy" and "social" and to a lesser extent "attractive/sexy", "intelligent" and "tough". Boys wanted to come across as "sporty", "tough", "beautiful", "attractive/sexy", and to a lesser extent "sweet", "rich", "intelligent", "hard working" and "computer savvy". These findings reveal how Moroccan-Dutch youth would ideally represent themselves. Striving to meet expectations of what is accepted as normal and standard in selfies and profile-page culture seems an important ideal. Meeting the normal standard is combined with the perpetuation of dichotomous gender ideals. Girls' ideals are being beautiful and sweet, while boys aim for a sporty image and toughness. Being expected to showcase certain attributes, these ideals reveal self-regulatory values young people negotiate with. Each of the chosen labels covers a distinct configuration of femininity and masculinity, stereotypical ideals that are not unproblematic.

During my interviews, informants described the stereotypically gendered practice of profile photo selection. Oussema described that most boys show themselves as follows: "look at how pretty I am, look at how nice my eyes are as a ray of light shines in it" or they pose in their pictures with "pumped up chests" and aimed to go for a "look at how tough I am, look at how muscled I am" impression, while girls "lean over", showed their bodily curves and "blow a kiss to the camera". Fourteen-year-old Ziham said boys "put up tough photos, where they put up their middle-fingers

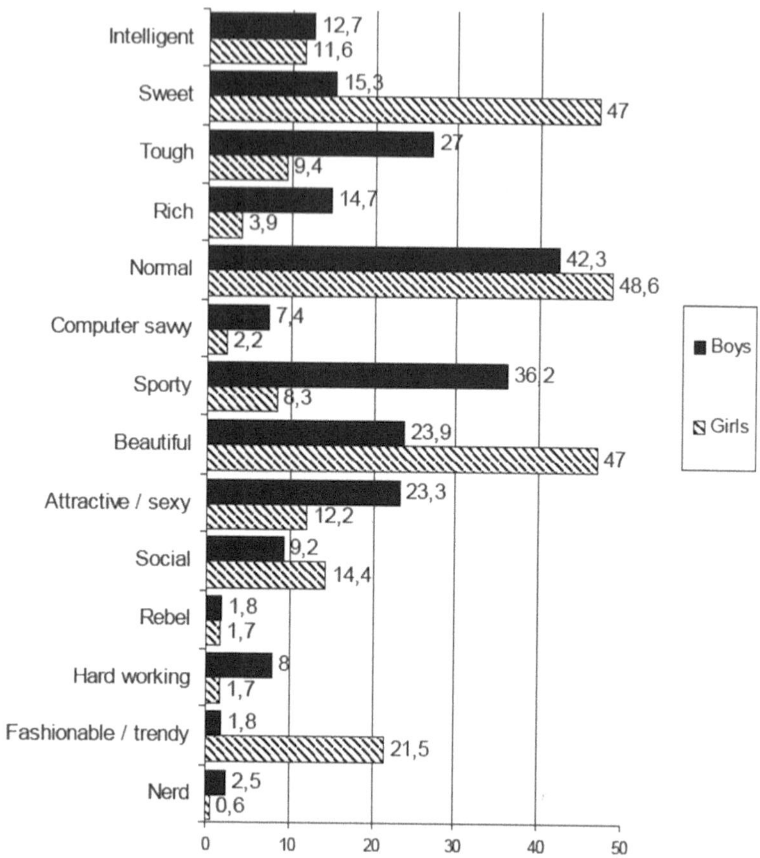

Fig. 2 Moroccan-Dutch youth self-reporting their selfie ideals (Graph shows percentages, n = 344)

and so on", she added that among her friends "girls don't do that. They just show themselves wearing tight clothes or so, with untied hair". According to 16-year-old Bibi, in some photos "girls show their boobs almost popping out of their bras". Fourteen-year-old Ayoub noted "girls put lots of make-up on" or showed pictures "when they have just come from the shower". Although individual informants often nuanced their own positioning, the majority of the informants gave a highly stereotypically gendered description of photograph ideals. Andra Siibak in Estonia (2009) and Michele Strano in the United States (2008) have found similar self-presentation strategies, for instance girls aim to display ideals of female beauty on their online social networking profile pages. These findings suggest that shared teenage norms of gender go beyond ethnic groups. Striving to meet expectations of what is accepted as normal and standard in profile-page culture seems an important ideal. Meeting these standards is one example of seeking sameness, stressing commonalities and aiming for acceptance among fellow white teenagers. As Moroccan-Dutch youth choose to adapt their profile picture to meet widely used gendered norms, they highlight commonalities and seek sameness instead of emphasising differences. In addition, taking charge of their own selfies for self-representation purposes, these minority subjects navigate the continuum between empowerment and objectification. In the case of uploading selfies to one's profile page, a female informant's internalisation of gendered stereotypes might indicate she seized the opportunity "to be in charge of her to-be-looked-at-ness" (Smelik 2009, p. 185). This opportunity, however, becomes increasingly difficult as the celebrated visual ideals of youth, fitness and beauty are becoming more and more unrealistic and unattainable, especially in the present era of widespread digital manipulation.

4.3 *Appropriating a Corner of One's Own*

> It is a sort of support. As a process of feeding [your emotions], by sort of reacting to each other. You'll have everyone who backs you up. It's like everyone is on the same side. You kind of become more sure of yourself. You just know, yes look we are not the only ones who think this way and so on. Thus you can express your opinion and just put everything up and you hear that others are similar to you. – Ilham, 13 years old.

During our interview, Ilham eloquently described the emotional support she received from being able to secure speaking power on the online discussion forum *Marokko.nl*. Message boards, also known as Internet forums, are digital spaces where users can engage in conversations by publicly posting messages in response to each other. Ilham noted that her self-confidence grew from being able to publish her opinions and connect with other like-minded people. She had the agency to publish her own opinions, in contrast with being positioned in certain ways by others. Seizing the opportunity to speak for herself and hearing others appreciate her voice, Ilham self-consciously claimed membership within a group of people of her choice. By doing so, she felt heard, she got confirmation that she was not the only one out there who felt a certain way. Through such discussions, similarity can actively be foregrounded and an alternative supportive community can be formed.

The *Wired Up* survey findings indicate a distinct preference for engaging with discussion boards among ethnic minorities in the Netherlands: Moroccan-Dutch youth reported visiting online discussion boards more than ethnic majority Dutch youth. One in every five Moroccan-Dutch youth reported visiting online discussion boards for at least 4 days per week, while only one in every ten ethnic majority Dutch respondents reported doing so. Moroccan-Dutch respondents also reported being more attached to visiting online discussion boards than ethnic majority Dutch youth are. Additionally, they would miss Internet forum discussions if they were no longer able to participate in them, more so than Dutch majority youth reported. These findings resonate with earlier studies that suggest that message boards are especially popular among minority subjects (Byrne 2008).

During the interviews I learned that forums like *Marokko.nl*, *Chaima.nl* and *Maroc.nl* are felt as a safe space to connect with fellow Moroccan-Dutch youth. As

15-year-old SouSou states: "Marokko.nl is a website where especially Moroccans come so to say". As Naoul, a 16-year-old girl notes: "Marokko.nl is a community", "it is your own circle, with all those Moroccan things" that are discussed and "the people there are like you, that's nice". Being a "corner of one's own", these sites are frequented to create a space where Moroccan-Dutch youth can become the majority. Boundary markers such as Moroccan images and symbols that include photos taken in Morocco, Arabic typing, visual references to Islam like a minaret and the Quran as well as photos of veiled women are circulated. Furthermore, in the discussion, users can reframe dominant stereotypical views circulating in news media. Sixteen-year-old Nevra finds that "different stories" are shared on Internet forums, where "there is often negative talk about Moroccan youth [in the newsmedia], I find that youth there can say what they want, showing it is not all bad". However, such moments of empowerment are not uncontested. When ethnic minorities find the opportunity to voice themselves, their contributions are often quickly pigeonholed or marginalised. Journalists and politicians seem to criticise and dismiss Internet forums such as *Marokko.nl*. Public news media link discussion sites frequented by Moroccan-Dutch individuals to extremism and radicalism, with newspaper items such as: *Cut-and-paste-Islam: how young Muslims in the Netherlands compose their radical worldview* (Oostveen 2004, my translation). Additionally, these sites are dismissed as the underbelly of the unknown, as encapsulating grimy spaces disconnected from mainstream society: "*Gettos on the web. On the Internet, every group creates its own truth*" (Hulsman 2005, my translation). As the site has no control over who subscribes and posts, anti-immigrant and Islamophobic users are also present on the site. It is estimated that 20 % of *Marokko.nl* visitors come from the Dutch right-wing blog Geenstijl.nl or are supporters of the right-wing PVV. Internet scholar Albert Benschop added that those visitors sometimes setup a profile like Mohammed21 and discredit the site with extremist statements, after which they can complain about the site (Knijff 2009). Nonetheless, it remains significant that the informants perceive the forums they frequent as safe zones where they can articulate alternative ways of being, although their acts simultaneously remain subject to tight scrutiny and control.

4.4 Hybridisation

Another commonly observed tactic is the *hybridisation of affiliations*. Inzaf, for instance, logged in to MSN Messenger using the display name "*El Hoceima is the bom, that's the place where I come from so just tell everyone that's the city number ONE*". Explaining its significance during our interview, she shared: El Hoceima "means a lot to me because that is the town in Morocco where I am from, I was not born there but my father was and I want to show that I am proud of it". She added, "it rhymes in English" and it is "nicer to say it in English than in Dutch". Through hybridisation, different loyalties can be combined. She signalled transnational affiliations with the city of El Hoceima in Morocco but she used the vocabulary of

English-language global hip-hop youth culture as well as Internetspeak. She used the nickname to emphasise her individuality, but also to connect with her peers. Consider also the display name of a young male informant consisting of both Latin and Arabic characters, *"Mø محمد BadBoy"*. In the latter netspeak, Mø is combined with Arabic alphabet characters to write the name Mohammed. The name also integrates a connection to mainstream global hip-hop culture by referencing BadBoy, the record label set up by Sean P. Diddy Combs. Similarly, circulating on groups like "Imazighen" on social networking sites such as the Dutch *Hyves* and *Facebook*, informants posted statements such as "Amazighen!! 4-Evaah" and "Amazigh. My Pride. My Life", referring to the Amazigh, or Berber people, the Moroccan ethnic minority group with which most Moroccan-Dutch migrant youth identify. Or take the example of the profile image circulating on various Moroccan-Dutch SNS group pages that showed Bart Simpson, the young and rebellious main character in the animated television series The Simpsons, dressed up in clothes with the Moroccan red and green starred national flag. Adored by young people across the world for his disrespect for adult authority, he was depicted wearing a hoody sweater and speaking into the microphone, again referencing urban and street youth culture. Such acts of hybridisation reflect active intercultural encounters. Similarly, Ayhan Kaya has argued that young Turkish-Germans in Berlin used hip-hop youth culture to mingle in the mainstream cultural field. These young people tapped into universal symbols such as rap, cool looks, graffiti and dance to mark a social, cultural and political space in the urban landscape. In their appropriation and recirculation of hip-hop youth culture, migrant youth may combine their "aesthetics of diaspora" and "global transcultural capital" (2002, p. 45). Hip-hop as such is a creative repository that enables ethnic minority youth to appropriate its elements, connect with their co-ethnics and peers, and insert themselves into global youth culture.

5 Conclusions

> What remains insufficiently addressed are the very real and material ways in which space constitutes a site and a medium for the enactment of cultural power – Raka Shome (2003, p. 40)

This chapter sought to move beyond understanding digital divides as a matter of ownership, access or literacy, by arguing participation in Internet platforms is characterised by forms of spatial power relations that are not yet sufficiently understood (Gilbert 2010; Halford and Savage 2010; Leurs 2015). The question then arises how subjects on the wrong side of the template and peer-produced digital divide invade prescriptive spaces, transforming them from within but also creating alternative platforms for communication and belonging.

To answer this question, I have extended Walter Benjamin 's writing on nineteenth century arcades and Nirmal Puwar's notion of "space invaders" by coupling their writings with empirical data on the digital practices of Moroccan-Dutch youth.

The optics of the arcade and space invaders can be developed further to empirically trace and theorise digital spatial biases and their subversion but also to intervene in dominant techno-determinist utopian and dystopian thinking about digital media potentialities. The empirical examples showcased that Internet platforms and their terrains are hierarchical territories and that they are uneven geographies marked by symbols and discursive borders. As the Google search auto-complete suggestions and informants' experiences of discrimination and exclusion I have discussed exemplify, mainstream (young, white, male and middle-class bodies) participating in mainstream digital spaces produce and occupy certain templates and reserved positions. When having to assert themselves against the grain, non-mainstream users such as ethnic minorities become space invaders of digital locations. Through racial passing, perpetuating common teenage gender selfie stereotypes and hybridisation, migrant youth show their offline and online "mixed embeddedness" by mobilising empowering opportunities to establish "bridging" and "bonding" relationships with fellow ethnic majority youth (Codagnone and Kluzer 2011; Peeters and D'Haenens 2005). Digital spaces are thus best considered as part of the everyday, real-life, uneven power relations, where offline and online spheres infuse each other with meaning.

References

Benjamin, W. (1999). *The arcades project*. Cambridge: Harvard University Press.

Bhabha, H. (1994). *The location of culture*. New York: Routledge.

Boyd, D. (2014). *It's complicated: The social lives of networked teens*. New Haven: Yale University Press.

Boyd, D. (2011). Guilt through algorithmic association. *Apophenia*. http://www.zephoria.org/thoughts/archives/2011/09/12/guilt-through-algorithmic-association.html. Accessed 13 Jan 2016.

Byrne, D. N. (2008). The future of (the) 'race': Identity, discourse, and the rise of computer-mediated public spheres. In A. Everett (Ed.), *Learning race and ethnicity: Youth and digital media* (pp. 15–38). Cambridge, MA: MIT Press.

Castells, M. (2001). *The internet galaxy*. Oxford: Blackwell.

CBS. (2014a). *ICT gebruik van personen naar persoonskenmerken*. http://statline.cbs.nl/StatWeb/publication/?DM=SLNL&PA=71098ned&D1=33-133&D2=0-3&D3=a&HDR=G1&STB=T,G2&VW=T. Accessed 13 Jan 2016.

CBS. (2014b, January 1). *Population; sex, age, origin and generation*. http://statline.cbs.nl/Statweb/publication/?DM=SLEN&PA=37325ENG&D1=0&D2=0&D3=0&D4=0&D5=139&D6=l&LA=EN&VW=T. Accessed 13 Jan 2016.

Codagnone, C., & Kluzer, S. (2011). *ICT for the social and economic integration of migrants into Europe*. European Commission, Institute for Prospective Technological Studies. http://ftp.jrc.es/EURdoc/JRC63183.pdf. Accessed 13 Jan 2016.

D'Haenens, L., & Ogan, C. (2013). Internet-using children and digital inequality: A comparison between majority and minority Europeans. *Communications-The European Journal of Communication Research, 38*(1), 41–60.

De Valk, H., & Crul, M. (2008). Education. In M. Crul & L. Heering (Eds.), *The position of the Turkish and Moroccan second generation in Amsterdam and Rotterdam* (pp. 63–85). Amsterdam: Amsterdam University Press.

Gilbert, M. (2010). Theorizing digital and urban inequalities. *Information, Communication & Society, 13*(7), 1000–1018.

Google. (2012). *Autocomplete. Inside search*. http://support.google.com/websearch/bin/answer.py?hl=en&answer=106230. Accessed 11 Sept 2013.

Graham, M. (2011). Time machines and virtual portals: The spatialities of the digital divide. *Progress in Development Studies, 11*(3), 211–227.

Halford, S., & Savage, M. (2010). Reconceptualizing digital social inequality. *Information, Communication & Society, 13*(7), 937–955.

Hulsman, B. (2005, January 8). Getto's op het web. Op internet heeft elke groep zijn eigen waarheid (p. 33). *NRC Handelsblad*.

Kaya, A. (2002). Aesthetics of diaspora: Contemporary minstrels in Turkish Berlin. *Journal of Ethnic and Migration Studies, 28*(1), 43–62.

Knijff, C. (2009, November 6). Marokko.nl: Nuttige kijk op de onderbuik. *Volkskrant*.

Lanier, J. (2010). *You are not a gadget: A manifesto*. London: Penguin Group.

Leurs, K. (2015). *Digital passages: Migrant youth 2.0. Diaspora, gender and youth cultural intersections*. Amsterdam: Amsterdam University Press.

Leurs, K., Midden, E., & Ponzanesi, S. (2012). Digital multiculturalism in the Netherlands: Religious, ethnic, and gender positioning by Moroccan-Dutch youth. *Religion and Gender, 2*(1), 150–175. http://www.religionandgender.org/index.php/rg/article/download/36/pdf_1. Accessed 13 Jan 2016.

Madden, A., Lenhart, A., Duggan, M., Cortesi, S., & Gasser, U. (2013). *Teens and technology 2013*. Pew Research Centre. http://www.pewinternet.org/files/old-media//Files/Reports/2013/PIP_TeensandTechnology2013.pdf. Accessed 13 Jan 2016.

Morozov, E. (2011). *The net delusion: The dark site of internet freedom*. New York: Public Affairs.

Murelli, E., & Okot-Uma, R. W. O. (2002). *Breaking the digital divide: Implications for developing countries*. London: Commonwealth Secretariat.

Nakamura, L. (2002). *Cybertypes: Race, ethnicity and identity on the Internet*. New York: Routledge.

Nakamura, L., & Lovink, G. (2005). Talking race and cyberspace: An interview with Lisa Nakamura. *Frontiers: A Journal of Women Studies, 26*(1), 60–65.

Oostveen, M. (2004, November 27). *De knip- en plak-islam; Hoe jonge moslims in Nederland hun radicale wereldbeeld samenstellen* (p. 38). NRC Handelsblad. http://vorige.nrc.nl//dossiers/moslimterreur/moslims_in_nederland/article1629224.ece/De_knip-_en_plak-islam. Accessed 13 Jan 2016.

Peeters, A., & D'Haenens, L. (2005). Bridging or bonding? Relationships between integration and media use among ethnic minorities in the Netherlands. *Communications-The European Journal of Communication Research, 30*(2), 201–231.

Puwar, N. (2004). *Space invaders: Race, gender and bodies out of place*. Oxford: Berg.

Selwyn, N. (2004). Reconsidering political and popular understandings of the digital divide. *New Media & Society, 6*, 341–362.

Shome, R. (2003). Space matters: The power and practice of space. *Communication Theory, 13*(1), 39–56.

Siibak, A. (2009). Constructing the self through the photo selection. *Journal of Psychosocial Research on Cyberspace, 3*(1). http://www.cyberpsychology.eu/view.php?cisloclanku=2009061501. Accessed 13 Jan 2016.

Smelik, A. (2009). Lara Croft, Kill Bill, and the battle for theory in feminist film studies. In R. Buikema & I. van der Tuin (Eds.), *Doing gender in media, art and culture* (pp. 178–192). Oxford: Routledge.

Strano, M. M. (2008). User descriptions and interpretations of self-presentation through Facebook profile images. *Cyberpsychology: Journal of Psychosocial Research on Cyberspace*, 2(2). http://cyberpsychology.eu/view.php?cisloclanku=2008110402&article=5. Accessed 13 Jan 2016.

Wajcman, J. (2007). From women and technology to gendered technoscience. *Information, Communication & Society, 10*(3), 287–298.

Walker Rettberg, J. (2014). *Seeing ourselves through technology: How we use selfies blogs and wearable devices to see and shape ourselves*. New York: Palgrave.

Wilders, P. (2005, October 18). En wederom van die laffe kankermarokkanen. Forum posting, *Meetholland*. https://web.archive.org/web/20120125074934/http://old.meetholland.com/message/708037.aspx. Accessed 13 Jan 2016.

Agentive Students Using Social Media – Spatial Positionings and Engagement in *Space2cre8*

Ola Erstad

Abstract During the last couple of years the tension between user-generated content creation and corporate power structures has become an important issue in research on young people and social media. The approach presented in this chapter is about the role of education and learning linked to issues of participation, creation and agency within spatial relationships online and offline. The activities studied are part of an online environment called *Space2cre8* with the specific purpose of engaging youngsters who are defined as at risk in communicative and collaborative activities. Different data sources are presented to shed light on the engagement of these youngsters. The research question is directed towards how students in a multicultural class in one community of Oslo engage themselves in the new spaces represented by *Space2cre8* made available through school activities, but also as part of their everyday life. Implications are discussed concerning media literacy, new activism and empowerment among youth.

1 Introduction

A key issue in contemporary research on young people and social media is the tension between user-generated content creation and corporate power structures. Since the massive diffusion of social media from around 2005 onwards much research has been directed towards the implications of the use of such media for young people concerning their social lives (Boyd 2010), personal interests (Ito et al. 2010), participation and engagement (Jenkins 2006). Until recently, social media have been perceived as an open, online environment for exploring interests and diverse forms of literacy practices, from short messages on Twitter, longer texts within special interest groups on Facebook or posting and sharing videos on YouTube. However, the corporate organisations behind some of these media developments now influence the ways we navigate and act within social media more

O. Erstad (✉)
Department of Education, University of Oslo, Oslo, Norway
e-mail: ola.erstad@iped.uio.no

M. Walrave et al. (eds.), *Youth 2.0: Social Media and Adolescence*,
DOI 10.1007/978-3-319-27893-3_5

directly following new business models. Some researchers and media activists (Pariser 2011) raise critical concerns about the implications of how organisations like Facebook and Google are using what we produce online for certain purposes and direct our activities in certain ways without us being aware.

For several reasons, schools constitute an important social institution in our media culture. Firstly, schools remain among the few social spaces in society where people come together face-to-face to conduct critical examinations and build knowledge about contemporary societies. Secondly, young people develop a reflective approach and meta-cognitive competencies about specific domains of life through learning and conceptual development. Thirdly, young people also gain skills in acting on their environment, especially through literacy skills in the broad sense, including media literacy.

The role of education in contemporary media cultures is not only about using technology as a tool for learning, which often seems to be the sole argument (Selwyn 2011). It is also about how people relate to technologies and how they develop the competence to be informed, critical and reflective citizens in this society. Umberto Eco pointed to the importance of these issues more than 20 years ago and we are still trying to approach these challenges in a mediatised society.

> The battle for the survival of man as a responsible being in the Communications Era is not to be won where the communication originates, but where it arrives. … The universe of Technological Communication would then be patrolled by groups of communications guerillas, who would restore a critical dimension to passive reception. The threat that "the medium is the message" could then become, for both medium and message, the return to individual responsibility. (Eco 1987, p. 142, 144)

In this chapter I will raise some issues about young people and new media, especially linked to the role of social media. My approach is framed within discourses about media and education and questions about the role of schools and learning in a media-saturated culture.

The case presented in this article is an online environment called *Space2cre8* developed as a social medium with the specific purpose of engaging youngsters who are defined as at risk in communicative and collaborative activities. As such, my interest, empirically, is not so much in the typical youngster using social media, but rather in the young people in our societies with fewer resources or less privileged positions. My research question is directed towards how students in a multicultural class in one community of Oslo engage themselves in the new spaces represented by *Space2cre8* made available through school activities, but also as part of their everyday life.

2 Issues of Participation, Creation and Sharing

In the early days of social media, *MySpace* was the main attraction, with a growth from zero to over 100 million registered users worldwide in just a couple of years. The site incorporated a variety of meeting places such as blogs, user forums, instant messaging, personal profiles, online photo albums and visitor comment spaces. Another site with great appeal to young people is YouTube, a site that enables anyone to produce and present private videos, pictures, and diverse media sources to other people. In recent years, *Facebook* has become the major social networking site worldwide, with an amazing growth in just a few years estimated at more than 700 million users.

The idea behind such online sites is not new. What is new is the ease with which people can upload and share their own digital stories and connect with others. Similar social networking sites have existed in Scandinavian countries before 2005. Some examples are *LunarStorm* in Sweden, *blink* in Norway, and *Skum.dk* in Denmark. The development of these sites started around 1999–2000 and since then, different social sites have gained increasing popularity among young people even though *Facebook* has become the main social networking site in these countries also. In a Scandinavian context, this development is partly explained by high degrees of access to technology amongst young people (Drotner 2001; Ling 2004).

These developments point towards what Jenkins et al. (2009, p. 5–6) describes as participatory culture:

1. Relatively low barriers to artistic expression and civic commitment
2. Strong support for creating and sharing one's creations with others
3. Some type of informal mentorship whereby what is known by the most experienced is passed along to novices
4. Where members believe that their contributions matter
5. Where members feel some degree of social connection with one another (at the very least they care what other people think about what they have created).

These descriptions are supported by the Pew Internet and American life study, which made several studies especially on user-generated content creation. For example, in one report (Lenhart et al. 2007), when social media and content creation was starting to boom, the researchers summarised their findings on the growth of these activities as:

- Content creation by teenagers continues to grow, with 64 % of online teenagers ages 12–17 engaging in at least one type of content creation, up from 57 % of online teens in 2004.
- 35 % of all teen girls blog, compared with 20 % of online boys and 54 % of wired girls post photos online compared with 40 % of online boys.
- Boys dominate one area – posting of video content online. Online teen boys are nearly twice as likely as online girls (19 vs. 10 %) to have posted a video online somewhere where someone else could see it.
- Many teen content creators do not simply plaster their creative endeavours on the Web for anyone to view; many teens limit access to content that they share.
- There is a subset of teens who are super-communicators – teens who have a host of technology options for dealing with family and friends, including traditional landline phones, cell phones, texting, SNSs, instant messaging and email. They represent about 28 % of the entire teen population and they are more likely to be older girls.

These activities have developed further (Ito et al. 2010). The main point here is the amazing impact social media have had on participation, creation and sharing of content among youth (Erstad 2013).

From a more qualitative perspective, Mizuko Ito and her research group have studied creative practices among youth using digital media in the *Digital Youth Project* (Ito et al. 2010). They show how digital media create new possibilities for young people in their expressive practices, and how they use social media both to pursue interests and to build *friendships*.[1] In this way they develop a collaborative strategy of communication and production of content, from simple SMS to complex multimodal expressions.

There are important cultural differences in how common these practices are. The US data presented above are not supported by data from Norway, where access to technology is good, but where young people are less active as advanced producers of content. Several studies have documented that in the age group 16–24, only 5–8 % respond that they write blogs or post photos and videos on the Internet, while about 50 % are just looking for information on different sites (Erstad 2010). We need to take account of differences between cultures, groups and people.

Still, in the above mentioned report by Jenkins et al. (2009, p. 16–27) he raises three concerns that relate directly to educational issues:

- *The Participation Gap* – the unequal access to the opportunities, experiences, skills, and knowledge that will prepare youth for full participation in the world of tomorrow.
- *The Transparency Problem* – The challenges young people face in learning to see clearly the ways that media shape perceptions of the world.
- *The Ethics Challenge* – The breakdown of traditional forms of professional training and socialisation that might have prepared young people for their increasingly public roles as media makers and community participants.

These concerns are of great importance and directly address how education might provide the social spaces for learning and critical reflection in a digital age. One challenge in doing so is related to the lack of agency among learners within our school systems today, a lack of experiencing relevance and authenticity in what and how they learn at school (Erstad and Sefton-Green 2013).

3 Spatial Literacies and Agentive Selves

Interesting work has been done on what has been termed as spatial literacies (Leander and Sheehy 2004; Comber and Nixon 2008) in emphasizing how places and spaces construct ways of speaking and writing, and how digital media challenge traditional spaces and places in what some describe as new mobilities (Leander et al. 2010). Learning in informal communities may similarly be studied with an

[1] See http://digitalyouth.ischool.berkeley.edu/

emphasis on the contextual, where complex interactions among participants who take on different roles as learners and tutors are studied in affinity groups, both online and offline (Pelletier et al. 2010; Pelletier 2009).

Learning and literacy is all about the ways we make sense of information from resources in our environment and how we communicate it by using different means, not just understood as the "reading" and "writing" of the written text. In this way, literacy is something that changes over time due to changes in the cultural tools we have available (Wertsch 1998). The foundational thoughts for this research orientation include the interrelationship between culture, cognition and communication and how this creates a way of connecting learning and people's lives. Historically, this can be related to Wilhelm Wundt and his concept of a "folk psychologie". The point is to place learning within the broader cultural processes in which people are involved. Schools are seen as an important social space in our society but, in a cultural historic sense, this changes over time.

The individual's access to different forms of knowledge, such as different experiences and interpretation opportunities, helps in developing various identities in different contexts. Identity is developed in the mutual relationship between individuals in activities, where individuals are dependent on how they perceive themselves and on how this perception is met by others. This means that the individual's perception of his or her position in the interaction is central to understanding how identity is developed. While the social and cultural spheres have to do with how actions are recognised and given meaning, social positions relate to how actions constitute relationships. Youngsters move back and forth between cultural worlds (Holland et al. 1998) addressing ways of using digital media by young people (Buckingham 2003; Hull and Greeno 2006), where different resources are in play. Through action and interaction, they make use of the available resources to "author" themselves in unique ways.

Recently, interest in linking learning and identity formation as interrelated practices has increased (Buckingham 2008, p. 1; Caldas-Coulthard and Iedema 2008; Hull and Greeno 2006). This is connected to the capacity to adapt to changing roles within different contexts (Holland et al. 1998; Moje and Luke 2009). Many of these studies have criticised the institutional practices of education, claiming that the resources, identities and experiences that students develop in other settings are not properly recognised or used as an anchor for developing their skills and knowledge in school (Heath 2012; Wortham 2011).

Holland et al. (1998) promote a more complex situated perspective on learning and identity, advocating that a person can be composed of many, often incoherent self-understandings and changeable identities embedded in the situated social context. As such, identity is not bound by pre-given categories such as ethnicity, nationality or gender, but is seen more as negotiated and socially produced *in situ*. All resources available for a person are then seen as important in his or her cultural identity work. Holland et al. (1998) developed conceptions of situated identity which weave together different actions, such as cultural resources in use (in what they describe as *figured worlds*), social relationships (*positioning*) and personal expression (*space of authoring*). From this perspective, identities are formed and reshaped in activities through individuals' perceptions of "who they might be" and this type of understanding is a tool for their targeted actions in new situations.

In line with the above, Etienne Wenger (1998, p. 149) has described identity as negotiated experience, community membership, learning trajectory, nexus of multi-membership and a relationship between the local and the global. Of special interest when trying to combine identity with learning is the point Wenger makes about "identity as learning trajectory".

Agency, in this context, becomes an important perspective to link overall issues of empowerment and participation and epistemological issues among students. Agency is located by some (Cooren 2004) in various relationships between self and structure, or used to explicate various forms of agency, including the technological, human and textual (Hardy 2004). The important point here is that agency implies "the capacity to make a difference" (Castor and Cooren 2006), linked to certain institutional and cultural practices. The concept of agency might be perceived as closely connected to the concept of identity (Hull and Greeno 2006). For example, by composing digital stories, young people get the opportunity to "craft an agentive self" (Hull and Katz 2006), where they actively take part in a social construction of their own identity.

However, at the same time agency is especially at stake these days where media systems are having an increased impact on ways of creating content. As shown above, the implication of the digital revolution has been an increased engagement of people in creating and sharing content online. Yet, during the last 5 years another development has become more apparent. New business models and corporate media structures have evolved that structure online activities in new ways, breaking with the fundamental ideas of the Internet as an open communicative space. This is seen, for example, in the ways companies like Facebook and Google are developing. Some describe this as *the power of algorithms* (Pariser 2011). This is, of course, not new since the Internet has always been based on certain algorithms that structure what we can and cannot do on it. The new development, however, is the way these companies use the content that people provide by posting multimodal content on these online sites in order to structure our actions in certain ways and for certain purposes, like advertising.

The examples mentioned by Eli Pariser in his TED talk[2] are illustrative. He refers to some personal experiences in using Facebook and Google. As an online activist he used Facebook to engage in discussions with people from the whole political spectrum, also with more conservative *friends*. However, for a certain period he engaged less with these conservative *friends* on Facebook, with the consequence that these friends were just deleted from his network of people. The algorithm in the way Facebook is structured had somehow just erased them since they were less actively connected. His other example is how he asked two friends to enter the same search word in Google, which was "Egypt". What appeared on their screens was very different. One received a series of links to sites for travel and holiday locations in Egypt, while the other received a series of updates on the uprising and the politi-

[2] www.ted.com/playlists/26/our_digital_lives.html

cal developments in Egypt. The browser had adjusted the same search word to their individual profiles and former online activities.

In his book *The Filter Bubble* (2011) Pariser uses examples like these to address important challenges we are facing at the moment in our dealings with social media like Facebook and search engines like Google. These are not innocent and neutral technologies best suited to provide for our personal online activities. More and more these corporations are directed towards structuring and filtering our access to information and using our content creation in certain ways. The programmers and engineers developing the algorithms for how these services function obtain a lot of impact on our activities in using such media (Bucher 2012).

4 Social Spaces of School and Media Use

There is a lot of interest in digital media in schools in general, and social media in particular (Erstad 2013). From within schools this is often experienced as a technology push for access to hardware and software (Selwyn 2011). An important question is, of course, what new affordances and options new technologies represent (Gibson 1986), and how these are framed (Goffman 1974/1987) within different social practices like school settings. The concept of affordances implies that the environment offers the individual different ways of acting. Through social interactions we might also learn how different environments provide different opportunities to act, for example in online versus offline environments. My point is that we need to move beyond issues of the learning outcomes of using digital media in classrooms. At present, the more important issues are about agency and technology use as means of participation in people's everyday life and the mobile aspect of time and space relationships across contexts.

The concept of learning environment is used to describe changes in the way we organise learning activities, both in real life settings in classrooms and virtual environments. This indicates a change away from learning environments where the teacher and the textbook structure, define and control the learning process, towards student-centred learning environments where the students themselves are the main frame of reference for defining the learning process (Jonassen and Land 2000, p. viii).

There has been an interest in elaborating on the concepts of "space" and "place" related to learning and the use of digital technologies (Bekerman et al. 2006). Technological developments during the last 20 years have created whole new ways of conceptualising learning spaces, from early attempts at virtual realities in the mid-1990s, to parallel worlds such as *Second Life* (Boellstorff 2008). There are also many online spaces developed for learning, either as e-learning courses or as a combination of face-to-face and online learning activities. However, it is necessary to be critical of these over-optimistic beliefs in these alternative learning spaces and what they can accomplish concerning learning. As Mark Nunes (2006) did in his book, *Cyberspaces of Everyday Life*, we need to study how online spaces, used by young people, function as continuations of their physical activities and doings in everyday life.

Leander et al. (2010), based on cultural developments in later years, have argued in favour of radically different ways of considering spaces for learning than has been the norm in educational research, referring to the works of Henri Lefebvre and Edward Soja. The aim is to challenge the "classroom-as-container" metaphor. This opens up ways of studying spatial relations in community settings, in the way that people engage with different resources. Space and place is then understood much more as embedded in, and being part of, the activities and practices of people in their everyday trajectories of participation, both face-to-face and online-offline (Leander and McKim 2003).

The main challenge today is to understand and study the interconnections between the different social spaces in which young people operate and the ways that digital media support and encourage these connections.

5 *Space2cre8* – Norway[3]

Space2cre8 (*S28*, www.space2cre8.com) connects 12–18 year-old students in the US, India, Norway, South Africa, Australia, the UK and various new countries that are joining. Students in these countries communicate about school-related issues as part of project activities as well as about leisure-time issues, such as interests, daily lives and about being young in different cultural settings. Even though *S28* is a closed social network, with username and password required, exclusive for youth affiliated with the specific schools and after-school programmes taking part in the project, it has many of the same functions and appearances as other commercial social networking sites such as *Facebook*. Each participant creates a personal profile from where she/he can be linked to other youths in the network by using what is called "the toolbox". This "toolbox" consists of different means for interacting with other people in the network, such as sending messages, writing blogs, creating groups, adding photos, music and/or videos to your profile for others to watch, and so forth. Just as in any other social networking site, you accept a friend's requests or add friends and post messages on the wall of another person's profile. There is also a chat function available, which makes it possible to participate in synchronous communication with other members of the network.

S28 differs from other social networking sites in some important ways. First, it is a restricted space to which only members of the community have access. Second, the site aims to include youth who have mostly not had access to the benefits of the digital revolution, from countries such as India and South Africa, together with youth from Western countries, such as the United States and Norway. Third, teachers, researchers or after-school staff encourage and initiate both offline and

[3]The collection and analysis of data from this project was done together with two of my PhD students, Kristin Vasbø and Kenneth Silseth.

online activities across the different sites in the network via their discussions and updates on email, online discussion groups and Skype talks. However, most cross-site activities develop from actions already taking place among the youngsters at one of the sites.

In our research project in Oslo, we studied one class of 8th-grade students (13–14 years old) at a lower secondary school during one academic year (2009–2010). Greendale, the school in this study, is located in the Eastern part of Oslo in a predominantly suburban area consisting of apartment blocks, but also with forests and green areas close by. Families, on average, have the lowest gross income of the whole city. This area also has the highest percentage of non-Western immigrants in the municipality and more than 40 % of those living in the area are under 19 years old.

The school, being a large concrete building, looked quite traditional from the outside. Inside it was a bit different from other Norwegian schools since it had no long corridors and most classrooms had some flexibility in being able to move walls to make smaller additional rooms for smaller group work. The technology infrastructure at the school was poor. They had a computer room but several of the machines did not work. In addition the school had a couple of class sets with laptops that could be rolled in from another securely locked room. One of these trollies with laptops was used for this project but was shared with three other classes. At the start of the project, access to technology and the Internet was a challenge, due to the lack of proper support at the school. This improved during the school year. The school had plans to upgrade its computer room and Internet connection, but not much happened during the year we were at the school. As such, this school can be characterised as below average in terms of access to, and use of, digital technology as part of the curriculum.

The class we studied had 29 students, evenly divided between boys and girls. Almost all the students had grown up in Norway, but the parents came from Tunisia, Pakistan, Kurdistan, Albania, Somalia, Vietnam, Korea, Iraq, China, Poland and Norway. The class sessions were primarily run by one teacher, sometimes two. All of the teachers were ethnic Norwegian. Our impressions from the first period spent at the school was that this was a very demanding student group. There were many conflicts between students and teachers and some of the boys received quite a lot of reprimands from the teachers for disruptive behaviour. To some extent these tensions between students were also expressed during classroom activities. In terms of the project this was an interesting class to work with.

Within the *Space2cre8* project we were particularly interested in how young people with a diversity of cultural backgrounds make use of social media and what they express through media production within a school context. Specifically, we were interested to know how this new online space plays a role in different ways of negotiating cultural identity and movement between different learning spaces. Socio-cultural theories of learning consider social interaction as central to how individuals learn and construct traditions within their cultural communities (Cole 1996; Rogoff 2003; Vygotsky 1978). Learning takes place when the learner is participating in a social practice and changes or develops his/her participation through interacting within the particular practice (Lave and Wenger 1991). When dealing with students who are learning in multicultural educational settings, the notion of cultural identity is often foregrounded. An often-used approach to cultural identity is to emphasise national belonging and ethnicity as the dominant categories in identification (Banks and Banks 2005; Hall 1959). Holland et al. (1998), on the other hand, promoted a more complex, situated perspective as regards learning and identity, advocating that a person consists of many, often incoherent self-understandings and changeable identities embedded in the situated social context. Participating in social networks such as *S28* represents a context for identity in practice where cultural resources can be combined and developed in new ways.

6 Methods and Data Collection

Approximately 60 full hours were spent at the school during one academic year, with the majority of these hours spent in the classroom. About 35 h were videotaped, both whole class sessions and group work using *S28*. Individual interviews and group interviews of students were carried out, focusing on their media consumption and different activities at school. Vasbø and Silseth also recorded several informal conversations with the teachers. Field notes were written after each session, throughout the year. In addition, the online activities were documented: the students' profiles at *S28*, digital stories, movies (both made by the students, but also downloaded from sites such as YouTube), chat sequences, blogs and the pictures taken by students themselves.

In the presentation below the analysis is directed towards "forms of interaction" and "identity markers", both in the physical space of the classroom and online on *Space2cre8*. Related to different spaces and activities this can be explained in Table 1.

6.1 Theme One: Drawing on Cosmopolitan Youth Cultures

One interesting activity that relates to identity work and agency are the special interest groups at *S28* set up by youth. For example, one of the students, Muhammed, started a group which he named "We who are from Asia", where three other students immediately obtained membership. Muhammed's parents are originally from

Table 1 Overview of data collected and contexts

	Classroom	Group work, making products	Interactions in front of computer	Activities on *space2cre8*
Forms of interaction	Whole group interactions	Small group interaction, formal-informal	2–3 people in dialogue	Building relationships (chat, profiles)
Identity markers	Voices, movements, cloths	Presenting themselves to others	Negotiating meaning	Understanding the other

Pakistan and he describes the group in the following way: "this group is for us who are from Asia". They used the option of special interest groups to create identity markers linked to their cultural backgrounds, making them different in certain respects from the other students in the class.

Other students started groups drawing instead on shared popular cultural issues. One girl (Kuyna) created what she called the "Drew Bieber group". She presents this group in the following way:

> Hi :D this group is about Justin Drew Bieber. Here you can learn about him, listen to his music, watch his video and see some pictures of him. Go to my page to see his pictures and you can go to videos and watch his video (if you want) If you want to learn about him, just ask questions and I or someone who knows about him can answer. :D

Another girl (Yasmin) made a group about the same artist and named it: "We who love Justin Drew Bieber". She introduces the group like this: "This is a group for us who love Justin Bieber. Here can we talk about how cute he is and we can put in video and look at videos." One boy (Steven) created a music group and called it: "We like music" and explained what this group was all about in the following way: "This group is for those who like music; it's just for fun. Join if you love music, all kinds of music."

When producing groups, the students use semiotic resources that connect to their parents' background and ethnic belonging, as well as to global popular youth culture. In this process, they are mixing voices from different sources that are important to them but which are seldom expressed within the classroom or recognised by the teachers.

The students' profiles are interesting in regard to identity work. When presenting themselves through their profile, the majority of the students chose to promote their ethnic identity more than their Norwegian belonging, even though the majority were born and raised in Norway. In addition to ethnic identity, they also promoted their interests and leisure activities, as illustrated by the following examples of student profile texts, written in English by the students (names have been changed to safeguard the anonymity of the students):

- Hi everybody, my name is Yasmin. I'm 13 years old and going on 8th grade on Greendale. My home country is Turkey. There I have a house and my aunts, uncles, grand-parents and my relative's lives there. My interest is to be with friends, shopping and much another fun things.
- My name is Kim. I am from Vietnam, but I live in Norway. I have 1 little sister and 1 big brother. I play the piano and I like it: D
- My name is Adil, I like football and my favorite team it's Manchester United FC. I play for Greendale IF. I'm born in Norway, but my parents are from Macedonia and Kosovo. I speak Albanian with my family, but with my teachers and friends I speak Norwegian.

These presentations are representative of how the students represent themselves through their profiles. Some of the students even chose profile names that connect them to their parent's homeland. For instance, Tarek calls himself "Iraqi", due to his

Fig. 1 Illustration made by Ahmed

parents originally coming from Iraq. Ahmed calls himself "Tunisiano", a name that connects him to his Tunisian father's homeland, but also to a French rapper of Tunisian origin who call himself "Tunisiano". He also made a visual representation of himself combining his cultural background from Tunisia with his interest in the French rapper. It was posted on the site the following way (Fig. 1).

Another boy, Khamil, has parents from Turkey and he calls himself "Turkish-B". He is a breaker, and the last letter "-B" might indicate a reference to hip hop music and break-dancing. This is interesting in regard to identity work because they make use of traditional categories of cultural identity, but as seen with "Tunisiano" and "Turkish-B", they also may transform and mix these traditional categories into new popular culture practices.

The *S28* group in the US (Oakland) made a movie called "Hello Norway", as a way of initiating communication and contact with the students in Norway. In the movie, the Oakland students talk about their favourite sports and favourite foods and pose questions such as: "Do you play basketball in Norway?" "What movies do you like?" and "How big are your houses?" The movie ended with a written request: "Please reply back!" As a response, the Norwegian students made a presentation where they filmed each other with Flip cameras and figured out by themselves how to make their individual presentations. In their replies, they presented themselves by name, favourite sports, other leisure activities and favourite foods, and then each put a question back to the youth in Oakland. The following are some of the examples of how the students presented themselves:

- Hi my name is Petter. I am from Norway and I like to play soccer and listen to music. And I wonder what kind of music you guys like?
- My name is Anita. I like to do shopping and I like to hang out with friends and play football. My question for you is: do you people like to play football?
- Hi my name is Mona and I like to be with friends. What do you do in your free-time?
- My name is Hanne. I ride a horse. Are there many horses in Oakland?

These presentations are important in building relationships with others and in initiating understandings across communities as well as on a personal level that develops into more contact over time. As shown above, they often start with simple questions and interests, often suggested by the teacher in the classroom. However, through this, they discover similarities and differences that create social networks.

6.2 Theme Two: New Spaces – Different Positions

Below I will focus on two girls, both non-ethnic Norwegian and both Muslim to illustrate how the new spaces represented by *Space2cre8* could result in two different positions for the students in the Norwegian class. About half of the students defined the spatial opportunities on *Space2cre8* as a prolongation of their school activities and as a school related project, while the other half defined it to a larger extent as an interest and friendship driven activity, and as different from school activities. Here is a short presentation of each of the two girls:

Girl 1: Kuyna	*Girl 2: Yasmin*
From Kurdistan (Iraq). Attends Koran school in the afternoons and weekends, and wears a hijab at school. At school, Kuyna appears to be a relatively quiet and withdrawn, but values being with friends. Uses her computer, at home, for a couple of hours per day, playing games, chatting via MSN, and doing homework. Likes Kurdish music and Arabic films. She does not use e-mail or Facebook profile, but chats with friends and family living in Iraq. She perceives *S28* as safer compared to other commercial sites. She had 75 friends out of a total of 162 members on *S28*.	Born and raised in Norway, family from Turkey. She neither wears a hijab nor goes to Koran school. An ambitious, active student and gets good grades. Interest in becoming an architect. Yasmin uses her computer for about two h per day, uses MSN to chat with her friends and visits Facebook and Biip.no frequently (one of the most popular Norwegian social networking sites). Her profile name in *S28* is Yasminx3u-. She has added an "x" and a "3" to her name to symbolise a heart, and a "u" and a "–" (hyphen) because she thinks it looks nice. She often changes her profile picture because she wants to use the most recent photo of herself.

The way the two girls represent the two different orientations and positionings towards *Space2cre8* as a new space of activity is seen in the following two remarks from each of them:

"If it had marks I would have been working much harder." Yasmin; school-oriented.

"If I had Facebook, I don't have, but if I had, and someone added me, and I didn't know the person, then I wouldn't talk to it, but this here is like school x or what it is, like from school, I feel that, it is like better to talk." Kunya; friendship-oriented.

This is further elaborated in the following extracts from online chats on *Space2cre8*.

Yasmin: School oriented

Ya:	hello check out the IUP thing (individual education plan) where you can see which grade you have in the different subjects and stuff, but only the subjects in where we had L (teacher) for example in religion and stuff
Ya:	She says what results we have got in tests.
Ya:	She says I am glaying [gligger] a 5 in written Norwegian :D:D:D:D:D.
Ya:	I am laying on, I ment.
Om:	Good.
Ya:	Check out you to.
Om:	I will og into my IUP thing (individual education plan) to check.
Ya:	Ok.
Om:	Just wait a little bit.
Ya:	Wait, I will check out Am`s.
Ya:	hahahaha
Om:	hahahaha
Om:	I am laying on 4+.
Om:	That`s because of not so good fantasy.
Om:	Where is Am laying?
Om:	Where is Amal laying?
Om:	Where are you in laying in natural science?
Om:	I`m laying on 5.
Ya:	Ahhaha.
Ya:	Am is laying in 2-3 in religion
Ya:	And 3- in Norwegian
Ya:	Hahahahahah
Ya:	Lol
Om:	hahahaha

Kunya: Friendship oriented

N:	Hi
N:	hi
Ku:	hi
Ku:	what time is it there
Ku:	?
N:	hi
N:	its 9 in da mornin
Ku:	:O
N:	wat time is it there?
Ku:	its 18.20
Ku:	18.30
N:	o
N	r u a boy or a girl
Ku:	i am a girl
N	o...nice
N	how old r u?
Ku:	13 how old are you
Ku:	??
N	13, too
N	where r u from?
Ku:	ok
Ku:	Iraq
N	really
Ku:	hehe yes
N	is it like really hectic there?
N	u kno, wit all da war and stuff
N	wats it like there?
Ku:	I'm not actually from iraq
N	wel...then where r u from?
Ku:	I am from kurdistan but it is not a country but but Kurdistan is in Iraq
N	o
Ku:	yes
N	so r u in kurdistan rite now?
Ku:	now i am in Norway
Ku:	i live in Norway

As the quotes above illustrate there is a division among the students. On the one hand, the ones that interpret their activities with *Space2cre8* as mainly framed within the school context are thereby seen as supporting working with school issues. These are often the well-established students who do well in the classroom and are actively engaging with the teacher. On the other hand, there are those that interpret *Space2cre8* as a new and alternative space opening new possibilities for relationships and are oriented towards friendship. These students are mainly the ones that are quiet in the classroom. They also work on school-related issues and content but they commit themselves to a larger extent than the former group to building relations with the other youngsters in the network.

6.3 Theme Three: Content Creation as Potential for Empowerment

The making of short films as part of a school project that could then be posted on *S28* illustrates how students use this activity to negotiate cultural and religious identities. The theme of the project was "Youth, alcohol and drugs". The students were divided into six groups, and each group was given information material about young people and substance abuse and some overall themes on the issue. However, each group was free to choose which angle they would take on the issue and how to present this in the film.

All of the films focused exclusively on the negative effects of alcohol, and all of them reflected religious elements, often involving a Muslim perspective on alcohol. One example is the movie by Khaled's group, which reflected on one moral dilemma that he had experienced, as he has a non-Muslim mother who drinks alcohol, thereby influencing her sons to start drinking even though they have a Muslim father who is against it.

In order to give a more in-depth understanding of the importance of these movies, I will focus on one girl, Kunya, in one of the groups that became central to the project and our data analysis. This group made a film called "Have you forgotten? I am a Muslim." There are several reasons for choosing this particular girl. One interesting fact is that she is one of the few students in the class that does not have a *Facebook* profile, but has been one of the most frequent users of *S28 (see above)*. In the interview she said that when she communicates with other students, she communicates primarily with those who are online at the same time as she is, using the chat function. On *S28*, she calls herself Deriia. In her profile text she writes:

> I am a girl who is 13 years old. my name is Kuyna but it pronounced (taken out for anonymity). I am from Kurdistan but live in Norway. I speak kurdish at home and Norwegian with my friends and teacher. I love to be with my friends and just have fun. I like to listen to Kurdish, Arabic, Turkish and English music. I am a BIIG fan of Justin Bieber.

Kuyna is very fond of her cousin who lives in Kurdistan, and therefore she makes use of the cousin's name as a profile name. The profile picture is taken at school, but she has used Picnic.com at home to edit it. She is one of the Norwegian students with the most friends on *S28* (75 friends) out of a total of 162 members of the community (the girl with the most friends has 117). In the interview, she explains that when she is logged onto *S28*, it is mainly in order to check out other student's pictures, but that she also has participated in several chat interactions with other students. Kuyna is a huge fan of Justin Bieber and has created two groups dedicated to him. The background of her profile on *S28* is an image of Justin Bieber. She is conscious about esthetics, something that becomes evident when she talks about whether the profile pictures match the background of the profile (e.g., colour, content of image, etc.). In the background picture of her profile, Bieber wears a purple t-shirt. She has decided to use this because it matches the purple sweater she wears on her profile picture. Kuyna has also uploaded several movies of different artists to her profile. These movies are mostly links to YouTube, but she also makes films herself at home, something she has learned from her sister.

Kuyna decided on the title for the film her group made as part of the project: "Have you forgotten? I am a Muslim!" The film is about a Muslim girl, Fatima, played by Kuyna, who is tempted by her Norwegian friend into tasting alcohol. Fatima is a Pakistani girl who lives together with her aunt and uncle in Norway. The film starts with a long sequence where Fatima sits in front of the computer communicating with her friends on *Space2cre8*. The rest of the film is about Fatima going out with her friend. They meet a boy hanging out on a corner drinking alcohol. They stop and chat with him and Fatima is pressured into tasting alcohol by the other two and talks about going to a party to meet other friends. Then Fatima's aunt and uncle come by and catch her drinking. Her friend runs away and does not support her. Fatima is hit by her uncle on the street and the next sequence shows her "uncle" on the phone, saying that he will send her back to the parents' homeland, Pakistan.

During the interactions in class when making this film, and also in an interview, Kuyna explained that she witnessed a Muslim girl being hit by her father. However, she explained that this type of punishment is not common among Muslims. She has also heard about girls in her community that have been sent back to the parent's country of origin, due to inappropriate behaviour. This movie becomes a resource for reflecting upon the challenges that take place in the intersection between Western and Muslim cultures in which she is situated. When this movie was uploaded to *S28*, it created a lot of discussion on the other sites, especially in the US.

7 Discussion

Through the presentation of the data above, I have tried to address the question of how students in a multi-ethnic classroom have been using *Space2cre8* as a space for negotiating cultural identities and positioning themselves as learners. Cultural resources such as ethnic and local belonging and global youth culture are mixed together in the different activities on *Space2cre8*. When presenting themselves in their profiles, the majority of the students focus on the connections to their parent's ethnic origins, but when presenting themselves for the Oakland kids, by sending their video-messages, it is interesting to observe that the students instead highlight their presumed shared interests, such as music, soccer and being with friends.

Many of the activities, such as making the "youth and alcohol" films, indicate how social identification and academic learning are interwoven processes in the classroom and are part of the individual learner's "learning identity" (Wortham 2006). Through the different cultural resources available, the youngsters can create their own combination and personal expression in what Holland, Lachicotte Jr., Skinner and Cain (1998) describe as a *space of authoring*. When, for example, Khamil calls himself "Turkish-B" and Ahmed calls himself "Tunisiano", they are communicating both ethnic belonging and their belonging to the global hip-hop culture. When re-mixing these resources and images representing music or artists, they are engaged in processes of meaning making and symbolic creativity (Willis 1990), expressing different aspects of their identities. To understand how students make use of social networking sites in educational settings, we have to study how students use them *in situ*, in between online and offline activities. It is simply not enough to solely study profiles or carry out surveys; we have to do ethnographic studies focusing on situations where these technologies are used and made meaningful by students.

Moreover, a social networking site such as *Space2cre8* becomes an important resource for reflecting upon cultural identities among students in a classroom setting. This is done by using and producing different modalities such as text, video, links, and so forth, on the site. This is also done by relating to the other students, both in how they present themselves to the "others" and through their conceptions of who the others are, which reflects back on themselves in the way that they draw on similar references in popular culture, such as Justin Bieber, but also on how they are different.

Lastly, social networking sites such as *Space2cre8* represent alternative and powerful spaces for learning in schools in the way they engage students in the processes of producing meaning and figurative worlds that go beyond regular classroom activities. This is very much a collective task in the way students negotiate different types of knowledge within a school context and forge identities, online and offline. When working with these semiotic resources, the students are involved in both academic and non-academic knowledge production, playing out various resources from different figurative worlds as well as creating new worlds and new meanings. As seen above, the students position themselves differently when using this site, some seeing it as an extension of the classroom activities of working with school content, while others see possibilities of extending and creating new spaces for relational connections with youth in other countries.

8 Media Literacy, New Activism and Empowerment

The presentation in this chapter raises some issues concerning young people in contemporary media culture and especially the challenges this poses to education and schooling. I have used the case of *Space2cre8* to make these issues a bit more concrete. Looking ahead I want to highlight two core issues.

One issue concerns media literacy. During the last decades this concept has moved from being at the margins linked to media studies in schools towards being defined as a core competence in the twenty-first century. One of the key competencies defined by the European Commission, for example, is digital competence that directly builds on definitions of media literacy. The important research issue is what we mean by this term, especially the critical media literacy of people living in contemporary media culture, as well as the role of education in building knowledge and competencies within this field (Erstad and Sefton-Green 2013).

The other issue builds on the former to raise some awareness of empowerment and new activism in contemporary culture. As a research approach this has implications for methodological developments in ways of studying the developments presented in this chapter and ways of doing research with communities rather than just specific users. This is seen in various ways of redefining audience research in Media and Communication studies and engaging the public as co-researchers when doing research into these issues. The important issue is to what extent people can develop real agency and empowerment in their dealings with digital media, supported by learning activities in schools, rather than that their activities of engagement and participation are subordinated to the corporate structures of the new media (Pariser 2011).

References

Banks, J. A., & Banks, C. A. M. (2005). *Multicultural education: Issues and perspectives*. Hoboken: Wiley.

Bekerman, Z., Burbules, N. C., & Silberman-Keller, D. (Eds.). (2006). *Learning in places: The informal education reader*. New York: Peter Lang.

Boellstorff, T. (2008). *Coming of age in second life: An anthropologist explores the virtually human*. Princeton: Princeton University Press.

Boyd, D. (2010). Social network sites as networked publics: Affordances, dynamics, and implications. In Z. Papacharissi (Ed.), *Networked self: Identity, community, and culture on social network sites* (pp. 39–58). New York: Routledge.

Bucher, T. (2012). *Programmed sociality: A software studies perspective on social networking sites*. PhD thesis, Department of Media and Communication, University of Oslo.

Buckingham, D. (2003). *Media education: Literacy, learning and contemporary culture*. Cambridge: Polity Press.

Buckingham, D. (Ed.). (2008). *Youth, identity, and digital media*. Cambridge, MA: The MIT Press.

Caldas-Coulthard, C. R., & Iedema, R. (Eds.). (2008). *Identity trouble: Critical discourse and contested identities*. New York: Palgrave Macmillan.

Castor, T., & Cooren, F. (2006). Organizations as hybrid forms of life: The implications of the selection of agency in problem formulation. *Management Communication Quarterly, 19*, 570–600.

Cole, M. (1996). *Cultural psychology: A once and future discipline*. Harvard: Harvard University Press.

Comber, B., & Nixon, H. (2008). Spatial literacies, design texts, and emergent pedagogies in purposeful literacy curriculum. *Pedagogies: An International Journal, 3*, 221–240.

Cooren, F. (2004). Textual agency: How texts do things in organizational settings. *Organization, 11*, 373–393.

Drotner, K. (2001). *Medier for fremtiden. Børn, unge og deg nye medielandskab* [Media for the future. Children and young people in the new media age]. København: Høst & Søns Forlag.

Eco, U. (1987). *Travels in hyper-reality*. London: Picador.

Erstad, O. (2010). *Digital kompetanse i skolen, 2. utgave* (Digital competence in the school, 2nd ed.). Oslo: Universitetsforlaget (University Press).

Erstad, O. (2013). *Digital learning lives: Trajectories, literacies, and schooling*. New York: Peter Lang.

Erstad, O., & Sefton-Green, J. (Eds.). (2013). *Identity, community, and learning lives in the digital age*. New York: Cambridge University Press.

Gibson, J. J. (1986). *The ecological approach to visual perception*. Hillsdale: LEA.
Goffman, E. (1974/1987). *Frame analysis: An essay on the organization of experience*. Boston: Northeastern University Press.
Hall, E. T. (1959). *The silent language*. Greenwich: Fawcett.
Hardy, C. (2004). Scaling up and bearing down in discourse analysis: Questions regarding textual agencies and their context. *Organization, 11*, 415–425.
Heath, S. B. (2012). *Words at work and play: Three decades in family and community life*. Cambridge: Cambridge University Press.
Holland, D., Lachicotte, Jr., W. J., Skinner, D., & Cain, C. (1998). *Identity and agency in cultural worlds*. Cambridge, MA: Harvard University Press.
Hull, G., & Greeno, J. G. (2006). Identity and agency in non-school and school worlds. In Z. Bekerman, N. C. Burbules, & D. Silberman-Keller (Eds.), *Learning in places: The informal education reader* (pp. 77–98). New York: Peter Lang.
Hull, G. A., & Katz, M.-L. (2006). Crafting an agentive self: Case studies on digital storytelling. *Research in the Teaching of English, 41*(1), 43–81.
Ito, M., et al. (2010). *Hanging out, messing around, and geeking out*. Cambridge, MA: The MIT Press.
Jenkins, H. (2006). *Convergence culture: Where old and new media collide*. New York: New York University Press.
Jenkins, H., Purushotma, R., Weigel, M., Clinton, K., & Robinson, A. J. (2009). *Confronting the challenges of participatory culture: Media education for the 21st century. The MacArthur Foundation*. Cambridge, MA: The MIT Press.
Jonassen, D. H., & Land, S. M. (Eds.). (2000). *Theoretical foundations of learning environments*. Mahwah: Lawrence Erlbaum Associates.
Lave, J., & Wenger, E. (1991). *Situated learning: Legitimate peripheral participation*. Cambridge: Cambridge University Press.
Leander, K. M., & McKim, K. K. (2003). Tracing the everyday "sitings" of adolescents on the Internet: A strategic adaptation of ethnography across online and offline spaces. *Education, Communication & Information, 3*(2), 211–240.
Leander, K., & Sheehy, M. (Eds.). (2004). *Spatializing literacy research and practice*. New York: Peter Lang.
Leander, K., Phillips, N. C., & Taylor, K. H. (2010). The changing social spaces of learning: Mapping new mobilities. *Review of Research in Education, 34*, 329–394.
Lenhart, A., Madden, M., Smith, A., & Macgill, A. (2007). *Teens and social media*. http://www.pewinternet.org/files/old-media/Files/Reports/2007/PIP_Teens_Social_Media_Final.pdf.pdf. Accessed 30 Jan 2015.
Ling, R. (2004). *The mobile connection: The cell phone's impact on society*. Amsterdam: Elsevier.
Moje, E., & Luke, A. (2009). Literacy and identity: Examining the metaphors in history and contemporary research. *Reading Research Quarterly, 44*(4), 415–437.
Nunes, M. (2006). *Cyberspaces of everyday life*. Minneapolis: University of Minnesota Press.
Pariser, E. (2011). *The filter bubble*. New York: Penguin.
Pelletier, C. (2009). Games and learning: What's the connection. *International Journal of Learning and Media, 1*(1), 83–101.
Pelletier, C., Burn, A., & Buckingham, D. (2010). Game design as textual poaching: Media literacy, creativity and game-making. *E-Learning and Digital Media, 7*(1), 90–107.
Rogoff, B. (2003). *The cultural nature of human development*. Oxford: Oxford University Press.
Selwyn, N. (2011). *Schools and schooling in the digital age: A critical analysis*. Oxon: Routledge.
Vygotsky, L. S. (1978). *Mind in society: The development of higher psychological processes*. Cambridge, MA: Harvard University Press.
Wenger, E. (1998). *Communities of practice: Learning, meaning and identity*. Cambridge: Cambridge University Press.
Wertsch, J. V. (1998). *Mind as action*. New York: Oxford University Press.

Willis, P. (1990). *Common culture: Symbolic work at play in the everyday cultures of the young*. Milton Keynes: Open University Press.

Wortham, S. (2006). *Learning identity: The joint emergence of social identification and academic learning*. Boston: Cambridge University Press.

Wortham, S. (Ed.). (2011). *Youth cultures, language, and literacy* (Review of research in education, 35). Washington, DC: American Educational Research Association.

Part II
Privacy: Balancing Self-disclosure & Privacy Concerns

The Paradoxes of Online Privacy

Sabine Trepte

Abstract Over the course of the last years, privacy in the Internet has attracted a lot of public attention and stimulated numerous scientific studies. When conducting research on privacy, the entire spectrum of human communication and interaction needs to be addressed. The core aspects are privacy related attitudes and privacy related behaviours. In addition, another pivotal aspect is the knowledge of privacy mechanisms that users now need to possess. In this chapter, I will elaborate on these three aspects. First of all, I am going to focus on those attitudes from which the particular behaviours arguably result. The fact that this seemingly sequential relation does not always hold and that several paradoxical notions can be observed will be addressed afterwards. Finally, possible explanations and solutions to address these paradoxes will be presented.

Privacy is commonly understood as a process of boundary management and of the ways individuals can control who has access to them (Altman 1975; Margulis 2011; Petronio 2002). Privacy is not a question of having it or not, but rather a process which is constantly in flux. Within this process we try to optimise the balance of an ideal level of privacy and the level of privacy currently achieved (Altman 1975). We assess the ideal and the achieved level of privacy during communication. Imbalance triggers motives for changing either the privacy context or privacy behaviour (Dienlin 2014). Ideal privacy can mean that individuals perceive they are in control of who is getting in touch with them and whom they can approach (social privacy, cf. Burgoon et al. 1989). It can also mean that they are in control of the physical boundaries such as their body, their home, even their country and can determine if and how these borders are crossed (physical privacy, cf. Burgoon et al. 1989). Most importantly, ideal privacy means that what we think and what we feel is exchanged only when it feels right (psychological privacy, cf. Burgoon et al. 1989), and only

This chapter reprints a section formerly published in Trepte, S. & Dienlin, T. (2014). Privatsphäre im Internet. In T. Porsch & S. Pieschl (Hrsg.), *Neue Medien und deren Schatten. Mediennutzung, Medienwirkung, Medienkompetenz (S. 53-80)*. Göttingen: Hogrefe.

S. Trepte (✉)
School of Communication, Dept. of Media Psychology, University of Hohenheim, Stuttgart, Germany
e-mail: sabine.trepte@uni-hohenheim.de

M. Walrave et al. (eds.), *Youth 2.0: Social Media and Adolescence*,
DOI 10.1007/978-3-319-27893-3_6

with regard to data and information that we are willing to share (informational privacy, cf. Burgoon et al. 1989). Achieved privacy analogously refers to social, physical, psychological and informational issues.

Psychological research has investigated privacy since the 1970ies. It is a broad and exciting field of research, too vast to summarise here (Margulis 2011). The most important milestones are that privacy is important for staying healthy, both physically and mentally (Margulis 2003; Vinsel et al. 1980). Only if people have the chance to control whom to get in touch with, where and what to share, are they satisfied with their lives. That said, sharing information about myself with others, something which can be termed as the most important behaviour of privacy, namely self-disclosure, is also required to stay healthy and happy (Trepte & Scharkow in press). People who are not able to self-disclose have been shown to have higher rates of depression, anxiety and somatic symptoms (Berg and Derlega 1987; Derlega and Berg 1987).

Privacy is part of the pedagogical routine. Children learn about privacy right from the start. They acquire the dialectics of privacy, e.g. when it is better to share and when it seems worthwhile to withhold (Finkenauer et al. 2002). Privacy has been demonstrated to be an important developmental task, because it is part of developing a personal identity, of initiating and maintaining relationships (Peter and Valkenburg 2011).

Since the rise of social media our understanding of privacy and the routines of privacy socialisation seem to be challenged (Boyd 2014). Furthermore, in social media, common boundaries of what has formerly been defined as public and private are blurred. Paradoxes and antagonisms of online privacy are an issue both in academic and anecdotal references (Murphy 2014; Trepte and Reinecke 2011). In the following I will try to shed light on some of the most pressing issues around online privacy paradoxes. First, I will refer to the conflict between social media affordances and our traditional understanding of privacy. While this conflict refers to the interaction of technology and psychology, my second point will refer to the seeming contradiction of privacy attitudes and behaviours, commonly known as the privacy paradox. After this, the risk paradox and the control paradox will be addressed. Finally, I will refer to why and how online privacy literacy might be a remedy for the antagonisms of online privacy.

1 Privacy in Conflict with Social Media Affordances

Social media in general and social network sites (SNSs) in particular seem to imply certain challenges to the definition and management of individual privacy. We can find a myriad of anecdotal references in the press which refer to how social media affordances defy traditional privacy expectations and habits. Also, academic outlets have underlined the risks and challenges which social media pose to privacy (Livingstone et al. 2013; Trepte et al. 2014a). It seems that social media, as a disruptive innovation, a mega-trend and one of the most successful technologies in terms of user numbers, trouble our familiar understanding of privacy. To better understand the apparent conflict, we need a fine-honed understanding of both. Psychological privacy has been outlined in the previous section, whereas social media affordances will be addressed in what follows. Media affordances refer to what media can do and have on offer, or in other words, "by suggesting possibilities for interaction" (Papacharissi 2010, p. 51). I propose to further differentiate the term social media affordances into social media functions and social media characteristics.

Social media functions refer to the purpose of social media, they describe what social media are made for and how they are used. As such they can be referred to as "warm" affordances, because they are immersive, deeply rooted in user behaviour and reflected by users' thoughts and emotions. Two functions define social media: (1) As digital online services social media allow the mutual connection of users and the exchange of content (Schmidt and Weichert 2012). They are set up for the interaction of at least two interaction partners (Ellison and Boyd 2013).

Social media characteristics refer to technological and structural properties, to its infrastructure and architecture (Papacharissi 2010). These can be termed as "cold" affordances as they are usually not thought of while using social media. Although social media characteristics determine user behaviour, they are not the purpose of social media. Three characteristics describe social media's nature (1) Social media may be defined as online communication media which at the same time offer services for one-to-one as for one-to-many communication. (2) They can be defined as communication media for personal as well as for mass communication. (3) Communication content can be read and heard by recipients known to the person communicating and by recipients which are either not consciously addressed (e.g. the wider network of friends) or others not known. This latter group may consist of website owners or third parties which have been authorised by website owners (e.g. website owners' clients using the users' data for marketing purposes). Social media comprise social network sites (e.g. Facebook, Google+), blogs, online games (e.g. World of Warcraft, Electronic Sports League) and web services which allow sharing and commenting of content (e.g. Instagram, YouTube).

Returning to the routines of privacy the question is what is so challenging about transferring it to social media? I suppose it is the interaction of privacy expectations with social media affordances that causes turbulence. To give an example, a status information on a social network site is usually posted to trigger interaction with others (cf. social media functions). Also, these posts may be read by friends of friends or by website owners or their clients (cf. social media characteristics). It seems that social media functions, as "warm" affordances, ask for privacy regulations accustomed to non-mediated contexts. Here, using social media feels like talking to friends in a private room. Disclosures might even be more authentic as compared to face-to-face situations, because social media block out physical appearance and can be thought about and edited (Trepte and Reinecke 2011). In contrast, social media characteristics, as "cold" properties of social media, suggest behaviours similar to privacy regulation in mass-mediated or public contexts. These properties are usually processed on a rational level which is more abstract and asks for cognitive elaboration. Social media characteristics are represented as terms and conditions whereas social media functions help us answering the most important questions in life such as: Who shares with me and with whom do I share?

By and large, I suggest that some social media affordances accommodate our traditional understanding of privacy and some do not. We have a hard time holding both apart, and based on blurred lines, some contradictory behaviours have been observed in social media research (Vitak et al. 2015). The most cited one is certainly the privacy paradox which I will refer to in the following.

2 The Privacy Paradox

In brief, the privacy paradox refers to privacy attitudes being inconsistent with privacy behaviours (Barnes 2006). It has often been demonstrated that although users are concerned about their privacy, they exhibit behaviours that seemingly feed these concerns. In other words, users report being concerned about publishing too much information online but in turn keep publishing information online. To better understand this contradiction, I will now examine both online privacy attitudes and online privacy behaviours.

2.1 Online Privacy Attitudes – Lost in Concerns

Regarding the attitudes toward online privacy, studies have demonstrated that people are particularly concerned with what happens with their data and how vulnerable they are on account of the large quantities that are publicly shared. In an EU-representative study, 64 % of all Germans and 58 % of all Europeans agreed with the statement that there are no alternatives to the disclosure of personal information when buying products or services in the Internet (Eurobarometer 2011). People also complain about lacking informational privacy. 68 % of all Germans and 63 % of all Europeans report that disclosure is perceived as a severe problem (Eurobarometer 2011). Especially people who think that they have already disclosed information which was not necessary for purchasing goods or services are concerned with the further processing of their data by unknown third parties. 73 % of all Germans and 72 % of all Europeans report that they are "very concerned" about these issues (Eurobarometer 2011).

Furthermore, in a study with 498 participants, it was found that concerns regarding privacy encompass computer viruses, spam, spyware or attacks by hackers (Paine et al. 2007). Less prevalent were concerns regarding identity theft or general safety. Moreover, in an EU-representative study, it was shown that a large part of Europeans (73 %) were concerned with what would generally happen to their data once transferred to companies. Finally, most Europeans would like to know the specific purposes for which their data were collected and think that for further data processing prior consent is required (Eurobarometer 2011).

Results from longitudinal studies have shown that privacy concerns have increased over time: Whilst in 1970, 30 % of respondents reported that they are concerned, in 2000, 80 % indicated their concern (Cho et al. 2010). In sum, it can be stated that privacy concerns are increasingly prevalent and pronounced. That said, it is important to ask which factors nurture these concerns and whether different patterns exist for particular groups, such as gender and culture.

In previous research on intercultural terms of privacy, is has often been suggested that people in individualistic cultures, in which the individual has a more valued status, show more privacy concerns in comparison to collectivist cultures, in which the community is more accentuated and in which organisations are more readily allowed to engage in personal private life (Cho et al. 2009; Jackson and Wang 2013). However, results are manifold and do not unequivocally support this simple hypothesis. In a study with users in New York, Singapore, Bangalore, Seoul and Sidney, for example, only marginal differences between users in these respective countries were found (Cho et al. 2009). Moreover, in a large study with 538 participants from 38 countries, no relation between individualism and privacy concerns have emerged (Bellman et al. 2004).

With respect to gender as an influencing factor with respect to privacy attitudes, it was shown that women show more pronounced privacy concerns (Cho et al. 2009; Christofides et al. 2009; Yao and Zhang 2008). In addition, women consider it more likely that they would become victims of hostile and aggressive messages in SNSs (Trepte et al. 2013). Thelwall (2011) showed comprehensively that women need to be more concerned because of the necessary preoccupation with their physical safety and because of gender-specific needs regarding communication. Whilst men generally spend more time online and disclose larger quantities of personal information, woman search for more intense interactions, which implies more self-disclosure and as such makes women more vulnerable in terms of online privacy (Thelwall 2008, 2011).

It is interesting to see that users seem to project their concerns to other users. They are convinced they are better informed and more in control of their privacy than other users (Debatin et al. 2009). In a study with 910 users in Singapore, Cho et al. (2010) showed that concerns on the one hand relate to the individual self and on the other hand to general societal consequences. Especially those people who are strongly convinced they have their privacy under control act according to the phenomenon of the so-called *positivity bias* (Reinecke and Trepte 2014). This bias expresses that positive disclosures get more and better feedback on SNSs and are therefore the most common (Utz 2011). In contrast, disclosures relating to negative events or feelings of regret are referred to less often on SNSs.

The aforementioned results demonstrate that people in Europe and beyond have substantial privacy concerns. In the following, I will turn to the question whether and how these concerns are translated into online privacy behaviours.

2.2 *Online Privacy Behaviours – A Question of Benefits and Gratifications*

Research often shows, for example, that privacy concerns are not translated into privacy behaviours. In order to be able to shop online, almost 90 % of all Europeans disclose their name, their postal address and even 18 % their personal ID's or passport's identification number (Eurobarometer 2011). On SNSs like Facebook or Google+, 51 % of all Europeans regularly post photos and 38 % provide their own postal address. Users in Germany are even more trusting. In a study with 327 participants, 93 % posted a photo and 83 % their postal address online (Trepte et al. 2013). Moreover, the readiness to disclose information on SNSs rose significantly in the course of 2 years. Heavy users and men are especially willing to post personal information on SNSs. Also, with respect to psychological privacy, it has been shown that over the course of 2 years people were more willing to disclose their emotions to others (Trepte et al. 2013). Based on the aforementioned results, the question arises: Why are people, despite their prevailing privacy concerns, increasingly willing to disclose online and to seemingly give up informational and psychological privacy? The theoretical assumption of the so called *privacy calculus* holds that people assess their present situation rationally and weigh which risks and benefits they can expect from disclosing information (Dinev and Hart 2006; Krasnova et al. 2012). If the uses and gratifications exceed the accompanying risks to a substantial degree, people will deliberately decide to take the associated risks (Ellison et al. 2011).

Regarding the gratifications relating to SNSs, current research mentions social support and social capital, identity management and self-presentation, as well as participation in the current sociopolitical discourse and current social life (for a more detailed elaboration, see Taddicken and Jers 2011). These gratifications do not only occur in online but also in offline contexts. Social support has been shown to be the major gratification and benefit of social media and SNS use (Ellison et al. 2011; Trepte et al. 2014b). Several studies have shown that in SNSs a substantial degree of immediate attention can be gained more easily, and that brief contacts as well as loose social network ties (*bridging social capital)* can be made and sustained more efficiently than outside of SNSs. When it comes to intensify loose ties and transfer them into profound friendships (*bonding social capital*) the situation changes. Several studies focusing on social capital have shown that although loose ties can be made easily, strong relationships cannot be established in the same way (Ellison et al. 2011; Steinfield et al. 2008). Hence, regarding strong relationships, empirical findings have drawn a more pessimistic picture (Trepte et al. 2014b). It is assumed that strong ties can solely be maintained if online contact is accompanied by *face-to-face* contact. In a study involving online gamers, it was found that face-to-face communication and physical proximity was a premise for strong friendships on the Internet as well as for social support in other contexts (Trepte et al. 2012). Moreover, for online role-playing games it was shown that only few of the users were able to establish strong social ties—and if that happened, it was necessarily connected with real life encounters (Williams 2007). Only in these cases have social network ties from the Internet become usable for offline contexts. A longitudinal study with 488 Internet-users has found that intensity of use, self-disclosure and social support can be considered a reciprocal and self-amplifying process: the more users engage in SNSs, the more they disclose of themselves. This is further amplified if users are able to generate social capital and only applies to those who are capable of initiating and sustaining friendships (Trepte and Reinecke 2013).

Identity-management and self-presentation are additional gratifications which are associated with an active engagement on SNSs, asking for disclosure of personal information (Krämer and Haferkamp 2011). Users manage their public image online and thereby also their own identity. It was shown that in this process, users tend to portray themselves in the most positive way (Toma and Hancock 2010, 2011; Toma et al. 2008). The genuine interests of self-presentation are often in stark contrast to privacy interests (Krämer and Haferkamp 2011).

2.3 *The Privacy Paradox and the Control Paradox*

So far, I have focused on behaviours relating to privacy issues on the Internet and how they are fostered by motives of social support and impression management. In sum, it can be concluded that people increasingly show privacy concerns and that these come along with an increasing willingness to regulate and to take care of online privacy; still, people are also disclosing more and more and thus reduce the degree of their informational, social and psychological privacy (Trepte et al. 2014a). The contradiction of lax privacy behaviours on the one hand, and amplified feelings of privacy concerns on the other, has been termed the *privacy paradox* (Barnes 2006). Current studies have shown that despite negative experiences users might alter their attitudes but not their behaviour. In a longitudinal study with 327 German Internet users who were interviewed across one year, the following was found: Users who had negative experiences (operationalised by having received hostile and aggressive mails and posts from fellow users) applied more safety mechanisms so as to protect their informational privacy compared to those who did not have negative experiences; moreover, they also assessed the risk of further privacy intrusions as being higher. Even so, users with negative experiences did not strengthen the protection of psychological or social privacy (Trepte et al. 2014a). Despite negative experiences on the Internet, users continued to share intimate content with others and did not block this content in terms of audiences.

Another inconsistency of privacy-related behaviours is termed the *control-paradox* (Brandimarte et al. 2010). It refers to the finding that users do not reflect on how (*use*) and by whom (*access*) their data are used as soon as they can control with whom they want to share (*release*). Brandimarte et al. (2010) conducted several experiments in which students were offered the possibility of providing personal data online for a new SNS of the local University. The experiment featured two groups: in the first one, students were told that the data of all participants would be publicly available online. In the second one, users were told that only 50 % of the profiles would be publicly available online. Results showed that compared to the second group, participants of the first one provided larger quantities and even more intimate content of private data online. Brandimarte et al. (2010) argued that users of the first group were willing to disclose more information because of having the impression that they possessed more control over their data. In a second experiment, a third group was told that their data would not only be featured on the SNS of their local university but also on another one. Despite the larger audience, users still disclosed more information as long as they were told that all of their data would be featured online. In a third experiment, participants were told that they would take part in a study on ethical behaviour and that, after the experiment, answers would be published in a "research bulletin". The audience and the content of the bulletin were not further elaborated. Participants were asked ten questions regarding whether, at some point in their lives, they had lied, committed theft or engaged in other behaviours that are considered socially deviant. Participants were offered three options to regulate their privacy: (1) no control: participants were told that they would automatically grant the researchers all rights to their answers; (2) partial control: users were able to tick off if they wanted to grant the researchers all the rights to their answers; and (3) high control: for each of the ten different questions, participants had the possibility of marking specifically if they wanted to grant researchers the rights to use the respective answers. Participants of the third group disclosed significantly more personal information compared to the other two groups. Participants neither reflected on how their data would be processed further, nor who would have access to their answers. The third condition simulated the typical privacy regulation context on SNSs: it can be argued that the control over privacy settings on SNSs—where privacy regulations have to be checked individually for a multitude of different actions—precisely echoes this empirical finding and corresponds to the control-paradox.

In recent years the privacy paradox has been criticised for being imprecise in several respects. Trepte et al. (2014a) suggested that it is not the behaviour and attitudes of users that is inconsistent, but the measurement thereof. They criticise the fact that in previous research privacy attitudes often refer to issues such as data fraud and identity theft, whereas behaviours deal more specifically with how privacy settings are used. They argue that these dimensions are not compatible and also that respondents might feel forced to answer that they are concerned on a more general level just because these concerns reflect current norms of disclosure. To solve some of these problems, Dienlin and Trepte (2014) measured attitudes and behaviours analogously. For instance, they asked for attitudes towards disclosing religious beliefs and how they are disclosed on SNSs. As expected, attitudes and behaviours did not differ. Masur and Scharkow (in press) argue that privacy behaviours have to be differentiated into "active" technology-centred strategies (e.g. using pseudonyms and encryption) and more "passive" strategies of how parsimoniously personal data are handled.

By and large, the privacy paradox has been refined and reconsidered, but still, users and consumers do not always act consistently when it comes to online privacy.

What are the future perspectives and what can we do about the paradoxes we are facing as an integral part of social media use?

3 Privacy Literacy as a Remedy for Paradoxical Behaviour?

At this point, it is essential to determine why users do not protect their privacy more efficiently. Trepte et al. (2015) suggest four hypotheses to answer the question of why users accept privacy risks although they have concerns: the gratification hypothesis which assumes that the gratifications obtained surmount privacy risks (cf. Sect. 2 of this chapter); the measurement bias hypothesis which suggests that attitudes were measured by asking for societal issues and behaviours for individual online uses (Sect. 3); the social desirability hypothesis which states that users do not report true attitudes but only what they expect to be socially desirable (Sect. 3); and finally, the knowledge gap hypothesis which posits that attitudes and behaviours would match, if only users knew more about online privacy. In fact, previous research almost unequivocally has shown that *knowledge* about online privacy is scant. A study with 65 participants, all of which were first interviewed regarding their intentions and priorities on SNSs (Madejski et al. 2012), showed that intentions and the factual settings were inconsistent. At least one disparity between privacy intentions and privacy settings was found for each participant. 94 % of the users shared information that they actually wanted to keep private; 84 % of the users restrained access to information that they actually wanted to share. In addition, users are not informed of the terms of the Internet service provider's underlying business model. In a study representative for US-citizens with 1500 young adults, participants were asked if they knew that their Internet behaviour would be recorded (Turow et al. 2005). The majority of participants (84 %) knew that their own surfing behaviour could be replicated by means of cookies and that Internet providers (e.g., SNSs, travelling portals, retailers) captured which websites were used. Half of the participants did *not* know that personal data, such as the postal address, can be sold to third party companies. They also did not know that no information was available about which data exactly were saved and stored, and that companies cannot be forced to return or erase that data. In sum, one can observe a significant knowledge gap for users in terms of how data are interchanged between providers and how data are used for actions like *targeting* (the personally specified allocation of advertisements by means of sociodemographic data or surfing habits), r*eal-time bidding* (the personally specified allocation of advertisements by means of surfing habits—with the special clause that the costs of advertisement are calculated according to success rates, this being how often advertisements are clicked on and how often items are bought) and *affiliate marketing* (so-called affiliates, thus advertisers, pay the providers a provision when advertisements are clicked or a purchase takes place). Hoofnagle et al. (2010) showed in a study with 975 US-Americans taking part in a telephone-interview that the knowledge of profit models was indeed very low. The following five questions were to be answered, and participants had to check if they were "true" or "false": Do the data-protection guidelines on a website include that (1) your data would not be shared with other providers without your consent?; (2) your data including purchases and postal addresses would not be shared with other providers without your consent?; (3) your data (name, purchases, etc.) would be erased if commanded?; (4) you have the possibility to file a lawsuit against the providers if they violated their data-protection guidelines?; (5) your consent has to be attained for providers if they wanted to track your surfing behaviours on other websites? The correct answer for all five questions was "false". Only 3 % of all participants were able to answer all questions correctly and 30 % were not even able to answer one single question correctly. Especially youths and young adults were seldom capable of assessing the legal and economical context adequately. Thus, it seems of the utmost importance for further research in this area to focus on privacy knowledge (Trepte et al. 2015). Increasing privacy knowledge seems a condition sine qua non to influences users' privacy behaviours.

References

Altman, I. (1975). *The environment and social behavior: Privacy, personal space, territory, crowding*. Monterey: Brooks/Cole Publishing Company.

Barnes, S. B. (2006). A privacy paradox: Social networking in the Unites States. *First Monday, 11*(9). http://firstmonday.org/htbin/cgiwrap/bin/ojs/index.php/fm/article/view/1394/1312. Accessed 30 Jan 2015.

Bellman, S., Johnson, E. J., Kobrin, S. J., & Lohse, G. L. (2004). International differences in information privacy concerns: A global survey of consumers. *The Information Society, 20*, 313–324. doi:10.1080/01972240490507956.

Berg, J. H., & Derlega, V. J. (1987). Themes in the study of self-disclosure. In V. J. Derlega (Ed.), *Self-disclosure: Theory, research, and therapy* (pp. 1–8). New York: Plenum Press.

Boyd, D. (2014). *It's complicated: The social lives of networked teens*. New Haven: Yale University Press.

Brandimarte, L., Acquisti, A., & Loewenstein, G. (2010). *Privacy concerns and information disclosure: An illusion of control hypothesis*. Paper presented at the Workshop on the Economics of Information Security (WEIS).

Burgoon, J. K., Parrott, R., Le Poire, B. A., Kelley, D. L., Walther, J. B., & Perry, D. (1989). Maintaining and restoring privacy through communication in different types of relationships. *Journal of Social and Personal Relationships, 6*, 131–158.

Cho, H., Rivera-Sanchez, M., & Lim, S. S. (2009). A multinational study on online privacy: Global concerns and local responses. *New Media & Society, 11*(3), 395–416. doi:10.1177/1461444808101618.

Cho, H., Lee, J.-S., & Chung, S. (2010). Optimistic bias about online privacy risks: Testing the moderating effects of perceived controllability and prior experience. *Computers in Human Behavior, 26*, 987–995. doi:10.1016/j.chb.2010.02.012.

Christofides, E., Muise, A., & Desmarais, S. (2009). Information disclosure and control on facebook: Are they two sides of the same coin or two different processes? *CyberPsychology & Behavior, 12*(3), 341–345. doi:10.1089/cpb.2008.0226.

Debatin, B., Lovejoy, J. P., Horn, A.-K., & Hughes, B. N. (2009). Facebook and online privacy: Attitudes, behaviors, and unintended consequences. *Journal of Computer-Mediated Communication, 15*, 83–108. doi:10.1111/j.1083-6101.2009.01494.x.

Derlega, V. J., & Berg, J. H. (Eds.). (1987). *Self-disclosure: Theory, research, and therapy*. New York: Plenum.
Dienlin, T. (2014). The privacy process model. In S. Garnett, S. Halft, M. Herz, & J.-M. Mönig (Eds.), *Medien und Privatheit [Media and privacy]* (pp. 105–122). Passau: Stutz.
Dienlin, T., & Trepte, S. (2014). Is the privacy paradox a relic of the past? An in-depth analysis of privacy attitudes and privacy behaviors. *European Journal of Social Psychology*. doi:10.1002/ejsp.2049.
Dinev, T., & Hart, P. (2006). An extended privacy calculus model for e-commerce transactions. *Information Systems Research, 17*(1), 61–80. doi:10.1287/isre.1060.0080.
Ellison, N. B., & Boyd, D. (2013). Sociality through social network sites. In W. H. Dutton (Ed.), *The oxford handbook of internet studies*. Oxford: Oxford University Press.
Ellison, N. B., Vitak, J., Steinfield, C., Gray, R., & Lampe, C. (2011). Negotiating privacy concerns and social capital needs in a social media environment. In S. Trepte & L. Reinecke (Eds.), *Privacy online: Perspectives on privacy and self-disclosure in the social web* (pp. 19–32). Berlin: Springer.
Eurobarometer. (2011). *Attitudes on data protection and electronic identity in the European Union*. Brussels: European Commission. http://ec.europa.eu/public_opinion/archives/ebs/ebs_335_en.pdf. Accessed 30 Jan 2015.
Finkenauer, C., Engels, R. C. M. E., & Meeus, W. (2002). Keeping secrets from parents: Advantages and disadvantages of secrecy in adolescence. *Journal of Youth and Adolescence, 31*(2), 123–136.
Hoofnagle, C., King, J., Li, S., & Turow, J. (2010). *How different are young adults from older adults when it comes to information privacy attitudes and policy*. http://ssrn.com/abstract=1589864. Accessed 31 Jan 2013.
Jackson, L. A., & Wang, J.-L. (2013). Cultural differences in social networking site use: A comparative study of China and the United States. *Computers in Human Behavior, 29*(3), 910–921. doi:10.1016/j.chb.2012.11.024.
Krämer, N. C., & Haferkamp, N. (2011). Online self-presentation: Balancing privacy concerns and impression construction on social networking sites. In S. Trepte & L. Reinecke (Eds.), *Privacy online: Perspectives on privacy and self-disclosure in the social web* (pp. 127–142). Berlin: Springer.
Krasnova, H., Veltri, N. F., & Günther, O. (2012). Self-disclosure and privacy calculus on social networking sites: The role of culture. *Business & Information Systems Engineering, 4*(3), 127–135. doi:10.1007/s12599-012-0216-6.
Livingstone, S., Ólafsson, K., & Staksrud, E. (2013). Risky social networking practices among "underage" users: Lessons for evidence-based policy. *Journal of Computer-Mediated Communication, 18*(3), 303–320. doi:10.1111/jcc4.12012.
Madejski, M., Johnson, M., & Bellovin, S. M. (2012). *A study of privacy settings errors in an online social network*. Paper presented at the tenth annual IEEE international conference on pervasive computing and communications, Lugano, Switzerland.
Margulis, S. T. (2003). Privacy as a social issue and behavioral concept. *Journal of Social Issues, 59*(2), 243–261.
Margulis, S. T. (2011). Three theories of privacy: An overview. In S. Trepte & L. Reinecke (Eds.), *Privacy online: Perspectives on privacy and self-disclosure in the social web* (pp. 9–17). New York: Springer.
Masur, P. K., & Scharkow, M. (in press). Disclosure management on social network sites: Individual privacy perceptions and user-directed privacy strategies. *Social Media and Society*
Murphy, K. (2014, October 14). We want privacy, but can't stop sharing. *New York Times*.
Paine, C., Reips, U.-D., Stieger, S., Joinson, A. N., & Buchanan, T. (2007). Internet users' perceptions of 'privacy concerns' and 'privacy actions'. *International Journal of Human-Computer Studies, 65*, 526–536. doi:10.1016/j.ijhcs.2006.12.001.
Papacharissi, Z. (2010). *A private sphere: Democracy in a digital age*. Cambridge: Polity Press.

Peter, J., & Valkenburg, P. M. (2011). Adolescents' online privacy: Toward a developmental perspective. In S. Trepte & L. Reinecke (Eds.), *Privacy online: Perspectives on privacy and self-disclosure in the social web* (pp. 221–234). Berlin: Springer.

Petronio, S. (2002). *Boundaries of privacy*. Albany: State University of New York Press.

Reinecke, L., & Trepte, S. (2014). Authenticity and well-being on social network sites: A two-wave longitudinal study on the effects of online-authenticity and the positivity bias in SNS communication. *Computers in Human Behavior, 30*, 95–102.

Schmidt, J.-H., & Weichert, T. (Eds.). (2012). *Datenschutz. Grundlagen, Entwicklungen und Kontroversen* (Vol. 1190). Bonn: Bundeszentrale für politische Bildung.

Steinfield, C., Ellison, N. B., & Lampe, C. (2008). Social capital, self-esteem, and use of online social network sites: A longitudinal analysis. *Journal of Applied Developmental Psychology, 29*, 434–445.

Taddicken, M., & Jers, C. (2011). The uses of privacy online: Trading a loss of privacy for social web gratifications? In S. Trepte & L. Reinecke (Eds.), *Privacy online: Perspectives on privacy and self-disclosure in the social web* (pp. 143–158). Berlin: Springer.

Thelwall, M. (2008). Social networks, gender, and friending: An analysis of myspace member profiles. *Journal of the American Society for Information Science and Technology, 59*(8), 1321–1330. doi:10.1002/asi.20835.

Thelwall, M. (2011). Privacy and gender in the social web. In S. Trepte & L. Reinecke (Eds.), *Privacy online: Perspectives on privacy and self-disclosure in the social web* (pp. 251–266). Berlin: Springer.

Toma, C. L., & Hancock, J. T. (2010). Looks and lies: The role of physical attractiveness in online dating self-presentation and deception. *Communication Research, 37*, 335–351.

Toma, C. L., & Hancock, J. T. (2011). A new twist on love's labor: Self-presentation in online dating profiles. In K. B. Wright & L. M. Webb (Eds.), *Computer-mediated communication in personal relationships* (pp. 41–55). New York: Peter Lang.

Toma, C. L., Hancock, J. T., & Ellison, N. B. (2008). Separating fact from fiction: An examination of deceptive self-presentation in online dating profiles. *Personality and Social Psychological Bulletin, 34*(8), 1023–1036.

Trepte, S., & Reinecke, L. (2011). The social web as shelter for privacy and authentic living. In S. Trepte & L. Reinecke (Eds.), *Privacy online: Perspectives on privacy and self-disclosure in the social web* (pp. 61–74). Berlin: Springer.

Trepte, S., & Reinecke, L. (2013). The reciprocal effects of social network site use and the disposition for self-disclosure: A longitudinal study. *Computers in Human Behavior, 29*(3), 1102–1112. doi:10.1016/j.chb.2012.10.002.

Trepte, S., Reinecke, L., & Juechems, K. (2012). The social side of gaming: How playing online computer games creates online and offline social support. *Computers in Human Behavior, 28*, 832–839. doi:10.1016/j.chb.2011.12.003.

Trepte, S., Dienlin, T., & Reinecke, L. (2013). *Privacy, self-disclosure, social support, and social network site use. Research report of a three-year panel study*. Stuttgart: University of Hohenheim. Available at University of Hohenheim website: https://opus.uni-hohenheim.de/volltexte/2013/889/pdf/Trepte_Dienlin_Reinecke_2013_Privacy_Self_Disclosure_Social_Support_and_SNS_Use.pdf

Trepte, S., Dienlin, T., & Reinecke, L. (2014a). Risky behaviors: How online experiences influence privacy behaviors. In B. Stark, O. Quiring, & N. Jackob (Eds.), *Von der Gutenberg-Galaxis zur Google-Galaxis [From the Gutenberg galaxy to the Google galaxy]* (pp. 225–244). Wiesbaden: UVK.

Trepte, S., Dienlin, T., & Reinecke, L. (2014b). The influence of social support received in online and offline contexts on satisfaction with social support and satisfaction with life: A longitudinal study. *Media Psychology*. doi:10.1080/15213269.2013.838904.

Trepte, S., & Scharkow, M. (in press). Friends and Live-Savers: How social capital and social support received in media environments contribute to well-being. In L. Reinecke & M. B. O. Oliver

(Eds.), *Handbook of media use and well-being: International perspectives on theory and research on positive media effects*. New York: Routledge.

Trepte, S., Teutsch, D., Masur, P. K., Eicher, C., Fischer, M., Hennhöfer, A., & Lind, F. (2015). Do people know about privacy and data protection strategies? Towards the "Online Privacy Literacy Scale" (OPLIS). In S. Gutwirth et al. (Eds.), *Reforming European data protection law* (Law, governance and technology series 20, pp. 333–366). Dordrecht: Springer.

Turow, J., Feldman, L., & Meltzer, K. (2005). *Open to exploitation: America's shoppers online and offline. Report from the Annenberg Public Policy Center of the University of Pennsylvania Annenberg School for Communication Departmental Papers (ASC)*. Philadelphia: University of Pennsylvania.

Utz, S. (2011). Social network site use among Dutch students: Effects of time and platform. In F. Comunello (Ed.), *Networked sociability and individualism: Technology for personal and professional relationships*. Hershey: IGI Global.

Vinsel, A., Brown, B. B., Altman, I., & Foss, C. (1980). Privacy regulation, territorial displays, and effectiveness of individual functioning. *Journal of Personality and Social Psychology, 39*(6), 1104–1115.

Williams, D. (2007). The impact of time online: Social capital and cyberbalkanization. *CyberPsychology & Behavior, 10*(3), 398–406.

Vitak, J., Blasiola, S., Patil, S., & Litt, E. (2015). Balancing audience and privacy tensions on social network sites. *International Journal of Communication, 9*, 1485–1504. doi: 1932–8036/20150005.

Yao, M. Z., & Zhang, J. (2008). Predicting user concerns about online privacy in Hong Kong. *CyberPsychology & Behavior, 11*(6), 779–781. doi:10.1089/cpb.2007.0208.

The Role of Informational Norms on Social Network Sites

Wouter Martinus Petrus Steijn

Abstract Still little is known concerning the role informational norms play in regulating the privacy of individuals on social network sites. Considering privacy during social interaction one can identify norms of appropriateness and norms of distribution. This study investigates the adherence to these informational norms on social network sites by young and old users. Data were collected by means of a survey amongst 1002 social network site users, including adolescents, young adults and adults. The results show that the normative expectations associated with a social network site indicate that these sites are considered to be public, that adolescents and young adults primarily differ from adults in their adherence to norms of appropriateness and that a strong relationship is found between informational norms and actual information sharing. It is concluded that the role informational norms play for understanding online behaviour should not be underestimated, but are not yet effective regulators for online behaviour.

1 Introduction

Social norms play an important role for our privacy in everyday life by regulating what information is shared during interactions (Schwartz 1968, p. 742; Nissenbaum 2004, 2010). As yet, little is known concerning the role such norms play in regulating individuals' privacy during online interaction on social network sites (SNSs). The behaviour of youth on SNSs has been established to be remarkably similar to offline behaviour; social interaction with friends that used to occur on the playing field now occurs on SNSs (boyd 2008; Herring 2008; Marwick et al. 2010). The norms regulating shared information during offline interactions might not have fully made this transition to online interactions. As a result, opinions may differ on what is appropriate to share on an SNS profile and whether this information can be shared outside of the SNS context. Discrepancies in normative expectations related to information sharing on SNSs could in part explain the differences between younger and older individuals' online privacy behaviour and why youth generally appear to

W.M.P. Steijn (✉)
Tilburg Institute for Law, Technology and Society, Tilburg University, Tilburg, Netherlands
e-mail: wouter.steijn@tno.nl

M. Walrave et al. (eds.), *Youth 2.0: Social Media and Adolescence*,
DOI 10.1007/978-3-319-27893-3_7

be more careless with respect to privacy (Debatin et al. 2009; Govani and Pashley 2005; Gross and Acquisti 2005).

This study intends to contribute to the existing knowledge concerning information sharing on SNSs and online privacy by investigating the adherence, or non-adherence, of users to online social norms with respect to the sharing of information (henceforth *informational norms*). Investigation of the role informational norms play on social network sites will not only provide a better understanding of online behaviour in general, but will also provide additional insight into often observed differences between younger and older individuals' behaviour on SNSs and their **experience of online privacy**, as norms may play a more important role for youth in establishing their online privacy (boyd and Marwick 2011). This study will therefore address three issues. First, has a distinct normative expectation been developed for sharing information on SNSs compared to sharing information during a public or private offline interaction? Second, how do younger and older SNS users differ in their adherence to informational norms associated with SNS profiles? Third, what is the relationship between actual information sharing and the reported adherence to informational norms when compared with privacy attitudes and using privacy settings?

1.1 Background

Norms have been identified as one of four external regulators of behaviour, the others being market, architecture and law (Lessig 1999). Law primarily regulates SNS users' privacy in relation to data collection practices by institutions, while playing little part in the day-to-day management by SNS users of their online privacy in relation to other users. From a market perspective, SNSs generally push into publishing as much information as possible since the business plan of online providers of SNSs are generally based on the sharing of information (Andrews 2012; Pekárek and Leenes 2009). As a result, the architecture of SNSs also invites us to share as much information as possible (Peterson 2010) while the actual audience of the shared information is difficult to determine (Bernstein et al. 2013). On top of that, public figures of SNSs downplay the importance of privacy among their users (Johnson 2010). Yet, numerous studies have shown that privacy is in fact still important for SNS users (boyd and Marwick 2011; Livingstone 2008; Marwick et al. 2010; Raynes-Goldie 2010) and the role of norms may be an important one in respect to the other regulatory forces.

Considering privacy during social interaction, both the nature of the information shared during the interaction and the degree to which the shared information is subsequently allowed to be shared with others is of interest (Derlega and Chaikin 1977; Nissenbaum 2004, 2010; Petronio 2002). Nissenbaum (2004) identified these norms concerning information sharing as norms of appropriateness and norms of distribution respectively. Norms of appropriateness, as the name suggests, concerns what kind of information is appropriate for sharing in a given context. Reciprocity can also be considered a norm of appropriateness in the sense of whether it is appropriate to reciprocate disclosures your conversation partner made and thus affect the nature of the information shared during the interaction. Norms of distribution concern whether the shared information should subsequently be shared with others who were not present during the interaction. Similarly, the degree to which it is (un-) desirable for others to overhear the conversation gives an indication of whether the shared information is considered suitable for distribution to others not part of the conversation.

In her discussion of privacy, Nissenbaum explains how these norms are associated with a certain context (2010). This way, we know in any given context what information is appropriate and whether this information is allowed to be shared (i.e. distributed) with others and thus transfer it from one context to another. While Nissenbaum is one of the first to explicitly emphasise the role of contextual norms in relation to privacy, previous privacy theories mentioned the importance of norms for privacy (Stein and Shand 1974; Johnson 1989; Moore 1984). Other privacy theories also addressed the dynamic nature of when certain kinds of information should be considered private. For example, Altman (1975) described privacy as "the *selective* control of access to the self"[1] and Westin (1967) described privacy as a dynamic process: we regulate privacy to fulfil momentary needs and requirements. Both definitions suggest that the context and the associated informational norms individuals themselves deem important determine the desired privacy.

During offline social interactions, we are normally able to identify what norms apply. Taking into account where (e.g. at work or at home) and in whose company (e.g. friends or family) we are, we know which kind of information is appropriate for sharing and which is not. In addition, we recognise conventional cues of confidentiality (e.g. when an announcement is whispered, shared behind closed doors) and know that we ought not to distribute the information to others. As all individuals involved in face-to-face interaction often experience the same context, the implicit privacy expectations of the interaction based on the associated norms are often met.

Norms are generally not explicitly learned; instead they originate as

> matters of mere convenience, repeated for their immediate value in reducing the costs involved in face-to-face influence and in smoothing out the course of the interaction. […] The rule is likely to take on the characteristic of a moral obligation (Thibaut and Kelley 1959, p. 128).

In other words, if a certain rule is consistently applied to a given situation, after sufficient repetition of that situation the rule becomes internalised and becomes implicit to that situation. This is especially apparent when new technologies are introduced to social interactions. Social norms need to develop and will change to accommodate these new technologies; a process which takes time. The introduction of mobile phones, for example, seems to have changed a norm over time, making it more acceptable to have intimate conversations in public. Almost everyone has experienced at some point overhearing an awkward telephone conversation in the

[1] Emphasis added by author.

train held by someone else. Similarly, these days it is hardly frowned upon anymore when a conversation partner takes out their mobile phone to check for the latest news or a message while you are talking with them.

Nowadays, norms have to adapt to interactions taking place online on SNSs as well. In contrast to offline interactions, the context during online interaction on SNSs is more ambiguous and conventional cues may not apply. Information on SNSs is shared between individuals who do not necessarily experience the same context. For example, some user may only share information with their closest friends on SNSs, whereas other users may by default share information with anyone on their friend list. Similarly, two users can differ in their privacy settings, one using the strictest privacy settings while the other has left his profile wide open. Both situations are not always transparent, resulting in users differing in what they consider appropriate and whether the shared information can be distributed outside of the SNS profile.

1.2 Related Work

Although it seems generally accepted that norms play an important role in online privacy regulation, relatively few studies have investigated the role of informational norms on SNSs. The studies that have generally focused on adolescents, show the importance of norms in online information sharing. Ito and colleagues concluded, based on their ethnographic approach, that online communications of youth, including those taking place on SNSs, are grounded in norms and reciprocity (2008). Similarly, boyd and Marwick identified an adherence to norms that condemned distribution of their online information on SNSs among youth (2011). Mesch and Beker explored the adherence of norms of appropriateness amongst 12 to 17-year-olds and concluded that there is a relationship between norm adherence and online disclosures (2010).

Most studies investigating the use of SNSs in relation to privacy focus on why users share information on SNSs and to what degree they manipulate their privacy settings in order to protect the shared information. Most of these studies focused on young adults (Acquisti and Gross 2006; Debatin et al. 2009; Govani and Pashley 2005; Gross and Acquisti 2005; Tufekci 2008), while some compared adolescents with adults (Christofides et al. 2012; Pfeil et al. 2009). Often the conclusion is drawn that young users do not care about their privacy since they share a lot of information online and do not change their privacy settings.

However, as argued before, norms may be the most important regulatory force for users to rely on to protect privacy on SNSs. The role of norms is often not taken into consideration when analysing online behaviour from a privacy perspective. Taking the adherence to informational norms into account could explain why previous studies often find no relationship between privacy concern and information sharing on SNSs (Acquisti and Gross 2006; Tufekci 2008) or often report the underuse of privacy settings by SNS users (Govani and Pashley 2005). Respondents may instead rely on informational norms to protect the information they share on their profile.

As mentioned before, one of the research goals of this chapter is to investigate the differences in norm adherence between SNS users of different age groups. boyd and Marwick (2011) have argued that for youth norms are an important element in safeguarding their privacy online. However, if these norms are not shared or recognised by older individuals they will have different privacy expectations regarding their online information. Subsequently, if younger individuals are indeed found to rely differently or more heavily on norms of appropriateness and distribution on SNSs compared to older individuals, this could help understand why young people often seem careless about their privacy, while they themselves report to be concerned with their privacy.

1.3 Current Study

The current study will contribute to existing knowledge by investigating the role informational norms of appropriateness and distribution play in relation to privacy on SNSs by addressing three research goals. First, the norms associated with sharing information on a SNS profile will be compared with the norms associated with a public and private offline interaction to determine if a distinct normative expectation has developed for information shared on a SNS profiles and how public or private the shared information on an SNS profile is considered. Second, the adherence to informational norms of adolescents (12 to 19-year-olds), young adults (20 to 30-year-olds) and adults (31-year-old and older) will be compared, to provide additional insight into the often observed differences in online behaviour between young and old. Third, the relationship between informational norms and actual information sharing on SNSs will be explored to assess the actual importance of informational norms in relation to the sharing of information on SNS profiles. Next, exact research hypotheses and questions will be formulated.

The first research goal concerns comparing the SNS profile context with a public and private offline context. It can be expected that there is a general consensus in how a public and private context in offline interaction are distinguished in relation to the associated norms. During a private offline interaction, i.e. a one-to-one talk with a friend, more information is appropriate for sharing, but what is shared during the interaction should not be distributed further. During a public offline interaction, i.e. a conversation with several friends, less content is appropriate for sharing, but it is less objectionable to distribute what is shared during the interaction with others. SNS profiles are generally considered public spaces, but at the same time young users can demand privacy in these areas claiming that parents and teachers should not look at the information shared on a profile just because they can (boyd 2007; Leenes 2010, p. 56). One could therefore wonder whether a distinct normative expectation has developed for the sharing of information on SNS profiles and whether this normative expectation suggests that the shared information is considered public or private. This study will therefore investigate how interactions on an SNS profile relate to a public or private offline context by addressing the following research question:

Research Question 1: How do informational norms associated with sharing information on an SNS profile relate to the informational norms associated with sharing information in an offline public or private context?

The second research goal concerns comparing adherence to the informational norms by three age groups. Adolescents (Christofides et al. 2012; Pfeil et al. 2009) and young adults (Debatin et al. 2009; Govani and Pashley 2005; Gross and Acquisti 2005) are generally found to disclose more information on SNSs than adults, and thus more likely to find this information appropriate for sharing as well. One possible explanation for this is that they consider SNSs to be more private places, as opposed to adults who may consider them more public, like everything else on the Internet (boyd and Marwick 2011). Therefore, younger individuals are expected to consider information shared on their SNS profile as not suitable for further distribution outside of the profile, as this is expected to be considered suitable only for information shared in a public context. The following hypotheses summarise the expectations in relation to the different age groups:

Hypothesis 1a: Compared to adults, adolescents and young adults will consider it more appropriate to share information on an SNS profile.

Hypothesis 1b: Compared to adults, adolescents and young adults will consider information shared on an SNS profile less suitable for further distribution beyond the original context.

Finally, the third goal is to explore the relationship between the informational norms and actual information disclosure. Respondents who consider more information is appropriate for sharing on their SNS profile are expected to actually share more information as well. This expectation matches the results of Mesch and Beker, who found positive correlations between self-disclosure and being all right with sharing offline or online personal information (2010). This chapter will expand on these findings by investigating a broader age group, but also by investigating norms of distribution. Individuals who consider what they share on their SNS profile to be suitable for further distribution are expected to disclose less. Again, these expectations have been summarised in two hypotheses:

Hypothesis 2a: Considering it more appropriate to share information on an SNS profile will be positively related to actual sharing of information on an SNS profile.

Hypothesis 2b: Considering the shared information on an SNS profile suitable for distribution beyond the original context will be negatively related to actual sharing of information on an SNS profile.

2 Method

2.1 Participants

Data were collected from 19 July to 4 August 2011 by the research institute TNS-NIPO[2] through an online survey, which allowed respondents to participate from their own computer at home. Respondents were recruited through a stratified sampling procedure. In total, 1008 respondents aged 12 to 83-years-old with a profile on an SNS completed the questionnaire. Six respondents were removed from the sample as they explicitly stated having created their profile merely for a different purpose (e.g. as requirement for using another site). Of the remaining 1002 respondents, 125 (12.5 %) only have a profile on Facebook, 365 (36.4 %) only have a profile on Hyves[3] and 512 (51.1 %) have a profile on both sites. Respondents using both Hyves and Facebook were prompted to answer the items for the SNS they used most. From the respondents reporting to use both, 268 respondents reported using Hyves the most (52.3 %) versus 244 using Facebook most (47.7 %).

Of all respondents, 372 were adolescents (12 to 19-year-olds, $M=14.60$, $SD=2.16$), 277 were young adults (20 to 30-year-olds, $M=25.55$, $SD=3.10$), and 353 were adults (31-year-olds and older, $M=46.22$, $SD=12.12$). Respondents were asked for their consent to participate in the research survey and parents provided consent for individuals younger than 18 years old. All respondents were rewarded with special credits upon completion of a survey which they can trade for various coupons with TNS-NIPO.

Gender distribution was uneven over the three age groups with males making up 47.0 %, 28.9 % and 41.1 % respectively. To control for possible gender differences when exploring the differences between the age groups, the analyses between age groups were done twice: once with the normal data and once with all cases weighted for gender distribution.[4] The weighted analysis did not show any meaningful deviations. Therefore, the data without weights have been used and will be reported here.

2.2 Measures

This study explored what norms exist on SNSs and their role in relation to information disclosure. Adolescents, young adults and adults were investigated to find differences in what norms they thought applied for information shared during a public conversation with a group of friends (*public context*), a private conversation with

---

[2] www.tns-nipo.nl

[3] www.hyves.nl; the most popular Dutch social network site.

[4] Weights were obtained by dividing the population distribution with the sample distribution. Information concerning the population gender distribution of the Netherlands was obtained from statline.cbs.nl in August 2011.

one friend (*private context*), or sharing information with contacts on an SNS profile (*profile context*). Of interest were norms of appropriateness, i.e. what information is deemed appropriate and whether reciprocity is expected and norms of distribution, i.e. how public the shared information is and whether information is allowed to be distributed to others. In addition, their role in relation to *information disclosure* on social network sites, when controlling for *privacy attitudes* and the *private profile* of respondents, was explored.

Norms of Appropriateness In order to assess the norms of appropriateness, respondents' adherence to reciprocity and the amount of information they considered appropriate in each context was assessed. Reciprocity was assessed through three items for each context on a four point Likert scale from 1 (completely disagree) to 4 (completely agree), and an option *don't know*. Respondents were asked for each context whether they agreed with the following statements[5]: I tell them (share) as much about myself as they (contacts) tell (share) about themselves, I believe everyone has (all contacts have) the right to know the same amount about each other, they (contacts) should tell (share) as much about themselves as I do. For each context, the three items were reduced to a single *reciprocity* scale with a Cronbach alpha of .773, .863 and .812, for the public, private and profile context respectively.

In addition, respondents were presented with a list of 15 topics and asked to mark the topics they thought appropriate to share in the context (*appropriateness*). Respondents had to judge the 15 topics separately for each of the three contexts. The list consisted of the topics: *health, educational or work results, current education or work, finance, relation, family, religion, political preferences, parties, sensitive topics, personal success, personal worries, home address, telephone number, interests.* The resulting scale ran from 0 to 15.

Norms of Distribution The norms of distribution were assessed through three items on a 4-point Likert scale from 1 (completely disagree) to 4 (completely agree), and one option: *don't know*. These items concerned the informational flow out of the context by the self (*information flow self*): I tell others what I have heard during the conversation (seen on Facebook/Hyves); the informational flow out of the context by others (*information flow others*): everything I tell during the conversation (share on my profile) about myself my friends (contacts) can tell to others (non-contacts); how public the conversation or information is considered to be (*publicity*): others are allowed to listen in on the conversation (non-contacts are allowed to look at the information I share).

Information Disclosure Profile information and information shared through public posts were addressed separately. Respondents were asked to indicate whether they shared each of the following 12 types of profile information using yes/no questions: *name*, *age*, *gender*, *birthday*, *address* (city), *address* (street name and number), *e-mail*, *relationship status*, *current work* or *school, religion*, *interests* and *phone*

[5] Deviations for the items in relation to the profile context added in parentheses.

number. Next, respondents were asked how frequently they shared a public post on their profile using a 7-point scale (*never, once a month, several times a month, once a week, several times a week, once a day*, or *several times a day*) with a lower score indicating less frequency. Furthermore, respondents were asked if they discussed the following 11 topics in their public posts using yes/no questions: *health, school/ work results, finance, relationships, family, religion, politics, parties, emotional topics, personal success* and *personal worries*.

Private Profile Of interest was whether respondents had manipulated their privacy settings to only allow contacts to access the information shared on the profile. Response possibilities were *I know how to and I have done so, I know how to but I did not do so, I don't know how, but I let someone do it*, and *I don't know how and I have not let someone do so*. The majority of respondents reported having manipulated the settings themselves or not at all. Therefore, responses were collapsed into the dichotomous variable *done* and *not done*.

Privacy Attitude Respondents' privacy attitudes were obtained through four items with a 4-point Likert scale from (1) completely disagree to (4) completely agree. The items assess to what degree respondents were concerned about privacy, think privacy important, feel they have too little privacy and consider the Internet a danger. The four items were combined into a single *privacy attitude* scale with an acceptable Cronbach alpha of .703.

3 Results

3.1 Online Versus Offline Context

The first research question concerned how the norms associated with information sharing on an SNS profile would relate to the norms associated with sharing information in an offline public or private context. Table 1 presents the responses of respondents to the norm items for all three contexts. A repeated measures ANOVA was used to test for differences in norm adherence between the three contexts. Results show that there was a significant effect of context on adherence to the norms; the critical statistical information for the analysis is provided in Appendix A. Bonferroni post hoc comparisons showed that all means presented in Table 1 differed significantly across the three contexts with $p < .001$, except for the difference between the public and profile context for information flow others, which differed with a $p = .011$.

The norms associated with the private or public context differed as would be expected. On the one hand, more topics are considered appropriate (*appropriateness*) and reciprocity (*reciprocity*) is considered more appropriate during a private conversation with a single friend (*private context*) as opposed to having a

Table 1 Mean descriptive of responses to norm items

	Private			Public			Profile		
	N	Mean	S.D.	N	Mean	S.D.	N	Mean	S.D.
Appropriateness	1002	8.17	4.726	1002	5.26	3.401	1002	3.84	2.397
Reciprocity	861	2.58	.714	844	2.44	.662	816	1.79	.677
Information flow self	914	1.77	.747	912	1.97	.766	872	2.66	.832
Information flow others	914	1.67	.725	920	2.27	.865	867	2.41	.848
Publicity	918	1.73	.738	929	2.33	.809	875	1.98	.889

Note. Scales for publicity, information flow self, information flow others, and reciprocity are 1 (disagree completely) to 4 (agree completely). Reciprocity is the average of three items. For appropriateness, respondents were asked about 15 topics in total

conversation with a group of friends (*public context*). On the other hand, it is considered less suitable for the information shared in a conversation with a single friend to be shared with others later on either by the self (*information flow self*) or by the conversation partner (*information flow others*). Similarly, it is considered less suitable for others to overhear the conversation (*Publicity*) in the private context.

Comparing the norms associated with sharing information on an SNS profile (*profile context*) with the offline public and private context suggests that SNSs are primarily considered to be very public places. It is considered even less appropriate to reciprocate information shared on an SNS profile and less information is considered appropriate for sharing on an SNS profile compared to the offline contexts. Furthermore, sharing the information shared on an SNS profile with non-contacts, either by oneself or others, is considered more suitable than the sharing of information heard in a public or private conversation. The only exception to this trend is that non-contacts looking at information shared on the profile is considered less suitable than others listening in on a conversation held with friends in public.

In answer to the research question, the comparison of the norms associated with sharing information on an SNS profile with both offline contexts indicates that SNS profiles are generally considered to be very public places. Even less information is considered appropriate for sharing on an SNS profile than during a public offline conversation and the shared information is considered even more suitable to be distributed outside of the context. *Publicity* is the only exception; although it is deemed more appropriate for non-contacts to overlook information shared on the profile than others overhearing a private conversation, it is deemed less appropriate compared to others overhearing a public conversation.

3.2 Age Related Differences

The first hypothesis investigated the differences between adolescents, young adults and adults with respect to norm adherence in profile context. Adolescents and young adults were expected to consider sharing information on an SNS profile more

Table 2 Comparison of norm adherence in the profile context between age groups

	Adolescents			Young adults			Adults		
Profile context	N	Mean	S.D.	N	Mean	S.D.	N	Mean	S.D.
Appropriateness	372	3.74	2.44	277	4.61[a]***	2.63	353	3.36[b]***	1.98
Reciprocity	280	1.93	.69	231	1.74[a]**	.66	305	1.70[a]***	.68
Information flow self	300	2.60	.83	248	2.80[a]*	.79	324	2.61[b]*	.83
Information flow others	302	2.31	.86	245	2.52[a]*	.79	320	2.41	.85
Publicity	303	1.94	.88	248	1.93	.86	324	2.04	.91

Note. Scales for publicity, information flow self, information flow others, and reciprocity are 1 (disagree completely) to 4 (agree completely). Reciprocity is the average of three items. For appropriateness, respondents were asked about 15 topics in total

The superscript *a* indicates a significant difference between 12 to 19-year-olds and the older categories, the superscript *b* indicates a significant difference between 20 to 30-year-olds and 31-year-old and older

Note. Reported p-values are based on post hoc analyses. * $p<.05$, ** $p<.01$, *** $p<.001$

appropriate compared to adults and to consider the information shared on an SNS profile less suitable for further distribution beyond the original context. Table 2 gives an overview of all the mean scores respondents from the various age groups scored on the informational norm items concerning the profile context.

Exploring the norms of appropriateness, a significant age effect was found for both *appropriateness*, $F(2, 999)=22.57$, $p<.001$, $\eta^2=.04$, and *reciprocity*, $F(2, 813)=10.17$, $p<.001$, $\eta^2=.02$. Post hoc analysis showed that young adults considered most topics to be appropriate for sharing on an SNS profile compared to adolescents and adults who did not differ from each other significantly, while adolescents considered reciprocating information shared on a SNS profile more appropriate compared to both young adults and adults who did not differ significantly. These results support the first part of the hypothesis; adolescents and young adults consider sharing information on a SNS profile more appropriate. While young adults consider more topics appropriate for sharing, adolescents consider reciprocation of information more appropriate on an SNS profile.

Next, the norms of distribution were explored. A significant age effect was found for *information flow self*, $F(2, 869)=5.00$, $p=.007$, $\eta^2=.01$, *information flow others*, $F(2, 864)=4.36$, $p=.013$, $\eta^2=.01$, but not for *publicity*, $F(2, 872)=1.50$, $p=.225$, $\eta^2=.00$. Post hoc analysis showed that young adults considered telling others about what their contacts shared on an SNS profile most suitable compared to adolescents and adults who did not differ significantly. Similarly, young adults considered their contacts sharing with others what they themselves shared on their SNS profile also as most suitable. This difference is only significant compared to adolescents who considered this least suitable. These results do not support the second part of the hypothesis; on the contrary, young adults considered the information shared on an SNS profile more suitable for further distribution, whereas adolescents and adults did not differ. The differences found for the norms of distribution were less significant than those for the informational norms of appropriateness.

Appendix B offers the tables for the public and private contexts and comparison will show similar differences between the age groups concerning norms associated with the offline contexts. This suggests that the observed differences between the age groups is not specific for norms associated with SNS profiles as similar differences also exist for norms associated with the offline contexts.

3.3 Norms and Online Information Sharing

The final research question concerned the actual relationship between the informational norms and information sharing on social network sites. Considering sharing information on an SNS profile to be more appropriate was expected to be positively related to actual information sharing, while considering the distribution of the shared information more appropriate was expected to be negatively related to actual information sharing on an SNS profile.

First, a comparison was made between the number of topics respondents deemed appropriate for sharing on an SNS profile and the number of topics respondents reported to have shared on their profile. The latter number was obtained by combining the responses to the relevant topics for *post content* and *profile* information together to obtain a similar list of topics that was presented to respondents for *appropriateness*. On average, respondents deemed 3.845 (SD=2.397) pieces of information appropriate for sharing on an SNS, while reporting to have actually shared 5.284 (SD=3.344) of these topics on their profile on average. Paired sample *t*-test shows that the amount actually disclosed is significantly more than what is deemed appropriate, t $(1001)=13.438$, $p<.001$, $d=0.42$. In other words, respondents generally post more information than they deem appropriate on SNSs.

Next, linear regression analysis was used to explore the relationship between the informational norms associated with an SNS profile and information sharing on SNS profiles. Respondents' *post frequency*, *post content* and *profile information* were analysed in turn, using a stepwise procedure. In the first step several background variables were included in the model: *age*, *gender*, *privacy attitude* and *private profile*. Age was included in the form of two dummy variables: *dummy YA* provides the difference between adolescents and young adults, and *dummy A* provides the difference between adolescents and adults. In the second step the informational norms relating to SNS profiles were added. This step allows the relationship between the informational norms associated with an SNS profile and information sharing to be determined while controlling for the variables included in step 1. Finally, in the third step the informational norms relating to the public and private context were added. This made it possible to assess to what degree information sharing on SNS profiles is primarily related to informational norms associated with SNS profiles or to informational norms in general. If the former is true, this last step should not cause a significant improvement of the model.

Table 3 gives an overview of the fit parameters of all three steps for the linear regression models. It can be seen that while every model was significant, only step

Table 3 Fit parameters of stepwise linear regression models

	Post frequency	Post content	Profile information
Step 1: Control variables			
R2Δ	.093***	.107***	.032***
F	14.215***	16.560***	4.599***
Step 2: Profile norms			
R2Δ	.032***	.063***	.059***
F	9.801***	14.009***	6.872***
Step 3: Public & private norms			
R2Δ	.013	.027*	.015
F	5.427***	8.273***	4.019***

Note. * $p<.05$, *** $p<.001$

1 and 2 were significant improvements of the model and step 3 only provided a marginal improvement for *post content*. Step 2 of the model was therefore rated as giving the best model, indicating that it is primarily the informational norms associated with an SNS profile which have a relationship with the actual information sharing as opposed to informational norms in general. The linear regression was done again omitting step 3 to increase the number of respondents included in the analysis (N=696 versus N=782).

In step 1 of the models, *private profile* had a significant relationship with *post content* and *post frequency*, and *privacy attitude* with *profile information* and *post frequency*. After inclusion of the informational norms associated with SNS profiles in step 2, only the significant relationship between *private profile* and *post frequency* remains. Table 4 provides an overview of the results from the final analysis. *Appropriateness, reciprocity* and *information self* have a significant relationship with two or all of the indices of information sharing on an SNS profile. Further inspection of Table 4 shows that females post more frequently and about more topics than males, and young adults post about more topics and share more profile information than adolescents, while adults post less frequently and about fewer topics compared to adolescents.

Testing the hypothesis, the results in Table 4 support the first part of the second hypothesis that considering it to be more appropriate to share information on an SNS profile would be positively related to actual information sharing. *Appropriateness* has a significant and positive relationship with all three indices of information sharing; respondents who consider more topics appropriate for sharing on an SNS profile post more frequently, about more topics and also share more profile information. Similarly, *reciprocity* has a significant positive relationship with *post frequency* and *post content*; respondents who deem reciprocity to be appropriate on an SNS profile post more frequently and about more topics.

Only partial support is found for the second part of the second hypothesis, that considering the distribution of the shared information more appropriate would be negatively related to actual information sharing on an SNS profile. Only for *Information flow self* was a significant negative relationship found with *Post fre-*

Table 4 Predictors of sharing information on SNS profile

	Post frequency	Post content	Profile information
N	782	782	782
R^2	.129	.180	.096
F	11.426***	16.941***	8.192***
Gender (male = 0)	.459 (.124)***	.400 (.195)*	−.152 (.159)
Age YA (Young adults = 1)	−.281 (.156)	.815 (.245)**	.825 (.199)***
Age A (Adults = 1)	−.806 (.144)***	−.848 (.226)***	.362 (.184)*
Private profile (not done = 0)	.377 (.144)**	.362 (.227)	.152 (.184)
Privacy attitude	.209 (.119)	−.004 (.176)	.203 (.143)
Appropriateness	.093 (.027)**	.301 (.042)***	.218 (.034)***
Reciprocity	.255 (.093)**	.437 (.147)**	.218 (.119)
Information flow self	−.317 (.082)***	−.098 (.128)	−.340 (.104)**
Information flow others	.151 (.086)	.151 (.135)	.128 (.110)
Publicity	.039 (.081)	−.075 (.127)	.020 (.103)
Constant	2.611	1.250	5.201

Note. Non-standardised coefficients with standard errors in parentheses
Profile information scored from 0 to 12 options revealed. Post content scored from 0 to 11 topics. Post frequency scored from 7 for *never* to 1 for *several times per day*. A higher score on *privacy attitudes* signifies more concern with privacy
* $p<.05$, ** $p<.01$, *** $p<.001$

quency and *Post content*; respondents who consider it suitable for themselves to share information shared by contacts on an SNS profile with non-contacts post less frequently and share less profile information.

4 Discussion

The goal of this study was to investigate the relationship between online informational norms and information sharing on SNSs and online privacy. The results presented in this chapter provide several insights. First of all, comparison of the reported adherence to informational norms in a public, private or profile context indicate that the normative expectations associated with an SNS profile is that of a very public place. Second, distinct differences were found in the normative expectations adolescents, young adults and adults associate with an SNS profile, which primarily concern norms of appropriateness. Third, the informational norms associated with an SNS profile showed a stronger relationship with actual information sharing on SNS profiles than privacy attitudes or using privacy settings. Next, these findings will be further discussed in turn.

The results indicated that SNS users are generally aware that SNSs are public spaces and have adjusted their normative expectations accordingly. SNSs even remain somewhat public when SNS users make use of the privacy settings to limit access to the information shared on their profile for contacts only, as these contacts can still include individuals from various social spheres (e.g. family, work and friends) and strangers (Binder et al. 2009; Lampinen et al. 2009). Respondents generally indicated that a few topics are appropriate for sharing on an SNS profile but that reciprocity is not appropriate. Concerning the norms of distribution, respondents appeared to make a distinction as to how shared information is allowed to be distributed from SNS profiles. While it was considered suitable for contacts to share the information with non-contacts (*information flow others*), non-contacts were absolutely not allowed to look at the shared information directly (*publicity*). Perhaps users expect that if the shared information is distributed by contacts, this information will be better contextualised than when non-contacts look at that information directly with little sense of the context.

The results further showed that compared to adults, adolescents and young adults consider it more appropriate to share information on an SNS profile, although adolescents and young adults differ in the way how. While young adults considered most topics to be appropriate for sharing on an SNS profile, adolescents disagreed the least with the suitability of reciprocating shared information on an SNS profile. In other words, when adolescents share more information than adults on an SNS profile (Christofides et al. 2012; Pfeil et al. 2009) this may in part have a reciprocal motivation. They share as much about themselves as their friends share about themselves and therefore consider it less troublesome than individuals outside of this reciprocal circle (e.g. adults or parents). For this latter group these disclosures on an SNS profile may seem to indicate a lack of concern for privacy.

Comparison of adherence to norms of distribution between adults, adolescents and young adults showed an opposite relationship than the one hypothesised; young adults considered the information shared on an SNS profile most suitable for further distribution by themselves or by their contacts. Only for the norm *publicity* no differences were found between the age groups. Previous studies generally observed a sentiment amongst younger respondents that parents have no business looking at their profiles (Leenes 2010, p. 56). In 2007, boyd also identified this sentiment amongst youth that parents and teachers should not visit their profiles just because they could. Indeed, the norm *publicity* was the only norm that indicated that SNS profiles are considered more private as a domain than a public conversation. However, with the rise of adult SNS users (Hampton et al. 2011), adults and teachers may now share this normative expectation with younger SNS users.

The differences between the age groups in norm adherence are not unique to the SNS profile context. The tables in Appendix B presented similar differences between the age groups for the offline public and private contexts. This suggests that the rise of SNSs as medium for interaction has not caused a difference in norm adherence between younger and older individuals. Instead, it seems likely that differences in informational norm adherence already existed in relation to offline conversations as well, but that the social overlap on SNSs magnifies these differences and creates a cause for conflict. In other words, when adolescents are interacting with friends face-to-face, they will act differently from an adult interacting with friends, but either group generally does not experience the conversation of the other.

Online, however, both adults and adolescents now interact on the same medium (e.g. SNSs) making the differing normative expectations all the more apparent.

The last analyses investigated the relationship between the informational norms and actual information sharing on SNS profiles. The results suggest that SNS users do not necessarily abide by the normative expectations they themselves report. Respondents generally reported to have disclosed more topics on their profile than they themselves deem to be appropriate. Despite this, a strong relationship was found between the informational norms and actual information disclosed. In fact, the informational norms associated with an SNS profile distinguished themselves from the informational norms associated with the other offline contexts as main predictors of the actual information shared on SNS profiles. This suggests that SNS users have a unique set of normative expectations which they associate with SNS profiles.

While only marginal support was found for the negative relationship between actual information sharing on an SNS profile and the norms of distribution, strong support was found for the positive relationship with the norms of appropriateness and actual information sharing on an SNS profile. In line with the findings of Mesch and Beker (2010), respondents who found more topics appropriate for sharing on an SNS profile, posted more frequently and about more topics and shared more profile information themselves. Similarly, respondents who adhere more to the norm of reciprocity also post more frequently and about more topics, but do not share more profile information. As a result, SNS users who strongly adhere to the informational norms of appropriateness and thus share a lot of information, will be seen as careless of privacy by those who do not adhere to this norm. Concerning the norms of distribution, respondents who believe they have the right to share information shared on a profile (*information flow self*), post less frequently themselves and share less profile information. The individuals adhering to this norm will experience SNS profiles differently compared to individuals who do not adhere to this norm. This can have important privacy implications when the shared information by SNS users who do not adhere to this norm becomes distributed by those who do adhere to this norm and therefore put a different privacy value on the shared information.

The adherence to these norms of appropriateness proved to be better predictors of actual information sharing than the privacy attitudes held by respondents or whether or not they had set their profile to private. These results are in line with previous studies which found no relationship between privacy attitudes and information disclosure on SNSs (Acquisti and Gross 2006; Tufekci 2008). Instead, the adherence to informational norms on SNSs had the strongest relationship with information sharing even when taking architectural regulators, which can affect how publicly or privately the profile is experienced (e.g. privacy settings), into account. This strongly supports the fact that norms play an important role in managing online privacy and the decision to disclose information (boyd and Marwick 2011). When SNS users share information on their profile, they have normative expectations of whether it is appropriate to do so or not on an SNS profile, distinct from their normative expectations from offline interactions.

To conclude, norms regulating privacy during social interaction appear to have made the transition to SNSs. Not only do SNS users report a unique set of normative expectations associated with SNS profiles compared to other contexts, but these informational norms associated with the SNS profile also have a strong relationship with actual information sharing on SNSs. These findings strongly suggest an important role for informational norms concerning individuals behaviour on SNSs. Considering that the architecture of SNS is designed to share as much information as possible (Peterson 2010) while the actual audience is often difficult if not impossible to determine (Bernstein et al. 2013), the role norms play in safeguarding online privacy may be an important one and should not be overlooked. However, because of the differences in norm adherence between different age groups and the fact that SNS users do not necessarily abide by their own norms, it is clear that norms in themselves are not enough as yet to safeguard the privacy of SNS users from each other.

4.1 Limitations and Recommendations

When interpreting the results presented in this chapter, it is important to consider that while the assumption is that informational norms influence information sharing, no causality was obtained in this study. As a result, the reported norm adherence observed here could also be a rationalisation of respondents' actual behaviour. In other words, their normative expectations associated with SNS profiles are the result of their initial behaviour when first introduced to the sites. Future studies might want to establish the causality between the normative expectations associated with SNS profiles and actual behaviour.

Secondly, the norm items used in this study primarily referred to interaction with friends. This was most likely interpreted by respondents as friends from an age group similar to their own. However, one of the problems of SNSs these days is that both adults and adolescents have joined the same online conversation. It would therefore be interesting to know what norms adolescents adhere to when interacting with an adult and vice versa. This would be able to provide further insights in relation to potential misunderstandings between younger and older individuals.

Appendixes

Appendix A

Table 5 Critical statistical information and effect sizes for the repeated measure ANOVA performed on the effect of context for the means reported in Table 1

	Mauchly's test			Huynh-Feldt estimates			
	χ^2 (DF=2)	p	ε	F	DF	p	$\eta^2_{partial}$
Appropriateness	98.66	.000	.89	562.79	1.8, 1230.2	.000	.45
Reciprocity	122.45	.000	.86	500.54	1.7, 1199.2	.000	.42
Information flow self	82.16	.000	.90	321.40	1.8, 1253.4	.000	.32
Information flow others	5.88	.053	.99	232.73	2.0, 1382.3	.000	.25
Publicity	36.83	.000	.95	119.68	1.9, 1325.2	.000	.15

Note. Huynh-Feldt estimates were used since the assumption of sphericity was violated according to the Mauchly's test

Appendix B

Table 6 Comparison of norm adherence in the public context between age groups

	Adolescents			Young adults			Adults		
Public context	N	Mean	S.D.	N	Mean	S.D.	N	Mean	S.D.
Appropriateness	372	4.81	3.14	277	6.37^{a***}	3.86	353	4.85^{b***}	3.08
Reciprocity	289	2.62	.63	234	2.42^{a**}	.62	321	2.30^{a***}	.68
Information flow self	321	2.01	.79	254	2.06	.76	337	1.88^{b**}	.74
Information flow others	323	2.20	.86	262	2.20	.84	335	2.40^{a**b*}	.87
Publicity	331	2.31	.81	262	2.33	.80	336	235	.82

Note. Scales for publicity, information flow self, information flow others, and reciprocity was 1 (disagree completely) to 4 (agree completely). Reciprocity is the average of three items. For appropriateness, respondents were asked about 15 topics in total

The superscript *a* indicates a significant difference between 12- to 19-year-olds and the older categories, the superscript *b* indicates a significant difference between 20- to 30-year-olds and 31-year-old and older

Note. * $p<.05$, ** $p<.01$, *** $p<.001$

Table 7 Comparison of norm adherence in the private context between age groups

	Adolescents			Young adults			Adults		
Private context	N	Mean	S.D.	N	Mean	S.D.	N	Mean	S.D.
Appropriateness	372	7.10	4.42	277	9.78[a***]	4.94	353	8.06[a*b***]	4.53
Reciprocity	295	2.77	.68	246	2.53[a***]	.67	320	2.45[a***]	.74
Information flow self	325	1.82	.78	254	1.87	.75	335	1.64[a*b**]	.70
Information flow others	327	1.65	.73	255	1.70	.73	332	1.67	.72
Publicity	328	1.79	.77	256	1.74	.73	334	1.67	.71

Note. Scales for publicity, information flow self, information flow others, and reciprocity was 1 (disagree completely) to 4 (agree completely). Reciprocity is the average of three items. For appropriateness, respondents were asked about 15 topics in total

The superscript *a* indicates a significant difference between 12- to 19-year-olds and the older categories, the superscript *b* indicates a significant difference between 20- to 30-year-olds and 31-year-old and older

Note. * $p<.05$, ** $p<.01$, *** $p<.001$

References

Acquisti, A., & Gross, R. (2006). *Imagined communities: Awareness, information sharing, and privacy on the Facebook.* Paper presented at the 6th Workshop on Privacy Enhancing Technologies, Cambridge, UK.

Altman, I. (1975). *The environment and social behavior.* Monterey: Brooks/Cole Publishing Company.

Andrews, L. (2012, February 4). Facebook is using you. *The New York Times.* http://www.nytimes.com. Accessed 5 July 2012.

Bernstein, M. S., Bakshy, E., Burke, M., & Karrer, B. (2013). *Quantifying the invisible audience in social networks.* Paper presented at the CHI, Paris, France.

Binder, J., Howes, A., & Sutcliffe, A. (2009). *The problem of conflicting social spheres: Effects of network structure on experienced tension in social network sites.* Paper presented at the CHI, Boston, MA.

boyd, d. (2007). Why youth (heart) social network sites: The role of networked publics in teenage social life. In D. Buckingham (Ed.), *Youth, identity, and digital media* (pp. 119–142). Cambridge, MA: MIT Press.

boyd, d. m. (2008). *Taken out of context: American teen sociality in networked publics.* PhD diss., University of California.

boyd, d. m., & Marwick, A. E. (2011). *Social privacy in networked publics: Teens' attitudes, practices, and strategies.* Paper presented at the A Decade in Internet Time: Symposium on the Dynamics of the Internet and Society, Oxford.

Christofides, E., Muise, A., & Desmarais, S. (2012). Hey mom, what's on your Facebook? Comparing Facebook disclosure and privacy in adolescents and adults. *Social Psychological and Personality Science, 3*(1), 48–54.

Debatin, B., Lovejoy, J. P., Horn, A., & Hughes, B. N. (2009). Facebook and online privacy: Attitudes, behaviors, and unintended consequences. *Journal of Computer-Mediated Communication, 15*(1), 83–108.

Derlega, V. J., & Chaikin, A. L. (1977). Privacy and self-disclosure in social relationships. *Journal of Social Issues, 33*(3), 102–115.

Govani, T., & Pashley, H. (2005). *Student awareness of the privacy implications when using Facebook*. http://lorrie.cranor.org/courses/fa05/tubzhlp.pdf. Accessed Sept 2010.

Gross, R., & Acquisti, A. (2005). *Information revelation and privacy in online social networks*. Paper presented at the proceedings of the ACM Workshop on Privacy in the Electronic Society, Alexandria, VA, USA.

Hampton, K. N., Gourlet, L. S., Rainie, L., & Purcell, K. (2011). *Social networking sites and our lives*. Pew Internet & American Life Project report. Available at: http://www.pewinternet.org/Reports/2011/Technology-and-social-networks.aspx

Herring, S. C. (2008). Questioning the generational divide: Technological exoticism and adult constructions of online youth identity. In D. Buckingham (Ed.), *Youth, identity, and digital media* (pp. 71–94). Cambridge, MA: MIT Press.

Ito, M., Horst, H. A., Bittani, M., boyd, d. m., Herr-Stephenson, B., Lange, P. G., Pascoe, C. J., & Robinson, L. (2008). *Living and learning with new media: Summary of findings from the digital youth project*. http://digitalyouth.ischool.berkeley.edu/files/report/digitalyouth-WhitePaper.pdf. Accessed 7 Mar 2013.

Johnson, J. L. (1989). Privacy and the judgements of others. *The Journal of Value Inquiry, 23*, 157–168.

Johnson, B. (2010, January 1). Privacy no longer a social norm, says Facebook founder. *The Guardian*. http://www.guardian.co.uk/technology/2010/jan/11/facebook-privacy. Accessed 14 Nov 2011.

Lampinen, A., Tamminen, S., & Oulasvirta, A. (2009). *"All my people right here, right now": Management of group co-presence on a social networking site*. Paper presented at the International Conference on Supporting Group Work, Sanibel Island, FL, USA.

Leenes, R. (2010). Context is everything. Sociality and privacy in online social network sites. *Privacy and Identity, 320*, 48–65.

Lessig, L. (1999). *Code and other laws of cyberspace*. New York: Basic Books.

Livingstone, S. (2008). Taking risky opportunities in youthful content creation: Teenagers' use of social networking sites for intimacy, privacy and self-expression. *New Media & Society, 10*(3), 393–411.

Marwick, A. E., Diaz, D. M., & Palfrey, J. (2010). *Youth, privacy and reputation*. Available at: http://ssrn.com/abstract=1588163

Mesch, G. S., & Beker, G. (2010). Are norms of disclosure of online and offline personal information associated with the disclosure of personal information online. *Human Communication Research, 36*(4), 570–592.

Moore, B. (1984). *Privacy: Studies in social and cultural history*. New York/London: M.E. Sharpe Inc.

Nissenbaum, H. F. (2004). Privacy as contextual integrity. *Washington Law Review, 79*(1), 119–158.

Nissenbaum, H. F. (2010). *Privacy in context. Technology, policy, and the integrity of social life*. Palo Alto: Stanford University Press.

Pekárek, M., & Leenes, R. (2009). *Privacy and social network sites: Follow the money*. Paper presented at the W3C Workshop on the Future of Social Networking, Barcelona, Spain

Peterson, C. (2010). *Losing face: An environmental analysis of privacy on Facebook*. Available at: http://works.bepress.com/cgi/viewcontent.cgi?article=1001&context=cpeterson

Petronio, S. (2002). *Boundaries of privacy: Dialectics of disclosure*. Albany: State University of New York Press.

Pfeil, U., Arjan, R., & Zaphiris, P. (2009). Age differences in online social networking – A study of user profiles and the social capital divide among teenagers and older users in MySpace. *Computers in Human Behavior, 25*(3), 643–654.

Raynes-Goldie, K. (2010). Aliases, creeping, and wall cleaning: Understanding privacy in the age of Facebook. *First Monday, 15*(1).

Schwartz, B. (1968). The social psychology of privacy. *American Journal of Sociology, 73*(6), 741–752.

Stein, P., & Shand, J. (1974). *Legal values in Western society*. Edinburgh: Edinburgh University Press.
Thibaut, J., & Kelley, H. (1959). *Social psychology of groups*. New York: Wiley.
Tufekci, Z. (2008). Can you see me now? Audience and disclosure regulation in online social network sites. *Bulletin of Science, Technology and Society, 28*(1), 20–36.
Westin, A. (1967). *Privacy and freedom*. New York: The Bodley Head.

iDisclose: Applications of Privacy Management Theory to Children, Adolescents and Emerging Adults

Stephen Cory Robinson

Abstract Protecting personal information in online environments is vital to most individuals, including those in the three distinct age groups of children, adolescents and emerging adults. As each group interacts online, they use different disclosure practices and protection mechanisms to manage and distribute their personal information. After describing self-disclosure and communication privacy management theory (CPM), this chapter examines how privacy management strategies and self-disclosure practices in online environments differ between children, adolescents and emerging adults. The chapter considers theoretical strengths and weaknesses of CPM and also explores the applicability of the tenets of CPM to online communication in self-disclosure. In concluding, the text argues that a greater understanding of the privacy protection mechanisms employed by children, adolescents and emerging adults will help to strengthen privacy regulation and protection of personal information for each of these specific groups. Implications for media literacy, privacy protection practices, online marketing and advertising are presented.

"You already have zero privacy. Get over it." Scott McNealy, former CEO of Sun Microsystems Inc.

Every day, individuals around the world use the Internet for a multitude of reasons, including product research, trip planning, socialising, leisure activities and more. Each of these individuals will interact with various websites and online entities as they embark on finding solutions or information to fulfil their varying end goals. Through the navigation of websites, individuals may find themselves divulging information in exchange for product discounts, educational information, or, in the case of social networks, recommendations as to whom to connect and socialise with. Connecting with users on social networks requires users to disclose important personal information, with this self-disclosed information providing the foundation of the business model employed by social network sites (SNSs), including Facebook.

S.C. Robinson (✉)
Department of Science and Technology, Linköping University, Norrköping, Sweden
e-mail: cory.robinson@liu.se

M. Walrave et al. (eds.), *Youth 2.0: Social Media and Adolescence*,
DOI 10.1007/978-3-319-27893-3_8

Through the collection of users' personal data, social network sites are able to target products and services to these users. As users interact with these targeted ads, they are disclosing additional information, including which ads they interact with or choose to ignore, and this cyclical gathering and utilisation of personal information further solidifies the SNS business model. Currently, the collection of information and the resulting targeted advertisements provide 85 % of Facebook's revenue (Sengupta 2012).

As individuals exchange information with websites, these are wrought by the constant need to initiate, implement and negotiate rules dictating the use and dissemination of their private information. These rules for private information exchange help to regulate who accesses the information, how the information is accessed and for what reasons the requesting entity accesses this potentially lucrative, and sometimes potentially damaging personal information.

Adults are thought to negotiate these information exchanges in a more complex and sophisticated manner than would adolescents or children (Petronio 2002). It is important to investigate how children (under the age of 13), adolescents (between 13 and 17 years of age), and emerging adults (between 18 and 25 years of age) implement and negotiate the solicitation and divulging of their personal information online. How do these three distinct age groups create appropriate protection mechanisms for the dissemination and protection of their private information? Does a theoretical framework exist for understanding how online self-disclosure differs amongst these age groups occurs? Additionally, do these distinct age groups conceptualise "privacy" differently?

While self-disclosure, or the act of providing personal information to another, has been studied extensively in interpersonal communication (Cozby 1972, 1973; Jourard 1971a, b; Wheeless 1976, 1978; Wheeless and Grotz 1976), a theory explaining self-disclosure in the realm of online communication has yet to be developed (Nguyen et al. 2012). A review of the literature shows a significant theoretical gap. Further insights are necessary concerning online self-disclosure and its implications for online marketing and advertising that targets children, adolescents and emerging adults.

Communication privacy management (CPM) theory (Petronio 2002), provides a "first step toward building a theory of online privacy management" (Metzger 2007, p. 21). Previously applied in interpersonal relationships, CPM presents a robust theory which can account for some elements of the multifaceted process of self-disclosure, especially the concept of privacy and its relation to self- disclosure, as well as the creation of boundaries and rules for which personal information can be shared and utilised.

This chapter explores the differences between children's, adolescents' and emerging adults' motivations for utilising the Internet and social networks, how they disclose information online, and how CPM may or may not explain differences in how each group establishes and make use of privacy boundaries. It begins with a review of the literature to provide definitions of self-disclosure and privacy management, as well as an examination of how each age group discussed in this chapter relates to these topics.

1 Literature Review

1.1 Self-Disclosure Defined

Self-disclosure (also referred to in literature as "self disclosure") is the process of divulging personal information to another individual (Cozby 1973; Petronio and Durham 2008; Wheeless 1976). Self-disclosure is an important aspect of relationships and is both an act of intimacy and a relationship management strategy (Cozby 1973; Sprecher and Hendrick 2004). Disclosiveness (Wheeless 1978), interpersonal solidarity (Brown 1965) and reciprocity (Miller and Kenny 1986) are all elements of the process of self-disclosure. Further, three parameters can be identified in self-disclosure: (1) breadth is the quantity of information disclosed, (2) depth is the intimacy of information and (3) duration is the amount of time spent describing information (Cozby 1973).

The exploration of the self-disclosure process originates in the study of interpersonal communication, but self-disclosure has also been applied to online relationships (Joinson 2001; Krasnova et al. 2009; Nguyen et al. 2012). In the use of social networking sites, self-disclosure is "the amount of information shared on user's profile as well as in the process of the communication with others" (Krasnova and Veltri 2010, p. 2). Research has shown how both gender (Punyanunt-Carter 2006) and culture (Chen 1992; Durand 2010) can regulate online self-disclosure. Compared to self-disclosure in offline environments, online self-disclosure occurs quicker and at a deeper level (Barak and Bloch 2006; McCoyd and Kerson 2006). Currently, a unified theory explaining online self-disclosure is absent (Nguyen et al. 2012) and a framework for understanding online privacy management strategies is lacking as well (Child and Petronio 2011). CPM can provide a framework for explaining the process of self-disclosure online, as well as how individuals use protection strategies to manage the flow of personal information.

1.2 Privacy Management

Individuals hold the ownership of their information and therefore have a right to regulate access to that information (Petronio 2002). Because of this right of individuals to own and regulate access to their information, this author argues that a privacy or disclosure management approach is well suited to analysing and explaining the phenomenon of the sharing of personal information, not just in face-to-face communication, but in digital environments as well. Metzger (2007) concurs and argues that Petronio's CPM theory is applicable to relationships in digital environments, including ecommerce. While the CPM model is not complete in terms of fully explaining self-disclosure, it does provide a starting point for analysing self-disclosure and privacy protection in both interpersonal and online communication (Metzger 2007). In CPM, self-disclosure is a dialectical process where an individual is constantly balancing both the disclosing and concealing of private information (Petronio and Durham 2008). To balance privacy and disclosure, CPM establishes a rules-based system for how individuals divulge or protect information (Petronio 2002). By following a rules-based system, individuals are able to minimise costs (i.e. embarrassment, privacy loss), while maximising rewards (i.e. entertainment, trust) (Metzger 2007).

Petronio's approach is grounded in six principles, three *assumption maxims*, and three *interaction maxims* (Petronio and Durham 2008). Assumption maxims define the managing of private disclosure, while the interaction maxims illustrate how interactions with others are managed during the revealing and concealing of information (Petronio and Durham 2008). *Public-private dialectical tension*, the first assumption maxim, is the previously mentioned push-pull of disclosure and privacy (Petronio and Durham 2008). *Conceptualisation of private information*, the second assumption maxim, asserts that individuals believe they have a right to own their information and are thus entitled to choose whether to keep it private or disclose it to others (Petronio and Durham 2008). The final assumption principle, p*rivacy rules*, are guidelines that create privacy boundaries that dictate the ebb-and-flow of private information; these are developed using the criteria of culture, gender, motivation, context and risk-benefit ratio (Petronio and Durham 2008).

As previously noted, interaction maxims illustrate how interactions with others are managed during the revealing and concealing of information. The first of three interaction maxims, *shared boundaries*, posits that when private information is shared, the recipient becomes a co-owner of that information. The discloser and recipient collaborate to create a "mutual boundary around the information" (Petronio and Durham 2008, p. 310), and different boundaries exist for sharing information (i.e. dyadic, group, family). *Boundary coordination*, the second interaction principle, refers to the co-managing and co-owning of information by individuals (Petronio and Durham 2008), whereby both parties become responsible for the co-managing of the information. *Boundary turbulence*, the final interaction maxim, is when information is co-owned (as in CPM) and must be collaboratively managed by the discloser and the recipient (Petronio and Durham 2008).

1.3 Children and Disclosure

Of the three groups explored in the chapter, children are the earliest in age, and, according to U.S. law, children are defined as individuals younger than age 13 (Federal Trade Commission 1998). The Internet provides a medium that is ripe for targeting and collecting personal information for marketing purposes; with 80 % of American children ages 0–8 utilising the Internet (at least) once each week (Gutnick et al. 2011), the Internet presents a concern that collecting personal information from children is an invasion of privacy (Kunkel et al. 2004). The number of children utilising the Internet increases year on year as more children join social networking sites. While the terms of usage for Facebook clearly state that no one under the age of 13 can use the service (Facebook 2012), 38 % of American children using Facebook are younger than 12 (Protalinski 2012), and in Britain, one million users aged 9–12 use the social media site (Rushton 2013).

In using the Internet, children, adolescents and emerging adults engage for different reasons. While teenagers primarily use the Internet for socialisation, children use email and online forums for educational purposes (Blau 2011). In addition to educational activities, children visit entertainment and media sites online, as children can consume over 10 h of media in 1 day (Kaiser Family Foundation 2010). One form of entertainment that can lure children online to websites is advergames (i.e. online games featuring branding); a 2006 study showed that 73 % of children's websites employ it (Kaiser Family Foundation). Disturbingly, advergames have been found to persuade children on an emotional, subconscious level (Nairn and Hang 2012). An even bigger concern is that advergames may no longer constitute a clear marketing tool, as marketing messages are combined with other forms of online media (An and Stern 2011) that blur the line between marketing and other online content (Walrave and Heirman 2012). While previous research found children could not distinguish between online advertisements and content (Nairn and Hang 2012; Gilutz and Nielsen 2002), contradicting research (Young 2003) found that by age 8, most children could distinguish between programme content and advertising and also acknowledge the persuasive intent of the advertising content. Compared with adults, children are more willing to disclose personal information in online settings (Turow and Nir 2000). Additionally, research has shown that younger users have less social and technical understanding of the intricate nature of the Internet (Yan 2006). As children may or may not be able to distinguish between online content and advertising, and as they are more vulnerable to online disclosure, how is children's privacy protected online and what kind of information is being collected from websites?

In the online realm, privacy is a highly regulated issue concerning children. Since children do not perceive privacy in the manner that older users do (Petronio 2002), there is a need for legislation to protect children's privacy. In the United States and Europe, key legislation exists to protect children online: Child Online Privacy Protection Act (1998), or COPPA, in the United States, and in the EU, the more general Data Protection Directive (1995). Recently, the United States' Federal Trade Commission strengthened COPPA by increasing parental protection over the disclosure of their children's privacy (Federal Trade Commission 2012). Even with the recent updates that regulate and restrict how websites and online marketers can target children, individuals of young age are still able to peruse online content and, in the process, expose themselves to online data mining. For example, even though websites state children younger than 13 need parental consent to register, their content targets children and requests personal information from them (Miyazaki et al. 2009). Various types of websites request personal information from children, but these sites can be generally categorised into entertainment sites, online retailers, brick and mortar online stores, and, finally, food and toy manufacturers (Miyazaki et al. 2009). As a result of the breadth and depth of information disclosed online, as well as the ease with which this information can be obtained, targeting and theft of an individual's profile (i.e. identify theft) has become commonplace. Identity theft is a major concern, even for children, as identity theft and credit report inconsistencies may not be discovered for years (Power 2011). Recently, it was discovered that 10 % of American children have experienced identity theft, while only 0.2 % of American adults have experienced identity theft (Power 2011).

Several studies have been conducted in an attempt to discover strategies for protecting children online. Miyazaki et al. (2009) demonstrated that the combination of a visual warning (i.e. content is not meant for children under 13) on a website and the threat of parental notification via email reduced the willingness of preteens to disclose information online. Surprisingly, a visual warning given to children visiting websites was shown to raise disclosure levels (Miyazaki et al. 2009). Parental mediation and education of children regarding online safety should be useful in reducing children's disclosure online (Miyazaki et al. 2009).

1.4 Adolescents and Disclosure

Second in chronological order of the three age groups addressed in this chapter, an adolescent is an individual in the adolescence stage of life, or "the transition stage between childhood and adulthood" (Kaplan 2004, p. 1). Youn (2005) defined teenagers as "children 13 and older" (p. 88). For practical reasons, this chapter defines adolescents as individuals between 13 and 17 years of age, as children are defined by American legislation, including COPPA, as 13 and under.

As 80 % of American adolescents use social networking (Purcell 2012), it is important to understand the functions of online self-disclosure and privacy management amongst this unique group. Self-disclosure amongst adolescents is an important developmental task (Steinberg and Morris 2001) and is used to form and maintain relationships (Buhrmester and Furman 1987); indeed, adolescents are better able to disclose online than offline (Schouten et al. 2007). Adolescents also disclose information differently than do adults, as adolescents disclose more information on social networking sites and are less likely than adults to use privacy settings (Christofides et al. 2011; Walrave et al. 2012).

Within the adolescent age bracket, it should be noted that differences exist in amount and type of disclosure. Older teenagers are more likely than younger teenagers to disclose addresses and telephone numbers (Livingstone et al. 2011) and older teens are more likely to reconsider posting content after considering the negative implications (Purcell 2012). Also, as adolescents grow older, their competence in managing online privacy settings increases (Walrave et al. 2012).

As 93 % of teenagers possess an account on an SNS (Purcell 2012), this age group is particularly desirable to marketers and online advertisers. Many websites function to sell products and services and many of these target teenagers and adolescents. Advertisers engage with adolescents through various practices, including the use of commercial incentives. The use of commercial incentives in exchange for information online is a common practice, and when adolescents are provided commercial incentives in exchange for information disclosure, behavioural intention is the most important predictor for disclosure (Heirman et al. 2012).

With regard to social networking sites, teenagers define privacy as being in control of who knows what about them, as well as controlling the managing of the disclosure, rather than privacy being tied to divulging certain types of information (Livingstone 2008). Adolescents, regardless of contradicting reports and research, are cognisant of maintaining online privacy (Purcell 2012) but to varying extents, depending on the type of personal information involved in the disclosure and the medium in which the online interaction occurs. One reason for a misconception about lack of privacy by adolescents may lie in what groups perceive as private information: what is private information to adults is not necessarily private information to adolescents (Christofides et al. 2011). While a majority of Belgian teenagers aged 12–18 (69 %) expressed concern about data collection practices on the Internet, a majority of those sampled provided simple demographics, such as gender (75 %) and even more lucrative marketing information, including brand preferences (68 %, Walrave and Heirman 2012). Additionally, the Belgian teenagers were also less likely to provide contact data versus profile data (Walrave and Heirman 2012). Adolescents disclose information differently depending on the Internet channel (i.e. instant message versus email) and Schouten et al. (2007) found that adolescents have higher degrees of disclosure in instant messaging when they feel less disinhibited. When adolescents have a higher perception of potential benefits, they are more willing to provide personal information to a website (Youn 2005). Conversely, when a higher level of risk perception of information disclosure is present, adolescents are less willing to provide personal information to online marketers (Youn 2005).

Furthermore, the concept of privacy among adolescents is complicated by their relationship with parents. During adolescence, the relationship between parents and teenagers are constantly being redefined as the adolescent seeks more independence and the establishing of their identity. Privacy, secrecy and trust are constant tensions that exist in these relationships. As teenagers develop self-identity and independence from their parents, they are likely to disclose online through responding to online marketing (Youn 2005). As noted, adolescents struggle in establishing independence and adolescent rebellion can be noted in social networking profiles; they see their profile as a private space, which is meant to be public with friends only and not shared with parents (Livingstone 2008). An ever-present tension between parents and teenagers over online privacy seems to exist, as both parents and teenagers have suggested that some secrets are necessary (Gillies et al. 2001). Frequently, both parties avoid conversing about secrecy, surveillance and disclosure, as they both seek to balance the delicate relationship between trust and privacy (Gillies et al. 2001).

Despite teen-parent conflicts in privacy, parents do serve as a positive mediating factor in helping establish online privacy practices. Parents monitoring and mediating teenager internet and mobile use can be viewed as one method of limiting a teen's negative experiences online, as well as increasing safe privacy practices online. Among Americans, more than 50 % of parents use parental controls to manage their teens' internet access (Purcell 2012) and 77 % of American parents monitor sites their teens visit, but conflicting data exist on the effectiveness of the mediating effect parents have on teens' disclosure levels (Walrave and Heirman 2012; Youn 2005). Parental influence on the value that adolescents place on privacy is of the utmost importance, as adolescents who value privacy in the face-to-face offline world are also less likely to disclose sensitive information online (De Souza and Dick 2009).

1.5 Emerging Adults and Disclosure

It should be noted that delimiting ages for adolescents and emerging adults is often difficult (Geiger and Castellino 2011), but for the purpose of this chapter, emerging adults are those defined as 18–25 years old, as used by Arnett (2000). Emerging adults are more likely than any other demographic to employ social media, with 83 % of American emerging adults owning a social media profile (Duggan and Brenner 2013). Emerging adults are also proficient at using multiple methods for using the Internet, as mobile app downloading is highest in emerging adults aged 18–29 within American demographics (Purcell 2012).

More than any other age group, emerging adults are interested in protecting their privacy. Compared to older users, emerging adults are more likely to delete unwanted comments from their social media profile, change privacy settings or take steps to limit the amount of their personal information online (Madden and Smith 2010). As Facebook has evolved over the years so too have trends in self-disclosure. In the public sphere, emerging adults have decreased public self-disclosures, while increasing both the scope and amount of private disclosures to connected friends (Stutzman et al. 2013). Among Americans, emerging adults are also more likely to not fully understand implications of privacy law, whereas older adults are more knowledgeable of existing privacy law (Hoofnagle et al. 2010).

More than any other age group, emerging adults also have a much broader interest in, and need for, going online. College students use Facebook for various reasons, including finding companionship or passing the time when bored (Sheldon 2008), but also to maintain relationships (Ellison et al. 2007; Sheldon 2008). In addition to social networking, emerging adults use the Internet to seek health information, obtain recent news, visit government sites, purchase products, bank online and make travel reservations (Zickuhr 2011).

Lastly, the literature shows that emerging adults have compelling reasons to practice a range of self-disclosure habits. For college students, self-disclosure is important in relationship quality, as those who disclosed more in CMC reported higher relationship quality (Yum and Hara 2005). However, emerging adults favour emotional self-disclosure through therapy in a face-to-face environment as opposed to online (Rogers et al. 2009).

2 Applicability of CPM Tenets to Child, Adolescent and Emerging Adult Disclosure

2.1 *Public-Private Dialectical Tension*

This dialectical push-pull of concealing or revealing privacy (Petronio and Durham 2008) seems to vary in amount between children, adolescents and emerging adults. Each of these groups, as they interact with websites or social environments online, must balance the desire to share personal information against the desire to also conceal it. While children do socialise on the Internet through social media (38 % under age 12) (MinorMonitor 2012), they do not socialise to the extent that adolescents or emerging adults do via social networking (Purcell 2012). As such, children do not experience the same dialectical tension of concealing/revealing that teenagers and emerging adults experience. The single greatest predictor of disclosure on SNSs by adolescents is the desire to communicate with peers outside of school hours (Walrave et al. 2012) and, with this, adolescents experience a significant desire to divulge information with peers, but also the pressure to conceal information as they interact with online marketers. Emerging adults, in contrast, balance dialectical tension in the same way that adolescents do, but as emerging adults are more developed in social identity compared to adolescents, they are less subjected to the strong social pressure to disclose compared to adolescents (Walrave et al. 2012).

2.2 *Conceptualisation of Private Information*

This privacy management tenet asserts that individuals believe they have a right to own their information and are thus entitled to keep it private or disclose it to others (Petronio and Durham 2008). Children, adolescents and emerging adults must cognitively process and understand this concept of ownership of their personal information. As children do not possess the complex cognitive capabilities of adolescents and emerging adults (Piaget 1964), children are not as aware of consequences and concerns related to information disclosure. Adolescents possess greater cognitive capabilities than do children, but adolescents do not always engage in self-protection of personal information. As previously mentioned, adolescents may therefore engage in risky activities online, as they may perceive marketing benefits as outweighing potential loss of privacy (Youn 2005). Emerging adults, possessing the greatest cognitive capacity of the three groups, are more likely to comprehend the notion of information ownership, as well as the consequences and concerns related to ownership.

2.3 Privacy Rules

Privacy rules are guidelines that create privacy boundaries that dictate the ebb-and-flow of private information and are developed using the criteria of culture, gender, motivation, context and risk-benefit ratio (Petronio and Durham 2008). Drawing on Piaget (1964) and cognitive development theory, this author believes that the implementation and complexity of privacy rules increase with age. For example, children will possess fewer strict and complex privacy rules than those of adolescents, while emerging adults will have more complex privacy rules than adolescents. This positive correlation of age with privacy rule complexity is present in many previous studies (Christofides et al. 2011; Fox et al. 2000; Walrave et al. 2012).

2.4 Shared Boundaries

Shared boundaries posit that when private information is shared, the recipient becomes a co-owner of that information. The discloser and recipient collaborate to create a "mutual boundary around the information" (Petronio and Durham 2008, p. 310) and different boundaries exist for sharing information (i.e. dyadic, group, family). The concept of sharing information may not be understood by children; while they definitely are targeted by online marketers and provide information, the concept that "information is no longer solely owned by the discloser" (Petronio and Durham 2008, p. 313) may be too technically complex for children. Adolescents use social media and the Internet to interact with peers and the sharing nature of websites like Twitter and YouTube encourage individuals to contribute to conversation or media creation. Identity formation, which is especially important during the adolescent years, encourages teenagers to engage in acts of sharing with their peers. Emerging adults, who have crafted more self-identity and are less prone to peer pressure than adolescents will share information with their peers but, unlike adolescents, are more likely to share with family members. In sharing with family members, emerging adults will create shared boundaries with these individuals, whereas adolescents are more likely to keep information private from family members, especially parents.

2.5 Boundary Coordination

Boundary coordination refers to the co-managing and co-owning of information by individuals (Petronio and Durham 2008), whereby both parties become responsible for the co-managing of the information. Metzger (2007) explains the processes involved in boundary coordination:

> As part of the coordination process, individuals enact rules to moderate boundary linkages (whether to link to others), boundary ownership rights (who should be included or excluded in the boundary), and boundary permeability (what information may be revealed to whom). (p. 336–337)

Children, as explored earlier, may not be able to cognitively process the concept of information ownership and may have their parents mediate boundary coordination on their behalf. Parents may mediate information solely on behalf of their children, whereas adolescents are more likely to mediate information by themselves, possibly without any parental involvement. As adolescents and emerging adults are more likely than children to institute privacy protection in their social network profiles, they directly engage in boundary permeability. Boundary linkages, or whether to link to others inside various social networking platforms, is a constant process inherent in social media profiles for all age groups. Complexity of those linkages seem to increase with age. In the process of creating groups in Google + or Facebook, individuals can allow information to be accessible to one group (i.e. friends), but not another group (i.e. co-workers). This complexity of sharing and defining individuals and placing them into appropriate groups for information dissemination is most likely not present in children's social media profiles.

2.6 *Boundary Turbulence*

Boundary turbulence can result when information is co-owned. To prevent it, both the discloser and the recipient can collaboratively manage the information (Petronio and Durham 2008). Turbulence can result from differences in privacy rules used by the discloser and recipient, or privacy rule violations by either party (Metzger 2007). Additionally, privacy violations and misconceptions about private information ownership are situations where boundary turbulence may occur (Petronio and Durham 2008). When boundary turbulence occurs, varying levels of breakdown occur and individuals may experience minor disruptions or complete collapse in managing their private information (Child and Westermann 2013). When a child's parent attempts to become a Facebook friend with their child, turbulence may occur as the child may see the friend request as an invasion of privacy (Petronio et al. 2003).

3 Limitations

While literature exists that compares each age group individually, there appears to be a lack of literature that compares online disclosure amongst all three age groups (i.e. children, adolescents and emerging adults). While a plethora of reports (Duggan and Brenner 2013; Evangelista 2012; Madden 2012; Madden and Smith 2010; Madden et al. 2012; Purcell 2012; Zickuhr 2011) document usage of various new media (apps, email, websites, etc.), there is a lack of reasoning about why and how these individual groups disclose online. Another limitation exists in operationalising each age group (i.e. children, adolescents and emerging adults); there currently exists difficulty in clearly defining age parameters for each specific group (Geiger and Castellino 2011). Clarifying the age parameters between children and adolescents is important as "younger children may not understand the safety and privacy issues created by the online collection of personal information" (Federal Trade Commission 2008).

Privacy management addresses the communication aspect of online disclosure but does not address the technical side of digital communication – the server-side process of collecting and then storing information in databases. Information technology theory is more conducive to explaining the technical aspects of digital communication, but a combination of the two areas might be beneficial in addressing weaknesses that each theoretical approach has individually.

4 Implications

The author has identified several implications related to Internet use, protection and disclosure of personal information that result from using CPM as a framework for understanding the distinct differences in self-disclosure practices among children, adolescents and emerging adults

Foremost, clear communication between parent and child must be initiated to provide clear guidelines for what is appropriate and safe when disclosing personal information online. Parental guidance for children may help to lessen online disclosure and strengthen online privacy protection, while it may backfire with adolescents, actually providing an incentive to the teenager to disclose more (disclosing information online provides risk and thus establishes independence by rebutting guidance provided by parent).

Secondly, children and adolescents are not intellectually stagnant, nor do they navigate the Internet in the same manner year after year. Children and teenagers are becoming more intelligent about how they use and interact with websites (Budiu and Nielsen 2010); this lends a need for greater, more targeted education campaigns. Conversely, marketers may employ more sophisticated marketing campaigns online, possibly to even confuse individuals about the purpose of the advertisement (is it content or advertisement?).

Thirdly, all age groups must be exposed to up-to-date media literacy practices and how to properly use and interface with the various channels online. Child identity theft presents a sound reason for media literacy, especially those of younger ages. Children cannot cognitively process the immediate threats of predation and manipulation online, so parents and guardians should act as mediators between the children's information and websites requesting access for the information. Privacy boundaries are not just created by children but also by their parent/guardian and they must constantly revisit them and adapt them as needed. When a child is 5 years old, and is aware of his email address, the parent must provide him with rules as to when he can divulge or not divulge that information: for example, he can provide that address for playing games online, but not provide it to strangers on social media.

In addition, at risk groups, including teens, should be made aware that advertisers and information collection schemes are not preferential to one group; every individual using the Internet is susceptible to data collection schemes. Teens do not initiate strict enough privacy boundaries, or provide enough clarification of the way they use personal information, as they do not consider themselves as vulnerable to identity theft as do emerging adults. As teens are strongly influenced by anticipated social pressure from peers and family (Heirman et al. 2012), public information campaigns regarding protection of online privacy should be directed not just at parents, but at all of the individual's peers (friends, instructors, etc.).

Lastly, users of the Internet are aware of the constant mechanisms used to collect and distribute personal information. With this knowledge, privacy and protection of personal information is a legitimate concern, regardless of age group. Caution needs to be exercised when assuming that adolescents are not concerned about privacy; their definition of private information is different than for those in other age groups. Further, adolescents do not always have the ability to assert control over privacy mechanisms, as parents may ultimately decide privacy decisions (which ironically, can counter the effort of adolescents to initiate privacy protections).

5 Conclusion

5.1 Theoretical Strengths

Privacy management is a robust theory for analysing online privacy and self-disclosure, as it is a practical theory that is "designed to provide an explanation for communicative issues about privacy that individuals face in the everyday world" (Petronio 2002, p. xvii). Further, dynamics of face-to-face communication are prevalent in online communication as well and therefore CPM is applicable in explaining online relationships (Metzger 2007).

Even though legislation continues to strengthen the protection of children's privacy online, children under the age of 13 are continuing to join and interact with websites, and, in the process, are illegally targeted by online marketers. No legislation can completely prevent children from interacting with marketers but CPM can highlight the need for marketers to adhere to the privacy boundaries created by COPPA and the European Union's Data Protection Directive.

5.2 Theoretical Weaknesses

Teens engage in various activities to establish independence (including disclosing private information online) and sometimes go against safe practices in attempts to establish independence. A rebellion effect can explain why teens have been found to not obey media consumption options that are recommended by guardians and parents (Walrave and Heirman 2011). As teenagers possess tendencies towards risk and rebellion, they are likely to focus on potential benefits offered by online marketers rather than the risks posed by privacy loss (Youn 2005). Studies have shown that peer influences on risk, specifically risk-taking and risky-decision making, are greater among adolescents than younger adults (Gardner and Steinberg 2005). The element of risk, or consciously seeking out risk, is not addressed by CPM. Instead, CPM defines risk as the losing of control of how others use private information once disclosed (Metzger 2007). CPM does not address risk in the sense of purposefully exposing oneself to loss of control. Since engaging in risky behaviours online has become normative for young users (Blau 2011), further urgency is given to developing a theoretical framework for explaining online disclosure.

Privacy management holds private information as central to the disclosure process. Petronio (2002) states that "CPM makes private information, as the content of what is disclosed, a primary focal point" (p. 3). As Christofides et al. (2011) note, what is defined as "private information" by one individual or group may not necessarily be the definition agreed upon by another individual or group. If what defines private information is not agreed upon or understood by both parties involved in the disclosure process, turbulence is most likely present from the onset. At the beginning of the disclosure process, the parties involved need to come to agreement on what information is constituted as private information.

Another weakness of Petronio's model lies in the control of privacy boundaries. CPM states that individuals create privacy boundaries to establish control over the use of private information, or, in inclusive boundary coordination, one person gives control of privacy to another individual (i.e. a child giving control of privacy to their parent) (Petronio 2002). But what occurs when an entity other than a disclosing individual establishes the privacy boundaries or the rules for disclosure? In the instance of COPPA, or other legislation, boundaries for what kind of information can be disclosed and collected are implemented on behalf of children. In the context of Facebook and third party applications, Facebook can make decisions as to how an individual's information is handled and distributed by third party applications: sometimes users interact directly with Facebook, while at other times Facebook may interact with the application *on behalf* of the user.

CPM also does not consider how a lack of technical understanding plays a role in establishing privacy boundaries. For example, children cannot always discern between content and advertising. As a result, this lesser technical competency influences the complexity of the privacy boundaries implemented. Adolescents and emerging adults possess more technical knowledge than children and this is likely to influence the complexity of the privacy boundaries they implement. Adolescents are aware that the use of deception is one method for protecting personal information; websites cannot always authenticate information, so individuals can falsify information (i.e. name, age, phone number) in order to preserve privacy. Metzger (2007) posits that individuals with high privacy concern may utilise privacy protection practices, including deception. Studies have shown that as many as 40 % of individuals may falsify information when interacting with websites (Metzger 2007).

While this author concurs that deception may be employed as a privacy protection mechanism, this author believes technical proficiency (i.e. mastery of computer technology, including hardware and SNS usage) also plays a key role and is distinct from deception as a privacy protection mechanism.

5.3 Closing

As adolescent and emerging adults balance the risk-benefit ratio of self-disclosure they may recognise that they have an opportunity to create the appropriate privacy boundaries for protecting and disclosing their personal information. After all, within the framework of ecommerce, these Internet users are merely consumers. As such, marketers and other organisations must, in turn, be willing to respect and adhere to the consumer-established boundaries. "It is in the industry's best interest to address and remedy privacy concerns via self-regulation before the current state of activities leads to increases in government regulation" (Miyazaki et al. 2009, p. 79). As consumers divulge personal information in exchange for both economic and entertainment benefits online (Krasnova et al. 2009), further consumer privacy education initiatives are required so that consumers can achieve minimal costs (loss of privacy) while maximising rewards (i.e. online entertainment, socialisation, knowledge-acquisition). A greater understanding of the privacy protection mechanisms employed by children, adolescents and emerging adults will help to strengthen privacy regulation and the protection of personal information for each of these specific groups.

References

An, S., & Stern, S. (2011). Mitigating the effects of advergames on children: Do advertising breaks work? *Journal of Advertising, 40*(1), 43–56. doi:10.2753/JOA0091-3367400103.

Arnett, J. (2000). Emerging adulthood: A theory of development from the late teens through the twenties. *The American Psychologist, 55*(5), 469–480.

Barak, A., & Bloch, N. (2006). Factors related to perceived helpfulness in supporting highly distressed individuals through an online support chat. *Cyberpsychology & Behavior: The Impact of The Internet, Multimedia and Virtual Reality on Behavior and Society, 9*(1), 60–68.

Blau, I. (2011). Application use, online relationship types, self-disclosure, and Internet abuse among children and youth: Implications for education and Internet safety programs. *Journal of Educational Computing Research, 45*(1), 95–116. doi:10.2190/EC.45.1.e.

Brown, R. (1965). *Social psychology*. Oxford: Free Press of Glencoe.

Budiu, R., & Nielsen, J. (2010). *Children's websites: Usability issues in designing for kids* (2nd ed.). Fremont: Nielsen Norman Group.

Buhrmester, D., & Furman, W. (1987). The development of companionship and intimacy. *Child Development, 58*, 1101–1113.

Chen, G. (1992). Differences in self-disclosure patterns among Americans versus Chinese: A comparative study. *Journal of Cross-Cultural Psychology, 26*, 84–91.

Child, J., & Petronio, S. (2011). Unpacking the paradoxes of privacy in cmc relationships: The challenges of blogging and relational communication on the Internet. In K. B. Wright & L. M. Webb (Eds.), *Computer-mediated communication in personal relationships* (pp. 21–40). New York: Peter Lang.

Child, J., & Westermann, D. (2013). Let's be Facebook friends: Exploring parental Facebook friend requests from a communication privacy management (cpm) perspective. *Journal of Family Communication, 13*(1), 46–59. doi:10.1080/15267431.2012.742089.

Children's Online Privacy Protection Act of 1998. (1998). 15 U.S.C. §§ 6501–6508 C.F.R. § 1302.

Christofides, E., Muise, A., & Desmarais, S. (2011). Hey mom, what's on your Facebook? Comparing Facebook disclosure and privacy in adolescents and adults. *Social Psychological and Personality Science*. doi:10.1177/1948550611408619.

Cozby, P. (1972). Self-disclosure, reciprocity and liking. *Sociometry, 35*(1), 151–160.

Cozby, P. (1973). Self-disclosure: A literature review. *Psychological Bulletin, 79*, 73–91.

De Souza, Z., & Dick, G. (2009). Disclosure of information by children in social networking—not just a case of "you show me yours and I'll show you mine". *International Journal of Information Management, 29*(4), 255–261. doi:http://dx.doi.org/10.1016/j.ijinfomgt.2009.03.006

Duggan, M., & Brenner, J. (2013). *The demographics of social media users – 2012*. Washington, DC: Pew Research Center. Retrieved May 7, 2013, from http://www.pewinternet.org/2013/02/14/the-demographics-of-social-media-users-2012/

Durand, C. (2010). *A comparative study of self-disclosure in face-to-face and email communication between Americans and Chinese*. University of Rhode Island: Senior Honor Projects (Paper 197).

Ellison, N., Steinfield, C., & Lampe, C. (2007). The benefits of Facebook 'friends:' Social capital and college students' use of online social network sites. *Journal of Computer-Mediated Communication, 12*(4), 1143–1168. doi:10.1111/j.1083-6101.2007.00367.x.

European Communities Commission. (1995). Directive 95/46 EC of the European Parliament and of the Council of 24 October 1995 on the protection of individuals with regard to the processing of personal data and the free movement of such data.

Evangelista, B. (2012, February 25). Facebook friend lists shrinking to guard privacy. *San Francisco Chronicle*. http://www.sfgate.com/cgi-bin/article.cgi?f=/c/a/2012/02/24/BUH11NC6HA.DTL. Accessed 24 Feb 2013.

Facebook. (2012). *Statement of rights and responsibilities*. http://www.facebook.com/legal/terms. Accessed 18 Feb 2013.

Federal Trade Commission. (1998). *Children's Online Privacy Protection Act of 1998*, 15 U.S.C. §§ 6501–6508 C.F.R. § 1302.

Federal Trade Commission. (2008). *Frequently asked questions about the Children's Online Privacy Protection Rule*. http://www.ftc.gov/privacy/coppafaqs.shtm. Accessed 24 Feb 2013.

Federal Trade Commission. (2012). *FTC strengthens kids' privacy, gives parents greater control over their information by amending Children's Online Privacy Protection Rule*. http://www.ftc.gov/opa/2012/12/coppa.shtm. Accessed 27 Feb 2013.

Fox, S., Rainie, L., Horrigan, J., Lenhart, A., Spooner, T., & Carter, C. (2000). Trust and privacy online: Why Americans want to rewrite the rules. *The Pew Internet & American Life Project*. http://www.pewinternet.org/files/old-media/Files/Reports/2000/PIP_Trust_Privacy_Report.pdf.pdf. Accessed 28 Feb 2013.

Gardner, M., & Steinberg, L. (2005). Peer influence on risk taking, risk preference, and risky decision making in adolescence and adulthood: An experimental study. *Developmental Psychology, 41*(4), 625–635.

Geiger, A., & Castellino, S. (2011). Delineating the age ranges used to define adolescents and emerging adults. *Journal of Clinical Oncology, 29*(16), 492–493.

Gillies, V., Ribbens McCarthy, J., & Holland, J. (2001). *The family lives of young people*. http://www.jrf.org.uk/sites/files/jrf/351.pdf. Accessed 23 Feb 2013.

Gilutz, S., & Nielsen, J. (2002). *Usability of websites for children*. Freemont: Nielsen Norman Group.

Gutnick, A., Robb, M., Takeuchi, L., & Kotler, J. (2011). *Always connected: The new digital media habits of young children*. http://www.joanganzcooneycenter.org/publication/always-connected-the-new-digital-media-habits-of-young-children/. Accessed 5 Mar 2013.

Heirman, W., Walrave, M., & Ponnet, K. (2012). Predicting adolescents' disclosure of personal information in exchange for commercial incentives: An application of an extended theory of planned behavior. *CyberPsychology, Behavior, and Social Networking, 16*(2), 81–87.

Hoofnagle, C., King, J., Li, S., & Turow, J. (2010). *How different are emerging adults from older adults when it comes to information privacy attitudes and policies*? http://papers.ssrn.com/sol3/papers.cfm?abstract_id=1589864. Accessed 6 Mar 2013.

Joinson, A. (2001). Self-disclosure in computer-mediated communication: The role of self-awareness and visual anonymity. *European Journal of Social Psychology, 31*(2), 177–192.

Jourard, S. (1971a). *Self-disclosure: An experimental analysis of the transparent self*. Oxford: Wiley.

Jourard, S. (1971b). *The transparent self* (2nd ed.). Oxford: Wiley.

Kaiser Family Foundation. (2006). *It's child's play: Advergaming and the online marketing of food to children*. http://www.kff.org/entmedia/upload/7536.pdf. Accessed 23 Feb 2013.

Kaiser Family Foundation. (2010). *Generation M2: Media in the lives of 8–18-year-olds*. http://www.kff.org/entmedia/mh012010pkg.cfm. Accessed 23 Feb 2013.

Kaplan, P. S. (2004). *Adolescence*. Boston: Houghton Mifflin Company.

Krasnova, H., & Veltri, N. (2010). *Privacy calculus on social networking sites: Explorative evidence from Germany and USA*. Paper presented at the Hawaii international conference on system sciences, Hawaii. http://doi.ieeecomputersociety.org/10.1109/HICSS.2010.307

Krasnova, H., Kolesnikova, E., & Guenther, O. (2009). *"It won't happen to me!": Self-disclosure in online social networks*. Paper presented at the Americas conference on information systems, San Francisco.

Kunkel, D., Wilcox, B., Cantor, J., Palmer, E., Linn, S., & Dowrick, P. (2004). *Report of the Apa Task Force on Advertising and Children*. http://www.sfu.ca/cmns/faculty/kline_s/320/06-spring/resources/sup_readings/childrenads.pdf. Accessed 15 Feb 2013.

Livingstone, S. (2008). Taking risky opportunities in youthful content creation: Teenagers' use of social networking sites for intimacy, privacy and self-expression. *New Media & Society, 10*(3), 393–411.

Livingstone, S., Ólafsson, K., & Staksrud, E. (2011). *Social networking, age and privacy*. http://eprints.lse.ac.uk/35849/. Accessed 9 Mar 2013.

Madden, M. (2012). Privacy management on social media sites. *Pew Internet & American Life Project*. http://www.pewinternet.org/Reports/2012/Privacy-management-on-social-media.aspx. Accessed 1 Mar 2013.

Madden, M., & Smith, A. (2010). *Reputation management and social media: How people monitor their identity and search for others online*. http://www.pewinternet.org/Reports/2010/Reputation-Management/Summary-of-Findings.aspx?view=all. Accessed 4 Mar 2013.

Madden, M., Cortesi, S., Gasser, U., Lenhart, A., & Duggan, M. (2012). Parents, teens, and online privacy. *Pew Internet & American Life Project*. http://www.pewinternet.org/Reports/2012/Teens-and-Privacy.aspx. Accessed 5 Mar 2013.

McCoyd, J., & Kerson, T. (2006). Conducting intensive interviews using email: A serendipitous comparative opportunity. *Qualitative Social Work: Research and Practice, 5*(3), 389–406. doi:10.1177/1473325006067367.

Metzger, M. (2007). Communication privacy management in electronic commerce. *Journal of Computer-Mediated Communication, 12*(2), 1–27. doi:10.1111/j.1083-6101.2007.00328.x.

Miller, L., & Kenny, D. (1986). Reciprocity of self-disclosure at the individual and dyadic levels: A social relations analysis. *Journal of Personality and Social Psychology, 50*(4), 713–719. doi:10.1037/0022-3514.50.4.713.

MinorMonitor. (2012). *Minormonitor surveys 1,000 parents of children on Facebook, shares results on realities, parental concerns*. http://www.minormonitor.com/2012/04/minormonitor-surveys-1000-parents-of-children-on-facebook-shares-results-on-realities-parental-concerns/. Accessed 2 Mar 2013.

Miyazaki, A., Stanaland, A., & Lwin, M. (2009). Self-regulatory safeguards and the online privacy of preteen children. *Journal of Advertising, 38*(4), 79–91.

Nairn, A., & Hang, H. (2012). *Advergames: "It's not an advert – it says play!": A review of research: Family and parenting institute*. http://www.bath.ac.uk/management/news_events/pdf/advergames-report-december2012.pdf. Accessed 29 May 2013.

Nguyen, M., Bin, Y., & Campbell, A. (2012). Comparing online and offline self-disclosure: A systematic review. *CyberPsychology, Behavior & Social Networking, 15*(2), 103–111. doi:10.1089/cyber.2011.0277.

Petronio, S. (2002). *Boundaries of privacy dialectics of disclosure*. Albany: State University of New York Press.

Petronio, S., & Durham, W. (2008). Communication privacy management theory. In L. Baxter & D. Braithewaite (Eds.), *Engaging theories in interpersonal communication: Multiple perspectives* (pp. 309–322). Thousand Oaks: Sage Publications, Inc.

Petronio, S., Jones, S., & Morr, M. (2003). Family privacy dilemmas: Managing communication boundaries within family groups. In L. R. Frey (Ed.), *Group communication in context: Studies of bona fide groups* (2nd ed., pp. 23–55). Mahwah: Lawrence Erlbaum Associates Publishers.

Piaget, J. (1964). Part I: Cognitive development in children: Piaget development and learning. *Journal of Research in Science Teaching, 2*(3), 176–186. doi:10.1002/tea.3660020306.

Power, R. (2011). *Child identity theft: New evidence suggests that identity thieves are targeting children for unused social security numbers*. http://jjie.org/children-at-higher-risk-for-identity-theft-than-adults-study-says/54303. Accessed 3 Mar 2013.

Protalinski, E. (2012). *38% of kids on Facebook are under the minimum age of 13*. http://www.zdnet.com/blog/facebook/38-of-kids-on-facebook-are-under-the-minimum-age-of-13/11745. Accessed 18 Feb 2013.

Punyanunt-Carter, N. (2006). An analysis of college students' self-disclosure behaviors on the Internet. *College Student Journal, 40*(2), 329–331.

Purcell, K. (2012). *Teens 2012: Truth, trends, and myths about teen online behavior*. Paper presented at the 27th annual ACT enrollment planners conference, Chicago. http://pewinternet.org/Presentations/2012/July/Teens-2012-Truth-Trends-and-Myths-About-Teen-Online-Behavior.aspx

Rogers, V., Griffin, M., Wykle, M., & Fitzpatrick, J. (2009). Internet versus face-to-face therapy: Emotional self-disclosure issues for emerging adults. *Issues in Mental Health Nursing, 30*(10), 596–602. doi:10.1080/01612840903003520.

Rushton, K. (2013). *Million young children ignore rules to become Facebook user.* http://www.telegraph.co.uk/technology/facebook/9822498/Million-young-children-ignore-rules-to-become-Facebook-user.html. Accessed 18 Feb 2013.

Schouten, A., Valkenburg, P., & Peter, J. (2007). Precursors and underlying processes of adolescents' online self-disclosure: Developing and testing an Internet-attribute-perception model. *Media Psychology, 10*(2), 292–315. doi:10.1080/15213260701375686.

Sengupta, S. (2012, July 22). Facebook advertising efforts face a day of judgment. *The New York Times*. http://www.nytimes.com/2012/07/23/technology/facebook-advertising-efforts-face-a--day-of-judgment.html?_r=0. Accessed 29 May 2013.

Sheldon, P. (2008). The relationship between unwillingness-to-communicate and students' Facebook use. *Journal of Media Psychology: Theories, Methods, and Applications, 20*(2), 67–75. doi:10.1027/1864-1105.20.2.67.

Sprecher, S., & Hendrick, S. (2004). Self-disclosure in intimate relationships: Associations with individual and relationship characteristics over time. *Journal of Social and Clinical Psychology, 23*(6), 857–877. doi:10.1521/jscp.23.6.857.54803.

Steinberg, L., & Morris, A. (2001). Adolescent development. *Annual Review of Psychology, 52*(1), 83.

Stutzman, F., Gross, R., & Acquisti, A. (2013). Silent listeners: The evolution of privacy and disclosure on Facebook. *Journal of Privacy and Confidentiality, 4*(2), 2.
Turow, J., & Nir, L. (2000). *The Internet and the family, 2000: The view from parents, the view from kids* (Report no. 33). http://www.annenbergpublicpolicycenter.org/downloads/information_and_society/20000516_internet_and_family/20000516_internet_and_family_report.pdf. Accessed 6 Mar 2013.
Walrave, M., & Heirman, W. (2011). Disclosing or protecting? Teenagers' online self-disclosure. In S. Gutwirth, Y. Poullet, P. De Hert, & R. Leenes (Eds.), *Computers, privacy and data protection: An element of choice* (pp. 285–307). Dordrecht, NL: Springer.
Walrave, M., & Heirman, W. (2012). Adolescents, online marketing and privacy: Predicting adolescents' willingness to disclose personal information for marketing purposes. *Children & Society, 27*(6), 1–14. doi:10.1111/j.1099-0860.2011.00423.x.
Walrave, M., Vanwesenbeeck, I., & Heirman, W. (2012). Connecting and protecting? Comparing predictors of selfdisclosure and privacy settings use between adolescents and adults. Cyberpsychology. *Journal of Psychosocial Research on Cyberspace, 6*(1), article 3.
Wheeless, L. (1976). Self-disclosure and interpersonal solidarity: Measurement, validation, and relationships. *Human Communication Research, 3*(1), 47–67.
Wheeless, L. (1978). A follow-up study of the relationships among trust, disclosure, and interpersonal solidarity. *Human Communication Research, 4*, 143–157.
Wheeless, L., & Grotz, J. (1976). Conceptualization and measurement of reported self-disclosure. *Human Communication Research, 2*(4), 339–346.
Yan, Z. (2006). What influences children's and adolescents' understanding of the complexity of the Internet? *Developmental Psychology, 42*(3), 418–428. doi:10.1037/0012-1649.42.3.418.
Youn, S. (2005). Teenagers' perceptions of online privacy and coping behaviors: A risk–benefit appraisal approach. *Journal of Broadcasting & Electronic Media, 49*(1), 86–110. doi:10.1207/s15506878jobem4901_6.
Young, B. (2003). Does food advertising make children obese? *Young Consumers: Insight and Ideas for Responsible Marketers, 4*(3), 19–26.
Yum, Y., & Hara, K. (2005). Computer-mediated relationship development: A cross-cultural comparison. *Journal of Computer-Mediated Communication, 11*(1), 133–152. doi:10.1111/j.1083-6101.2006.tb00307.x.
Zickuhr, K. (2011). Generations 2010. *Pew Internet & American Life Project.* http://www.pewinternet.org/Reports/2010/Generations-2010.aspx. Accessed 7 Mar 2013.

Part III
Risks & Empowerment: Supporting & Empowering Youth

Social Relations: Exploring How Youth Use Social Media to Communicate Signs and Symptoms of Depression and Suicidal Ideation

Jennifer L. Laffier

Abstract Over the last decade it has become apparent that social media may act as a vehicle for youth to communicate signs and symptoms of mental health distress. Therefore, this qualitative case study explored (1) how signs and symptoms of suicide ideation and severe depression can present within the context of social media and (2) how on-line signs and symptoms can be used to create screening tools for the general public. Content analysis of media reports, newspapers, and social media sites revealed several themes such as (1) loneliness, depression and hopelessness were key symptoms, (2) personality characteristics and frequency of social media use acted as mediators to identifying escalation of mental health distress, and (3) engaging in social media may provide both support and further pain for a person experiencing depression. These insights are used to make recommendations for future studies and the development of online screening tools.

1 Introduction

Over the last decade it has become apparent that social media may act as a vehicle for youth to communicate signs and symptoms of mental health distress, in particular suicide ideation and severe depression (Luxton et al. 2012). The media has covered numerous cases of youth who committed suicide and communicated their mental health distress through social media such as Facebook, Twitter, Tumblr and YouTube (Curry 2012). For example, a recent Canadian case was that of Amanda Todd, a 15 year old who communicated her depression and suicide ideation on YouTube over several months before taking her own life (National Post 2012). Suicide is a leading cause of death for youth in many countries including Canada, the United States, Norway, Japan and Belgium (Wasserman et al. 2005). Previous research has indicated warning signs and symptoms for severe depression and

J.L. Laffier, Ph.D. (✉)
Institute of Technology, University of Ontario, Oshawa, ON, Canada
e-mail: Jennifer.Laffier@uoit.ca

M. Walrave et al. (eds.), *Youth 2.0: Social Media and Adolescence*,
DOI 10.1007/978-3-319-27893-3_9

suicidal ideation, which has aided prevention and intervention programmes (American Association of Suicidology 2013; Centre for Addiction and Mental Health 2010). It is the early recognition of these warning signs that is essential to preventing suicide (Sakinofsky and Webster 2010).

However, further exploration of how mental health distress is communicated online, especially on social media sites, is needed. Social media sites such as Facebook, Twitter and YouTube are indicative of the way in which youth today communicate and socialise (Brown et al. 2006). There is an increasing amount of self-disclosure online because adolescents report they are better able to express themselves authentically online perhaps due to the anonymity they feel (Lenhart et al. 2001). Thus, social media have become a key expressive tool for youth where they may express signs and symptoms of depression and suicidal ideation.

This two-phase study explored how youth use social media to communicate mental health distress. The research questions were identified as (1) how can signs and symptoms of suicide ideation and severe depression present themselves within the context of social media and (2) how can on-line signs and symptoms be used to create screening tools for the general public using social media. Phase one involved creating a checklist of signs and symptoms of suicidal ideation from the research, while phase two involved exploring several youth suicide cases reported in the media to examine how these youth used social media during times of mental health distress and what signs of suicide ideation and escalation were presented. Using content analysis of media reports, public interviews and online communications, common themes related to the checklist were identified. Finally, recommendations are made for the development of screening tools and educational programmes for non-professionals, such as youth or parents, to help youth in times of mental health distress.

2 Literature Review

Suicide is a worldwide public health problem amongst adolescents (Bertera 2007). Global statistics for youth suicide (15–19 years. old) show that suicide is the second most common cause of death after road-traffic accidents (Wasserman et al. 2005). There are 164,000 recorded suicide deaths of individuals under 25 years old in the world every year (Bertera 2007). Researchers are quick to point out that this number is a gross underestimate considering the number of unsuccessful suicide attempts every year that are not recorded (Skinner and McFaull 2012) and the misclassification of suicide of young people (Hawton et al. 2012). The suicide rates have increased for several youth populations such as females, youth that identify as lesbian, gay, bisexual or transgender (LGBT), as well as aboriginal youth (Hawton et al. 2012; Wasserman et al. 2005). The suicide methods that youth may choose vary and may include medication, guns, hanging or suffocation (Apter 2010).

There are a number of identified risk factors for suicidal ideation and this includes social factors such as bullying or break-ups, pre-existing mental health problems and alcohol or drug abuse (Apter 2010; Bertera 2007; Skinner and McFaull 2012). However, depression and loneliness were identified as the most influential risk factors for adolescent suicide (American Foundation for Suicide Prevention 2012; Apter 2010; Sun and Hui 2007). Researchers speculated that these two risk factors had a reciprocal relationship resulting in increased negative impacts on mental health (Lasgaard et al. 2011; Sun and Hui 2007). Depression, an overwhelming feeling of sadness and hopelessness, is associated with social withdrawal and self-perceived social failure which can increase the risk of loneliness (Lasgaard et al. 2011). Being lonely in adolescence may not only include feeling alienated from peers but also the feeling of having failed in the critical task of being socially connected (Apter 2010). This in turn causes greater depression. Perpetuating this cycle is the fact that many people tend to respond negatively to people suffering depression (Bertera 2007), thus increasing the depressed individual's feelings of loneliness. The term thwarted belongingness was used by researchers (Lasgaard et al. 2011) to describe a sense that one does not belong to or feel connected with a valued group or relationship; this may cause anger as well as loneliness.

The signs and symptoms of suicide have been recorded by many organisations and research centres such as the American Association of Suicidology (2013), the Centre for Addiction and Mental Health (2010), and the Mental Health Commission of Canada (2012). Signs and symptoms of suicide behaviour are often classified into three categories; behavioural, cognitive and emotional. Behavioural signs and symptoms, the visible behaviours and actions that identify suicidal thoughts and emotions, include (a) giving possessions away, (b) getting affairs in order (bank accounts, wills), (c) excessive crying, (d) agitation, (e) isolating oneself, (f) writing goodbye letters, (g) reaching out to apologise to people, (h) sleeping problems, (i) changes in eating habits, (j) directly or indirectly expressing a wish to die, (k) developing a plan for suicide that includes where, how and when the act will happen (American Association of Suicidology 2013; American Foundation for Suicide Prevention 2012; Apter 2010; Bertera 2007). Emotional signs and symptoms of suicidal ideation include (a) depression, (b) a sense of hopelessness, (c) emotional pain and (d) feeling out of control (American Association of Suicidology 2013; Centre for Addiction and Mental Health 2010). Cognitive signs and symptoms of suicidal ideation, i.e. the thought processes, include (a) being unable to imagine the future, (b) negative or pessimistic thoughts, (c) imagining oneself as worthless and (d) memory and concentration difficulties (American Association of Suicidology 2013; American Foundation for Suicide Prevention 2012; Apter 2010; Bertera 2007; Canadian Association for Suicide Prevention 2014; Hawton et al. 2012; Luxton et al. 2012). These signs and symptoms may progress in intensity and duration as a person moves from suicidal thoughts to ideation (Hawton et al. 2012).

Recently researchers have noted the role that social media play in the lives of adolescents and thus also their potential part in mental health, including suicidal ideation (Luxton et al. 2012). Social networking sites such as MySpace, Facebook, Twitter, blogs and MySpace are particularly popular among young people (Mitchell and Ybarra 2009). Such sites represent a new facet of young people's environments, a place where they spend time exploring their identities and communicating with friends (Mitchell and Ybarra 2009; Robertson et al. 2012). Social media sites such as Facebook can offer an outlet for personal expression and reflection (Blais et al. 2008). Adolescents report that they are better able to be their "true selves" when communicating on the internet than when communicating face-to-face (Lenhart et al. 2001). This increased amount of self-disclosure may be due to the limited availability of other social cues (Blais et al. 2008). Adolescents are better able to experiment with social skills, identities, strategies and receiving support that might have proven more risky in a face-to-face context (Sun and Hui 2007). However, some researchers have pointed out the different effects this increased self-disclosure and social experimenting can have on adolescents; communicating with known others may have a beneficial impact while communicating with strangers may have no impact or a negative impact on relationship quality (Blais et al. 2008).

The role of the internet in suicidal behaviour has been a topic of recent interest (Robertson et al. 2012). Researchers present two views on the link between social media and adolescent suicide: (1) social media increase the risk for youth suicides (Biddle et al. 2008; Lenhart et al. 2001) and (2) social media can be a protective factor against youth suicide (Apter 2010; Luxton et al. 2012; Skinner and McFaull 2012). The first view, more prominent in the literature, suggests that when considering the role of social media in youth suicide, social media increase the risk in several ways. First, social media can offer a "how to" dictionary for youth considering suicide. A number of studies have found that some internet sites promote suicide (Apter 2010; Hawton et al. 2012). These are called "pro-suicide" websites, social media or chat rooms because they offer ideas and support for the act of suicide. Second, social media can cause suicide contagion; when others learn and mimic suicide behaviour through social modelling (Biddle et al. 2008). An adolescent's friends are influential in terms of social modelling with respect to suicidal behaviour and social media may increase the size of a person's circle of influence, thus resulting in an increase in suicide clusters (Robertson et al. 2012). A suicide cluster is defined as an excessive number of suicides or attempted suicides occurring more closely together in time and space than would typically be expected in a particular community (Robertson et al. 2012). In past studies researchers (Luxton et al. 2012) found that social media allowed for the rapid spread of information and rumours within communities.

Recent literature suggests the need to explore social media and the Internet as a protective factor for young people (Hawton et al. 2012; Luxton et al. 2012; Robertson et al. 2012; Skinner and McFaull 2012). Social media may be able to act as a prevention aid by offering online support groups or crisis centre information (Skinner and McFaull 2012). In addition, if people were getting help online this would reduce the number of suicides, thus reducing the contagion effect. However, more controlled studies are required to explore how these information and support sites are utilised and give support to people at risk (Hawton et al. 2012). Some researchers (Luxton et al. 2012; Robertson et al. 2012) noted one possible benefit of social media is the ability to screen people at risk. The monitoring of social networking sites by suicide prevention agencies would allow detection of conversations after a suicide that might give cause for concern. This in turn could lead to a posting from the agency to remind people they are there to help if needed (Robertson et al. 2012). Key words could be identified as high-risk words when typed into computers allowing suicide support groups to send messages to posters. Some social media sites such as Twitter and Facebook are already engaging in such activities (Curry 2012). However, privacy settings on social networking sites, the differentiated words that could be used to signify suicidal ideation and available resources for online crisis support may present barriers for this to happen.

The risks and benefits of social media related to suicide warrants further investigation (Skinner and McFaull 2012) and a number of gaps have been identified. First, although there are self-reports for reporting risk factors and the presence of suicide ideation, there are still major problems in the objective assessment of suicidal adolescents (Bertera 2007). Second, there is a need to understand the time sequence that affects suicidal ideation; this includes how individuals escalate from minor thoughts to frequent ideation (Apter 2010). Third, there is a need for greater understanding of the factors that contribute to suicide in young people (Hawton et al. 2012). Lastly, – and this is the gap this study aims to address, – there is a need to understand the role that social media play in the communication of suicidal ideation by adolescents (Hawton et al. 2012; Luxton et al. 2012).

3 Methods

3.1 Research Design and Method

In order to accomplish the research aim of this study, which was to explore how signs and symptoms of suicide ideation and severe depression can present within the context of social media, a qualitative case study was used with four public cases of adolescent suicides in North America. A case study design was chosen as being conducive to describing context and illustrating participants' realities and actions, both essential to fulfilling the purpose of this study (Yin 2009). Using small sample sizes such as this allows for detailed descriptions that can uncover patterns of meanings that might be lost with larger sample sizes (Eisenhart and Graebner 2007). Data from the four case studies allowed for comparison and congruence. However, as is typical in exploratory and interpretative case study research (Yin 2009), each case was reviewed individually before cross-case comparisons were made. Although generalisation is difficult with small sample sizes, the purpose of this study was to explore potential themes in order to guide and conduct further studies in this area.

In order to understand how the four adolescents used social media, public information, such as media releases and social media communications, was explored. Content analysis, – a qualitative data reduction method that attempts to identify core themes and meanings from text or images, – was used as it provided the opportunity to understand the adolescents' social reality in a subjective yet scientific manner (Zhang and Wildemuth 2009). In order to create the themes a directed content analysis approach was used whereby initial coding was developed from theories and relevant research findings related to signs and symptoms of depression and suicidal ideation (Berg and Lune 2011). Thus, this study involved two phases of research: (1) creating a checklist of signs and symptoms of suicide and severe depression from a review of the literature in order to guide analysis of case studies (2) content analysis of each case to review how the signs and symptoms of suicide or severe depression were communicated.

3.2 Sample

Purposeful sampling was applied in this study in order to select participants who could provide insight and in-depth information about this phenomenon of central importance (Fletcher and Plakoyiannaki 2010). Selection criterion included (1) current or prominent cases in the media to increase available data sources on each case, (2) adolescents similar in age range in order to increase reliability of cross-case comparisons, (3) adolescents from Canada and United States to increase cultural similarities and (4), adolescents who used social media. Based on these criteria four cases were selected for this exploratory study: (1) Amanda Todd, 15 years old from British Columbia, Canada, (2) Jamie Humbly, 14 years old from Ontario, Canada, (3) Felicia Garcia, 15 years old from New York, United States and (4) Amanda Cummings, 15 years old from New York, United States. These cases were explored to understand the role that social media play in the lives of adolescents suffering from suicidal ideation and depression.

3.3 Data Analysis

Phase One In order to understand the communication of suicide and severe depression in an online environment the signs and symptoms of suicide were first reviewed. Phase one involved completing a literature review of the signs and symptoms of suicide ideation identified by experts in the field. To conduct this literature review the following methods were used: (1) an internet search of key words "suicide", "adolescents", "depression", suicide risk factors, "suicidal signs and symptoms", (2) an internet search for major organisations and associations related to suicide and mental health and (3), a review of suicide intervention and prevention training manuals. All of the signs and symptoms identified in the related documents were recorded and then re-examined to identify the most common cited signs and symptoms or overlapping ideas. Upon completion a checklist was created of common suicidal signs and symptoms (Table 1).

Table 1 Suicide checklist: Signs and symptoms identified from literature review

Symptoms	Signs
Hopelessness	Expressing wish to die
Depression/emotional pain	Has a suicide plan
Desperation	Isolation/social withdrawal
Loneliness	Getting affairs in order
Thwarted belongingness (perception of social failure, not belonging)	Inability to cope (self-medication, confusion, risky behaviour)
Pessimism/negative thoughts	Making amends
Anxiety/agitation	Preoccupation with death
Low self-esteem/feelings of worthlessness	Giving items away
Anger	Saying goodbyes
	Excessive crying
	Sleeping/eating difficulties

Phase Two Interpretative content analysis was conducted on the data sources for each adolescent. First data were collected by searching the public records for each case through websites, news archives, public interviews with family and friends and recorded online communications. These data were separated for each case and put into chronological order to piece together a timeline of events. Second, the unit of analysis was defined as words or images from the data that communicated themes of suicidal ideation and severe depression. Third, the coding schemes for the units of analysis were developed; each sign/symptom from the checklist was defined as a potential theme and created as a code (i.e. depression or loneliness). Fourth, the data were coded by going through each data source and reviewing what the adolescent did on social media sites, including what they wrote, posted, liked, created or browsed. Once a theme was identified from their use of words, images or behaviours it was coded and then entered into a construct table that contained columns for each theme, case and date (Zhang and Wildemuth 2009; Berg and Lune 2011). In order to ensure reliability, direct comments made by the adolescents were recorded the way they were written, including slang and grammar or spelling mistakes (Yin 2009). An extra column was created titled *new themes* for any emerging themes not identified by the literature review. Fifth, the consistency of coding schemes was evaluated by re-checking the coded items and their relationship to each other. Through this process it was noted that several units of analysis needed to have more than one code because they fitted into several categories. Lastly, conclusions were drawn from the data (first on a case by case basis and then using a cross-case comparison). This involved adding a separate column to the construct table that summarised the case evidence and indicated how the construct was measured (Yin 2009) (Table 2).

Table 2 Sample of construct table used for evidence of each case

Theme	Evidence	Date	Summary notes
Depression			
Loneliness			
Anger			
Hopelessness			
Desperation			
New theme?			

4 Results

The results of this analysis are presented in narrative case presentations. First, each case is presented individually and then a brief cross-case comparison is presented. These results are then followed by a discussion of the findings as well as the implications and recommendations from this study.

4.1 *Individual Case Presentations*

Case 1: Amanda Todd Amanda, a grade ten student from British Columbia had suffered mental health issues, including anxiety, depression and eating disorders, as well as peer victimisation, prior to her suicide in October 2012 (Grenoble 2012). A series of events involving harassment and cyber-bullying from a specific male and peers had increased her mental health anguish. Through a video chat room in 2007 she met a male who convinced her to post semi-nude pictures of herself. This male later distributed the photos on the Internet and used them to create a fake Facebook page (Shaw 2013). This resulted in ridicule and bullying from peers that caused Amanda to move two times; she began to experience anxiety, taking drugs and alcohol, practising self-harm behaviours and suffering depression (National Post 2012). A later incident involving a sexual encounter with a past boyfriend caused an altercation with Amanda and a group of girls led by the male's girlfriend. Amanda was assaulted and shortly afterwards attempted suicide (Grenoble 2012). Derogatory remarks and insults were left on Amanda Todd's Facebook page after her suicide attempt. Although Amanda received mental health treatment she continued to experience anxiety and depression up to the time of her death (Shaw 2013).

During this time Amanda had used social media sites, such as chat-rooms, Facebook and YouTube, and expressed herself with technological tools such as prezi and video recordings on her phone (National Post 2012; Todd 2012a, b, c). She created a prezi about bullying to bring awareness to others and this made her feel better for a short time (Todd 2012a, b, c). One month prior to her death she posted a 9 min video clip to YouTube titled *My Story: Struggling, bullying, suicide and self-harm* (National Post 2012). In the video she used flashcards, without any verbal communication, to tell of her ordeal. Through her narrative she expressed many signs and symptoms of suicide and severe depression. Amanda hinted at feeling *lonely* in one of her slides "I have no one" (Todd 2012a, b, c). In addition to direct statements of feeling lonely she demonstrated signs of *isolation.* Amanda suffered from agoraphobia, barely leaving the house for months due to anxiety and peer victimisation (Shaw 2013); she also frequently posted photos and videos on her own. She demonstrated a *wish to die* by stating: "I wanted to die so bad" and describing her previous attempt "when he brought me home I drank bleach" (Todd 2012a, b, c). *Emotional pain* and *depression* was communicated in her words "I started cutting", "I am constantly crying now", "I cried every night", "Constantly cutting, very depressed.", "It killed me inside" (Todd 2012a, b, c). She was demonstrating constant and uncontrollable *crying*, a sign of depression (American Association of Suicidology 2013). Signs of *depression* were also evident in the video in Amanda's body language. Amanda shared feelings of *hopelessness;* "Life's never getting better" and "every day I think...why am I still here" (Todd 2012a, b, c). Amanda's *desperation* was evident in her YouTube video where she attempted to ask for help: "I have no one, I need someone" (Todd 2012a, b, c). Because this cry for help was made to the public it could be assumed that Amanda was desperate for someone to help her. In this 9-min video she also communicated the *inability to cope*; she wrote about drinking, self-cutting, risky behaviour and confusion (Shaw 2013). Prior to her death Amanda left a *goodbye message* for her mother by creating a video on her phone (Shaw 2013).

Amanda Todd demonstrated numerous signs and symptoms of suicidal ideation not only through her words, but also through her body language and actions. She demonstrated depression, emotional pain, loneliness, hopelessness, desperation, crying, isolation and a wish to die. Her use of technology may have also indicated an escalation of depression. Her prezi, created on 7 September 2012 was about bullying and was meant to be informative; the focus was not on her personal experiences of bullying. However, her YouTube video clip created on 11 October 2012 about bullying was very personal and expressed many signs and symptoms of severe depression and suicide. In the video she directly asked for help. Although technology and social media may have given Amanda a method of expressing herself, they also became a source of negativity; she experienced cyber-bullying and harassment from peers and strangers on chat rooms, Facebook and YouTube. This negative feedback from her social environment often triggered or escalated Amanda's feelings of depression and loneliness (Shaw 2013).

Case 2: Jamie Hubley Jamie a grade ten student from Ottawa, Canada was openly gay and took his own life in 2011 after years of experiencing bullying, depression and loneliness (CBC 2011). Being an openly gay male at a Catholic school in a small town in Canada was hard for Jamie (CTV News 2011). In grade seven Jamie was harassed on a school bus for participating in figure skating. A group of boys on the bus tried shoving batteries down his throat (CBC 2011). His parents moved him to a public school in the hope that things would get better but according to his parents things did not improve (CBC 2011). Jamie was teased and harassed for his sexuality. He tried to advocate for gay rights through his school rainbow club (a gay-straight alliance group). However, shortly after putting posters up to support the club the posters were torn down (CTV News 2011).

Jamie often engaged with social media sites; he had his own blog page on tumblr and used YouTube to post comments or videos of himself (Tumblr 2011). Earlier online communications from Jamie were positive as he discussed such topics as his love for music and hopes of meeting someone (CTV News 2011). However, with time his posts became more negative; he expressed frustration and *anger* for being the only openly gay male at his school and wanting to find a boyfriend; "I hate being the only open gay guy in my school… It f***ing sucks" (CBC 2011). He expressed feelings of *depression* on his blog; "Being sad is sad… I'v been like this for way to long" (Tumblr 2011). He also made direct comments of being on medication for depression; "Iv been on 4 different anti -depressants, none of them worked. I'v been depressed since January, How f***ing long is this going to last" (CTV News 2011). Jamie communicated feelings of *hopelessness* and *inability to cope*; "How do you even know It will get better? its not" and "I really want to end it. Like all of it, I not getting better theres 3 more years of highschool left" (CTV News 2011). Shortly before his death he wrote; "I'm tired of life, really. It's so hard, I'm sorry, I can't take it anymore" and "I don't want to wait 3 years" (Tumblr 2011). He demonstrated *emotional pain* in his communications; "It's just too hard. This hurts too much." (Tumblr 2011). *Emotional pain* was also evident in the way he described himself as broken; "You can't break what is already broke" and "You bent me until I broke" (CTV News 2011). This may also demonstrate *low self-esteem* since he sees himself as damaged. Jamie often posted video clips of himself alone, either signing or dancing and this could demonstrate *isolation. Anger* was demonstrated in several posts: "f-ck hig school and f—ck having shitty friends" (Burke 2011) and in his final post "like me (many) a big f--k you. Go ride a unicorn" (Tumblr 2011). As time went on Jamie's posts of depression and loneliness became more frequent (Burke 2011) demonstrating escalation of his depression. Indirect *wishes to die* were expressed several times in his blogs "I really want it to end", "I am tired of life", and "Maybe in my next life I will be a flying squirrel" (Tumblr 2011).

Jamie Hubley demonstrated several signs and symptoms of suicidal ideation and severe depression on social media sites such as tumblr and YouTube; emotional pain, depression, anger, loneliness, wish to die, inability to cope and isolation. Jamie used social media as an outlet to express himself. Over time his expressions of hopelessness, loneliness and depression became more frequent, demonstrating an escalation of depression and suicidal ideation. There were fewer and fewer "good day" announcements. Similar to Amanda Todd, Jamie used his social media to indirectly seek help; he posed the question "how do you even know it will get better?" as if seeking a response. Signs and symptoms of Jamie's depression were not only evident in his direct communications (words), but also in his body language portrayed in his videos and pictures; he appeared sad and lethargic. Like Amanda Todd, Jamie left a suicide note on his blog page instead of a hand written note.

Case 3: Felicia Garcia Felicia was from New York and took her own life in October 2012 by jumping in front of a subway train in front of her classmates (Pow

2012). Felicia had a difficult childhood. Her parents died when she was young and she went to live with her aunt. However, her aunt was unable to care for her and Felicia moved in and out of foster care homes where she frequently ran away (Chapman et al. 2012). In high school Felicia experienced a number of events that impacted on her mental health. Rumours were spread at the high school that Felicia had had sexual relations with several boys on the football team at a party. The encounters were recorded and quickly spread throughout the school. Felicia experienced bullying and harassment because of this event and suffered depression (Driskill 2012). School personnel attempted a mediation session with her and one of the males on the football team however the male denied harassing Felicia in the session. Immediately after the session she exchanged words with another football player (Chapman et al. 2012). She took her life that same day by falling backwards onto the subway track after school where many classmates stood (Pow 2012).

Felicia liked to use social media sites such as Twitter, Facebook, Instagram and YouTube. Although Felicia was described as a private and tough person (Pow 2012) she did demonstrate some signs and symptoms of depression and suicide ideation on these sites. She posted a photo of herself on Instagram that demonstrated *depression;* the photo was of her smiling, however the word depressed was cut and pasted across her eyes. The caption read "Just because someone is smiling does not make them happy" (Driskill 2012). This photo may have been a call for help. In another photo she wore makeup to look like she had stitches going through her mouth to keep her mouth closed and makeup to look like blood and injuries on her face. Although no caption was included, this photo might have portrayed the *anger*, *isolation* and *depression* she was feeling. The tweets on her Twitter account demonstrated *anger* and *thwarted belongingness* from the treatment she was receiving from peers; "treat me like a joke and I will leave you like it's funny", "guys who play with girls head #BLOWME!", "when bitches are pussy and cannot handle their own problems, or when they continue talking shit on facebook and twitter", "I hate when people are in my business, you don't even know what's going on, mind ya neck!", and "people should really consider wearing a diaper around their mouth considering all the shit they talk" (Driskill 2012). These last two tweets were posted less than 2 weeks before Felicia took her own life (Pow 2012). Two days before Felicia died by suicide she posted her last tweet saying "I cant, ım done, I give up" (Pow 2012). The message communicated several signs and symptoms; a *wish to die*, *saying goodbye, hopelessness* and *inability to cope*. After Felicia's death strangers and peers her age posted derogatory remarks and images on Facebook YouTube and other social media sites.

Felicia Garcia demonstrated some signs and symptoms of depression, including a clear message of suicidal ideation 2 days before she took her life. Her tweets and photos on Instagram demonstrated *anger*, *depression* and *isolation*. Her final message demonstrated a sense of *hopelessness* that things would not get better and she could not *cope* with her situation. Escalation of her anger and frustration was demonstrated by more negative posts and less happy communications about football or friends. According to her family and friends Felicia demonstrated toughness; she rarely cried, showed her pain or reacted to bullies (Driskill 2012). The need to appear tough or in control may have been due to her upbringing She often reacted to her situation with expressions of anger instead of sadness. Such behaviour may mask signs and symptoms of depression and suicidal ideation on social media sites. However, this case demonstrates that underlying feelings of depression can be communicated, not only in written text, but also through images.

Case 4: Amanda Cummings Amanda, also from New York, was described as sensitive and artistic. She died by jumping in front of a city bus with a suicide note in her pocket 2 days after Christmas (Chapman and Boyle 2012). Speculation about the causes of Amanda's death focused on bullying, a history of depression, self-harm and heart break over boys (Mackenzie 2012). Amanda had received psychological treatment for her self-cutting at an earlier time (Chapman and Boyle 2012). She was in a relationship with an older boy that ended soon before her death (Mackenzie 2012). Her suicide note mentioned not being able to live without him (mydeathspace 2012). Family members reported that Amanda was being bullied and harassed by classmates due to her relationship with the male; one of the girls liked the boy as well.

For weeks leading up to her death Amanda posted messages on Facebook chronicling her feelings and thoughts. Signs of *depression* were evident in several posts; "worst sat. nite evr I cnt believe this is happening what did I do to deserve this?", "im spending this sat nite alone in my room crying", and "I am so tired-__________-fml depressed mood too" (Chapman and Boyle 2012). Amanda demonstrated *desperation* for help through her Facebook message posted 11 days before her death; "When I say Im ok I want that one person to look me in the eye, hug me, and say no you are not". She expressed feelings of *loneliness*; "mad people are turning against me, I am spending this sat nite alone in my room" (Chapman and Boyle 2012). This sense of *thwarted belongingness* caused anger and loneliness. Her *anger* was evident in her post "ur gunna catch a cold from the ice inside ur heart" (Mackenzie 2012). Thoughts of suicide, including a potential *plan*, were evident in several posts; "ill go kill myself with these pills, this knife, this life had already done half the job", "getting ready then im outa here, im off this" (McKenzie and Keneally 2012). On the day she died she posted a message on Facebook "Nd, I'll die tonight crying over you". After seeing this message her family and friends frantically tried calling her, texting her and posting messages on Facebook to get her to come home (Mackenzie 2012). She jumped in front of a city bus at 7:30 pm that evening but did not die from her injuries until a week later (McKenzie and Keneally 2012). While she was in the hospital, and even after her death, derogatory messages were left on her Facebook page and posted to Youtube.

Amanda Cummings demonstrated signs of depression, loneliness, anger, a wish to die, thoughts of suicide, as well as a plan for suicide. She made several direct remarks about ending her pain and killing herself. Although Amanda used Facebook to express her feelings and perhaps gain support from peers she also received negative feedback, similar to Amanda Todd. Even after her death people posted derogatory remarks on her Facebook site. Her symptoms escalated with more frequent posts of depression and loneliness throughout December, although there were periodic posts of happily anticipating Christmas.

Cross-Case Comparison When a cross-case comparison was conducted of the four cases several similarities and differences were noted. The most common and notable symptoms expressed by the teenagers were depression, emotional pain, loneliness, thwarted belongingness and hopelessness. Three of the teenagers left a final goodbye on a social media site; Amanda Cummings on Facebook, Jamie Hubley on his blog, Felicia Garcia on Twitter. Jamie, Felicia and Amanda Cummings all died within 2 days of their final posts. In all four cases there were allegations that bullying contributed to the teenagers' suicides. This coincides with findings from researchers that bullying can be a contributing factor in youth suicides (Sun and Hui 2007). For three of the adolescents, Amanda Todd, Amanda Cummings and Felicia Garcia, the very social media sites they used to express themselves became a vehicle on which others could post derogatory remarks about their deaths and personal characters. Three of the four youth, Amanda Todd, Amanda Cummings and Jamie Hubley, directly or indirectly reached out for help through social media. The one youth described as "tough", Felicia Garcia, did not make any requests or appeals for help. She often portrayed only anger and did not point out the trouble in her life. The two teenagers described as "sensitive", Jamie Hubley and Amanda Cummings, used their social media sites more frequently and expressed more private emotions and thoughts. These findings and other insights of this exploratory study are discussed further.

4.2 *Discussion*

Several insights as to how youth can use social media to communicate signs and symptoms of suicide ideation and how screening tools could be developed were gained from this exploratory study. It was evident that social media sites could record information like a personal journal, demonstrating mood patterns and activities over a period of time. Such online journals can be useful for detecting escalation of mental health problems, such as depression. When experiencing suicidal ideation, thoughts of suicide, death or emotional pain become more frequent; the person has less good days and becomes preoccupied with their symptoms (Livingworks.com). This was particularly evident for Jamie Hubley and Amanda Cummings whose negative posts escalated. However, the findings from this study suggest that personality characteristics may affect the amount of personal and sensitive information that a person shares. Individuals similar to Felicia Garcia for instance, may not demonstrate a clear escalation process if they are not revealing as much information. In addition, differences in personality characteristics or conflict styles may impact the way a person reacts to feelings of thwarted belongingness. Some teenagers may convey sadness due to being left out where others convey anger; this difference was evident between Felicia Garcia and Amanda Todd. Depression in the guise of anger should be considered in screening tools and awareness programmes. Time spent on social media sites will also affect signs of the escalation of mental health problems; if a person is not using social media frequently the patterns will be disrupted. Therefore, online screening tools for suicide should consider the dates and frequency of engagement on social media sites as mediators for the signs or symptoms.

The most prominent signs and symptoms of suicidal ideation in the four cases were depression, loneliness and hopelessness and these three symptoms may need to be highlighted in suicide programmes. Researchers (Lasgaard et al. 2011; Sun and Hui 2007) suggested that depression and loneliness act in a cyclical fashion; people tend to isolate others with depressions causing more feelings of loneliness for the person. This may have happened for the youth in this study; the more they presented depression or their need for help the more they risked isolation from their peer group. There were indications that this was the case for Amanda Todd; after she posted her YouTube video clip she received numerous derogatory and hurtful remarks on her Facebook page and YouTube comments section (Grenoble 2012). This would have increased her feelings of isolation and thwarted belongingness. Hence, social media may act as a double-edged sword for people experiencing depression; it can cause pain as well as provide support. This coincides with research that suggests communicating with known others may have a beneficial impact while communicating with strangers may have a negative impact on relationship quality (Blais et al. 2008). Suicide screening tools or programmes should include this information in order to inform people of how the type of support individuals are receiving or not receiving online can make their symptoms escalate. In addition, key words or phrases representing loneliness, depression or hopelessness should be provided as examples in online screening tools for the general public.

Social media and online technology also bring a new realm of communication not seen in face-to-face interactions. That includes communication through pictures, images or videos as we saw with Felicia Garcia, Amanda Todd and Jamie Hubley. Many social media sites such as Facebook, Instagram, YouTube and tumblr allow users to be creative and create videos, pictures, collages or personal pictures. Choices in pictures and creative displays can be revelations of emotions according to research in the field of creative therapies (Malchiodi 2011). Feelings of loneliness and depression can be communicated through images, as seen in the way Felicia Garcia communicated her feelings of depression in her photo of herself with the word depression cut and pasted over her eyes. Most suicide intervention and awareness programmes do not consider online adaptations of signs and symptoms of suicide or severe depression, especially considerations for visual presentations such as videos and pictures. Methods of reviewing or analysing photos for signs or symptoms of suicide or depression should be examined, especially for social media sites geared towards youth that are naturally exploring their creative instincts (Malchiodi 2011).

Posting suicide notes on social network sites in place of hand-written notes appears to be a recent phenomenon that is not clearly understood (Ruder et al. 2011). In this study, social media provided the means for three of the four youth to leave a suicide note or final message. Jamie posted a message on his blog site, Felicia Garcia left a message on twitter and Amanda Cummings left a message on Facebook. Although it is not a social media site, Amanda Todd left her mother a message on her phone in the form of a video (Shaw 2013). A consideration for future studies and suicide screening tools is the fact that Jamie, Felicia and Amanda Cummings all died within 2 days of their final posts. This may indicate the severity of their feelings and seriousness of such posts or remarks on social media sites. In addition, posting a suicide note or goodbye message on a public site may put greater pressure on teens to follow through with their actions. A hand-written note can be kept private and discarded if the teenagers change their mind but messages on social media sites remain forever once posted. Teenagers, who value toughness or credibility, may feel they need to walk to the talk amongst their peer groups. It was also noted from this analysis that the word "*can't*" was used by three of the four youth close to the end of their lives. The word can't is associated with a feeling of `no alternative (dictionary.com). Such key words could be provided as examples in screening tools for the general public to give them direction on how emotions and feelings may be described.

4.3 Limitations

This study is limited in the ability to generalise its results to larger population sizes because of the small sample size. However, this study could be used for generalisation to theoretical propositions or populations that share commonalities of experience through interpretation of the data (Kapitan 2010). In addition, analytical and theoretical generalisations could be explored with future studies using larger sample sizes. There are several possible limitations to using qualitative data, as identified in the literature and applicable to this study: (1) the meaning of words or phrases could be misinterpreted by researchers (Yin 2009), (2) the contextual nature of statements may not be understood (Stake 2010) and (3), visual images are subjective (Malchiodi 2011). In addition, information was limited for each of the cases because social media sites are often shut down when the user is deceased. This prevents a full review of their historical online activity.

4.4 Implications/Recommendations

This exploratory study has a number of implications for future research. By exploring how warning signs and symptoms of suicide are presented online, screening tools may be developed to assist in the prevention of suicide. Such screening tools can be combined with current screening methods that do not consider virtual signs and symptoms, and with aid of professionals and non-professionals, such as parents or peers, in identifying mental health distress. Current initiatives by social media such as Facebook, Twitter and Tumblr are limited in what they screen, assess and how they can provide interventions (Luxton et al. 2012). Thus, friends, families and the online community can learn how to identify warning signs. Giving the general public the resources and tools to identify severe depression and suicidal ideation may help fill the mental health service gap (Sakinofsky and Webster 2010). Of even greater value is helping adolescents, the population group most at risk and the highest consumers of social media, learn how to identity mental health distress in their peers and assist in the prevention and intervention of adolescent suicide.

The findings from this study suggest future research directions, as well as recommendations for the development of online screening tools and awareness programmes related to suicide. These include: (1) loneliness, depression and hopelessness should be highlighted as key symptoms related to suicidal ideation, (2) examples of key words or phrases representing signs and symptoms should be researched and provided on screening tools, (3) methods of reviewing and evaluating images, videos and pictures should be further researched and provided on screening tools, (4) personality characteristics and frequency of social media use should be discussed as mediators for identifying the escalation process, (5) methods of identifying and immediately addressing goodbye messages should be included in screening tools and awareness programmes, (6) methods for reviewing timelines of events to assess the escalation process should be included on screening tools, (7) methods of assessing the types of support a person is receiving online (positive vs. negative) should be discussed and included and (8), a full checklist of signs and symptoms should be developed with examples of online adaptations. Considering the insights from this preliminary study, future research in these areas will be conducted in a third phase in order to develop an online screening tool for suicide to be used by the general public.

References

American Association of Suicidology. (2013). *Stats & tools: Warning signs*. www.suicidology.org/web/guest/stats-and-tools/warningsigns. Accessed May 2013.

American Foundation for Suicide Prevention. (2012). *About suicide: Facts and figures*. http://www.afsp.org/index.cfm?page_id=04EA1254-BD31-1FA3-C549D77E6CA6AA37. Accessed May 2013.

Apter, A. (2010). Suicidal behavior in adolescence. *The Canadian Journal of Psychiatry, 5*(55), 271–273.

Berg, B. L., & Lune, H. (2011). *Qualitative research methods for the social sciences* (8th ed.). Los Angeles: Allyn and Bacon.

Bertera, E. M. (2007). The role of positive and negative social exchanges between adolescents, their peers and family as predictors of suicide ideation. *The Child and Adolescent Social Work Journal, 24*, 523–538.

Biddle, L., Donovan, J., Hawton, K., Kapur, N., & Gunnell, D. (2008). Suicide and the internet. *British Medical Journal, 336*, 800–802.

Blais, J. J., Craig, W. M., Peplar, D., & Connolly, J. (2008). Adolescents online: The importance of internet activity choices to salient relationships. *Youth Adolescence, 37*, 522–536. doi:10.1007/s10964-007-9262-7.

Brown, K., Cassidy, W., & Jackson, M. (2006). Cyber-bullying: Developing policy to direct responses that are equitable and effective in addressing this special form of bullying. *Canadian Journal of Educational Administration and Policy, 57*. http://umanitoba.ca/publications/cjeap/articles/brown_jackson_cassidy.html. Accessed 20 Sept 2011.

Burke, A. (2011, October 18). Gay Ottawa teen who killed himself was bullied. *CBC News, Ottawa*. http://www.cbc.ca/news/canada/ottawa/story/2011/10/18/ottawa-teen-suicide-father.html. Accessed May 2013.

Canadian Association for Suicide Prevention. (2014). *Suicide prevention*. http://suicideprevention.ca/understanding/what-is-suicide-prevention-intervention-and-postvention/. Accessed June 2013.

Canadian Broadcasting Centre. (2011). *Gay Ottawa teen who killed himself was bullied*. http://www.cbc.ca/news/canada/ottawa/story/2011/10/18/ottawa-teen-suicide-father.html. Accessed May 2013.

Canadian Mental Health Association. (2012). *Mental health first aid manual*. Ottawa: Canadian Mental Health Association.

Centre for Addiction and Mental Health. (2010). *Suicide prevention and assessment handbook*. Toronto: Author.

Chapman, B., & Boyle, C. (2012, January 3). Staten Island teen Amanda Cummings kills self by jumping in front of bus after being bullied. *The NY Daily News*. http://www.nydailynews.com/new-york/staten-island-teen-kills-jumping-front-bus-family-cites-bullies-article-1.1000243. Accessed May 2013.

Chapman, B., Kemp, J., Siemasko, C., & Tasch, J. (2012, October 25). Tormented 15 year-old Felicia Garcia jumped to death in front of train after bullying over sex with football players. *The NY Daily News*. http://www.nydailynews.com/new-york/15-year-old-throws-front-train-staten-island-article-1.1191808. Accessed May 2013.

CTV News. (2011, October 7). *Ottawa teen details final suicidal thoughts on blog*. http://www.ctvnews.ca/ottawa-teen-details-final-suicidal-thoughts-on-blog-1.712337. Accessed June 2013.

Curry, C. (2012, March 29). Facebook taking proactive stance against suicides. *ABC News*. http://abcnews.go.com/US/facebook-social-media-sites-working-offer-suicide-users/story?id=16029673. Accessed June 2013.

Driskill, K. (2012, October 28). Another tragic result of bullying, Felicia Garcia jumps in front of train. *The Examiner*. http://www.examiner.com/article/another-tragic-result-of-bullying--felicia-garcia-jumps-front-of-train. Accessed June 2013.

Eisenhart, K. M., & Graebner, M. E. (2007). Theory building from cases: Opportunities and challenges. *Academy of Management Journal, 50*(1), 25–32.

Fletcher, M., & Plakoyiannaki, E. (2010). *Sampling in case study research: Encyclopedia of case study research*. Thousand Oaks: Sage Publications. http://reference.com/casestudy/Article_n307.html. Accessed June 2013.

Grenoble, R. (2012, October 11). Amanda Todd: Bullied Canadian teen commits suicide after prolonged battle online and in school. *The Huffington Post*. http://www.huffingtonpost.com/2012/10/11/amanda-todd-suicide-bullying_n_1959909.html?utm_hp_ref=amanda-todd#slide=1637677. Accessed June 2013.

Hawton, K., Saunders, K. E. A., & O'Connor, R. (2012). Self-harm and suicide in adolescents. *Centre for Suicide Research Series, 379*, 2373–2383.

Kapitan, L. (2010). *Introduction to art therapy research*. London: Routledge.

Lasgaard, M., Goossens, L., & Elklit, A. (2011). Loneliness, depressive symptomatology, and suicide ideation in adolescence: Cross-sectional and longitudinal analyses. *Journal of Abnormal Child Psychiatry, 39*, 137–150. doi:10.1007/s10802-010-9442-x.

Lenhart, A., Rainie, L., & Lewis, O. (2001). *Teenage life online: The rise of the instant- message generation and the internet's impact on friendships and family relationships*. Washington, DC: Pew Internet and American Life Project.

Luxton, D., June, J., & Fairall, J. (2012). Social media and suicide: A public health perspective. *American Journal of Public Health, Supplement 2: Framing Health Matters, 102*(S2), 195–200.
Mackenzie, C. (2012, January 7). Heartbreak for family at funeral of 15 year-old who killed herself because of bullying- and are still bombarded with hate messages on tribute page. *The Daily Mail.* http://www.dailymail.co.uk/news/article-2083504/Amanda-Cummings-suicide-Hate-messages-Facebook-tribute-page.html#axzz2JhfcgBnC. Accessed June 2013.
Malchiodi, C. (2011). *Handbook of art therapy*. New York: Guildford Press.
McKenzie, C., & Keneally, M. (2012, January 17). *Bullying NOT the reason why 15-year-old girl jumped in front of the bus even though her death was taunted online.* http://www.dailymail.co.uk/news/article-2087854/Amanda-Cummings-suicide-Bullying-NOT-reason-15-year-old-jumped-bus.html#ixzz2fg9ay9sJ. Accessed June 2013.
Mitchell, K., & Ybarra, M. (2009). Social networking sites: Finding a balance between their risks and benefits. *Archives of Pediatric Adolescent Medicine, 163*, 87–89.
Mydeathspace. (2012, January 7). *Amanda Cummings (15) jumped in front of a bus after posting suicide threats on Facebook.* http://mydeathspace.com/article/2012/01/07/Amanda_Cummings_%2815%29_jumped_in_front_of_a_bus_after_posting_suicide_threats_on_Facebook. Accessed June 2013.
National Post. (2012, October 12). *Weeks after posting haunting YouTube video on her years of torment at classmates' hands, 15-year-old B.C. girl commits suicide.* http://news.nationalpost.com/2012/10/12/amanda-todd-suicide-2012/. Accessed June 2013.
Pow, H. (2012, October 25). "I can't. I'm done. I give up": Bullied teen jumps to her death in front of train as schoolmates look on in horror just days after harrowing tweet. *The Daily Mail.* http://www.dailymail.co.uk/news/article-2223133/Felicia-Garcia-suicide-Bullied-teen-jumps-death-train-schoolmates-look-horror-just-days-harrowing-tweet.html#axzz2JhfcgBnC. Accessed June 2013.
Robertson, L., Skegg, K., Poore, M., Williams, S., & Taylor, B. (2012). An adolescent suicide cluster and the possible role of electronic communication technology. *Crisis, 33*(4), 239–245.
Ruder, T. D., Hatch, G. M., Ampanozil, G., Thalil, M. J., & Fischer, N. (2011). Suicide announcement on Facebook. *Crisis, 32*(5), 280–282.
Sakinofsky, I., & Webster, G. (2010). The epidemiology of suicide in Canada. In J. Cairney & D. L. Streiner (Eds.), *Mental disorder in Canada: An epidemiological perspective*. Toronto: University of Toronto Press.
Shaw, G. (2013, March 13). Amanda Todd's mother speaks out about her daughter, bullying. *The Vancouver Sun.* http://www.vancouversun.com/news/Amanda+Todd+speaks+about+daughter+death/7384521/story.html. Accessed June 2013.
Skinner, R., & McFaull, S. (2012). Suicide among children and adolescents in Canada: Trends and sex differences, 1998–2008. *Canadian Medical Association Journal, 184*(9), 1029–1034.
Stake, R. (2010). *Qualitative research: Studying how things work*. New York: Guilford Press.
Sun, R. C. F., & Hui, E. K. P. (2007). Psychosocial factors contributing to adolescent suicidal ideation. *Journal of Youth Adolescence, 36*, 775–786.
Todd, A. (2012a, September). *Cyber Bullying* [Prezi Presentation]. http://prezi.com/atoa68w-rotkm/cyber-bulling/. Accessed June 2013.
Todd, A. (2012b, October). *Amanda Todd's story: Struggling, bullying, suicide, self-harm*. (video file). http://www.youtube.com/watch?v=ej7afkypUsc. Accessed June 2013.
Todd, C. (2012c). *Amanda Todd legacy webpage*. http://amandatoddlegacy.org/. Accessed June 2013.
Tumblr. (2011). *Tumblr tagged Jamie Hubley.* http://www.tumblr.com/tagged/jamie-hubley. Accessed May 2013.
Wasserman, D., Cheng, Q., & Jiang, G. (2005). Global suicide rates among young people aged 15 to 19. *World Psychiatry, 4*(2), 112–120.
Yin, R. K. (2009). *Case study research: Design and methods*. Los Angeles: Sage Publications.
Zhang, Y., & Wildemuth, B. M. (2009). Qualitative analysis of content. In B. Wildemuth (Ed.), *Applications of social research methods to questions in information and library science* (pp. 308–319). Westport: Libraries Unlimited.

Compulsive Use of Social Networking Sites Among Secondary School Adolescents in Belgium

Jolien Vangeel, Rozane De Cock, Annabelle Klein, Pascal Minotte, Omar Rosas, and Gert-Jan Meerkerk

Abstract Some Internet users find it difficult to control the time spent on the Internet, which can lead to a negative impact on school, work and relationships with friends and family. The main goal of the present study was to assess the prevalence of compulsive social networking using the Compulsive Social Networking Scale (CSS) and to determine the profile of compulsive versus non-compulsive users of SNSs by means of a cross-sectional survey among 1002 Belgian adolescents. The results indicate that respondents had an average score of 0.85 on the CSS (range 0–4). When applying a cut off of 2 and more, this resulted in 7.1 % compulsive users. Results showed that both personality traits (6 %) and psychosocial well-being (7.3 %) explain significant amounts of variance above gender and age. In sum, the block of age and gender together with personality and psychosocial well-being explains 15.8 % of the variance.

The research that led to these results was commissioned by Belgian Science Policy Office (Belspo) through the contract number [DR/00/064].

J. Vangeel (✉) • R. De Cock
Institute for Media Studies (IMS), KU Leuven, Leuven, Belgium
e-mail: Jolien.Vangeel@soc.kuleuven.be; Rozane.Decock@soc.kuleuven.be

A. Klein
Research Centre in Information, Law and Society (CRIDS), FUNDP, Namur, Belgium
e-mail: Annabelle.Klein@unamur.be

P. Minotte
Reference Centre in Mental Health (CRéSaM), Namur, Belgium
e-mail: p.minotte@cresam.be

O. Rosas
Institute for Culture and Society (ICS), University of Navarra, Navarra, Spain
e-mail: orosas@unav.es

G.-J. Meerkerk
IVO Addiction Research Institute Rotterdam, Erasmus Medical Centre Rotterdam, Rotterdam, Netherlands
e-mail: meerkerk@ivo.nl

M. Walrave et al. (eds.), *Youth 2.0: Social Media and Adolescence*,
DOI 10.1007/978-3-319-27893-3_10

1 Introduction

Social networking sites (SNSs)[1] are a very popular online activity among children in Belgium. In 2011, 39 % of 9–12-year-olds and 86 % of 13–16-year-olds had a profile on a SNS. Facebook appears to be the most popular SNS with 70 % of the 9–16-year-olds having a profile, designating the site as their only or most used SNS (Livingstone et al. 2011). 95 % of the Belgian children between 9 and 16 years old go online at least once a week and 66 % do this (almost) every day (d'Haenens and Vandoninck 2012). Boyd and Ellison (2007) define SNSs as

> web-based services that allow individuals to (1) construct a public or semi-public profile within a bounded system, (2) articulate a list of other users with whom they share a connection, and (3) view and traverse their list of connections and those made by others within the system.

According to the authors SNSs are unique not because of the possibility to meet strangers but because they allow users to show their connections to others. This view is also supported in an extended literature review by Kuss and Griffiths (2011). The results indicate that SNSs are mostly used to maintain offline connections rather than to make new friends. Although the Internet and new online technologies such as SNSs have several advantages, the increasing amount of time spent online can lead to maladaptive use, certainly among young people (Echeburua and de Corral 2010). In some cases Internet users are not able to control the time spent online, which can have negative consequences for relationships with family and friends and can lead to problems at school (Young 1998).

1.1 Terminology and Definition

Several authors have referred to the maladaptive use of Internet by using the term "Internet addiction" (Griffiths 1998; Young 1998), whereas others prefer "problematic" (Caplan 2002), "pathological" (Davis 2001), "excessive" (Suhail and Bargees 2006) or "compulsive" (Meerkerk 2007) Internet use. In line with Meerkerk, the term compulsive Internet use will be used in the current study. The author states that the term addiction implies an addiction to the Internet itself, whereas in reality "addicts" mostly have a problem dealing with the use of a specific type of Internet application such as gaming, pornography and online communication.

Furthermore the definition of this type of behaviour varies considerably from one study to another. Kandell (1998) defines Internet addiction as:

> a psychological dependence on the Internet that is characterised by (a) an increasing investment of resources on Internet-related activities, (b) unpleasant when offline, (c) an increasing tolerance to the effects of being online, and (d) denial of the problematic behaviours.

[1] For readability reasons 'social networking sites' will be abbreviated to 'SNSs' in the rest of the chapter.

Kandell remarks further that people who suffer from these symptoms are often also dealing with underlying psychological problems (comorbidity). Beard and Wolf (2001) define the phenomenon as "use of the Internet that creates psychological, social, school, and/or work difficulties in a person's life" and put a stronger emphasis on the negative consequences for everyday life. Griffiths (1998) uses the criteria of the Diagnostic and Statistical Manual Fourth Edition (DSM-IV) to come to a definition of Internet addiction including salience, mood modification, tolerance, withdrawal symptoms, conflict and relapse. The author states that any behaviour that meets all these criteria can be defined as an addiction. Despite the lack of a standardised terminology and definition most researchers do agree that the phenomenon exists (Chou et al. 2005) and the problem has received a lot of attention from researchers from different fields of expertise such as psychology, psychiatry and sociology (Chou and Hsiao 2000).

This chapter focuses specifically on the compulsive use of SNSs. According to Kuss and Griffiths (2011) an addiction to SNSs is part of what is described by Young et al. (1999) as a cyber-relationship addiction, which is characterised by over-involvement in online relationships. SNS addiction can be defined as a disorder that is "urge-driven" and includes a compulsive component. This type of addiction is a specific category in the spectrum of addictions related to Internet use (Karaiskos et al. 2010).

1.2 SNSs and Personality

Although literature on the topic is still scarce, some studies have linked personality traits to the use of SNSs using the Five-Factor model that divides personality into five dimensions: openness, extraversion, neuroticism, conscientiousness and agreeableness (Costa and McRae 1992). Extraversion and conscientiousness appear to be significantly related to the use of SNSs. Individuals with high scores on extraversion and low scores on conscientiousness make use of SNSs more often and report more addictive tendencies (Wilson et al. 2010). Correa et al. (2010) also found higher levels of SNS use among extraverts, especially among young adults. Results of a study conducted among university students show that people scoring high on extraversion belong to more Facebook groups, but no difference was found regarding the number of Facebook friends and use of communicative functions. Students scoring high on neuroticism had a preference for using the Facebook wall. Those with low scores on this trait preferred posting pictures on their own profile. Agreeableness and openness did not appear to be related to Facebook features (Ross et al. 2009). Amichai-Hamburger and Vinitzky (2010) found a higher number of friends among people with high scores on extraversion supporting the results of Ross et al., but found no difference regarding the membership of Facebook groups.

1.3 SNSs and Psychosocial Well-Being

The literature examining the link between SNSs and psychosocial well-being is equally scarce. Valkenburg et al. (2006) investigated whether the use of SNSs influences social self-esteem and the well-being of adolescents. Results indicated that there was no direct relationship, but the use of SNS did influence social self-esteem and well-being in an indirect way through received feedback on the SNS profile and the tone of that feedback. Negative feedback on the profile led to lower social self-esteem and well-being, while positive feedback led to an increase of the social self-esteem and well-being of the adolescents. The link between psychosocial factors and (compulsive) Internet use in general has been addressed more often by researchers. Young and Rogers (1998) found a link between high levels of depression and the chance of developing an Internet addiction. Ceyhan and Ceyhan (2008) identified loneliness and depression as important predictors of problematic Internet use with loneliness explaining 21.8 % of the variance and depression adding another 3.3 %. Caplan (2002) found significant correlations between problematic Internet use and psychosocial variables such as loneliness, depression and self-esteem. Furthermore Chak and Leung (2004) found a negative association between perceived control over one's life and Internet addiction.

1.4 SNS Use and Academic Performance

Few studies have examined the impact of SNS use, or Facebook in particular, on academic performance. A study among university students showed, for example, that Facebook users report a lower Grade Point Average (GPA) compared to non-users. Furthermore, the average study time per week is lower among users of this SNS compared to university students that do not use Facebook (Kirschner and Karpinski 2010). A comparable result is found in a study of Junco (2012) which shows that large increases in the time spent on Facebook is related to lower overall GPAs. Kolek and Saunders (2008) on the other hand found no negative correlation between grades and Facebook use. This outcome is supported by the results of a study conducted by Pasek et al. (2009) that also did not point in the direction of a negative impact of Facebook use on grades. The results of these studies show that there is as yet no consensus on the possible impact of Facebook on academic performance.

2 Focus of the Current Study

This study is the first to collect data about the compulsive use of SNS sites among youngsters in Belgium. The main goal is to assess the prevalence of compulsive SNS use among adolescents in secondary schools in Belgium and to ascertain the profile of compulsive versus non-compulsive users of SNSs. Based on the scientific literature and emerging research gaps, the following research questions were formulated:

Research question 1: What is the prevalence of secondary school children scoring high on the Compulsive Social Networking Scale (CSS) in Belgium?

Research question 2: What is the profile of secondary school children scoring high on the CSS in Belgium (compulsive SNS users) compared to children that are non-compulsive SNS users?

Research question 3: What are important predictors of compulsive SNS use among adolescents in secondary schools?

3 Methodology

3.1 Data Collection

This study is part of a broader research project on the topic of compulsive computer and Internet use in Belgium. A paper-and-pencil survey was distributed to adolescents of the first, third and fifth year of secondary school. The principals of the schools were contacted by letter or e-mail and by telephone a few weeks after mailing. During this conversation the potential participation of the school was discussed. Seventeen secondary schools in Flanders and Wallonia agreed to participate in this research, which allowed for a total sample of 1002 respondents. Since Dutch and French are both official languages in Belgium, the surveys were drafted in the two languages. 591 respondents filled in the Dutch version of the survey and 411 completed the French version. All questionnaires were filled in in the classroom during one lesson (in this case 50 min) in the presence of one of the researchers and a teacher or supervisor of the school. The children were allowed to ask questions for clarification when items or questions were unclear.

3.2 Sample Description

The sample contains 59 % Flemish and 41 % Walloon adolescents. The average age is 15.21 years. The sample consists of 50.6 % girls and 49.4 % boys. Most of the respondents are of Belgian origin: 72.7 %. The remaining part of the respondents has at least one parent from a different origin. 39.6 % of the secondary school pupils in the sample are in general education and 26.8 % are in technical education. 24.7 % are in vocational education and 8.9 % are in art education. The education level of the respondents in the sample is comparable to that of adolescents in secondary education in Flanders where 45.3 % are in general education, 30 % in technical education, 2.1 % in art education and 22.6 % in vocational education (VONC 2012).

3.3 *Variables and Measures*

To measure compulsive use of SNSs, the Bergen Facebook Addiction scale (Andreassen et al. 2012) was adapted to a compulsive SNS scale (CSS) measuring not only compulsive use of Facebook, but of SNSs in general.[2] This scale consists of 18 items that are rated on a 5-point scale ranging from never (=0) to very often (=4). Items to assess CSS included: "How often during the last year have you felt an urge to use SNSs more and more?", "How often during the last year have you spent more time on SNSs than initially intended?" and "How often during the last year have you used SNSs in order to reduce restlessness?". In analogy with the Compulsive Internet Use Scale (CIUS) which has shown to be reliable (Meerkerk 2007; Meerkerk et al. 2009), an average score of at least "sometimes" (≥ 2) is considered as an indication of compulsive use of the SNSs. The CSS was used to measure the degree to which an individual shows signs of salience, tolerance, withdrawal, relapse, mood modification and conflict. The scale showed good consistency in the current sample ($\alpha = .94$).

An important focus of the current study is to assess whether CSS scores are related to personality traits and psychosocial well-being. Therefore several measures were included in the survey in order to operationalise these variables. Personality traits were measured by the Quick Big Five (Vermulst and Gerris 2005), which divides personality into five different aspects: extraversion, resourcefulness, conscientiousness, agreeableness and emotional stability. Variables included for measuring psychosocial well-being were self-esteem, depression, perceived control and loneliness. Self-esteem was assessed by using the Rosenberg Self-Esteem Scale (Rosenberg 1965) and depression was measured using the Depressive Mood List (Kandel and Davies 1982). The Mastery Scale measured perceived control (Pearlin and Schooler 1978) and loneliness was assessed by using the Rasch-Type Loneliness Scale (de Jong-Gierveld and Kamphuis 1985).

Furthermore, respondents were asked to indicate the amount of time they spent on the Internet on an average day (measured per day: Monday, Tuesday, …). Respondents had to indicate on a 6-point scale ranging from "never" to "multiple times a day" the extent to which they engaged in several types of online activities. The following activities were included: e-mail, information seeking, chatting, online gaming, online pornography, downloading, video watching and online shop-

[2] The 18 items of the Bergen Facebook Addiction Scale (BFAS) were translated by two researchers into Dutch and French. To widen the applicability of the scale the items were reformulated by using the term 'social networking site' in general instead of the mentioning of a specific SNS brand name such as Facebook. The adapted Compulsive Social Networking Scale (CSS) was pilot tested together with other questions and scales in a paper-and-pencil survey administered in the classroom to 134 scholars of the first, third and fifth year of secondary school in Flanders and Wallonia. The internal consistency (Cronbach's alpha) was .95 for the Dutch version and .94 for the French version of the CSS. Tests for convergent validity point at high correlations between our CSS and for example, the Compulsive Internet Use Scale (CIUS).

ping. Another question focused on the respondents' attitude towards school by asking them to indicate on a 10-point scale ranging from "not at all" to "very much" how much they liked going to school. The respondents were also asked to give an indication of how they were doing at school on a 10-point scale ranging from "not well at all" to "very well". In addition, they were also asked whether they had an SNS profile and on which SNS in particular. Also the average time spent on SNSs on school days and non-school days was asked for. In the final socio-demographic part of the survey, respondents were asked about gender, age, nationality, position in line of siblings, education level and financial situation at home.

3.4 Statistical Analyses

T-tests were calculated in order to compare compulsive users of SNSs to non-compulsive users. Correlation analyses and hierarchical multiple regression analyses were conducted with the average score on the CSS as the dependent variable. Age and gender were entered in the first block of the regression analyses, personality traits in the second block and psychosocial scales in the last block.

4 Results

4.1 General SNS Use in Belgium

Most of the secondary school children have a profile on one or more SNSs: 88.2 %. Facebook is by far the most popular SNS with 95.5 % of all SNS users having a profile. Twitter (20.4 %) and Netlog (20.3 %) are used to a lesser extent. MySpace does not seem to arouse the interest of Belgian adolescents with only 1.8 % of SNS users having a profile on that site. 33.1 % of SNS users indicated they had a profile on other SNSs that were not mentioned in the examples specified in the survey. Other examples include Google+ (1.2 %) and Tumblr (3.7 %). Skype (7.1 %) and MSN (14.7 %) were also mentioned by adolescents as examples of SNSs, even though it is arguable whether they really can be seen as SNSs since Skype is mostly used to make online phone calls and MSN as a chat tool. The average amount of SNS profiles is 1.72. On a school day SNS users spent on average 1 h and 15 min on a SNS. During the weekend or holidays this average rises to 2 h and 16 min.

4.2 Prevalence of Compulsive SNS Use

Respondents had an average score of 0.85 on the CSS with a range from 0 (= never) to 4 (= very often). A cut off score of 2 and more was used to determine the number of compulsive users of SNSs. This resulted in a prevalence of 7.1 % of compulsive users of SNSs out of the 1002 secondary school pupils. Compulsive users have a significantly higher CSS score ($M=2.3$, $SD=0.42$) compared to non-compulsive SNS users ($M=0.66$, $SD=0.51$), $t(92.067)=-30.908$, $p<.01$. This study is part of a broader research project focusing on the compulsive use of the Internet as well as games. A prevalence of 9.5 % compulsive Internet users and a prevalence of 11 % compulsive gamers were found in this study.

4.3 Profile of Compulsive SNS Users

To answer our second research question the group of compulsive users of SNSs was compared to the group of non-compulsive users in order to assess the profile of both groups. The group of compulsive users consists of 48.6 % boys and 51.4 % girls. The average age is 14.84 years. As expected, compulsive users of SNSs spent more time on this type of online activity than their non-compulsive counterparts. Compulsive users spent 2 h and 38 min on SNSs on a typical school day, which is significantly higher than the average of 1 h and 7 min found in the group of non-compulsive users ($t(69.824)=-3.714$, $p<.01$). During the weekend or the holidays the time spent on SNSs was higher for both groups. Again, compulsive users ($M=4$ h and 35 min) spent significantly more time on SNSs than the non-compulsive group ($M=2$ h and 1 min) ($t(70.751)=-4.447$, $p<.01$). Both groups do not seem to differ regarding the personality traits of resourcefulness and conscientiousness. Compulsive SNS users did show significantly lower scores on the personality dimension of agreeableness ($M=22.67$) compared to the non-compulsive users ($M=23.65$), $t(100.069)=2.240$, $p<.05$, cohen's $d=0.31$. Lower scores were also found in the compulsive group regarding emotional well-being ($M=22.67$ versus $M=23.65$), $t(745)=2.26$, $p<.05$, cohen's $d=0.29$. Also for the personality trait of extraversion non-compulsive users of SNSs reported higher scores ($M=21.26$) compared to compulsive SNS users ($M=20.08$), $t(739)=-2.132$, $p<.05$, cohen's $d=0.27$.

Differences were found for all variables measuring psychosocial well-being. Compulsive SNS users show significantly higher scores on loneliness ($M=29.36$ versus $M=24.63$, $t(746)=-5.741$, $p<.01$), cohen's $d=-0.73$ and depressive feelings ($M=12.53$ versus $M=8.99$, $t(90.294)=-7.569$, $p<.01$, cohen's $d=-0.87$) than their non-compulsive counterparts. Scores on perceived control ($M=22.3$ versus $M=24.5$, $t(741)=4.454$, $p<.01$, cohen's $d=0.6$) and self-esteem ($M=32.55$ versus $M=36.21$, $t(734)=4.885$, $p<.01$, cohen's $d=0.6$) are significantly lower in the compulsive group.

Respondents were also asked to indicate on a scale from 1 to 10 how much they liked going to school. Results indicate that compulsive users have a significantly lower score ($M=5.31$) than the non-compulsive users ($M=6.04$), $t(80.218)=2.218$, $p<.05$, cohen's $d=0.30$. No difference was found between both groups when we look at the indication respondents gave about their grades on a scale from 1 to 10 ($t(79.478)=1.766$, $p>.05$). The indication of grades did, however, appear to be negatively correlated ($r=-.107$, $p<.01$) to CSS score (see correlation Table 2).

4.4 Predictors in CSS Outcome

To provide an answer to the third and last research question, we tried to establish predictors of the CSS score by using hierarchical regression. Gender and age were entered in the first block. Their betas and significance levels are reported as Step 1 in Table 1. This first block of age and gender explains 2.5 % of the variance, $F(2, 592)=8.608$, $p<.05$. Personality traits of the Quick Big Five were entered in Step 2 and explain an extra 6 % of the variance in the average CSS score, $F(7, 587)=8.902$, $p<.05$. Another 7.3 % is explained when entering psychosocial well-being predictors in the third step (Step 3), $F(11, 583)=11.136$, $p<.05$. In sum, the block of age and gender together with personality traits and variables related to psychosocial well-being explains 15.8 % of the variance in the average CSS score. Agreeableness appears to be the only personality predictor related to the average score on the CSS,

Table 1 Predictors of an average CSS score

	Beta	*p*	ΔR^2
STEP 1			
Gender	–.121	.003	2.5 %
Age	–.084	.031	
Adjusted R^2	**2.5 %**		
STEP 2			
Extraversion	.056	.174	6 %
Agreeableness	–.124	.005	
Conscientiousness	.016	.706	
Emotional stability Resourcefulness	–.067	.149	
	.029	.487	
Adjusted R^2	**8.5 %**		
STEP 3			
Loneliness	.113	.024	7.3 %
Perceived control	–.155	.003	
Self-esteem	–.113	.046	
Depressive feelings	.219	.000	
Adjusted R^2	**15.8 %**		

Table 2 Correlation table

	1	2	3	4	5	6	7	8	9	10	11	12	13	14
1 CIUS score	–													
2 VAT score	.533**	–												
3 CSS score	.490**	.351**	–											
4 Attitude school	–.184**	–.216**	–.057	–										
5 Grades	–.175**	–.187**	–.107**	.317**	–									
6 Loneliness	.242**	.193**	.247**	–.188**	–.161**	–								
7 Perceived control	–.272**	–.196**	–.256**	.113**	.132**	–.559**	–							
8 Self-esteem	–.299**	–.154**	–.230**	.173**	.204**	–.492**	.591**	–						
9 Depressive feelings	.429**	.280**	.326**	–.133**	–.166**	.380**	–.500**	–.561**	–					
10 Extraversion	–.120**	–.059	–.060	.067*	.063	–.336**	.311**	.294**	–.203**	–				
11 Conscientiousness	–.173**	–.211**	–.055	.293**	.368**	–.134**	.145**	.240**	–.169**	–.029	–			
12 Agreeableness	–.139**	–.236**	–.120**	.306**	.225**	–.320**	.211**	.290**	–.078*	.187**	.379**	–		
13 Emotional Stability	–.227**	–.089*	–.186**	–.052	.131**	–.236**	.381**	.381**	–.475**	.234**	.028	–.032	–	
14 Resourcefulness	–.139**	–.171**	–.061	.184**	.167**	–.150**	.157**	.310**	–.115**	.149**	.222**	.379**	–.071*	–
N	925	604	775	996	982	941	945	933	957	942	943	964	946	959
Mean	1.02	1.1	0.80	5.98	7.01	25.2	24.19	35.7	9.34	20.95	19.2	23.59	18.3	20.72
c	0.70	0.86	0.69	2.38	1.62	6.81	4.04	6.19	4.55	4.35	4.58	2.94	3.99	3.90

**. Correlation is significant at the 0.01 level (2-tailed)
*. Correlation is significant at the 0.05 level (2-tailed)

$\beta = -.124$, $p < .05$. All psychosocial well-being predictors are related to the CSS score. Loneliness and depressive feelings are positively related to the average score on the CSS: $\beta = .113$, $p < .05$ and $\beta = .219$, $p < .05$ respectively. Perceived control and self-esteem relate in a negative way to CSS score, $\beta = -.155$, $p < .05$ and $\beta = -.113$, $p < .05$ respectively.

5 Conclusion

The goals of the current study were to assess the prevalence of compulsive SNS use, to ascertain the profile of compulsive and non-compulsive users and to distinguish several important predictors of the CSS score. The results of the current study indicate that secondary school children have an average score of 0.85 on the CSS with a range from 0 to 4. When a cut-off score of 2 and more was applied, a prevalence of 7.1 % compulsive SNS users was ascertained among secondary school children in our sample. Several t-tests were calculated in order to compare compulsive users of SNSs to non-compulsive users. As could be expected compulsive SNS users spent significantly more time on SNSs compared to non-compulsive users, both on school and non-school days. Furthermore we specifically focused on differences regarding personality traits, psychosocial well-being and attitude towards school. Compulsive and non-compulsive users showed no differences when comparing the average score on the personality traits of extraversion, resourcefulness, conscientiousness and emotional stability. A difference was found for agreeableness with compulsive users having significantly lower scores on this dimension. In addition both groups differed with respect to all variables integrated in the study to measure psychosocial well-being. Higher scores were found in the compulsive group for loneliness and depressive feelings, lower scores were found for perceived control and self-esteem. Furthermore, respondents in the compulsive group gave a significantly lower indication on a scale from 1 to 10 asking how much they liked going to school and the indication of the respondents about their grades correlated negatively to the CSS score. Hierarchical multiple regression analyses identified personality traits and psychosocial well-being as important predictors of CSS scores. Gender and age were entered in the first block and explained 2.5 % of the variance in CSS scores. When entering personality traits in the second step another 6 % was explained and psychosocial well-being predictors in the third and last step explained an extra 7.8 % of the variance in the CSS score. Overall, the block of age and gender in combination with personality traits and variables indicating psychosocial well-being was able to account for 16 % of the variance in CSS scores.

This study was the first to focus on the compulsive use of SNSs among secondary school children in Belgium. Moreover, it is one of the few studies linking personality traits and psychosocial well-being to the compulsive use of SNSs. Previous research did already focus on the link between those variables and compulsive Internet use, but literature focusing on the link with compulsive SNS use is still scarce. Due to space constraints the current study was not able to test for all possible personality traits and variables that indicated psychosocial well-being. The integration of certain other variables such as shyness, life satisfaction and narcissism might help to predict the extent to which an individual has the tendency to use SNSs in a compulsive way. Follow-up research on the topic of the different forms of compulsive computer and Internet use is of great importance. Future studies should certainly focus on the link between those variables and the use of SNSs. In the same vein, the link between attitude towards school and grades should be investigated more extensively. The use and importance of the Internet is still on the rise worldwide, particularly with the current widespread rise in tablet and smartphone use. These new mobile devices make it possible to be online anywhere and anytime. Free mobile applications such as WhatsApp are already used by many people as an alternative to texting, indicating that activities in which the Internet is used are still expanding. Therefore longitudinal research needs to be conducted to register the evolution of computer and Internet use and its repercussions for problematic use (prevalence and mean age of problematic users) in Belgium over time.

References

Amichai-Hamburger, Y., & Vinitzky, G. (2010). Social network use and personality. *Computers in Human Behavior, 26*, 289–1295.

Andreassen, C., Torsheim, T., Brunborg, G., & Pallesen, S. (2012). Development of a Facebook addiction scale. *Psychological Reports, 110*, 1–17.

Beard, K. W., & Wolf, E. M. (2001). Modification in the proposed diagnostic criteria for Internet addiction. *Cyberpsychology & Behavior, 4*(3), 377–383.

Boyd, D. M., & Ellison, N. B. (2007). Social network sites: Definition, history, and scholarship. *Journal of Computer-Mediated Communication, 13*(1), 210–230.

Caplan, S. (2002). Problematic Internet use and psychosocial well-being: Development of a theory- based cognitive-behavioral measurement instrument. *Computers in Human Behavior, 18*, 552–575.

Ceyhan, A., & Ceyhan, E. (2008). Loneliness, depression, and computer self-efficacy as predictors of problematic Internet use. *Cyberpsychology & Behavior, 11*, 699–701.

Chak, K., & Leung, L. (2004). Shyness and locus of control as predictors of Internet addiction and Internet use. *Cyberpsychology & Behavior, 7*, 559–568.

Chou, C., & Hsiao, M. (2000). Internet addiction, usage, gratification, and pleasure experience: The Taiwan college students' case. *Computers & Education, 35*, 65–80.

Chou, C., Condron, L., & Belland, J. C. (2005). A review of the research in Internet addiction. *Educational Psychology Review, 17*(4), 363–388.

Correa, T., Hinsley, A. W., & de Zúñiga, H. G. (2010). Who interacts on the Web? The intersection of users' personality and social media use. *Computers in Human Behavior, 26*(2), 247–253.

Costa, P. T., & McRae, R. R. (1992). Normal personality assessment in clinical practice: The NEO personality inventory. *Psychological Assessment, 4*(1), 5–13.

d'Haenens, L., & Vandoninck, S. (2012). Digitale geletterdheid en omgaan met online risico's: positie van Belgische kinderen en jongeren in vergelijking met leeftijdsgenoten in Europa. In L. d'Haenens & S. Vandoninck (Eds.), *Kids Online: Kansen en risico's van kinderen en jongeren op het internet* (pp. 7–27). Ghent: Academia Press.

Davis, R. (2001). A cognitive-behavioral model of pathological Internet use. *Computer in Human Behavior, 17*, 187–195.

de Jong-Gierveld, J., & Kamphuis, F. (1985). The development of a Rasch-type loneliness scale. *Applied Psychological Measurement, 9*(236), 289–299.
Echeburua, E., & de Corral, P. (2010). Addiction to new technologies and to online social networking in young people: A new challenge. *Adicciones, 22*, 91–95.
Griffiths, M. (1998). Internet addiction: Does it really exist? In J. Gackenbach (Ed.), *Psychology and the Internet; intrapersonal, and transpersonal applications* (pp. 61–75). New York: Academic.
Junco, R. (2012). Too much face and not enough books: The relationship between multiple indices of Facebook use and academic performance. *Computers in Human Behavior, 28*, 187–198.
Kandel, D., & Davies, M. (1982). Epidemiology of depressive mood in adolescent. *Archives of General Psychiatry, 39*, 2105–2212.
Kandell, J. (1998). Internet addiction in campus: The vulnerability of college students. *Cyberpsychology & Behavior, 1*(1), 11–17.
Karaiskos, D., Tzavellas, E., Balta, G., & Paparrigopoulos, T. (2010). Social network addiction: A new clinical disorder? *European Psychiatry, 25*, 855.
Kirschner, P. A., & Karpinski, A. C. (2010). Facebook and academic performance. *Computers in Human Behavior, 26*, 1237–1245.
Kolek, E. A., & Saunders, D. (2008). Online disclosure: An empirical examination of undergraduate Facebook profiles. *NASPA Journal, 45*, 1–25.
Kuss, D., & Griffiths, M. (2011). Online social networking and addiction – A review of the psychological literature. *International Journal of Environmental Research and Public Health, 8*, 3528–3552.
Livingstone, S., Ólafsson, K., & Staksrud, E. (2011). *Social networking, age and privacy*. London: EU Kids Online.
Meerkerk, G. (2007). *Pwned by the Internet. Explorative research into the causes and consequences of compulsive Internet use*. Rotterdam: Erasmus Universiteit Rotterdam.
Meerkerk, G., Van den Eijnden, R., Vermulst, A., & Garretsen, H. (2009). The compulsive Internet use scale (CIUS): Some psychometric properties. *Cyberpsychology & Behavior, 12*(1), 1–6.
Pasek, J., More, E., & Hargittai, E. (2009). Facebook and academic performance: Reconciling a media sensation with data. *First Monday, 14*.
Pearlin, L., & Schooler, C. (1978). The structure of coping. *Journal of Health and Social Behavior, 19*, 2–21.
Rosenberg, M. (1965). *Society and the adolescent self-image*. Princeton: Princeton University Press.
Ross, C., Orr, E., Sisic, M., Arseneault, J., Simmering, M., & Orr, R. (2009). Personality and motivations associated with Facebook use. *Computers in Human Behavior, 25*, 578–586.
Suhail, K., & Bargees, Z. (2006). Effects of excessive Internet use on undergraduate students in Pakistan. *Cyberpsychology & Behavior, 9*, 297–307.
Valkenburg, P., Peter, J., & Schouten, A. (2006). Friend networking sites and their relationship to adolescents' well-being and social self-esteem. *Cyberpsychology & Behavior, 9*, 584–590.
Vermulst, A., & Gerris, J. (2005). *QBF: Quick Big Five persoonlijkheidstest handleiding* (Quick Big Five personality test manual). Leeuwarden: LDC Publications.
VONC. (2012). *Het Vlaamse onderwijs in cijfers 2011–2012*. Brussel: Vlaams Ministerie van Onderwijs en Vorming. http://www.vlaanderen.be/nl/publicaties/detail/vlaams-onderwijs-in-cijfers-2011-2012. Accessed 30 Mar 2014.
Wilson, K., Fornasier, S., & White, K. M. (2010). Psychological predictors of young adults' use of social networking sites. *Cyberpsychology, Behavior and Social Networking, 13*(2), 173–177.
Young, K. (1998). *Caught in the net: How to recognize the signs of Internet addiction and a winning strategy for recovery*. New York: Wiley.
Young, K., & Rogers, R. (1998). The relationship between depression and Internet addiction. *Cyberpsychology & Behavior, 1*, 125–128.
Young, K., Pistner, M., O'Mara, J., & Buchanan, J. (1999). Cyber disorders: The mental health concern for the new millennium. *Cyberpsychology & Behavior, 2*, 475–479.

(Cyber)bullying Perpetration as an Impulsive, Angry Reaction Following (Cyber)bullying Victimisation?

Sara Pabian and Heidi Vandebosch

Abstract This chapter starts from the unclear relation between impulsivity and (cyber)bullying perpetration and investigates the potential explanatory value of Agnew's (1992) General Strain Theory. This theory posits that individuals who experience strain and angriness (as a result of strain) are more at risk of engaging in deviant behaviour, moderated by conditioning variables. In the current chapter, we tested whether (cyber)bullying victimisation leads to (cyber)bullying perpetration, mediated by anger and impulsivity. Analyses were performed on a longitudinal dataset (two time points, 6 months in between) among 1590 Belgian 11–17-year-olds. Path analyses showed direct relations between victimisation and perpetration. Indirect relations were found via anger and via the interaction term between anger and impulsivity. Victims who were angrier were more involved in bullying perpetration at time 2. This relation was slightly stronger for angry, impulsive victims. The results provide further insight into the determinants of (cyber)bullying behaviour.

1 Literature Overview

1.1 Introduction

The literature on computer-mediated-communication (CMC) suggests that studying the link between impulsivity and cyberbullying behaviour might be especially relevant, since features of the online environment (e.g. the lack of cues, the *indirectness* and the perceived anonymity) are believed to potentially "trigger" negative behaviours (Walrave and Heirman 2010). Previous research on cyberbullying behaviour already found a (moderate) direct effect of impulsivity on cyberbullying perpetration (Fanti et al. 2012) and a more substantial indirect effect of impulsivity on (cyber)bullying perpetration via previous (cyber)bullying victimisation (Fanti et al. 2012; Vazsonyi et al. 2012). In this chapter, we explore how impulsivity

S. Pabian (✉) • H. Vandebosch
MIOS, University of Antwerp, Antwerp, Belgium
e-mail: sara.pabian@uantwerpen.be; heidi.vandebosch@uantwerpen.be

M. Walrave et al. (eds.), *Youth 2.0: Social Media and Adolescence*,
DOI 10.1007/978-3-319-27893-3_11

mediates the relation between previous (cyber)bullying victimisation and (cyber) bullying perpetration. Therefore the General Strain Theory (GST), which is a general theory of crime and has been successful in explaining a wide variety of antisocial and deviant behaviours, is used as a guiding framework. The theory posits that individuals who experience strain, and as a result of that strain are angry or frustrated (negative affect), are more at risk to engage in criminal or deviant behaviour (Agnew 1992). We hypothesise that angriness on peers mediates the relation between (cyber)bullying victimisation (as social stressor) and (cyber)bullying perpetration, whereas the relation between angriness and perpetration is moderated by level of impulsivity. In order to test the hypotheses, analyses were performed on a longitudinal dataset (two time points, 6 months in between) among 1606 Belgian 11–17 year olds. The results provide further insight into the determinants of cyberbullying behaviour.

1.2 Impulsivity and (Cyber)bullying

Impulsivity or low self-control can be defined as a tendency toward rapid, unplanned reaction to stimuli, without taking into account the negative consequences (Stanford et al. 2009). Previous research on traditional bullying shows that current perpetrators or those who had perpetrated in a recent reference period are more impulsive compared to those who had not bullied (Griffin and Gross 2004; Pontzer 2010). Also bully/victims or aggressive victims, individuals that are concurrently bullies and victims, have higher levels of impulsivity (O'Brennan et al. 2009; Unnever 2005).

A few recent studies indicate that impulsivity is also relevant in the context of cyberbullying (Fanti et al. 2012; Holt et al. 2012; Vazsonyi et al. 2012). In the longitudinal study of Fanti et al. (2012, p. 175) impulsivity (at time 1) predicted cyberbullying perpetration (at time 2) 1 year later. Moreover, the authors tested whether impulsivity has an interaction effect on cyberbullying perpetration with demographic characteristics, previous involvement in school bullying and cyberbullying as a victim and/or a bully, risk variables (media violence exposure, callous-unemotional traits and narcissism) and protective variables (family, friend, and school social support). No significant interaction effects were found. Holt et al. (2012) also tested the relation between low self-control, personal characteristics (deviant peer association) and deviant behaviour online. Posting mean or threatening messages about another person for others to see was included among other online deviant behaviours (no general cyberbullying measure was included). A significant positive relation between low self-control and posting mean or threatening messages online was found. No evidence was found for mediating or conditioning effects of associating with deviant peers on low self-control (Holt et al. 2012, p. 392). In line with the previous mentioned studies, Vazsonyi et al. (2012) found a positive direct relation between low self-control and cyberbullying perpetration.

However, the authors found a more substantial indirect effect via offline victimisation and offline perpetration. Put differently, offline victimisation and perpetration are mediators between low self-control and cyberbullying perpetration (and victimisation) (Vazsonyi et al. 2012, p. 222). This literature overview demonstrates the importance of impulsivity or low self-control for explaining (cyber)bullying perpetration. The current chapter will take into account impulsivity as a predictor of (cyber)bullying perpetration and will compare the predictive value for both traditional bullying and cyberbullying.

As shown, research on bullying and, more broadly, research on (online) deviant and risky behaviour, seldom investigates impulsivity as a predictor in isolation from other conditioning or mediating variables, such as personality traits and emotions (Holt et al. 2012; Vazsonyi et al. 2012). Other examples of conditioning or mediating variables of impulsivity are anger (Colder and Stice 1998), anxiety (Miller et al. 2012) and being depressed (e.g., Clarke 2006). For instance, high levels of anger were associated with delinquency for impulsive but not for low impulsive adolescents (Colder and Stice 1998, p. 265). In the current chapter, we will further examine the relation between impulsivity and cyberbullying by making use of a theoretical framework in which anger is a central concept.

1.3 General Strain Theory

In the early 1990s, Agnew argued that strain theory has a central role to play in explanations of crime and delinquency, provided that the strain models developed earlier by Merton (1938), Cohen (1955) and Cloward and Ohlin (1960) are substantially revised (Agnew 1992, p. 47). Agnew's General Strain Theory (GST) builds upon this traditional strain theory in criminology. The focus of the GST is on adolescents and their negative relationships in which the individual is not treated as he or she wants to be treated (negatively valued stimuli) (Agnew 1992, pp. 48–49). Agnew (1992) describes three theoretically distinct types of strains (but they may overlap in practice), each referring to a different type of negative relationship with others: "Other individuals may (1) prevent one from achieving positively valued goals, (2) remove or threaten to remove positively valued stimuli that one possesses, or (3) present or threaten to present one with noxious or negatively valued stimuli" (p. 50). Experiencing strain increases the likelihood that individuals will feel one or more of a range of negative emotions, such as disappointment, depression, fear and anger. Agnew (1992) describes anger as the most critical emotional reaction for the purposes of the GST, as it "creates a desire for retaliation/revenge, energises the individual for action, and lowers inhibition" (p. 60). The GST posits that adolescents are "pressured" into delinquency by the negative emotions experienced – most notably anger – which result from the negative relationships (Agnew 1992, p. 49). In other words, this negative affect creates (temporary) pressure for corrective action and may lead adolescents to respond in an anti-social and delinquent way.

Later on, Agnew and colleagues (2002) examined the extent to which certain personal characteristics condition the effect of strain. Such traits may have a major impact on the emotional reaction to strain, because they are relatively stable fixtures of the person's temperament and individuals bring these traits into almost every social encounter they experience (Agnew et al. 2002; Miller and Lynam 2001). One of these traits is "constraint". As described by Agnew et al. (2002), individuals low in constraint are impulsive, they are involved in risk-taking and sensation-seeking behaviour, they reject conventional social norms and are unconcerned with the feelings or rights of others. They have a higher likelihood of perceiving events as adverse or stressful and to experience strain (Agnew et al. 2002; Hay and Evans 2006).

1.4 General Strain Theory to Explain (Cyber)bullying

A large amount of studies have examined a wide variety of deviant behaviours as a source of strain, including bullying (Agnew et al. 2002). Being bullied (victimisation) is a negatively valued stimulus which can cause strain and which may subsequently lead to delinquency or anti-social behaviour as the adolescent tries to escape from, avoid, terminate or alleviate the negative stimulus, or seeks revenge against it (or against related targets) (Agnew 1992, p. 58, 2001, p. 346). Besides studying bullying as a source of strain, researchers also focus on bullying perpetration as a potential result of being exposed to strain. A few empirical studies have provided evidence of the potential for GST to explain traditional bullying and cyberbullying perpetration (as a result of strain) (Moon et al. 2010; Patchin and Hinduja 2011).

Previous research on traditional bullying perpetration showed that angry youth are more likely to bully others (Espelage and Swearer 2003), which is consistent with GST's emphasis on anger as the key negative emotion that mediates the relation between strain and deviant behaviour. Moon and colleagues (2010) empirically tested whether the General Strain Theory could explain school bullying in South Korea. The results showed that youth who experienced victimisation by peers were more likely to engage in bullying. A positive association with anger was found, but it was not found to be a mediating variable between victimisation and perpetration. The authors argue that other potentially influential emotions (anxiety, shame, frustration) might be relevant to Korean youth and bullying (Moon et al. 2010, p. 20).

First research has already proven the potential for GST to explain cyberbullying. Victims and perpetrator-victims of internet harassment are more associated with a propensity to respond to stimuli with anger (Ybarra et al. 2007, p. S36). Cyberbullies (especially those who target a prior perpetrator), in their turn, are found to be more vengeful, that is, the degree to which individuals tend to inflict harm or demand retribution for a perceived wrong (König et al. 2010, p. 217). In the study of König et al. (2010), 83.3 % of the traditional victims were also cyberbullies. In fact, the authors found that victims of traditional bullying and cyberbullying tended to choose their former perpetrator as cybervictim (König et al. 2010, p. 215): in their study 14.7 % of all cyberbullies indicated choosing a target who had traditionally bullied them before. One study empirically tested the GST to explain (cyber)bullying perpetration (Patchin and Hinduja 2011). First of all, the results suggest that strain (measured as a broad variety of (negative) experiences that are common among adolescents) is positively related to anger (Patchin and Hinduja 2011, p. 739). The more strained an adolescent was, the more anger and frustration he/she reported. Second, adolescents who experienced strain were more likely to (cyber) bully others than those who had not experienced strain. Also those adolescents who reported to feel anger/frustration were more likely to (cyber)bully others than those who had not experienced anger/frustration. However, the hypothesised mediating relationship purported by GST (anger mediates relation between strain and bullying perpetration) was not found (Patchin and Hinduja 2011, p. 739). The authors conclude that strain and anger/frustration have an influence on both types of bullying perpetration (cyberbullying and traditional bullying) independently of each other (Patchin and Hinduja 2011, p. 741). Though the cross-sectional nature of the data might cause the absence of a significant mediator effect, the authors could not ensure proper temporal ordering of the independent and dependent variables.

1.5 Current Study

Previous research on cyberbullying shows first evidence for the use of GST as a theoretical framework for the explanation of (cyber)bullying perpetration. However, only partial support for GST's explanatory power was found. The current study further examines the relation between strain (previous (cyber)bullying victimisation), anger and (cyber)bullying perpetration. Impulsivity or low-self control will be added to the model as a conditioning variable. Until now, it is still not clear how to integrate conditioning variables to the theory (Huck et al. 2012). Some include conditioning variables as interaction terms with strain (Agnew et al. 2002; Hay and Evans 2006), while others place conditioning variables as a mediator between strain and delinquent behaviour (e.g. Huck et al. 2012, p. 30). Based on previous research on deviant behaviour that showed a significant interaction effect of impulsivity and anger (Colder and Stice 1998), we expect that the interaction effect between anger and impulsivity mediates the relation between strain and (cyber)bullying perpetration. In other words, we expect that (cyber)bullying victimisation (as a source of strain) has an indirect effect on and leads to (cyber)bullying perpetration (outcome) via anger (negative effect), only or especially for those who have high levels of impulsivity (conditioning variable). As this study is part of a large scale longitudinal study on (cyber)bullying, other sources of strain or deviant outcomes could therefore not be incorporated into the model.

Specifically, we test the following hypotheses: (a) previous involvement in (cyber)bullying, as a victim will be positively associated with the experience of the negative affect anger; (b) anger will be positively associated with (cyber)bullying perpetration at time 2; (c) impulsivity will be positively associated with (cyber)bullying perpetration at time 2; (d) anger and impulsivity will interact such that high levels of both anger and impulsivity will predict (cyber)bullying perpetration at time 2 beyond what is expected on the basis of an additive effect; (e) the interaction between anger and impulsivity will mediate the relation between (cyber)bullying victimisation at time 1 and (cyber)bullying perpetration at time 2.

2 Method

2.1 Sample

The data that are used in this chapter stem from a large-scale longitudinal study in Belgium (Flanders), with four waves of data collection. In total 1814 students participated in a paper- and-pencil school survey at baseline (October 2011). They filled out the same questionnaire every 6 months. The last wave of data gathering took place in April-May 2013. A random stratified cluster sample was applied to select the respondents. The sampling criteria were grade and type of schooling (general, technical and vocational secondary education). For each educational grade, three schools were selected to participate in the study. Due to an overrepresentation of certain grades, schooling types and sexes, all the results were weighted based on their proportions in the population. Before the survey was administered, the parents of the students were notified by letter in order to receive (passive) parental consent. Students filled in the questionnaire during school time in their school in the presence of a researcher. Students were assured verbally and in writing that their responses would be anonymous and confidential.

The analyses that were performed in this chapter are based on data from the first and the second wave in order to establish causal relationships. Because some students preferred not to fill in identification information (date of birth and first letter of the names of their biological parents) for one of the two waves, it was sometimes impossible to connect the data from both waves. Students could also drop out due to being absent at time 2. Therefore the analytical sample consisted of 1590 students (44.9 % males, 55.1 % females; Mean Age = 13.73, SD = 1.14, age range 11–17 years; 95.6 % had Belgian nationality).

2.2 Instrument

Descriptive statistics of and correlations between the main variables are presented in Table 1. All variables were measured in each wave in exactly the same formulation and question sequence. However, all variables discussed below come from the

Table 1 Pearson correlations and descriptive statistics for dependent and independent variables

	1	2	3	4	5	6
Time 1 measures						
1. Cyberbullying victimisation	1.0					
2. Traditional bullying victimisation	.283***	1.0				
3. Anger	.109***	.139***	1.0			
4. Impulsivity	.041	.025	.161***	1.0		
Time 2 measures						
5. Cyberbullying perpetration	.110***	.167***	.133***	.135***	1.0	
6. Traditional bullying perpetration	.077**	.205***	.100***	.158***	.399***	1.0
Mean	.10	.25	2.63	2.32	.11	.15
Standard deviation	.30	.43	1.53	.44	.32	.36
Min./Max.	0/1	0/1	1/7	1/4	0/1	0/1
N	1379	1371	1373	1348	1389	1389

Note. **$p<.01$, ***$p<.001$

first wave of the study, whereas cyberbullying perpetration and traditional bullying perpetration come from the second wave. This ensures proper temporal ordering of the impact of the independent measures on the two dependent measures.

Self-Reported Cyberbullying Victimisation and Perpetration Cyberbullying was defined in the questionnaire as

> saying or doing intentionally mean or hurtful things via the internet or mobile phone, meant to make others feel bad. In addition, the victim cannot easily defend him- or herself. Friends who are teasing each other or who are having a quarrel are not bullying each other.

Following this definition, some examples of cyberbullying were given and respondents were asked how often they were bullied via the Internet or mobile phones in the past 6 months. The options ranged from never (1) to weekly (6). Next, they were asked how often they bullied others via the Internet or mobile phones in the past 6 months (never (1) – weekly (6)). Self-reported cyberbullying perpetration and victimisation were entered in the analyses as dichotomous variables with zero as a score for "never in the past six months" and one as a score for "at least once in the past six months".

Self-Reported Traditional Bullying Victimisation and Perpetration In line with the measurement of cyberbullying, a definition of traditional bullying was first provided:

> The previous questions involved bullying via the internet or mobile phones. Bullying can also happen in the "real world", for example, in school, in the street, in youth movements or in sport clubs. Someone who bullies in the real world can, for example, say mean things,

laugh at others, exclude or ignore others, hit or push someone or tell lies about someone. The next questions involve bullying in the real world.

Respondents were asked how often they were bullied "in the real world" in the past 6 months (never (1) – weekly (6)). Subsequently, they were asked how often they bullied others "in the real world" (never (1) – weekly (6)). Dichotomous variables were used in the analyses.

Anger One item measured anger in relation to peers: "I am often angry at peers". The item was assessed using a 7-point Likert scale with item responses ranging from 1 (strongly disagree) to 7 (strongly agree).

Impulsivity A shortened version of the Barrat Impulsiveness scale (BIS-11) was used to measure impulsivity (Stanford et al. 2009). Exploratory factor analysis using Varimax Rotation showed no different factors. Ten items compose together a reliable scale (alpha = .64) and a mean score for all the items was used for later analysis. A high mean score indicates a high level of impulsivity.

3 Results

11.7 % (N = 161) of the respondents indicated that they bullied someone at least once in the previous 6 months via the Internet or mobile phone and 21.6 % (N = 296) "in the real world" at time 1. The prevalence of cyberbullying did not change at time 2 (measured 6 months later), so in total 11.4 % (N = 158) of respondents reported at time 2 that they had cyberbullied someone in the past 6 months. The prevalence of traditional bullying decreased (significantly) at time 2, 14.9 % (N = 206) perpetrated bullying "in the real world" (matched-pair $t(1368) = 5.65$, $p < .001$). For victimisation, measured at time 1, 10.2 % (N = 140) was involved in cyberbullying and 25.1 % (N = 344) in traditional bullying as a victim. At time 2, victimisation was slightly lower: 9.0 % (N = 124) for cyberbullying (decrease is not significant) and 18.7 % (N = 260) for traditional bullying (significant decrease: $t(1370) = 5.18$, $p < .001$).

In order to test our hypotheses, we conducted path analyses in two steps. In a first step we tested the GST without the conditioning variable impulsivity. Based on the theory, we expected that previous victimisation would lead to perpetration at time 2, mediated by anger. As Fig. 1 and Table 2 illustrate, previous victimisation (both traditional bullying and cyberbullying) is a significant predictor for later perpetration (also both traditional bulling and cyberbullying) and anger. The latter is also a significant predictor for perpetration. Based on the conditions of Baron and Kenny (1986) and on mediation analyses (Preacher and Hayes 2004), we can conclude that anger functions as a (partial) mediator between victimisation and perpetration: (1) variations in levels of victimisation significantly accounts for variations in anger; (2) variations in anger significantly accounts for variations in perpetration; (3) with anger in the equation, the regression coefficient between victimisation and perpetration reduced significantly. Anger accounts for some but not all of

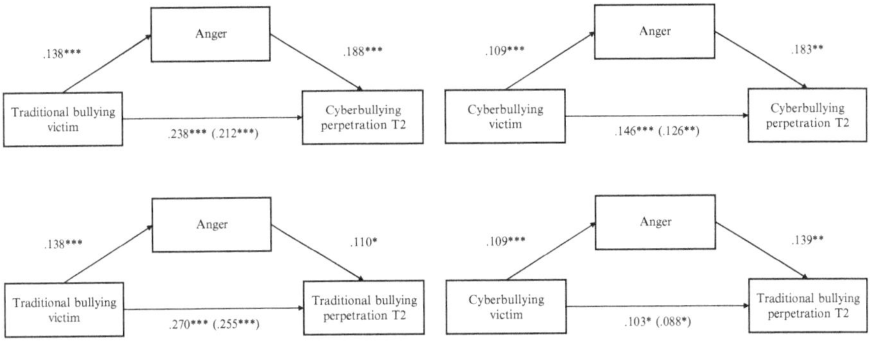

Fig. 1 Standardised regression coefficients for the relationships between victimisation and perpetration, mediated by anger (*Note.* The Betas between victimisation and perpetration controlling for anger are in parentheses. *p<.05, **p<.01, ***p<.001)

the relationship between victimisation and perpetration (no full mediation, the relation between victimisation and perpetration remains significant after adding anger to the model). The sums of the indirect effects are all significant (Betas: .015–.026, $p<.05 - p<.001$).

In a second step impulsivity was taken into account for explaining perpetration. In other words, a moderated mediation effect was tested, whereby impulsivity is tested as moderator for the mediated relation between victimisation and perpetration via anger. Based on our hypotheses, we expected that (1) impulsivity will be positively associated with (cyber)bullying perpetration at time 2; (2) anger and impulsivity interact such that high levels of both anger and impulsivity will predict (cyber)bullying perpetration at time 2 beyond what is expected on the basis of additive effect; and (3) the interaction between anger and impulsivity mediates the relation between (cyber)bullying victimisation at time 1 and (cyber)bullying perpetration at time 2.

First of all our results show a significant association between impulsivity and anger (cf. Table 1). Adolescents who are more impulsive, also score higher on angriness. Figure 2 shows that the angry, impulsive adolescents have the highest probability to be involved in cyberbullying perpetration: The slope of the curve of impulsive respondents is steeper when the predicted probability of cyberbullying behaviour at time 2 and angriness at time 1 is taken into account. For further analyses, a new variable was created, formed by the product of anger and impulsivity (Wang and Wang 2012, p. 134).

The full model with (cyber)bullying victimisation and (cyber)bullying perpetration and the interaction term between impulsivity and anger is presented in Fig. 3. The model has a good fit for the data and is in line with our expectations: RMSEA=.015 (90 % CI: .000–.055), CFI=.997, $\chi^2(9)=266.86$, $p<.001$. About 11 % of the total variance of cyberbullying perpetration at time 2 (11.4 %) and 10.5 % of the total variance of traditional bullying perpetration at time 2 was explained. Previous victimisation is a significant predictor of anger*impulsivity. The interaction term is a good predictor for later bullying perpetration. A strong correlation was found between both forms of perpetration at time 2. Traditional bullying victimisation

Table 2 Unstandardised and standardised regression coefficients of direct and indirect effects of the model with anger as mediator (cf. Fig. 1)

Path	β	B	S.E.	Two-tailed p-value
Model traditional victim – cyberbully				
Traditional bullying victim to Cyberbullying perpetration T2 (without Anger in model)	.238	.566	.122	.000
Traditional bullying victim to Cyberbullying perpetration T2 (when Anger is added)	.212	.504	.119	.000
Traditional bullying victim to Anger	.138	.487	.065	.000
Anger to Cyberbullying perpetration T2	.188	.127	.033	.000
Indirect effect	*.026*	*.062*	*.020*	*.002*
Model traditional victim – traditional bully				
Traditional bullying victim to Traditional bullying perpetration T2 (without Anger in model)	.270	.647	.108	.000
Traditional bullying victim to Traditional bullying perpetration T2 (when Anger is added)	.255	.610	.112	.000
Traditional bullying victim to Anger	.138	.487	.097	.000
Anger to Traditional bullying perpetration T2	.110	.075	.031	.014
Indirect effect	*.015*	*.037*	*.018*	*.037*
Model cybervictim – cyberbully				
Cyberbullying victim to Cyberbullying perpetration T2 (without Anger in model)	.146	.491	.137	.000
Cyberbullying victim to Cyberbullying perpetration T2 (when Anger is added)	.126	.423	.135	.002
Cyberbullying victim to Anger	.109	.554	.124	.000
Anger to Cyberbullying perpetration T2	.183	.121	.035	.001
Indirect effect	*.020*	*.067*	*.024*	*.005*
Model cybervictim – traditional bully				
Cyberbullying victim to Traditional bullying perpetration T2 (without Anger in model)	.103	.345	.133	.010
Cyberbullying victim to Traditional bullying perpetration T2 (when Anger is added)	.088	.294	.133	.027
Cyberbullying victim to Anger	.109	.555	.124	.000
Anger to Traditional bullying perpetration T2	.139	.091	.031	.004
Indirect effect	*.015*	*.051*	*.020*	*.013*

also directly predicts (cyber)bullying perpetration at time 2. The model, as it is presented in Fig. 3, resulted after adding the interaction term between anger and impulsivity (anger*impulsivity) and omitting the main effects of anger and impulsivity (due to insignificance and low predictive value). Although there exists some disagreement in the literature, some authors state that it is possible to include interaction effects by themselves if this is based on expectations (e.g., Cleves et al. 2008). Lastly, Fig. 4 and Table 3 represent the standardised regression coefficients for the direct and indirect relations (via anger*impulsivity) between the different bullying forms separately. The sums of the indirect effects were all significant (Betas: .022–.029, $p<.01 - p<.001$). A comparison between (1) the coefficients and sums of the

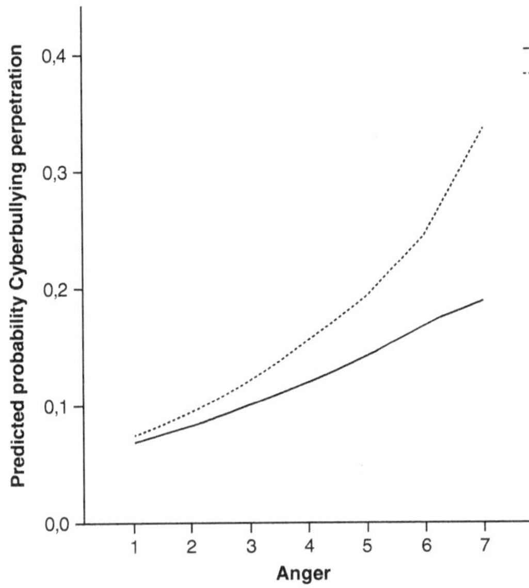

Fig. 2 Interaction between impulsivity and anger with regard to cyberbullying perpetration

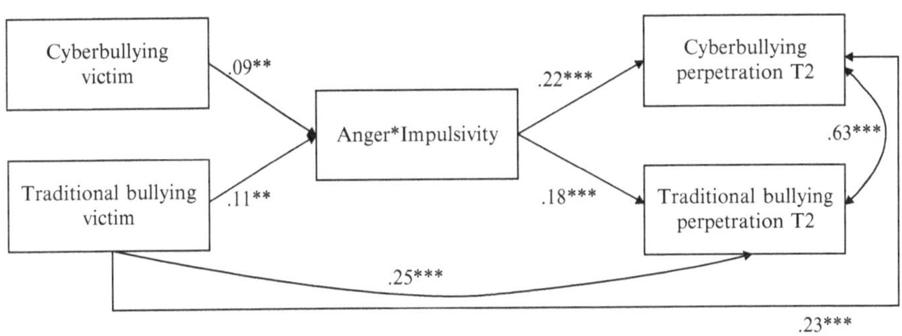

Fig. 3 Full model with standardised parameter estimates and their two-tailed p-value (*Note.* *p<.05, **p<.01, ***p<.001)

indirect effects of the model with anger as mediator (Fig. 1 and Table 2) and (2) the coefficients and sums of the indirect effects of the model with anger*impulsivity as mediator (Fig. 4 and Table 3), shows that the mediation effect of anger*impulsivity is slightly stronger.

4 Discussion and Conclusion

Although theoretical frameworks are rather absent in a large proportion of (early) research on cyberbullying, recent studies have included different theories to explain cyberbullying perpetration (Bauman et al. 2013), for instance: the Theory of Planned

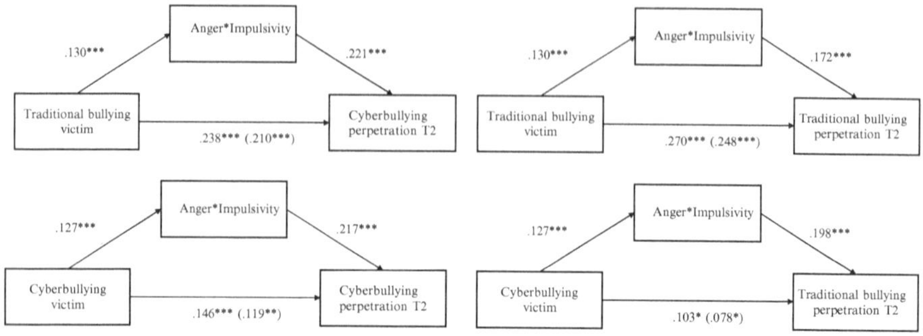

Fig. 4 Standardised regression coefficients for the relationships between victimisation and perpetration, mediated by anger and impulsivity (*Note.* The Betas between victimisation and perpetration controlling for anger*impulsivity are in parentheses. *p<.05, **p<.01, ***p<.001)

behaviour (Heirman and Walrave 2012; Pabian and Vandebosch 2014); the Routine Activities theory (e.g. Navarro and Jasinski 2012) and the General Strain theory (GST) (e.g. Patchin and Hinduja 2011). In this chapter we started from (1) the observation that cyberbullying perpetration might be motivated by negative emotions such as anger (apart from, for instance, revenge, fear, jealousy, boredom); (2) findings showing higher rates of impulsivity amongst perpetrators of cyberbullying and (3) evidence suggesting that victims might become perpetrators (e.g. findings with regard to coping strategies referring to retaliation and evidence regarding the existence of so-called "bully-victims"), in order to further test the predicted value of the GST and the potential moderating role of impulsivity in the process suggested by this theory. More specifically, the current study tested whether: (a) previous involvement in (cyber)bullying as a victim is positively associated with the experience of the negative affect anger; (b) anger is positively associated with (cyber) bullying perpetration at time 2; (c) impulsivity is positively associated with (cyber) bullying perpetration at time 2; (d) anger and impulsivity interact such that high levels of both anger and impulsivity will predict (cyber)bullying perpetration at time 2 beyond what is expected on the basis of additive effect; (e) the interaction between anger and impulsivity mediates the relation between (cyber)bullying victimisation at time 1 and (cyber)bullying perpetration at time 2.

The data used in this chapter stem from a large-scale longitudinal study in Belgium amongst 1590 students (44.9 % males, 55.1 % females; Mean Age = 13.73, age range 11–17 years). The analyses that were performed in this chapter are based on data from the first and the second wave (6 months interval) in order to establish causal relationships. All hypotheses, except for (c), were confirmed. The results indicate that a previous experience with cyberbullying victimisation is positively related to the self-reported frequency of being angry with peers. This angriness, especially amongst pupils with higher rates of impulsivity, explains later involvement with (cyber) bullying perpetration. In other words, these findings suggest that (at least in some instances) cyberbullying may be regarded as a negative externalising coping strategy of (especially impulsive) youngsters. This knowledge is

Table 3 Unstandardised and standardised regression coefficients of direct and indirect effects of the model with anger*impulsivity as mediator (cf. Fig. 4)

Path	β	B	S.E.	Two-tailed p-value
Model traditional victim – cyberbully				
Traditional bullying victim to Cyberbullying perpetration T2 (without Anger*impulsivity in model)	.238	.566	.122	.000
Traditional bullying victim to Cyberbullying perpetration T2 (when Anger*impulsivity is added)	.210	.495	.119	.000
Traditional bullying victim to Anger*impulsivity	.130	1.202	.254	.000
Anger*impulsivity to Cyberbullying perpetration T2	.221	.057	.012	.000
Indirect effect	*.029*	*.069*	*.020*	*.001*
Model traditional victim – traditional bully				
Traditional bullying victim to Traditional bullying perpetration T2 (without Anger*impulsivity in model)	.270	.647	.108	.000
Traditional bullying victim to Traditional bullying perpetration T2 (when Anger*impulsivity is added)	.248	.592	.112	.000
Traditional bullying victim to Anger*impulsivity	.130	1.202	.254	.000
Anger*impulsivity to Traditional bullying perpetration T2	.172	.045	.011	.000
Indirect effect	*.022*	*.054*	*.019*	*.004*
Model cybervictim – cyberbully				
Cyberbullying victim to Cyberbullying perpetration T2 (without Anger*impulsivity in model)	.146	.491	.137	.000
Cyberbullying victim to Cyberbullying perpetration T2 (when Anger*impulsivity is added)	.119	.394	.133	.003
Cyberbullying victim to Anger*impulsivity	.127	1.677	.309	.000
Anger*impulsivity to Cyberbullying perpetration T2	.217	.055	.013	.000
Indirect effect	*.027*	*.092*	*.026*	*.000*
Model cybervictim – traditional bully				
Cyberbullying victim to Traditional bullying perpetration T2 (without Anger*impulsivity in model)	.103	.345	.133	.010
Cyberbullying victim to Traditional bullying perpetration T2 (when Anger*impulsivity is added)	.078	.263	.132	.046
Cyberbullying victim to Anger*impulsivity	.127	1.679	.309	.000
Anger*impulsivity to Traditional bullying perpetration T2	.198	.050	.011	.000
Indirect effect	*.025*	*.083*	*.024*	*.001*

important for (cyber)bullying interventions, because it suggests that it is wise to pay special attention to youngsters that are at "high risk" (i.e. impulsive youngsters) and to focus on teaching them the right coping strategies.

An additional interesting finding of the current research is that cyberbullying victimisation appears to lead to on- and offline perpetration only via the abovementioned mediating interaction, while traditional victimisation also appears to have a direct effect on cyber and traditional bullying perpetration. Different factors might explain these findings. On the one hand, cyberbullying victimisation and the experienced anger, in combination with the readily available ICT channels, might facilitate aggressive behaviour (cf. the online disinhibition effect) especially among youngsters who also have fewer internal regulation mechanisms (e.g. impulsive persons). On the other hand, the link with consecutive traditional bullying might be related to the fact that some of those who have become the target of online bullying might not have less social, physical or other "real-life" power (like many traditional victims) than their online perpetrators (the latter might just be in a privileged position because they can act anonymously, for instance). Therefore they might also be better capable of showing offline bullying behaviour. In the case of traditional victimisation there appears to be a direct effect on (both traditional and cyber) bullying perpetration, suggesting that there are also other explanations for why (offline) victimisation can lead to (off- and online) bullying. For instance, (some) traditional victims might experience negative emotions but cannot react impulsively (on- or offline) because this entails too many risks for them (e.g. because they are physically too weak) or because ICT might not be readily available (e.g. in a school context with strict guidelines regarding the personal use of mobile phones or computers). In their case bullying perpetration might be a more deliberate, "rational" reaction. Future research might further try to investigate this and also focus on the specific targets of the reactions following victimisation: in what cases do youngsters really "retaliate" (implying a circle of aggression) and in what cases do youngsters look for a scapegoat (in example, someone other than their original aggressor) to (cyber)bully (implying the extension of (cyber)bullying)?

With regard to the main variables in our research, the following observations and suggestions for future research can be made. The *strain* that our research focused on was the strain caused by peer aggression. As the GST and the earlier study of Patchin and Hinduja (2011) which tests this theory in the context of cyberbullying, suggest, there might also be other sources of strain for adolescents. Negative experiences with teachers or parents, for instance, might *trigger* the same maladaptive coping mechanism. A similar remark can be made with regard to the behavioural outcomes. While we studied (cyber)bullying perpetration as externalising behaviour, other negative behaviours are also possible (e.g. smoking, drinking, drug use, …). Earlier research on cyberbullying already suggests, for instance, that some perpetrators have declining school performances (Kowalski and Limber 2013), which might cause strain. Other studies show that perpetrators are often involved in other negative or delinquent behaviour, for instance being violent towards peers (Mishna et al. 2012).

As regards the emotions that play an important role in the underlying mechanism connecting bullying victimisation and bullying perpetration, we only focused on "anger with peers", as the GST suggests that this emotion is a key motivator. An important shortcoming in our study is the fact that we only measured this emotion using a single item and at the same time that we measured the respondents' experience of (cyber)bullying during the previous 6 months. Therefore the temporal (and causal) order of the variables might be questioned. For instance, it is not excluded that respondents who are often angry with peers in fact score high on trait angriness while also showing a stronger tendency to interpret peers' actions as (cyber)bullying (cf. the idea of "hostile attribution", which is present in the GST and in research and theories on (cyber)bullying). Future research should therefore try to distinguish between state and situation angriness, using multiple-item scales, and try to capture the temporal and causal order between victimisation and anger. Furthermore, attention can be paid to other emotions that might mediate the relationship between victimisation and perpetration.

As mentioned earlier, an important innovation in the current study was the inclusion of *impulsivity* as a possible moderator. The results show that those who are more impulsive are indeed more likely to become (cyber)bullies when being angry at peers (after supposedly being victimised by peers). Impulsivity is regarded as a personal characteristic that for most adolescents peaks during early or mid-adolescence and decreases during late adolescence (Romer 2010). Thus, the ability to deal with potential triggers might grow over time. This might also partly explain the decline in cyberbullying perpetration after early adolescence (Kowalski et al. 2012; Tokunaga 2010). Again, future longitudinal research should try to provide evidence for this.

Finally, longitudinal panel studies might also try to disentangle the different paths that youngsters follow (bullies/victims; offline/online) and their determinants: how do youngsters become (habitual) perpetrators, victims, or both? Under what conditions do these early experiences "fade away" by the transition to adulthood, and under which circumstances and in what forms do early (cyber)bullying experiences have (life)long consequences?

References

Agnew, R. (1992). Foundation for a general strain theory of crime and delinquency. *Criminology, 30*(1), 47–88. doi:10.1111/j.1745-9125.1992.tb01093.x.

Agnew, R. (2001). Building on the foundation of general strain theory: Specifying the types of strain most likely to lead to crime and delinquency. *Journal of Research in Crime and Delinquency, 38*(4), 319–361. doi:10.1177/0022427801038004001.

Agnew, R., Brezina, T., Wright, J. P., & Cullen, F. T. (2002). Strain, personality traits, and delinquency: Extending general strain theory. *Criminology, 40*(1), 43–72. doi:10.1111/j.1745-9125.2002.tb00949.x.

Baron, R. M., & Kenny, D. A. (1986). The moderator-mediator variable distinction in social psychological research: Conceptual, strategic, and statistical considerations. *Journal of Personality and Social Psychology, 51*(6), 1173–1182.

Bauman, S., Cross, D., & Walker, J. L. (Eds.). (2013). *Principles of cyberbullying research: Definitions, measures, and methodology*. New York: Routledge.

Clarke, D. (2006). Impulsivity as a mediator in the relationship between depression and problem gambling. *Personality and Individual Differences, 40*(1), 5–15. doi:10.1016/j.paid.2005.05.008.

Cleves, M. A., Gould, W. W., & Gutierrez, R. G. (2008). *An introduction to survival analysis using stata* (2nd ed.). College Station: Stata Press.

Cloward, R. A., & Ohlin, L. E. (1960). *Delinquency and opportunity*. New York: Free Press.

Cohen, A. K. (1955). *Delinquent boys*. New York: Free Press.

Colder, C. R., & Stice, E. (1998). A longitudinal study of the interactive effects of impulsivity and anger on adolescent problem behaviour. *Journal of Youth and Adolescence, 27*(3), 255–274. doi:10.1023/A:1022889202419.
Espelage, D. L., & Swearer, S. M. (2003). Research on school bullying and victimisation: What have we learned and where do we go from here? *School Psychology Review, 32*(3), 365–383.
Fanti, K. A., Demetriou, A. G., & Hawa, V. V. (2012). A longitudinal study of cyberbullying: Examining risk and protective factors. *European Journal of Developmental Psychology, 9*(2), 168–181. doi:10.1080/17405629.2011.643169.
Griffin, R. S., & Gross, A. M. (2004). Childhood bullying: Current empirical findings and future directions for research. *Aggression and Violent Behavior, 9*(4), 379–400.
Hay, C., & Evans, M. M. (2006). Violent victimisation and involvement in delinquency: Examining predictions from general strain theory. *Journal of Criminal Justice, 34*(3), 261–274. doi:10.1016/j.jcrimjus.2006.03.005.
Heirman, W., & Walrave, M. (2012). Predicting adolescent perpetration in cyberbullying: An application of the theory of planned behavior. *Psicothema, 24*(4), 614–620.
Holt, T. J., Bossler, A. M., & May, D. C. (2012). Low self-control, deviant peer associations, and juvenile cyberdeviance. *American Journal of Criminal Justice, 37*(3), 378–395. doi:10.1007/s12103-011-9117-3.
Huck, J. L., Lee, D. R., Bowen, K. N., Spraitz, J. D., & Bowers, J. H. (2012). Specifying the dynamic relationships of general strain, coping, and young adult crime. *Western Criminology Review, 13*(2), 25.
König, A., Gollwitzer, M., & Steffgen, G. (2010). Cyberbullying as an act of revenge? *Australian Journal of Guidance and Counselling, 20*(2), 210–224.
Kowalski, R. M., & Limber, S. P. (2013). Psychological, physical, and academic correlates of cyberbullying and traditional bullying. *The relationship between youth involvement in bullying and suicide, 53*(1, Supplement), S13–S20. doi:10.1016/j.jadohealth.2012.09.018.
Kowalski, R. M., Limber, S. P., & Agatston, P. W. (2012). *Cyberbullying: Bullying in the digital age* (Vol. 2). West Sussex: Wiley-Blackwell.
Merton, R. (1938). Social structure and anomie. *American Sociological Review, 3*(5), 672–682.
Miller, J. D., & Lynam, D. (2001). Structural models of personality and their relation to antisocial behaviour: A meta-analytic review. *Criminology, 39*(4), 765–798. doi:10.1111/j.1745-9125.2001.tb00940.x.
Miller, D. J., Vachon, D. D., & Aalsma, M. C. (2012). Negative affect and emotion dysregulation: Conditional relations with violence and risky sexual behaviour in a sample of justice-involved adolescents. *Criminal Justice and Behavior, 39*(10), 1316–1327. doi:10.1177/0093854812448784.
Mishna, F., Khoury-Kassabri, M., Gadalla, T., & Daciuk, J. (2012). Risk factors for involvement in cyber bullying: Victims, bullies and bully–victims. *Children and Youth Services Review, 34*(1), 63–70. doi:10.1016/j.childyouth.2011.08.032.
Moon, B., McCluskey, J. D., & McCluskey, C. P. (2010a). A general theory of crime and computer crime: An empirical test. *Journal of Criminal Justice, 38*(4), 767–772. doi:10.1016/j.jcrimjus.2010.05.003.
Moon, B., Morash, M., & McCluskey, J. D. (2010b). General strain theory and school bullying: An empirical test in South Korea. *Crime & Delinquency*. doi:10.1177/0011128710364809.
Navarro, J. N., & Jasinski, J. L. (2012). Going cyber: Using routine activities theory to predict cyberbullying experiences. *Sociological Spectrum, 32*(1), 81–94. doi:10.1080/02732173.2012.628560.
O'Brennan, L. M., Bradshaw, C. P., & Sawyer, A. L. (2009). Examining developmental differences in the social-emotional problems among frequent bullies, victims, and bully/victims. *Psychology in the Schools, 46*(2), 100–115. doi:10.1002/pits.20357.
Pabian, S., & Vandebosch, H. (2014). Using the theory of planned behaviour to understand cyberbullying: The importance of beliefs for developing interventions. *European Journal of Developmental Psychology, 11*(4), 463–477. doi:10.1080/17405629.2013.858626.

Patchin, J. W., & Hinduja, S. (2011). Traditional and non-traditional bullying among youth: A test of general strain theory. *Youth & Society, 43*(2), 727–751. doi:10.1177/0044118X10366951.

Pontzer, D. (2010). A theoretical test of bullying behaviour: Parenting, personality, and the bully/victim relationship. *Journal of Family Violence, 25*(3), 259–273. doi:10.1007/s10896-009-9289-5.

Preacher, K. J., & Hayes, A. F. (2004). SPSS and SAS procedures for estimating indirect effects in simple mediation models. *Behavior Research Methods, Instruments, & Computers, 36*(4), 717–731. doi:10.3758/BF03206553.

Romer, D. (2010). Adolescent risk taking, impulsivity, and brain development: Implications for prevention. *Developmental Psychobiology, 52*(3), 263–276. doi:10.1002/dev.20442.

Stanford, M. S., Mathias, C. W., Dougherty, D. M., Lake, S. L., Anderson, N. E., & Patton, J. H. (2009). Fifty years of the Barratt Impulsiveness Scale: An update and review. *Personality and Individual Differences, 47*(5), 385–395. doi:10.1016/j.paid.2009.04.008.

Tokunaga, R. S. (2010). Following you home from school: A critical review and synthesis of research on cyberbullying victimisation. *Computers in Human Behavior, 26*(3), 277–287.

Unnever, J. D. (2005). Bullies, aggressive victims, and victims: Are they distinct groups? *Aggressive Behavior, 31*(2), 153–171. doi:10.1002/ab.20083.

Vazsonyi, A. T., Machackova, H., Sevcikova, A., Smahel, D., & Cerna, A. (2012). Cyberbullying in context: Direct and indirect effects by low self-control across 25 European countries. *European Journal of Developmental Psychology, 9*(2), 210–227.

Walrave, M., & Heirman, W. (2010). Towards understanding the potential triggering features of technology. In S. Shaheen & A. H. Churchill (Eds.), *Truths and myths of cyber-bullying: International perspectives on stakeholder responsibility and children's safety* (pp. 28–49). New York: Peter Lang Publishing.

Wang, J., & Wang, X. (2012). *Structural equation modeling: Applications using Mplus* (3rd ed.). West Sussex: Wiley Press.

Ybarra, M. L., Espelage, D. L., & Mitchell, K. J. (2007). The co-occurrence of internet harassment and unwanted sexual solicitation victimisation and perpetration: Associations with psychosocial indicators. *Journal of Adolescent Health, 41*(6, Supplement 1), S31–S41.

Changing Unsafe Behaviour on Social Network Sites. Collaborative Learning vs. Individual Reflection

Ellen Vanderhoven, Tammy Schellens, and Martin Valcke

Abstract Recently, a lot of safety interventions have been developed about teenagers' privacy and security on social network sites (SNSs). However, these interventions often do not have an impact on attitudes and behaviour. Possibly, the instructional principles that guided their development only lead to better knowledge-construction and are not adequate in changing reputation-related behaviour. Following the theory of planned behaviour and theories about peer pressure during adolescence, it was hypothesised that interventions emphasising collaborative learning are less effective in changing attitudes and behaviour than interventions emphasising individual reflection. A quasi-experimental intervention study using a pre-test post-test design was set up in 115 classes. It was found that both a course with collaborative learning and a course with individual reflection raised awareness about contact risks on SNSs. However, only a course with an emphasis on individual reflection had a consistent impact on attitudes and behaviour. Implications of these results are discussed.

1 Introduction

Children and adolescents are one of the main user groups of social network sites (SNSs). For instance, in July 2012 33 % of the Facebook users in the US, 35 % of its users in Australia, 47 % of its users in Brazil and 38 % of its users in Belgium were under 24 years old (checkfacebook.com). Concerns about the privacy and security of these youngsters are growing, since SNSs are based on providing personal information in order to connect and communicate with others. Media

E. Vanderhoven (✉)
Department of Educational Studies & iMinds-MICT, Ghent University, Gent, Belgium
e-mail: Ellen.Vanderhoven@UGent.be

T. Schellens • M. Valcke
Department of Educational Studies, Ghent University, Ghent, Belgium
e-mail: Tammy.Schellens@UGent.be; Martin.Valcke@UGent.be

M. Walrave et al. (eds.), *Youth 2.0: Social Media and Adolescence*,
DOI 10.1007/978-3-319-27893-3_12

education at school has been put forward as a possible solution (Livingstone and Haddon 2009). However, it was found that courses about online safety in secondary education are effective in increasing awareness about these risks, but they do not change the attitudes with regard to these risks, and they only have a limited impact on teenagers' behaviour (Mishna et al. 2010; Vanderhoven et al. 2014a). The study described in this chapter, explores the possibilities for improving educational materials about risks on SNSs in such a way as to enhance their immediate impact on unsafe attitudes and behaviour.

2 Theoretical Framework

2.1 Risks on SNSs

As stated, SNSs are based on providing and sharing personal information. Therefore, children face different kinds of risks while using SNSs. One of the categories of risks teenagers face while using SNSs are contact risks (De Moor et al. 2008). These are risks that find their source in the fact that one of the most important features of an SNS is the possibility of communicating and having contact with others. Examples of contact risks are cyberbullying, sexual solicitation and all kinds of privacy risks (De Moor et al. 2008). Indeed, next to instant messaging, SNSs are the most popular media used for cyberbullying (Livingstone et al. 2011). Additionally, they can also be used for sexual solicitation, as is seen in the process of grooming, where an adult with sexual intentions manages to establish a relationship with a minor by using the internet (Choo 2009). The possibility of obtaining contact information by surfing on SNSs also increases the risk of offline sexual solicitation. Moreover, teenagers face privacy risks, since they post a lot of personal and sometimes risky information online (Livingstone et al. 2011). Additionally, 29 % of the teens maintain a public profile or do not know about their privacy settings and 28 % opt for partially private settings so that friends-of-friends can see their page (Livingstone et al. 2011). While friends-of-friends may sound reasonable familiar, these people are nevertheless mostly strangers.

Although a lot of teenagers develop resilience in coping with these online risks (Vandoninck et al. 2012), exposure still causes harm and negative experiences in a significant number of cases (Mcgivern and Noret 2011; Livingstone et al. 2011). Unintended consequences of revealing too much personal information include damaged reputation, rumours and gossip, harassment or stalking, hacking, identity-theft and the use of personal data or information by third parties such as advertisers or superiors, teachers or the potential employer (Debatin et al. 2009; Livingstone and Brake 2010).

Furthermore, some theories predict that young teens are more impatient and are less likely to recognise the risks and future consequences of their decisions (Lewis 1981). Additionally, it was found that they have a harder time controlling their impulses and have higher thrill-seeking and disinhibition scores than adults (Cauffman and Steinberg 2000). This could increase risk-taking by teens (Gruber 2001), especially since SNSs are used to construct an online identity (Madden and Smith 2010; Zhao et al. 2008), and posting pictures and interests helps in both building and revealing one's identity (Hum et al. 2011). The process of personal and social identity construction is inherently linked to the development of teenagers but SNSs give it a new dimension. The profile pages used to build an identity are often available to more people than just the peers they were built for, thereby complicating the process of privacy protection.

2.2 The Role of School Education

Because of all these risks teenagers face while using SNSs, many authors have emphasised the role of school education in raising awareness about these online risks (Livingstone and Haddon 2009; Marwick et al. 2010; Patchin and Hinduja 2010). Also, parents and young people report that they consider the school as an important place to receive online safety information (Safer Internet Programme 2009). This is in line with the general belief that schools have a broad educational agenda, including the enhancement of pupils' character, health and civic commitment (Greenberg et al. 2003). School education needs to enable pupils to participate fully in public life (The New London Group 1996). In the twenty-first century, this means that teaching media literacy at school has become a necessity. While traditionally media literacy referred to the ability to analyse and appreciate literature, the focus has been enlarged and for some time now it also includes skills with regard to computers (Brown 1998). With the rise of web 2.0, this covers not only interactive exploration of the Internet, but also the critical use of social media and SNSs. Livingstone (2004a) therefore describes media literacy in terms of four skills, namely as the ability to access, analyse, evaluate and create messages across a variety of contexts. It appears that teens are better at accessing and finding information online than they are at avoiding risks posed to them by the Internet (Livingstone 2004b). Therefore, a focus on this aspect during any form of media literacy education is invaluable.

However, although the topic of online safety has been formally included in school curricula in many European countries, the implementation is inconsistent (Safer Internet Programme 2009; Vanderhoven et al. 2013). Previous survey-studies with teachers in England indicate that 42 % of the teachers never lecture about online safety and only 11 % reported to do so frequently (Sharples et al. 2009). Additionally, despite the fact that a variety of educational packages about safety and security in SNSs has been developed (for an overview see Insafe 2014), there is a lack of consistent evaluation of any educational efforts in this field (Safer Internet Programme 2009). This causes uncertainty about the effectiveness of these initiatives. In other words, it is not known whether these materials achieve their goal, which is often to raise awareness about risks, but also to change attitudes and unsafe behaviour (Martens 2010).

The few evaluation studies that could be found, delivered promising results. A survey study in secondary education showed that while there was no direct impact on the attention in schools to the topic of safe use of SNSs on pupils' behaviour, school efforts did have an indirect impact on unsafe behaviour by raising privacy concern (Vanderhoven et al. 2013). Moreover, a recent intervention study found that courses about the risks of SNSs in secondary education are immediately effective in increasing awareness about these risks (Vanderhoven et al. 2014a). However, the same study revealed that these courses are not effective in changing the attitudes with regard to these risks, and they only have a limited impact on teenagers' behaviour immediately after the intervention. This is in line with other studies showing that (primary) school-based measures do not immediately influence the online safety behaviour of children (Valcke et al. 2007).

This lack of impact on actual behaviour can also be found in the more general research field of media education and media literacy education (Martens 2010). While research about online safety education in particular is rather scarce, more research has been done in the field of media literacy education. In this field, quantitative intervention studies in classroom settings typically find that media literacy education increases knowledge about the specific topic of the course, but that attitudes and behaviour are usually not measured (Martens 2010). Empirical research about media literacy education that did take into account these measures, indicates that attitudinal and behavioural changes are much harder to obtain (Cantor and Wilson 2003), and often not found immediately after the intervention (Duran et al. 2008; Steinke et al. 2007).

As can be concluded, media literacy curricula as well as online safety interventions appear to have more immediate success in changing knowledge than in changing attitudes or behaviour (Austin et al. 2005; Vanderhoven et al. 2014a). This is a striking verdict, considering that changing (unsafe) behaviour as soon as possible is one of the primary goals of most developed educational tools (Martens 2010). Therefore, a short-term impact is very valuable.

2.3 Changing Behaviour

Because education about the risks of SNS use is aimed at changing risky behaviour, one should look beyond mere cognitive learning. The trans-theoretical model of behaviour change (Prochaska et al. 1992) states in this context that a contemplation phase, in which people recognise that a problem exists, precedes the preparation phase and action phase, in which behaviour is changed. Considering this model, if we want to change the behaviour of teenagers who behave unsafely online, we first need to make sure that they are in a contemplation stage, that is, that they recognise the problem. We might state that this "recognition" contains a logic-based aspect (awareness of the problem) and an emotional-based aspect (concern about the problem). Indeed, one can state that children or adolescents who do not know about the risks of SNS use are in a pre-contemplation stage. Moreover, those who know about the risks, but do not recognise them as a problem as they do not care about them, are in a pre-contemplation stage as well. Therefore, a first goal of any educational material needs to be to change awareness of and concern about the risks.

Further, it seems necessary to change existing interventions so they have more chance of achieving their final goal of changing behaviour. While investigating how interventions should be changed, it is important to have a look at the precedents of behaviour. The Theory of Planned Behaviour (Ajzen 1991) states that attitudinal beliefs, subjective norms and perceived behavioural control predict behavioural intentions, which in turn predict behaviour. Meta-analytic reviews show that this theory has been confirmed in many empirical studies (Armitage and Conner 2001). With regard to safe behaviour on SNSs, this means that teenagers need to believe that safe behaviour is the best thing to do, that their significant others think so as well, and that they believe that they are able to behave safely on SNSs.

Considering their significant others, it has been found that teenagers are particularly sensitive to peer pressure and that resistance to peer influence only increases when getting older (Sumter et al. 2009). Therefore, it does not come as a surprise that peer pressure is a major motivator for revealing information online (De Souza and Dick 2009). It has been found that peers have a significant impact on different forms of decision-making of teenagers online (Heirman and Walrave 2012; Marwick et al. 2010). We might therefore hypothesise that during adolescence, the opinion of significant others (=social norm), and mainly of their peers, has a particularly important role in teenagers' decision-making online.

Because of the opportunities SNSs offer when sharing information – e.g. communicating (Pruulmann-Vengerfeldt and Runnel 2012) and creating an online identity (Hum et al. 2011; Madden and Smith 2010) – risky behaviour might be desirable between peers. Interventions that are aimed at changing unsafe behaviour need to take this into account. It might be hypothesised that this knowledge can be integrated into the development of school interventions by: (1) trying to decrease the social desirability of unsafe behaviour for teenagers and their peers as well and (2) lowering the impact of the opinion of teenagers' peers on their behaviour, at least during the intervention. The first is part of most classroom interventions, by influencing all peers at once (i.e. all peers in class; it is more difficult to reach external peers). The latter can be integrated in any intervention, by increasing the time for individual reflection during the intervention and by decreasing the "peer time" in which they can be influenced by their classmates.

However, since recent educational theories (e.g. constructivism) emphasise the importance of collaborative and active learning (Duffy and Cunningham 1996), these didactical principles have been part of many safety interventions (e.g., Insafe 2014). Therefore, the possibility that peers negatively influence their classmates' attitudes and thereby prevent behavioural change is rather high. One might hypothesise that when there are more opportunities during the intervention for individual reflection, immediate attitudinal and behavioural changes might be more plausible. However, no research could be found that explores the immediate impact of interventions with collaborative learning versus interventions with an emphasis on individual reflection on reputation-related behaviour such as using SNSs. To counter this shortcoming, a quasi-experimental intervention study has been set up to find out whether there is indeed a different short-term impact on the evaluation of contact risks on SNSs in courses with an emphasis on individual reflection rather than an emphasis on collaborative learning.

3 Method

3.1 Participants

In total 1564 pupils out of 115 secondary school classes filled in the surveys. The answers on pre- en post-test were screened for unreliable answers, such as no variance in answers to items. Unreliable cases were deleted, as were 2 classes in which implementation of the materials did not happen correctly, leaving the data of 1497 pupils between 11 and 19 years old (M = 14.90, SD = 1.88) that were used for analysis. However, 63 only responded to the post-test and 460 only responded to the pre-test. This large dropout was probably due to the long and time-consuming questionnaire. Several teachers reported not to have had time to let their pupils fill in the post-test questionnaire. Yet there was no significant difference in pre-test scores between the group who filled in both surveys and those who filled in only one survey ($F(9595) = 1.49$, $p = .15$), indicating that both groups were drawn from the same population with regard to the dependent variables.

3.2 Design

A pre-test post-test design was used, with three different conditions, as depicted in Fig. 1.

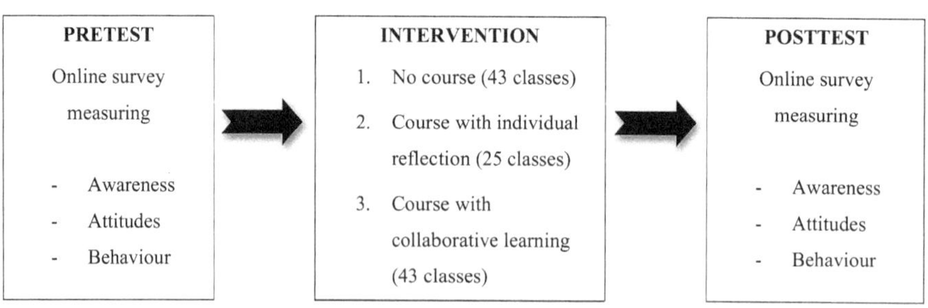

Fig. 1 Pre-test post-test design with three conditions

Table 1 Description of the different phases of the interventions in the three conditions of the study

	Condition with collaborative learning	Condition with individual reflection	Control condition
Phase 1: Introduction	The subject is introduced to the pupils		No lesson
Phase 2: simulated profile	Students receive a simulated SNS-profile on paper and have to fill in questions about the profile together with a peer	Students receive a simulated SNS-profile on paper and have to fill in questions alone	
Phase 3: class discussion	Answers of the exercise are discussed, guided by the teacher		
Phase 4: voting game	Different statements with regard to the specific content of the course are given. Students show their peers whether they agree or not by raising green and red cards. Answers are discussed guided by the teacher	Different statements with regard to the specific content of the course are given. Students write down individually whether they agree or not. Afterwards, answers are discussed guided by the teacher	
Phase 5: Theory	Some real-life examples are discussed. All the necessary information is summarised		

In one condition, the lesson was given with an emphasis on collaborative learning. In another condition, the given lesson had more emphasis on individual reflection. Apart from this, both lessons were similar. These two conditions were compared to a third, control condition where no lesson was given. The interventions are further explained in Table 1.

3.3 Measures

Before and after the intervention pupils' awareness, attitudes and behaviour towards contact risks on SNSs were measured. Therefore, a pre- and post-test was developed based on the contact risks as described by De Moor et al. (2008). Three different scales were developed, one for awareness, one for attitudes and one for behaviour, all built on the base of the means of six or more items. They all had a satisfactory reliability as measured by Cronbach's alpha (see Table 2). While the behavioural scale measures a broad set of behaviours, – including reflection before posting, acting safely (e.g. using privacy settings, not posting risky information) and reporting (e.g. cyberbullying), – a direct binary measure of behavioural change was conducted by the question "Did you change anything on your profile since the first questionnaire?". Where the latter was answered affirmatively, an open question about what they changed exactly gave us more qualitative insight into the type of behavioural change.

Table 2 Dependent variables with an indication of reliability and an example item

Variable	Items	Cronbach's α	Example item	Meaning
Awareness	6	.78	With sexy pictures or messages people might think you have sexual intentions	1 = low awareness, 7 = high awareness
Attitude	6	.77	How concerned are you that someone might approach you on SNSs with sexual intentions?	1 = low concern, 7 = high concern
Behaviour	10	.83	I use my SNS to gossip	1 = unsafe behaviour, 7 = safe behaviour

3.4 *Procedure*

To assure external validity, an authentic class situation, where the regular teacher was giving the lesson, was necessary. Therefore, only where teachers accepted cooperating with the research, were pupils given the link to an online survey. The teacher manual and the syllabus for students were distributed to all those teachers who were willing to participate. Approximately 1 week after pupils filled in the first survey, the course was given under the experimental conditions described. Every class participated in one course. The manual for teachers described in detail how the teacher should give the lesson (i.e. step by step instructions for the progress of the course). Two independent observers verified whether the lesson was indeed given as instructed, with special attention to the emphasis on collaborative learning vs. individual reflection. After having followed the course, pupils received the link to the second online survey. Pupils in the control condition did not receive any course but did get the link to the second online survey at the same time as the pupils out of the experimental conditions.

4 Results

4.1 *Analysis*

Since our data clearly have a hierarchical structure, i.e. pupils in classes, the data obtained from pupils in the same class might be dependent, and so might disturb the assumptions of simple regression analysis. In this respect Multilevel Modelling (MLM) is suggested as an alternative and adequate statistical approach. Consequently, a two-level structure is used: pupils (level 1) are nested within classes (level 2).

Moreover, since the effect of a course on three different dependent variables has to be verified, multiple models need to be tested. Therefore, a multiple testing correction is appropriate. In all analysis, a Bonferroni-correction was applied to the significance level $\alpha=0.05$, resulting in a significance of effects at the level $\alpha=0.02$. This correction results in a conservative significance level, ensuring that any significant effects observed reflect a real existing impact of the courses given.

Three different models were tested consecutively, with respectively the measured awareness, attitudes and behaviour in the post-test as dependent variables. For every dependent variable, a null model was built in which the intercept β_0 represents the mean post-test score for conditions. Second, we controlled for pre-test score by adding it as a covariate to the model. The resulting model (Model 1) shows the impact of the pre-test score on the post-test score. Finally, and most interestingly, the main effect of the intervention was added, with the control condition as a reference category (Model 2). Therefore, estimates of the courses give the difference in post-test-score on the dependent variable for pupils who followed this specific course compared to those who did not follow a course, when controlled for pre-test scores. Only the results of this last model will be discussed.

Furthermore, the answers to the open question (what did you change on your profile since the last survey?) were divided over different categories, depending on the nature of the reported change.

4.2 Results

The results of the quantitative multilevel analysis can be found in Table 3. It was found that both the course with individual reflection and the course with collaborative learning had a positive impact on awareness of contact risks, as compared to the control condition ($\chi^2(1)=8.91$, $p<.02$ and $\chi^2(1)=7.24$, $p<.02$ respectively). However, with regard to teenagers' attitudes and behaviour, a change could only be

Table 3 Results of the multilevel regression analysis on all three dependent variables

	Awareness	Attitudes	Behaviour
Fixed			
Intercept	4.54 (0.06)	4.96 (0.06)	5.16 (0.06)
Pre-test	0.61^{***}(0.03)	0.62^{***}(0.03)	0.67^{***}(0.04)
Course with individual reflection	0.23^{**} (0.09)	0.27^{**} (0.09)	0.21^{**} (0.09)
Course with cooperative learning	0.29^{**} (0.10)	0.17 (0.10)	0.17 (0.10)
Random			
Level 2 – Class			
σ^2_{u0}	0.03 (0.02)	0.05^{**}(0.02)	0.05^{*}(0.02)
Level 1 – Pupil			
σ^2_{e0}	0.68^{***}(0.04)	0.44^{***}(0.03)	0.38^{***}(0.03)

Note. Standard errors are in parentheses. * $p<.05$ ** $p<.02$ *** $p<.001$

observed when the course gave the opportunity for individual reflection as compared to the control group ($\chi^2(1)=9.91$, $p<.02$ for attitudes and $\chi^2(1)=5.67$, $p<.02$. for behaviour). The course with an emphasis on collaborative learning did not have any different impact compared to either the control group on attitudes ($\chi^2(1)=3.09$, $p>.02$) or behaviour ($\chi^2(1)=2.69$, $p>.02$).

However, the results of the answers to the binary question whether pupils changed anything on their profile since the last survey, show that both courses have some influence on the behaviour of teenagers (Table 4). Indeed, no significant difference could be found between both groups in the number of pupils who changed something ($\chi^2(1)=2.54$, $p=.11$), while both groups differed significantly from the control group ($\chi^2(1)=15.60$, $p<.001$ for collaborative learning and $\chi^2(1)=6.70$, $p<.01$ for individual reflection). In Table 4, it can be seen that most pupils who reported having changed anything, mostly changed their privacy settings, or adapted the personal information on their profile page.

5 Discussion

In previous literature, school education has been put forward as an important factor to protect children against the possible risks they face when using SNSs (Livingstone et al. 2011; Marwick et al. 2010; Patchin and Hinduja 2010). However, although safety interventions regularly have an impact on knowledge and awareness (Martens 2010; Mishna et al. 2010), an immediate impact on attitudes and behaviour is often lacking in general media education interventions (e.g. Duran et al. 2008) and Internet safety interventions in particular (Vanderhoven et al. 2014a). A possible reason for this lack of impact on attitudes and behaviour is that interventions are often developed following instructional guidelines from recent educational theories (e.g. constructivism), such as collaborative learning (Duffy and Cunningham 1996). These guidelines might only lead to better knowledge-construction, which is often the most important outcome of classroom teaching. However, to change reputation-related behaviour, such as those related to risks using SNSs, some of these instructional guidelines might not be adequate. It has been hypothesised, following the theory of planned behaviour (Ajzen 1991) and theories about peer pressure during adolescence (e.g. Sumter et al. 2009), that the opinion of peers during classroom interventions might have a negative impact on their attitudes and might prevent behavioural change. Therefore, interventions with an emphasis on collaborative learning would be less effective than interventions with an emphasis on individual reflection. To test this hypothesis, a quasi- experimental intervention study was set up. It was found that both a course with collaborative learning and a course with individual reflection achieved the goal of raising awareness about contact risks on SNSs. However, as was hypothesised, only a course with an emphasis on individual reflection had a consistent impact on attitudes and behaviour. Still, while the course using collaborative learning did not have an impact on the quantitative scales, pupils in this condition reported significantly more that they changed something on their

Table 4 The results of the qualitative analysis

Condition	Changed something (%)	Privacy settings (%)	Account settings with regard to commercial risks (%)	Personal information (%)	Pictures/videos/ interests (%)	Password (%)	Cyberbullying (%)	Report button (%)	Other (%)
Control (no course)	7	56	0	24	16	8	0	0	0
Course with collaborative learning	17**	75	0	14	3	0	6	3	3
Course with individual reflection	13**	57	0	32	5	2	0	0	2

Note: **$p<.01$

profile than pupils in the control condition (see Table 4). This difference can be explained by the fact that the quantitative scales measured a broader range of behaviour instead of just "changing something (anything) on your profile". For example, the quantitative scale also included behaviours such as reflection before posting and reporting information (e.g. cyberbullying). This way, a mean was calculated for safe behaviour in general, rather than counting every change a teenager may have made. It can be concluded that the intervention which leaves room for individual reflection rather than one using collaborative learning, is more consistent with regard to obtaining this outcome of changing attitudes and behaviour in general.

Our findings have several implications for practice and for further research. First of all, they show that education concerning the risks of using SNSs is not pointless, but that the format and implementation should be a well-advised choice. Too often a lot of money and time are spent on materials that are developed without any theoretical or empirical basis, and without any subsequent empirical evaluation (Vanderhoven et al. 2014b). Our results show that empirical research for defining critical aspects of development and implementation is just as invaluable as empirical evaluation for the definition of the impact of safety interventions. This latter is in agreement with previous research about prevention research in general (Nation et al. 2003).

Secondly, the results of this research give a first insight into one of the critical aspects that influences the degree of impact of a safety intervention on the awareness, attitudes and behaviour of teenagers with regard to existing risks on SNSs. As could be expected from the theory of planned behaviour, the opinion of significant others has an important influence on teenagers' behaviour. The results of this study give empirical evidence that this should be taken into account when developing educational materials concerning the safe use of SNSs, by increasing the possibilities for individual reflection and decreasing the moments of collaborative learning. The materials developed can therefore be used in practice to raise awareness about the risks and to change negative attitudes and unsafe behaviour of teenagers in secondary schools.

Thirdly, it seems plausible that the same reasoning might apply to interventions involving other reputation-related behaviour where peers might negatively influence each other, using some form of peer pressure. This might be the case for typical prevention-based interventions, focusing on behaviours such as drug abuse, smoking and aggressive behaviour. Further research should point this out.

Finally, further research should also focus on other critical factors that have a positive influence on the effectiveness of educational materials concerning the risks on SNSs. Indeed, in this study, we focused on peers as important significant others for teenagers. However, parents also have an important role in the life of adolescents. Therefore, involving parents in interventions might have a positive impact on their effectiveness. Following the theory of planned behaviour (Ajzen 1991), other aspects can be put forward that might have a positive impact as well, such as influencing their perceived behavioural control (e.g. increasing their confidence in using privacy settings). Ideally, further research will follow a design-based approach, i.e. starting from the practical problems observed (e.g. unsafe behaviour), and using iterative cycles of testing of solutions in practice. By refining of the problems, solutions and methods, design principles can be developed that can guarantee that next to a gain on knowledge, behaviour will be safer as well (Phillips et al. 2012).

Despite the invaluable contribution of this impact evaluation study, some limitations need to be taken into account. First of all, the given courses were short interventions, in the form of a 1-hour class. A longer intervention might lead to a stronger impact. Indeed, research in the field of prevention shows that campaigns need to be sufficiently dosed to be effective (Nation et al. 2003). However, a choice was made to develop short interventions to limit the workload of teachers who reported they did not have much time to spend on this cross-curricular topic (Vanderhoven et al. 2014b).

As a consequence of this decision, the course focused on teenagers in general, regardless of individual characteristics such as gender, age or the amount of online activity. It has been found, however, that some children are significantly less likely than others to respond adequately when exposed to online risks. Moreover, children reporting more psychological difficulties and a low self-esteem are often more upset by the risks they encounter (Vandoninck et al. 2012). Therefore, it would be interesting to take these individual differences into account in future research, in order to know what kind of impact the intervention has on these "vulnerable" teenagers.

Second, based on previous research, it was hypothesised that peers might have a negative influence on each other with regard to risk behaviour (De Souza and Dick 2009; Heirman and Walrave 2012; Marwick et al. 2010). Therefore, collaborative learning activities were substituted by exercises which had time for individual reflection. However, this way a possible positive influence of peers was excluded as well. One can argue that individual reflection and collaborative learning are not mutually exclusive and that both can be combined in one intervention. For example, by starting with an exercise giving attention to individual reflection and afterwards trying to increase the positive impact peers might have on each other by integrating forms of collaborative learning into the intervention, the positive impact of individual reflection and the possible positive impact of collaborative learning might be combined. However, an intervention combining both didactical principles would take more time. For the same reason as described above (i.e. the teachers' time constraints), the intervention was kept as short as possible. Still, future research could point out the added value of extending the course by integrating a focus on the possible positive influence of peers.

Finally, this study only focused on an immediate and hence short-term impact. This is in line with previous media literacy research (Martens 2010), but it has important consequences for the interpretation of the results. For example, it could reasonably be argued that the intervention with collaborative learning had a delayed impact on attitudes and behaviour, so that this impact was not observable in the post-test scores that were measured immediately after the intervention. Of course, although no conclusions could be drawn about long-term effects in our study, the finding that an intervention with more time for individual reflection has the potential to attain an immediate impact on attitudes and behaviour is very valuable. It surely is desirable that the impact of interventions concerning risks on SNSs is observable as soon as possible. Still, given the growing importance of sustainable learning (e.g. it is the main theme of the EARLI 2013 conference, which is one of the most important educational conferences), future research using a longitudinal approach might be interesting, not only to find out if an intervention with collaborative learning has a delayed impact but also to find out whether the impact of the intervention with individual reflection is persistent over time.

As a conclusion, it can be stated that while collaborative learning is described as an important instructional strategy for increasing knowledge (Duffy and Cunningham 1996), it is less effective in immediately changing reputation-related behaviour. This has important implications for prevention strategies, especially with regard to changing unsafe SNS-behaviour. Courses in secondary education should give the possibility for individual reflection if they want to attain an immediate change in attitudes and behaviour. Since teaching children how to act on SNSs is a desirable goal, our results are a clear indication of the importance of empirical research for evaluating educational materials and to define critical implementation formats. For now, we can conclude that, in this particular case, a problem shared is not a problem halved.

References

Ajzen, I. (1991). The theory of planned behavior. *Organizational Behavior and Human Decision Processes, 50*(2), 179–211. doi:10.1016/0749-5978(91)90020-T.

Armitage, C. J., & Conner, M. (2001). Efficacy of the theory of planned behavior: A meta-analytic review. *British Journal of Social Psychology, 40*(4), 471–499. doi:10.1348/014466601164939.

Austin, E. W., Pinkleton, B. E., Hust, S. J. T., & Cohen, M. (2005). Evaluation of an American legacy foundation/Washington State Department of Health media literacy pilot study. *Health Communication, 18*(1), 75–95. doi:10.1207/s15327027hc1801_4.

Brown, J. (1998). Media literacy perspectives. *Journal of Communication, 48*(1), 44–57. doi:10.1111/j.1460-2466.1998.tb02736.x.

Cantor, J., & Wilson, B. J. (2003). Media and violence: Intervention strategies for reducing aggression. *Media Psychology, 5*(4), 363–403. doi:10.1207/S1532785XMEP0504_03.

Cauffman, E., & Steinberg, L. (2000). (Im)maturity of judgment in adolescence: Why adolescents may be less culpable than adults*. *Behavioral Sciences & the Law, 18*(6), 741–760. doi:10.1002/bsl.416.

Choo, K.-K. R. (2009). *Online child grooming: A literature review on the misuse of social networking sites for grooming children for sexual offences*. Canberra: Australian Institute of Criminology.

De Moor, S., Dock, M., Gallez, S., Lenaerts, S., Scholler, C., & Vleugels, C. (2008). *Teens and ICT: Risks and opportunities*. Belgium: TIRO. http://www.belspo.be/belspo/fedra/TA/synTA08_en.pdf. Accessed 6 July 2010.

De Souza, Z., & Dick, G. N. (2009). Disclosure of information by children in social networking—Not just a case of "you show me yours and I'll show you mine". *International Journal of Information Management, 29*(4), 255–261. doi:10.1016/j.ijinfomgt.2009.03.006.

Debatin, B., Lovejoy, J. P., Horn, A.-K., & Hughes, B. N. (2009). Facebook and online privacy: Attitudes, behaviors, and unintended consequences. *Journal of Computer-Mediated Communication, 15*(1), 83–108. doi:10.1111/j.1083-6101.2009.01494.x.

Duffy, T., & Cunningham, D. (1996). Constructivism: Implications for the design and delivery of instruction. In D. Jonassen (Ed.), *Handbook of research for educational communications and technology* (pp. 170–198). New York: Simon & Schuster Macmillan.

Duran, R. L., Yousman, B., Walsh, K. M., & Longshore, M. A. (2008). Holistic media education: An assessment of the effectiveness of a college course in media literacy. *Communication Quarterly, 56*(1), 49–68. doi:10.1080/01463370701839198.

Greenberg, M. T., Weissberg, R. P., O'Brien, M. U., Zins, J. E., Fredericks, L., Resnik, H., & Elias, M. J. (2003). Enhancing school-based prevention and youth development through coordinated social, emotional, and academic learning. *American Psychologist, 58*(6–7), 466–474. doi:10.1037/0003-066X.58.6-7.466.

Gruber, J. (2001). Risky behavior among youths: An economic analysis. *NBER*. http://www.nber.org/books/grub01-1. Accessed 24 Sept 2012.

Heirman, W., & Walrave, M. (2012). Predicting adolescent perpetration in cyberbullying: An application of the theory of planned behavior. *Psicothema, 24*(4), 614–620.

Hum, N. J., Chamberlin, P. E., Hambright, B. L., Portwood, A. C., Schat, A. C., & Bevan, J. L. (2011). A picture is worth a thousand words: A content analysis of Facebook profile photographs. *Computers in Human Behavior, 27*(5), 1828–1833. doi:10.1016/j.chb.2011.04.003.

Insafe. (2014). *Educational resources for teachers*. http://lreforschools.eun.org/web/guest/insafe. Accessed 28 Jan 2014.

Lewis, C. C. (1981). How adolescents approach decisions: Changes over grades seven to twelve and policy implications. *Child Development, 52*(2), 538. doi:10.2307/1129172.

Livingstone, S. (2004a). Media literacy and the challenge of new information and communication technologies. *The Communication Review, 7*(1), 3–14. doi:10.1080/10714420490280152.

Livingstone, S. (2004b). What is media literacy? *Intermedia, 32*(3), 18–20.

Livingstone, S., & Brake, D. R. (2010). On the rapid rise of social networking sites: New findings and policy implications. *Children & Society, 24*(1), 75–83. doi:10.1111/j.1099-0860.2009.00243.x.

Livingstone, S., & Haddon, L. (2009). *EU kids online: Final report* (EC Safer Internet Plus Programme Deliverable D6.5). London: EU Kids Online: LSE.

Livingstone, S., Haddon, L., Görzig, A., & Olafsson, K. (2011). *Risks and safety on the internet: The perspective of European children. Full findings*. London: LSE: EU Kids Online.

Madden, M., & Smith, A. (2010). *A reputation management and social media*. Washington, DC: Pew Internet & American Life Project.

Martens, H. (2010). Evaluating media literacy education: Concepts, theories and future directions. *The Journal of Media Literacy Education, 2*(1), 1–22.

Marwick, A. E., Murgia-Diaz, D., & Palfrey, J. G. (2010). Youth, privacy and reputation (Literature review). *Berkman Center Research Publication, 5*, 10–29.

Mcgivern, P., & Noret, N. (2011). Online social networking and E-safety: Analysis of risk-taking behaviors and negative online experiences among adolescents. *British Conference of Undergraduate Research 2011 special issue*. www.warwick.ac.uk/go/reinventionjournal/issues/BCUR2011specialissue/mcgivernnoret. Accessed 24 Sept 2012.

Mishna, F., Cook, C., Saini, M., Wu, M.-J., & MacFadden, R. (2010). Interventions to prevent and reduce cyber abuse of youth: A systematic review. *Research on Social Work Practice, 21*(1), 5–14. doi:10.1177/1049731509351988.

Nation, M., Crusto, C., Wandersman, A., Kumpfer, K. L., Seybolt, D., Morrissey-Kane, E., & Davino, K. (2003). What works in prevention. Principles of effective prevention programs. *The American Psychologist, 58*(6–7), 449–456. doi:10.1037/0003-066X.58.6-7.449.

Patchin, J. W., & Hinduja, S. (2010). Changes in adolescent online social networking behaviors from 2006 to 2009. *Computers in Human Behavior, 26*(6), 1818–1821. doi:10.1016/j.chb.2010.07.009.

Phillips, R., McNaught, C., & Kennedy, G. (2012). *Evaluating e-learning: Guiding research and practice* (Connecting with e-learning). New York: Routledge, Taylor & Francis Group.

Prochaska, J. O., DiClemente, C. C., & Norcross, J. C. (1992). In search of how people change. Applications to addictive behaviors. *The American Psychologist, 47*(9), 1102–1114. doi:10.1037/0003-066X.47.9.1102.
Pruulmann-Vengerfeldt, P., & Runnel, P. (2012). Online opportunities. In S. Livingstone, L. Haddon, & A. Görzig (Eds.), *Children, risk and safety on the internet: Research and policy challenges in comparative perspective*. Bristol: The Policy Press.
Safer Internet Programme. (2009). *Assessment report on the status of online safety education in schools across Europe*. http://ec.europa.eu/information_society/activities/sip/docs/forum_oct_2009/assessment_report.pdf. Accessed 24 Sept 2012.
Sharples, M., Graber, R., Harrison, C., & Logan, K. (2009). E-safety and web 2.0 for children aged 11–16. *Journal of Computer Assisted Learning, 25*(1), 70–84.
Steinke, J., Lapinski, M. K., Crocker, N., Zietsman-Thomas, A., Williams, Y., Evergreen, S. H., & Kuchibhotla, S. (2007). Assessing media influences on middle school–aged children's perceptions of women in science using the draw-a-scientist test (DAST). *Science Communication, 29*(1), 35–64. doi:10.1177/1075547007306508.
Sumter, S. R., Bokhorst, C. L., Steinberg, L., & Westenberg, P. M. (2009). The developmental pattern of resistance to peer influence in adolescence: Will the teenager ever be able to resist? *Journal of Adolescence, 32*(4), 1009–1021. doi:10.1016/j.adolescence.2008.08.010.
The New London Group. (1996). A pedagogy of multiliteracies: Designing social futures. *Harvard Educational Review, 66*(1), 60–93.
Valcke, M., Schellens, T., Van Keer, H., & Gerarts, M. (2007). Primary school children's safe and unsafe use of the Internet at home and at school: An exploratory study. *Computers in Human Behavior, 23*(6), 2838–2850. doi:10.1016/j.chb.2006.05.008.
Vanderhoven, E., Schellens, T., & Valcke, M. (2013). Exploring the usefulness of school education about risks on social network sites: A survey study. *The Journal of Media Literacy Education, 5*(1), 285–294.
Vanderhoven, E., Schellens, T., & Valcke, M. (2014a). Educating teens about the risks on social network sites: Useful or pointless? An intervention study in secondary E-education. *Comunicar, 43*, 123–132. doi:10.3916/C43-2014-12.
Vanderhoven, E., Schellens, T., & Valcke, M. (2014b). Educational packages about the risks on social network sites: State of the art. *Procedia – Social and Behavioral Sciences, 112*, 603–612. doi:10.1016/j.sbspro.2014.01.1207.
Vandoninck, S., d' Haenens, L., & Segers, K. (2012). Coping and resilience: Children's responses to online risks. In S. Livingstone, L. Haddon, & A. Görzig (Eds.), *Children, risk and safety on the internet research and policy challenges in comparative perspective* (pp. 205–218). Bristol/Chicago: Policy Press.
Zhao, S., Grasmuck, S., & Martin, J. (2008). Identity construction on Facebook: Digital empowerment in anchored relationships. *Computers in Human Behavior, 24*(5), 1816–1836. doi:10.1016/j.chb.2008.02.012.

Empowering Children Through Labelling in Social Networks: Illusion or Solution?

Ellen Wauters, Eva Lievens, and Peggy Valcke

Abstract In order to protect minors from the risks associated with exposure to content which is deemed unsuitable (e.g. sexually implicit images, violence, offensive language) and potentially harmful, many countries have adopted systems of labelling or content classification. The purpose is to provide parents and carers with reliable and useful information so that they can make informed and well-balanced decisions about which content is appropriate for their children. This chapter identifies a number of key issues related to the development of labelling systems for the online and social networking environment, such as the rationale behind labelling, the object of the labelling systems and the types of labelling that could be used. Focusing mainly on policy documents and proposals at the European level (European Union and Council of Europe), references are made to specific national systems to illustrate good practices or recently developed schemes.

1 Introduction

In order to protect minors from the risks associated with exposure to content which is deemed unsuitable and/or potentially harmful (e.g. sexually implicit images, violence, offensive language), most countries have adopted certain labelling, rating or classification systems for media content. One of the most well-known examples for instance is the Dutch *Kijkwijzer* rating scheme, a cross-media rating system which was launched by NICAM (Netherlands Institute for the Classification of Audiovisual Media/*Nederlands Instituut voor de Classificatie van Audiovisuele Media*) in 2002. *Kijkwijzer* is a single content classification system for television programmes,

E. Wauters • P. Valcke
CiTiP – KU Leuven, Leuven, Belgium
e-mail: Ellen.Wauters@law.kuleuven.be; Peggy.Valcke@law.kuleuven.be

E. Lievens (✉)
Faculty of Law, Ghent University, Ghent, Belgium
e-mail: E.Lievens@ugent.be

M. Walrave et al. (eds.), *Youth 2.0: Social Media and Adolescence*,
DOI 10.1007/978-3-319-27893-3_13

videos, films, games and mobile content. The purpose of these kinds of systems is to provide parents and carers with reliable and useful information so that they can make informed and well-balanced decisions about which content they deem appropriate or suitable for their children.[1]

However, in order to achieve this goal effectively it is vital that potential users are, firstly aware of these systems and, secondly able to understand and use these systems in an efficient way. This was already recognised by the European Commission in 1996:

> Neither the strict application of laws, nor blind reliance on technology will entirely solve the issue of illegal and harmful content on the Internet. Public education will play a crucial role. Awareness activities should therefore be encouraged so that users understand the opportunities as well as the drawbacks of the Internet. Parents and educators, in particular, should be sufficiently informed so as to be able to take full advantage of parental control software and rating systems (European Commission 1996).

The importance of media literacy[2] in this context is increasingly stressed in a wide array of policy documents. In 2006, Commissioner Viviane Reding stressed that media literacy is a key element in the protection of minors:

> The Commission has not only proposed legislation laying down rules for audiovisual service providers: it firmly believes that rating and labelling of content combined with media literacy and technological solutions, such as user controlled filtering, are key tools to address these important issues (Reding 2006).

Increasingly, the proposals are to apply labelling systems in the online and social networking environment as well. Globalisation, convergence and the development of new technologies such as *social network services* (SNSs), however, pose several challenges for existing systems of labelling and content classification. First, the phenomenon of convergence has blurred the lines between traditionally separate audiovisual content delivery platforms and has increased the potential of users having access to information anytime and anywhere. This has resulted in a continually growing amount of content that is uploaded, mainly by individual, non-professional users, making it extremely difficult for platform providers to rate content on an *ex ante* basis. Secondly, the incompatibility of national systems may confuse parents and minors in making the right decisions. For instance, the same movie can have a different classification in different countries. Given the borderless nature of the Internet, it is easier for minors to buy or come across products which are not suitable for their age. A uniform system across Europe would prove helpful, but differences in cultural sensitivities between countries make it difficult to install a harmonised system.

---

[1] Cf. see also: Department of Homeland Security and the European Commission (2012). Joint declaration to make the Internet safer for kids, available at http://europa.eu/rapid/press-release_MEMO-12-881_en.htm.

[2] For more information, see Lievens et al. (2011). State of the art on regulatory trends in media. Identifying whether, what, how and who to regulate in social media, available at http://emsoc.be/wp-content/uploads/2012/01/State-of-the-art-on-regulatory-trends-in-media.Identifying-whether-what-how-and-who-to-regulate-in-social-media.pdf.

Taking these challenges into account, it is the aim of this chapter to identify a number of key issues that should be considered when developing labelling systems that could be used in the online and social networking environment.

Given the cross-border nature of the subject, the chapter mainly focuses on policy documents and initiatives at the European level. By means of illustration of a good practice, we discuss the Dutch *Kijkwijzer* system in detail. *Kijkwijzer* is widely regarded as a successful classification system for protecting minors against harmful media content and also served as an inspiration for the labelling system for games, PEGI (Pan-European Game Information).

2 Why Should Content Be Labelled in an SNS Environment?

The question that has to be answered first is: why should content be labelled in an SNS environment? Traditionally, rating and labelling systems were mainly intended to inform parents and caregivers about the suitability of movies, television programmes and video games.[3] These systems allow parents to make an informed choice about certain media products and enable the restriction of access, should they want to do this.

Studies have shown that many parents find this helpful. When developing *Kijkwijzer*, two consumer surveys were conducted: a survey in which parents indicated their major concerns about children and the media and a survey in which parents were asked whether they would like the establishment of a rating system. The latter showed that more that 75 % of parents would like such a system and 70 % of them indicated that they would actually use such a rating system (Valkenburg et al. 2002). Indeed, a 2012 survey in the Netherlands about *Kijkwijzer* indicated that about 92 % of the Dutch parents with children up to 16 years use *Kijkwijzer* and about 8 % never use it. Moreover, 96 % of parents found *Kijkwijzer* a useful warning system (Gosselt et al. 2012). In 2015, a repeat study confirmed that 91 % of parents use Kijkwijzer (Kijkwijzer.nl 2015). A Dutch survey about video game ratings showed that 77 % of parents found it necessary to have an age rating and 78 % were in favour of a rating for potentially harmful content (Nikken et al. 2007).

However, due to technological developments, the blurring boundaries between different media platforms and the increasing borderless nature of the Internet, it is not only much more difficult for parents to control their children's media consumption, but the implementation of these systems in the online environment seems much more difficult. In our opinion, this does not imply that content rating and labelling should be abandoned as possible instruments for empowering parents, educators and minors themselves to make decisions about which content is suitable for certain age groups. It is, however, very important that policymakers can base

[3] Note that in certain systems, ratings are also used to prohibit access to certain types of content, for instance certain film classification systems include access restrictions for movie theatres.

their decision whether to label content, also in the digital and SNS environments, on thorough social science research into the use of SNSs by young people and the possible impact of content and rating labelling systems.[4] In this context, the EU Kids Online study, which examined the use of online technologies by children and young people on a pan-European scale,[5] also suggested that further research should be conducted in order to test and evaluate effective content classification systems (Livingstone et al. 2012). Because the effectiveness of certain mechanisms may differ according to the platform they are used on, it is important to test, evaluate and refine possible mechanisms on a continuous basis. The study also found that in today's society, in general, parents support a universal rating system that can be applied across media. However, at the same time, parents indicated that they prefer detailed content ratings rather than simple age-based ratings (Livingstone et al. 2012).

3 What Should Be Labelled in an SNS Environment?

A second relevant question is which element(s) of SNSs could be subjected to labelling. On the one hand, content items, such as videoclips, games, pictures or apps could be labelled. On the other hand, a general quality label for the SNS platform as a whole could be introduced, one that would not only guarantee compliance with rules regarding the protection of minors but also with rules regarding privacy, inappropriate content, copyright issues, etc.

3.1 Labelling the Content

With regard to labelling the content itself, the question arises which content available on SNSs should/could be labelled: e.g. professional content, User Generated Content (UGC) or all content. In this context, UGC poses a specific concern. Traditional professional content has been relatively easy to label as there were a limited number of producers that needed to comply with the classification scheme in place. With regard to the enormous number of creators of UGC on SNSs, the

[4] Cf. for instance, theories such as the 'forbidden fruit effect' or the 'tainted fruit effect': Bushman and Stack (1996). Forbidden fruit versus tainted fruit: effects of warning labels on attraction to television violence. *Journal of Experimental Psychology: Applied*, *2*(3), 207–226; Gosselt et al. (2012). Effects of media ratings on children and adolescents: A Litmus test of the forbidden fruit effect. *Journal of Communication*, *61*, 1161–1178.

[5] More information is available at http://www2.lse.ac.uk/media@lse/research/EUKidsOnline/Home.aspx.

most significant question is whether creators will/should rate their own content?[6] In this context, a proposal put forward by the Dutch NICAM, and further developed in the framework of the CEO Coalition in cooperation with the British Board of Film Classification (BBFC), is a European-wide rating system for User Generated Audiovisual Media (You Rate It) with the purpose of enabling parents and children to make well-informed online viewing decisions.[7] The You Rate It tool is conceived as a simple rating mechanism which delivers solid ratings based on the experience of BBFC and NICAM as national film classifiers. The tool is stand-alone, implicating it can be embedded into any website which allows for UGC to be uploaded, and language and appearance can be customised to any website or national rating system.[8] The ratings in the cloud can be used by websites, apps, parental controls, search engines, etc. and can also be translated into local ratings. This implies that every country can receive an adjusted rating and a symbol which is recognisable in that particular country, reflecting different national sensitivities and concerns over content.[9] The developers stress the flexibility of You Rate It because it can be adapted to meet the different needs of countries, publics and platforms. For instance, the content could be rated while the user is uploading his content and/or the content could be rated by those viewing the content.[10] Also, the scope of the role of existing classifications systems can be adapted, for instance, countries can choose to let their national classification bodies act as an independent administrator who could check a proportion of the ratings and could handle complaints about incorrect ratings.[11] Finally, depending on the choices of different countries or platforms, it is possible to use either existing age ratings and labels or new, simplified ratings. The tool consists of six questions about the content of the UGC: behaviour, drugs, horror, language, sex/nudity and violence. There is also the possibility of including a facility that would enable viewers to report to an appropriate law enforcement body if they considered the content to be illegal. Video upload websites could mark the content as "not yet rated" and provide a rating button in order to rate it using the same rating form as when a video is uploaded for the first time. NICAM and BBFC are convinced that this tool would empower and involve uploaders, parents and children in

[6] For instance, the Internet Content Rating Association (ICRA), a self-regulatory initiative for online content, expected content providers to label the content of their own website according to the suitability for different groups of online users (for instance, minors). ICRA created a rating system based on the vocabulary that functions on PICS (Platform for Internet Content Selection), a standardised machine-readable format for describing content in an HTML file. One of the reasons given for the failure of ICRA is that companies were not willing to rate their own content. See, for instance, Archer (2009). ICRA*fail*, a lesson for the future. http://philarcher.org/icra/ICRAfail.pdf. He states that most members of ICRA did not even label their websites.

[7] http://www.yourateit.eu. See also the Miracle project: http://www.miracle-label.eu/.

[8] http://www.yourateit.eu.

[9] Internal document, available with the author.

[10] Internal document, available with the author.

[11] Internal document, available with the author.

the rating process and would create media awareness (NICAM, Wim Bekkers, Safer Internet Forum 2012).[12]

Although this tool sounds very promising, and the flexibility of the proposed system provides many opportunities, a number of questions can be raised with regard to its operationalisation in practice. For instance, given the fact that 72 h of content is uploaded every minute on YouTube,[13] how would national agencies cope with a possible overload in reports? Again, which national agency would have the competence to deal with the complaints? How would one deal with false reports, initiated by "competitors" of the uploader? Would the uploader have the right to appeal against the decision of a national agency? What about the cost of the system? For instance, is only one language sufficient, or does it need to be translated into every language in which a platform is available? Also, do non-professional uploaders have the necessary skills to judge and rate their own content in a correct way? The coders for *Kijkwijzer*, for instance, receive special training by NICAM in order to make a correct classification. Also, when in doubt about a particular classification, the coders have the possibility of asking for advice (NICAM 2011). Then there is perhaps the most important question: what would be the incentive for UGC platform providers, such as YouTube or Facebook, to embed this tool in their sites? Would this need to be imposed by government or would they be willing to do this on a voluntary basis? These are questions that would need to be taken into account if such a rating system were to be operationalised to rate UGC in online and social media environments. Although this initiative is still in a exploratory phase, it is a very interesting reflection on how rating systems could function in a very complex media environment.

Another issue relates to possible inconsistencies in labelling systems when different types of content are labelled. For instance, *Kijkwijzer* uses age categories AL, 6, 9, 12 and 16 (www.kijkwijzer.nl). In contrast, the PEGI system, which is the dominant model for self-regulation of the video game industry on a pan-European level, although inspired by the *Kijkwijzer* system, uses age categories 3, 7, 12, 16, 18.[14] Again, content descriptors of existing systems use different symbols (e.g. for sex, coarse language). These inconsistencies have the potential to confuse users and as a consequence could weaken the effectiveness of labelling systems. Traditionally, there was a clear separation between different audiovisual content (e.g. movies, television, video games). However, the phenomenon of media convergence has blurred the lines between traditionally separate audiovisual content delivery platforms and different types of audiovisual content that is now available on one single platform (e.g. on YouTube you can watch movies, video games sequences, extracts from television programmes as well as video clips).

---

[12] In September 2013 a pilot started with Italian company Mediaset for their UGC platform. Also, the European Commission has invited a number of Internet companies to investigate whether You Rate It can be an effective classification tool for non-professional content (http://www.kijkwijzer.nl/now-you-can-rate-it-/page18-0-258.html).

[13] http://www.youtube.com/t/press_statistics.

[14] www.pegi.info.

Therefore, in our opinion, the concept of platform neutrality could be a solution to avoid inconsistencies and confusion. This implicates a shift away from platform-specific modes of content regulation, based on a clear distinction between different audiovisual content delivery platforms and a clear distinction of content into particular technological "silos", which have been the basis of media policy in the past (Australian Law Reform Commission 2012). In its report "Classification – Content regulation and convergent media" the Australian Law Reform Commission argued that

> Classification should focus on media content rather than platforms or delivery technologies. In the context of media convergence, we have argued that attempts to apply different regulatory frameworks to media based upon their delivery platform has proven to be unsustainable over time, and has generated significant distortions in classification outcomes (Australian Law Reform Commission 2012).

The European Union introduced technology-neutrality in the Audiovisual Media Services Directive (AVMS Directive) (European Parliament and Council 2010). This implies common rules for all audiovisual media services,[15] irrespective of which transmission platform or technology is used. As a consequence new types of delivery modes such as Internet or mobile platforms can also fall under the scope of the AVMS Directive. However, depending on the interpretation of the notion "audio-visual media services", it has been argued that services such as Facebook and YouTube fall outside of that scope (Valcke et al. 2008, p. 112).[16]

However, introducing a new technology-neutral labelling system for cross-media types of content implies the abolishment of existing rating and labelling schemes and this can have consequences for users. Currently, they are familiar with the practices used at the national level. One possibility could be introducing a system that is based on PEGI (*supra*). Introducing a completely new cross-media system would take a lot of effort and need considerable time in order to gain the necessary trust and awareness.

3.2 *Quality Label or Trustmark for SNSs*

Another option, instead of labelling individual content items, is to develop a quality label or trustmark for SNSs, which implies that SNS providers agree to adhere to certain principles. In the area of e-commerce, a trustmark has been defined as

> any third-party mark, logo, picture, or symbol that is presented in an effort to dispel consumers' concerns about Internet security and privacy and, therefore, to increase firm specific trust levels (Aiken and Boush 2006).

[15] Defined as "a service as defined by Articles 49 and 50 of the Treaty which is under the editorial responsibility of a media service provider and the principal purpose of which is the provision of programmes in order to inform, entertain or educate, to the general public by electronic communications networks within the meaning of Article 2(a) of Directive 2002/21/EC".

[16] The AVMS Directive is currently under review. A first public consultation was closed in September 2015. See http://ec.europa.eu/digital-agenda/en/news/public-consultation-directive-201013eu-audiovisual-media-services-avmsd-media-framework-21st.

This is a more general solution, implicating that such a label is not necessarily specifically intended to protect minors from inappropriate content and could encompass more general principles such as privacy, the use of copyrighted material, offensive language, hate speech, etc.[17] For instance, such a labelling scheme could include rules about transparent information about the label itself, a clear and effective complaints procedure, effective report-abuse and notice and take-down procedures based on detailed criteria, clear information about which content is allowed on the SNS platform, procedures for the adoption of existing classifications of professional content (such as e.g. the PEGI OK label for small games that are available on the platform), etc.

The use of trustmarks poses benefits and risks for both users and SNS providers themselves. For users, a trustmark can act as a guarantee from an independent party as to the quality of a platform. Furthermore, trustmarks are easy to recognise. However, when a trustmark does not guarantee accuracy, independence or trustworthy information, and a user suffers damage because of his or her reliance on the trustmark concerned, the validity and the reliability of the whole system will be called into question. Moreover, once the user's trust is lost it will be very difficult to get it back (Balboni 2006, p. 101). There are some potential benefits and risks for SNS providers as well. Via a trustmark on their website, an SNS provider can provide certain information, increase the chance of gaining the user's trust and enhance the chances of doing business with him or her. But, at the same time, there are also risks associated with joining a trustmark scheme. For instance, a fellow platform that is part of the trustmark scheme can violate the rules of the trustmark thereby causing damage to users who rely on that particular trustmark. Consequently, the reputation of the trustmark will be violated and the investments made by the parties involved will be made meaningless (Balboni 2006, p. 101). In addition, the diversity in quality and credibility of trustmarks may have a negative impact on the use of trustmarks in general. It has been found that if a user sees a trustmark on a website which does not meet the user's expectations, this could also have a negative effect on other trustmark initiatives (DG for Internal Policies 2012, p. 21).

Although there are many differences between trustmark schemes, the one thing they do have in common is the certification by a third party. A certificate is commonly perceived as giving some form of guarantee, for instance quality and dependability. A certificate is attributed after completing a certification procedure which implies that

> a third party gives a written assurance that a product, process or service conforms to specific characteristics (Rae et al. 1995, p. 191).

Paolo Balboni distinguishes five stages in the certification process (Balboni 2008, pp. 49–55). The first step is the setting of standards for products and services. It is important to use uniform standards in this context, thus creating a level playing field in order to allow comparison and evaluation between products and services.

---

[17] In theory it would be possible to develop a quality label just for minors, just for privacy, etc., but in our opinion, it would be very complex for users if this would be the case.

The second step is the assessment or evaluation of the product, the service or the policy that has to be certified. The most common mechanism is an audit, which refers to a systematic quality procedure. The quality level of this procedure will have an important impact on the quality level of the certification in general. There are various ways to organise audits:

- One possibility is an internal procedure based on internal standards. The company itself sets out the procedure, its standards and the responsible employees and issues a guarantee, a sort of internal quality certificate, indicating that it complies with its internal standards. The weak point of this approach is that any statements made by the companies have not been independently verified by a third party. There can also be an internal audit based on third-party standards, an internal company audit and a third-party countercheck. This procedure cannot be identified as a certification because this implies the presence of a third party (*supra*).
- The procedure of an external audit entails that the company will be evaluated on the basis of official standards by external professional auditors who will issue a statement. The entity in charge of the certification will decide on the basis of this statement whether a company will receive the certificate or not (Balboni 2008, pp. 49–55). This may provide strong(er) warranties of accuracy and reliability.

Depending on the positive or negative outcome of the evaluation procedure, the certificate will be issued or denied, which is the third stage.

The fourth stage implies that after the certificate has been issued, compliance with the standards has to be monitored. This can be done by active or passive monitoring. In the case of passive monitoring, the monitoring will start after the certifier has received a complaint about the non-compliance of a company. In the case of active monitoring, the certifier will check the compliance of the certificate holders on a proactive and periodical basis.

Finally, depending on the positive or negative outcome of the monitoring procedure, a certificate may be confirmed or revoked. The certificate may also be suspended pending further enquiries or to give the certified entity the chance to restore its compliance with the standards (Balboni 2008, pp. 49–55). On the basis of this analysis, Balboni further identifies five key elements for trustworthy certification practice. The first is the independence of the certifier, which must be an unbiased, independent entity. There cannot be a conflict of interest with the companies applying for a certificate. Secondly, it is necessary to have impartiality in the auditing procedure. This entails that an external audit is more likely to be impartial than an internal audit (*supra*). Thirdly, because a company will display the certificate as a quality label, it is necessary to install an active monitoring procedure in order to assure the trustworthiness of the certificate and to ensure that the certified quality of the company meets the standards. Fourthly, it is essential that a certifier can take appropriate measures when confronted with the non-compliance of one of the certified companies. This again implies the necessary independence from the certified companies. If a certifier is not able to suspend, revoke a certificate or impose sanctions, the certificate could be perceived as ineffective. It may also lead to certain risks: for people who rely on the certificate, unfair competition between companies, allowing non-compliant companies to convey trust by means of the certificate and finally a risk for the certificate as such. The last key element is the accountability of the certifier. If a certifier is liable towards third parties, it can enhance the accuracy of the information provided by the certificate and thus improve its trustworthiness. If the certifier can be held accountable for the provision of inaccurate information, this can be a reassurance for people who rely on the certificate and enhance the chances of fostering trust in the certificate (Balboni 2008, pp. 55–58).[18]

From this description of the certification process we can deduct that the success of a quality label scheme for SNS platforms will to a significant extent depend on the way in which such a label is established, taking into account safeguards with regard to audits of platforms, the monitoring of compliance and the accountability of the certifier.

The goal of a quality label or trustmark scheme for SNS platforms would be to generate and enhance the trust of users in the services that are offered by the platform. This approach was proposed by the Council of Europe (CoE), in the appendix of the Recommendation on measures to protect children against harmful content and behaviour. In this document, the CoE set out guidelines for Member States regarding the development of a pan-European trustmark and labelling systems (Council of Europe 2009). According to the CoE, the labelling of online content contributes to the development of safe and secure spaces for children on the Internet. However, it further acknowledges that the effectiveness and trustworthiness of labelling systems greatly depend on the accountability of those responsible for these systems and their interoperability. For this reason, the CoE is of the opinion that the development of a pan-European trustmark for responsible labelling systems would enhance these systems and initiatives, facilitate the provision of safe and secure spaces for children on the Internet and avoid and/or mitigate their exposure to content and behaviour carrying a risk of harm. Importantly, the following criteria for such a trustmark were identified:

- adherence to human rights principles and standards, including the right to provide for effective means of recourse and remedy, for example the possibility to re-assess labelling when users and/or creators/authors of online content claim that content has been incorrectly labelled;
- labelling systems are provided and used on a voluntary basis, both by creators/authors and users;
- the inadmissibility of any form of censorship of content;
- respect for the editorial independence of media and media-like online content services;
- regular review of the labelled content, for example by introducing a maximum length of time of the validity of the label (Council of Europe 2009).

---

[18] A step beyond certification is the process of accreditation which adds an overarching layer to certification in order to ensure the supervision and quality of performance of certification bodies. In relation to the marketing of products and the process of repealing, the European Union adopted a Regulation in which it sets out the requirements for accreditation and market surveillance: Regulation (EC) No 765/2008 of the European Parliament and of the Council of 9 July 2008 setting out the requirements for accreditation and market surveillance relating to the marketing of products and repealing Regulation (EEC) No 339/93.

4 What Types of Content Labelling Should Be Used?

With regard to the option to label (items of) content, it is also important to assess how content should be labelled. Labelling can be done on an *ex ante* or *ex post* basis, for instance by users or via a complaints procedure.

As we already mentioned above, labelling all content in SNSs on an *ex ante* basis seems almost impossible given the vast amount of content that is uploaded, not only by professional content providers but also by a variety of different and often anonymous users. A more viable solution could possibly be found in adopting a reactive approach by encouraging users to report content which they find offensive or content that violates the terms and conditions or community guidelines of the platform in question. This approach, which is used by platforms such as YouTube, demands clear procedures to follow when reports are made, with appropriate safeguards to deal with abusive reports. SNSs are encouraged to adopt reporting mechanisms at various levels. The CoE for instance, stressed that

> while not being required to control, supervise and/or rate all content uploaded by its users, social networking service providers may be required to adopt certain precautionary measures (for example, comparable to "adult content" rules applicable in certain member States) or take diligent action in response to complaints (ex-post moderation) (Council of Europe 2012).

One of the measures suggested by the CoE is to

> set up easily accessible mechanisms for reporting inappropriate or apparently illegal content or behaviour posted on social networks (Council of Europe 2012).

The European Commission also perceives simple and robust reporting tools as a means to empower minors when confronted with risks on the Internet. These tools should

> be visible, easy to find, recognisable, accessible to all and available at any stage of the online experience where a child may need it (European Commission 2012).

Reporting mechanisms have been advocated by industry as well. For instance, it is one of the five action domains that was put forward by the Coalition to make the Internet a better place for kids (Coalition to make the Internet a better place for kids 2011). These reporting mechanisms should be single-click buttons or icons and have to be visible and easy to find. One of the key objectives of the Coalition was

> to make these reporting mechanisms work with equal facility across – computer screens, smart phones, television or games consoles (Coalition to make the Internet a better place for kids 2012).

The Safer Social Networking Principles also emphasised easy-to-use mechanisms to report conduct or content that violates the terms and conditions as one of the main principles. Again, these mechanisms need to be easily accessible to users at all times and the procedure should be easily understandable and age-appropriate (European Social Networking Task Force 2009).[19]

However, this approach has some limitations. First, considerable attention should be paid to the manner in which report-abuse, notice and removal procedures are drafted. They have to be specific enough about alleged infringements, while at the same time they need take into account the lack of expertise and experience of users in judging content in a correct manner. Ill judgement by users can lead to abuse, false accusations and irreparable reputational damages, so it is necessary to implement appropriate safeguards in the phase of the procedure where reports or complaints are assessed (IDate et al. 2008, p. 288).

5 How Should Labels Be Designed?

The purpose of a label or a content rating scheme is to transmit information in a simplified manner, often by means of icons or pictograms. Providing users with lengthy texts with regard to topics such as privacy has been found not to be very helpful in informing them. In order to offer users information about what data are collected about them, how these data are used and with whom they are shared, providers of services usually adopt a privacy policy or a privacy statement. These texts, however, are often very extensive and drafted in a language that is hard to understand for individuals who are not acquainted with the terms. The result is that these privacy policies are often not read by users.[20, 21] A 2008 study showed that if consumers were to take the time and effort to read all privacy policies of companies they interact with, it would cost an estimated 365 billion dollars per year in lost productivity (McDonald and Cranor 2008). Therefore, in order to be effective, the information provided must be clear, concise and informative.

At the same time it is important to be aware of the limitations of individuals with respect to processing information. Traditionally, legal and economic approaches have perceived consumers as rational beings who are “reasonably well informed and reasonably observant and circumspect” (European Parliament and Council

---

[19] Another industry initiative, the ICT Coalition for Children Online, also clarifies that members should provide a clear and simple process whereby users can report content (or behaviour). See http://www.ictcoalition.eu/.

[20] For instance Jensen et al. (2005). Privacy practices of Internet users: Self-reports versus observed behaviour. *International Journal of Human-Computer Studies*, *63*(1–2), 203–227; Gordon (2003). Privacy: A study of attitudes and behaviours in US, UK and EU Information Security Professionals. *Symantec Security Response,* 12. http://www.symantec.com/avcenter/reference/privacy.attitudes.behaviors.pdf, Grimmelman (2009). Saving Facebook. *Iowa Law Review*, *94*, 1182.

[21] However, contrary to these studies, a special Euro barometer survey found that almost 6 out of 10 internet users usually read privacy statements and that the majority of those who read them adapt their behaviour on the Internet: European Commission (2011). Special Eurobarometer 359, Attitudes on Data Protection and Electronic Identity in the European Union, Report. http://ec.europa.eu/public_opinion/archives/ebs/ebs_359_en.pdf.

2005). This assumes that consumers observe information, rationally process it and act in predictable ways. In this view, vulnerable consumers are atypical. Behavioural economics approaches, however, challenge these assumptions of rational action by studying how individuals make decisions and respond to law and policy, showing that the predictions based on a rational approach often do not hold (Luth 2010, p. 43). For instance, one limitation according to this approach is the limited ability of individuals to understand and process information. In this regard, we can refer to several EU Directives which require labels to be easy to understand, conspicuous, easily visible, clearly legible and indelible.[22] Another insight from behavioural economics is that individuals have the tendency to be too optimistic about their own capacity of avoiding a risk, in particular when they feel they have control over the situation. When using an informational approach, this could imply that consumers will often not attach the proper significance to the information provided to them (Howells 2005, p. 361). This over-optimism can have important repercussions when it comes to warnings. There is also a time-related bias, meaning that consumers have the tendency to emphasise immediate benefits, while downplaying delayed costs, such as possible infringements of rights in the future (Luth 2010, p. 53). This can further reduce the impact of warnings and is, for instance, very relevant with regard to the reluctance of SNS users to read the privacy policies or terms and conditions.[23]

Finally, it is important to note that a survey by Van den Berg and van der Hof concluded, perhaps surprisingly, that when offered a choice users favoured information about data collection and processing through visualisation (pictograms, icons, etc.) the least. They indicated a preference for the use of everyday language and/or the use of examples (Van den Berg and van der Hof 2012).

6 How Should Content Labelling in SNSs Be Integrated Within the Regulatory Framework?

A final relevant question is how the use of SNS (content) labelling could or should be integrated into the regulatory framework.

A first important issue is to consider which existing regulation may have an impact on labelling of SNS (content). A review of all legal issues with regard to the

---

[22] See for instance, European Parliament and Council (2000). Directive 2000/13/EC of 20 March 2000 on the approximation of the laws of the Member States relating to the labelling, presentation and advertising of foodstuffs, *OJ* 06.05.2000, L 109, 29; Council (1967). Directive 67/548/EEC of 27 June 1967 on the approximation of laws, regulations and administrative provisions relating to the classification, packaging and labelling of dangerous substances, *OJ* 16.08.1967, L 196, 1; European Parliament and Council (2010). Directive 2010/30/EU of 19 May 2010 on the indication by labelling and standard product information of the consumption of energy and other resources by energy-related products, *OJ* 18.06.2010, L 153, 1.

[23] See for instance Van Alsenoy (2012). SPION Project, D6. Legal requirements for privacy-friendly model privacy policies (not published).

Internet and SNSs is beyond the scope of this chapter. Therefore we focus on specific regulatory issues in the domain of the protection of minors against harmful content in online and SNS environments.

The European e-Commerce Directive (European Parliament and Council 2000), in principle, could be applicable to SNS providers. In a copyright related matter, in 2012, the European Court of Justice confirmed that an SNS provider could be qualified as a hosting service under article 14 of the Directive (European Parliament and Council 2000). However, the e-Commerce Directive is not applicable to information society service providers established in third countries (European Parliament and Council 2000). This would imply that companies located in the USA, such as Facebook and Google's YouTube, would fall outside of the scope of the e-Commerce Directive. In this respect it is useful to examine the definition of an "established service provider":

> a service provider who effectively pursues an economic activity using a fixed establishment for an indefinite period. The presence and use of the technical means and technologies required to provide the service do not, in themselves, constitute an establishment of the provider (European Parliament and Council 2000).

Recital 19 of the e-Commerce clarifies that the place of establishment involves the

> actual pursuit of an economic activity through a fixed establishment for an indefinite period; this requirement is also fulfilled when a company is constituted for a given period.

However, at the same time, the Recital states that the

> place of establishment of a company providing services via an Internet website is not the place at which the technology supporting its website is located or the place at which its website is accessible but the place where it pursues its economic activity (European Parliament and Council 2000).

When a service provider operates in several locations, it is important to determine from which location the actual service is provided. When it proves to be difficult to establish the exact location in such cases, it will be the location in which the service provider has the centre of its activities (European Parliament and Council 2000). Depending on the interpretation of concrete circumstances, in theory SNS providers who have their origins in a third, non-EU country but who provide their services in the EU market, who operate in the EU and who have offices and personnel in the EU, could thus possibly fall under the scope of the e-Commerce Directive.[24]

Being qualified as a hosting service under the e-Commerce Directive implies that an SNS provider falls under the "safe harbour" provisions of the e-Commerce

[24] See for instance the Terms of Facebook: "If you are a resident of or have your principal place of business in the US or Canada, this Statement is an agreement between you and Facebook, Inc. Otherwise, this Statement is an agreement between you and Facebook Ireland Limited. References to "us," "we," and "our" mean either Facebook, Inc. or Facebook Ireland Limited, as appropriate."

Directive, which exempts providers of information society services[25] from liability for unlawful acts in certain circumstances. These provisions are only applicable when the activity of the provider of information society services is limited to a mere technical functionality, i.e.,

> the technical process of operating and giving access to a communication network over which information made available by third parties is transmitted or temporarily stored, for the sole purpose of making the transmission more efficient (European Parliament and Council 2000).

The exemption is also dependent on the level of knowledge and the form of legal action with which the service provider is being confronted. In case of a criminal action, there has to be evidence that the service provider has actual knowledge of the illegal information, for example when he is aware that a discussion forum is being used to exchange data, to download works illegally or that links are being posted to racist websites, etc. In case of a civil action, the mere knowledge of facts or circumstances which indicate the illegal character ("constructive knowledge") could preempt a claim to the exemption (Lievens 2010, p. 360).

Article 14 of the e-Commerce Directive stipulates that

> where an information society service is provided that consists of the storage of information provided by a recipient of the service, the service provider is not liable for the information stored at the request of a recipient of the service, on condition that:
>
> (a) the provider does not have actual knowledge of illegal activity or information and, as regards claims for damages, is not aware of facts or circumstances from which the illegal activity or information is apparent; or
> (b) the provider, upon obtaining such knowledge or awareness, acts expeditiously to remove or to disable access to the information.[26]

Hosting providers thus have the difficult task of judging themselves when a complaint is credible enough or when a content provider is clearly exceeding certain legal limits before undertaking action and swiftly removing the information or disabling access to it. This may give rise to a "chilling effect": providers might remove content which is legal, just to make sure they are not found liable.

Article 15 of the e-Commerce Directive specifies that providers of information society services do not have a general obligation to monitor.[27] The rationale is that it would be impossible for them to monitor all information which is being stored or transmitted. Moreover, imposing a general monitoring system could also give rise to privacy issues. The European Court of Justice (ECJ) has judged in several cases

---

[25] Article 1 (2) e-Commerce Directive: "Any service normally provided for remuneration, at a distance, by electronic means and at the individual request of a recipient of services",

[26] The other two situations that are covered by the "safe harbour" provisions are caching and mere conduit. We will not discuss these situations as they are less relevant for SNSs.

[27] Article 15, e-Commerce Directive. However, Article 15 does not affect the possibility of injunctions of different kinds, such as orders by courts or administrative authorities requiring the termination or prevention of any infringement, including the removal of illegal information or the disabling of access to it: Recital 45 and 47. Article 12 para. 3, article 13 para.2 and article 14 para. 3 e-Commerce Directive.

that information society service providers, amongst which SNS providers, cannot be obliged to install a general filtering system on their platforms (ECJ 2008, 2011).

However, it is necessary to keep in mind that the e-Commerce Directive mainly focuses on illegal content. The liability for content which can be harmful to minors is not explicitly regulated.[28]

Despite the fact they do not have a general obligation to monitor, information SNS providers can voluntarily carry out spontaneous actions of (editorial) control, use filters, etcetera, for example because they want to protect their image or market their services as being "child-friendly". This could be risky, however, because in this situation they can be assumed to be active instead of passive players and may consequently lose their exemption from liability (Lievens 2010, p. 361). To reduce the risk of being qualified as an active actor, suggestions have been made to engage third parties to monitor the content on websites and explicitly inform the provider of information society services when there is a breach of the platform's terms and conditions (Byron 2008).

Secondly, and crucially, it is also necessary to consider which type of regulation is best suited to SNSs. Previous research has shown that types of regulation in which different actors are involved, such as self- and co-regulation, seem better adapted to fast-changing, complex environments, and hence are probably the way forward to achieve policy goals in the SNS environment (Lievens et al. 2011). In the European Union, for instance, the protection of minors against harmful content on the Internet began to raise concerns around 1996. However, the EU was convinced the issue was best addressed by alternative regulatory instruments rather than through legislation. This attitude fitted in with the more general trend towards "good governance" or "better law-making" that was the subject of regulatory initiatives at that time (European Commission 2001, 2002; European Parliament, Council and Commission 2003). At first, the EU focus in the audiovisual and online context was on self-regulation but gradually a shift towards co-regulation could be discerned.

There is no general accepted definition of self-regulation. Definitions range from the very narrow to the very broad.[29] However, in the different definitions we can distinguish two common elements: first, a group of actors who create, implement and enforce rules, second, that the involvement of the government is minimal (Lievens et al. 2011, p. 28). The benefits of self-regulation often cited are flexibility, the capacity to adapt quickly to fast-developing technologies and increasingly global issues, the high degree of expertise and a lower cost (Lievens et al. 2011, p. 29). However, there are also several drawbacks. A frequent criticism is the lack of effective enforcement. Sanctions are often mild and imposed in a reluctant manner. The reach of the self-regulatory scheme can be limited because it only applies to those who voluntarily participate and not all members of industries are therefore included (Latzer et al. 2013, p. 375). Another criticism is the lack of transparency,

---

[28] Article 16 of the e-Commerce Directive does encourage the development of codes of conduct for the protection of minors and human dignity, but does not impose an obligation to do so.

[29] For a detailed overview, cf. Lievens (2010). *Protecting children in the digital era: The use of alternative regulatory instruments*. Leiden/Boston: Martinus Nijhoff Publishers, 189 *et seq.*

the lack of accountability as well as legal certainty, all resulting in a decrease in democratic quality of regulation. Also, self-regulatory schemes could result in anticompetitive behaviour because of the close cooperation between companies (Latzer et al. 2013, p. 375). Furthermore, it is argued that self-regulation does not protect the fundamental rights of users and citizens in the same adequate way as traditional government legislation does, as private interests may be put before the public interest.

Since the mid-2000s, self-regulatory initiatives in the area of online child safety have indicated that the industry is committed to make the Internet a safer place for minors. However, the implementation of these initiatives has not been evaluated on a regular basis and often information about the processes and results are lacking. With regard to content rating and labelling in particular, the work of the CEO Coalition seemed promising in its initial 12-month plan of action, but since 2015 very little information has been communicated about the status of the Coalition.

For co-regulation, as for self-regulation, there is no generally accepted definition and there is no consensus on its exact scope. Usually, the "co-" indicates involvement of both governmental and private actors in the regulatory scheme (Latzer et al. 2013, p. 377). Depending on the particular combination of public authority and private sector elements, a distinction can be made between a top-down approach (where the public authority creates a legal framework for co-regulation) and a bottom-up approach (where the public authority incorporates an existing self-regulatory system into the legal framework) (Lievens et al. 2011, p. 39). Benefits attributed to co-regulation are often a combination of the advantages of self-regulation (flexibility, responsiveness, expertise and commitment of the industry) with the advantages of traditional state legislation (legal certainty, democratic guarantees and efficient enforcement) (Lievens et al. 2011, p. 43). An explanation for the success of *Kijkwijzer* for instance, may be found in the co-regulatory nature of the system. The Dutch Media Act stipulates that the television offer of the public and commercial broadcasters is only permitted to contain content which is potentially harmful for individuals younger than 16 years old if the organisation responsible for the content of the offer has joined an organisation certified by the government (*in casu* NICAM, cf. *supra*) (Dutch Media Act 2008, p. 4.1). This (self-regulatory) organisation has the task to create classification criteria, to decide on the timeframe when potentially harmful content can be broadcast and to develop symbols which indicate that such content is being broadcast (Dutch Media Act 2008, p. 4.2). These provisions, together with the supervisory function of the Dutch Media Authority, thus create important incentives for members of NICAM to comply with *Kijkwijzer*. However, co-regulation can also suffer from drawbacks. Normative requirements such as transparency, adequate participation and independence must be respected and a clear division of tasks between the different actors must be established. Furthermore, it is necessary to construct the combination of public authority and private actor elements in such a way that the advantages of self-regulation and traditional state legislation are not lost (Lievens et al. 2011, p. 43).

Finally, when opting for self- or co-regulatory labelling schemes instead of traditional top-down regulation, crucial aspects that have to be taken into account are certification, enforcement and compliance, which are related to the credibility and trustworthiness of a label (Helberger 2011, p. 362). Certification by a third party can provide assurance for users that the information supplied is correct. In addition, in order to enhance trust it is important that violations of the labelling or content rating scheme are sanctioned (Golan et al. 2001, p. 131). Possible means to follow up on compliance are regular monitoring measures, annual audits of the services and random checks or mystery shopping exercises, as well as a cascade of robust sanctions in case of non-compliance, including withdrawal of the label or financial sanctions (DG for Internal Policies 2012, p. 78). Effective verification of compliance, with and proper enforcement of, the requirements of the labelling and content rating schemes hold the key to a trustworthy system. Users could also be involved in the compliance process, for instance by reporting inappropriate content violations.

7 Conclusion

Labelling mechanisms are not new phenomena and have been used in many countries to achieve various objectives. Relating to the protection of minors, this has resulted in different classification systems for audiovisual products (e.g. television programmes or films) at national level, often inspired by cultural and social values that reflect how children are seen and approached in that particular society. These systems result from an era in which distribution of physical media was only effected by retailers (brick and mortar stores) and involved a mainly one-sided way of communicating on the part of content providers who could set restrictions on access to content. At that time, there was no need for a cross-media and cross-border system, since measures at a national level were sufficient to protect minors against harmful content.

The Internet has dramatically changed this situation. New intermediaries have arisen in the form of hosts and access providers who do not usually influence or control the content that is transmitted through their gateways and platforms. Moreover, a shift from one-way to two-way communication has occurred and access restrictions with respect to time and place are largely a thing of the past. In addition, information and content is easily and increasingly transmitted across borders, blurring the distinct line between jurisdictions and applicable national regulatory systems. SNSs are exemplary of these evolutions.

The purpose of this chapter was to identify key issues and questions related to the potential use of labelling systems originating in the changed media environment in order to empower parents, educators and minors.

Our analysis has shown that policymakers have various options for adopting labelling in the SNS environment: from a strict paternalistic approach, which could include *ex ante* labelling of (various items of) content that is available on SNSs, with incentives and safeguards included in (top-down) regulation, to more lenient approaches which could vary from *ex post*, complaints-based types of content labelling initiated by SNS providers to the use of (quality) labels which provide users with clear, understandable and relevant information about the policies that SNS providers adopt, possibly inspired by co-regulatory principles. The latter approach probably embodies user-empowerment principles in a manner that is most relevant in the SNS environment. However, in order to decide which system may be desirable, more social science and legal research is necessary, as well as a thorough and realistic cost-benefit analysis of various systems. Perspectives and best practices from other disciplines, such as consumer protection and privacy and data protection, may also be useful in this respect.

References

Aiken, D. K., & Boush, D. M. (2006). Trustmarks, objective-source ratings, and implied investments in advertising: Investigating online trust and the context-specific nature of internet signals. *Journal of the Academy of Marketing Science, 34*, 308–323.

Archer, P. (2009). ICRA*fail*, a lesson for the future. http://philarcher.org/icra/ICRAfail.pdf. Accessed 10 July 2013.

Australian Law Reform Commission. (2012, February). *Classification – Content regulation and convergent media, Final report.* http://www.alrc.gov.au/sites/default/files/pdfs/publications/final_report_118_for_web.pdf. Accessed 7 Mar 2012.

Balboni, P. (2006). Model for an adequate liability system for trustmark organisations, privacy and security issues. *Information Technology, 1*, 97–111.

Balboni, P. (2008). *Trustmarks – Third-party liability of trustmark organisations in Europe*. PhD dissertation, University of Tilburg, The Netherlands.

Bushman, B. J., & Stack, A. D. (1996). Forbidden fruit versus tainted fruit: Effects of warning labels on attraction to television violence. *Journal of Experimental Psychology: Applied, 2*(3), 207–226.

Byron, T. (2008). *Safer children in a digital world: The report of the Byron review.* http://media.education.gov.uk/assets/files/pdf/s/safer%20children%20in%20a%20digital%20world%20the%202008%20byron%20review.pdf. Accessed 10 July 2013.

Coalition to make the Internet a better place for kids. (2011). *Statement of purpose.* http://ec.europa.eu/information_society/activities/sip/docs/ceo_coalition/ceo_coalition_statement.pdf. Accessed 10 July 2013.

Coalition to make the Internet a better place for kids. (2012). *Action 3, wider use of content classification systems, Progress report* http://ec.europa.eu/information_society/activities/sip/docs/ceo_coalition/classif_progress_report.pdf. Accessed 10 July 2013.

Council of Europe (Committee of Ministers). (2009). *Recommendation CM/Rec(2009)5 of the Committee of Ministers to member states on measures to protect children against harmful content and behaviour and to promote their active participation in the new information and communications environment.* https://wcd.coe.int/ViewDoc.jsp?id=1470045&Site=CM. Accessed 10 July 2013.

Council of Europe (Committee of Ministers). (2012). *Recommendation CM/Rec(2012)4 on the protection of human rights with respect to social networking services.* https://wcd.coe.int/ViewDoc.jsp?id=1929453&Site=CM. Accessed 23 Jan 2013.

DG for Internal Policies. (2012). *Policy department economic and scientific policy*. Study: A Pan-European trustmark for e-commerce: Possibilities and opportunities. http://www.europarl.europa.eu/committees/hu/studiesdownload.html?languageDocument=EN&file=75183. Accessed 10 July 2013.

Dutch Media Act. (2008, December 29). *Act of 29 December 2008 to establish a new Media Act* (Wet van 29 december 2008 tot vaststelling van een nieuwe Mediawet (Mediawet 2008)).

ECJ. (2008). Productores de música de España (Promusicae) v telefónica de España SAU, C-275/06.
ECJ. (2011). Scarlet extended v SABAM, C-70/10.
European Commission. (1996). Communication to the European Parliament, the Council, the Economic and Social Committee and the Committee of the Regions, illegal and harmful content on the Internet, COM(96) 487 final. http://eurlex.europa.eu/LexUriServ/LexUriServ.do?uri=COM:1996:0487:FIN:en:PDF. Accessed 10 July 2013.
European Commission. (2001). *European Governance – A white paper*, COM (2001) 428 final, 25.07.2001. http://eurlex.europa.eu/LexUriServ/site/en/com/2001/com2001_0428en01.pdf. Accessed 10 July 2013.
European Commission. (2002). Communication action plan 'Simplifying and improving the regulatory environment'; COM (2002) 278 final, 05.06.2002. http://eurlex.europa.eu/LexUriServ/LexUriServ.do?uri=COM:2002:0278:FIN:en:PDF. Accessed 10 July 2013.
European Commission. (2011). Special Eurobarometer 359, attitudes on data protection and electronic identity in the European Union, Report. http://ec.europa.eu/public_opinion/archives/ebs/ebs_359_en.pdf. Accessed 10 July 2013.
European Commission. (2012). *Communication from the Commission to the European Parliament, the Council, the European Economic and Social Committee and the Committee of the Regions, European strategy for a better Internet for children.* http://eur-lex.europa.eu/LexUriServ/LexUriServ.do?uri=COM:2012:0196:FIN:EN:PDF. Accessed 10 July 2013.
European Parliament and Council. (2000). Directive 2000/31/EC of 8 June 2000 on certain legal aspects of information society services, in particular economic commerce, in the Internal Market (Directive on electronic commerce), *OJ* 17.07.2000, L 178, 1.
European Parliament and Council. (2005). Directive (EC)2005/29 concerning unfair business-to-consumer commercial practices in the internal market and amending Council Directive 84/450/EEC, Directives 97/7/EC, 98/27/EC and 2002/65/EC of the European Parliament and of the Council and Regulation (EC) No 2006/2004 of the European Parliament and of the Council [2005] OJ L149/22 (Unfair Commercial Practices Directive), *OJ* 11.06.2005, L 149/22.
European Parliament and Council. (2010). Directive 2010/13/EU of 10 March 2010 on the coordination of certain provisions laid down by law, regulation or administrative action in Member States concerning the provision of audiovisual media services (Audiovisual Media Services Directive), *OJ* 15.04.2010, L 95, 1.
European Social Networking Task Force. (2009). *Safer social networking principles for the EU.* https://ec.europa.eu/digital-agenda/sites/digital-agenda/files/sn_principles.pdf. Accessed 10 July 2013.
European Parliament, Council and Commission. (2003). Inter-institutional agreement on better law-making, *OJ* 31.12.2003. http://eurlex.europa.eu/LexUriServ/LexUriServ.do?uri=OJ:C:2003:321:0001:0001:EN:PDF. Accessed 10 July 2013.
Golan, E., Kuchler, F., & Mitchell, L. (2001). Economics of food labelling. *Journal of Consumer Policy, 24*, 117–184.
Gordon, S. (2003). Privacy: A study of attitudes and behaviours in US, UK and EU Information Security Professionals. *Symantec Security Response, 12.* http://www.symantec.com/avcenter/reference/privacy.attitudes.behaviors.pdf. Accessed 10 July 2013.
Gosselt, J., Van Hoof, J., & De Jong, M. (2012). Media rating systems: Do they work? Shop floor compliance with age restrictions in The Netherlands. *Mass Communication and Society, 15*(3), 335–359.
Grimmelman, J. (2009). Saving Facebook. *Iowa Law Review, 94*, 1182.
Helberger, N. (2011). Diversity label: Exploring the potential and limits of a transparency approach to media diversity. *Journal of Information Policy, 1*, 337–369.
Howells, G. (2005). The potential and limits of consumer empowerment by information. *Journal of Law and Society, 32*(3), 349–370.
IDate, TNO, & IViR (Helberger, N., Guibault, L., Janssen, E., van Eijk, N., Angelopoulos, C., van Hoboken, J., Swart, E., de Munck, S., Limonard, S., Poel, M., Kool, L., Le Borgne-Bachschmidt, F., Girieud, S., & Leiba, M.). (2008). *User-created-content: Supporting a participative infor-*

mation society – Final report. http://www.ivir.nl/publicaties/download/233. Accessed 5 Feb 2015.
Jensen, C., Potts, C., & Jensen, C. (2005). Privacy practices of Internet users: Self-reports versus observed behaviour. *International Journal of Human-Computer Studies, 63*(1–2), 203–227.
Kijkwijzer.nl. (2015). *91% ouders gebruikt Kijkwijzer*. http://www.kijkwijzer.nl/91-ouders-gebruikt-kijkwijzer/page18-0-409.html. Accessed 1 Feb 2016.
Latzer, M., Just, N., & Saurwein, F. (2013). Self –and co –regulation. Evidence, legitimacy and governance choice. In E. P. Monroe, S. G. Verhulst, & L. Morgan (Eds.), *Routledge handbook of media law* (pp. 373–397). Oxon: Routledge.
Lievens, E. (2010). *Protecting children in the digital era: The use of alternative regulatory instruments*. Leiden/Boston: Martinus Nijhoff Publishers.
Lievens, E., Valcke, P., & Valgaeren, P. J. (2011). *State of the art on regulatory trends in media. Identifying whether, what, how and who to regulate in social media*. https://lirias.kuleuven.be/bitstream/123456789/350852/1/EMSOC_ICRI_D+1+2+1_2011.pdf. Accessed 10 July 2013.
Livingstone, S., Olafsson, K., O'Neill, B., & Donoso, V. (2012). EU Kids Online: Towards a better Internet for children. http://www2.lse.ac.uk/media@lse/research/EUKidsOnline/EU%20Kids%20III/Reports/EUKidsOnlinereportfortheCEOCoalition.pdf. Accessed 10 July 2013.
Luth, H. A. (2010). *Behavioural economics in consumer policy, the economic analysis of standard terms in consumer contracts revisited*. PhD thesis, Erasmus University Rotterdam, The Netherlands.
McDonald, A., & Cranor, L. F. (2008). The cost of reading privacy policies. *I/S: A Journal of Law and Policy for the Information Society. 2008 Privacy Year in Review issue*. http://lorrie.cranor.org/pubs/readingPolicyCost-authorDraft.pdf. Accessed 10 July 2013.
NICAM. (2011). *Jaarverslag 2011*. http://www.kijkwijzer.nl/upload/zijbalk1/59_Nicam2011.pdf. Accessed 10 July 2013.
Nikken, P., Jansz, J., & Schouwstra, H. (2007). Parents' interest in videogame ratings and content descriptors in relation to game mediation. *European Journal of Communication, 22*, 315–336.
Rae, A., Robert, P., & Hausen, H.-L. (1995). *Software evaluation for certification: Principles, practice and legal liability*. London: McGraw Hill Book Company.
Reding, V. (2006). Freedom of the media, effective co-regulation and media literacy: Cornerstones for an efficient protection of minors in the European Union, speech at ICRA round table Brussels 'Mission Impossible', Brussels. http://europa.eu/rapid/press-release_SPEECH-06-374_en.htm?locale=en. Accessed 10 July 2013.
Safer Internet Forum. (2012). Wim Bekkers (NICAM), Brussels.
Valcke, P., Stevens, D., Lievens, E., & Werkers, E. (2008). Audiovisual media services in the EU: Next generation approach or old wine in new barrels? *Communications & Strategies, 71*, 103–118.
Valkenburg, P., Beentjes, H., Nikken, P., & Tan, E. (2002). Kijkwijzer: The Dutch rating system for audiovisual productions. *Communications, 27*(1), 79–102.
Van Alsenoy, B. (2012). SPION project, D6. Legal requirements for privacy-friendly model privacy policies (not published).
Van den Berg, B., & van der Hof, S. (2012). What happens to my data? *First Monday, 17*(7). http://www.uic.edu/htbin/cgiwrap/bin/ojs/index.php/fm/article/view/4010/3274. Accessed 10 July 2013.

Index

M. Walrave et al. (eds.), *Youth 2.0: Social Media and Adolescence*,
DOI 10.1007/978-3-319-27893-3

D

Kolibri 360 GmbH
Ferdinand-Jühlke-Straße 7
99095 Erfurt, Deutschland
produktsicherheit@kolibri360.de